W9-ADP-352

WITHDRAWN

Social Transformation in Modern China

The State and Local Elites in Henan, 1900–1937

The sources and nature of China's transformation from a traditional to modern society – accelerated in the early twentieth century by the downfall of the Qing dynasty, the advent of foreign technology, and increasing commercialization – are critical issues for the study of modern China. In this book, Xin Zhang uses the case of local elites and the power structure of Henan province, in north-central China, to demonstrate how local politics first transformed local society, challenged the state, and eventually influenced change across China. Rather than focusing separately on elite mobility, or social mobilization, or state making, as other studies of the subject have done, Zhang observes changes in all three categories as interrelated aspects of what he views as a single, self-generating phenomenon of social change.

Henan, the front-line province between northern and southern forces during the transition from imperial to Republican China, was an important source of new modes of political and social behavior. Zhang's access to original archival materials from this region offers rich, new empirical data. Using the most up-to-date social science theory, the author sets forth a holistic and contextualized view of the Chinese historical experience, making a contribution beyond the field of China studies, to the intellectual discourse on modernity in non-Western countries.

Xin Zhang is Associate Professor in the Department of History at Indiana University at Indianapolis.

Cambridge Modern China Series

Edited by William Kirby, Harvard University

Social Transformation in Modern China

The State and Local Elites in Henan, 1900–1937

XIN ZHANG

Indiana University

CAMBRIDGE
UNIVERSITY PRESS

149395

PUBLISHED BY THE PRESS SYNDICATE OF THE UNIVERSITY OF CAMBRIDGE
The Pitt Building, Trumpington Street, Cambridge, United Kingdom

CAMBRIDGE UNIVERSITY PRESS
The Edinburgh Building, Cambridge CB2 2RU, UK   http://www.cup.cam.ac.uk
40 West 20th Street, New York, NY 10011-4211, USA   http://www.cup.org
10 Stamford Road, Oakleigh, Melbourne 3166, Australia
Ruiz de Alarcón 13, 28014 Madrid, Spain

© Xin Zhang 2000

This book is in copyright. Subject to statutory exception
and to the provisions of relevant collective licensing agreements,
no reproduction of any part may take place without
the written permission of Cambridge University Press.

First published 2000

Printed in the United States of America.

Typeface Times New Roman 10/13 pt.   *System* QuarkXPress™ [BTS]

A catalog record for this book is available from the British Library.

Library of Congress Cataloging in Publication data

Zhang, Xin, 1956–
    Social transformation in modern China: the state and local elites in Henan,
    1900–1937/Xin Zhang.
        p.   cm. – (Cambridge modern China series)
    Includes bibliographical references and index.
    ISBN 0-521-64289-2
        1. Elite (Social sciences) – China.   2. China – Social conditions – 1912–1949.
    3. China – Politics and government – 20th century.   I. Title.   II. Series.
    HN740.Z9 E476 2000
    305.5′2′0951 – dc21   99-051370

ISBN   0 521 64289 2   hardback

To my beloved Guangming

Contents

Contents

Contents

Part IV
Modern State Making and the Interaction
between State and Society

List of Illustrations

List of Tables

Acknowledgments

This book began as a doctoral dissertation at the University of Chicago, and I thank the university for the Century Fellowship that enabled me to complete my doctoral degree. I also thank Guy Alitto for introducing me to the study of Henan, and Tang Tsou for encouraging me to pursue this research. During my years at Chicago, I received guidance from Barry D. Karl, Leo Ou-fan Lee, and William L. Parish, to all of whom I will always remain grateful. Mary Rankin, Prasenjit Duara, Elizabeth Perry, Joseph Esherick, Roger Des Forges, and Oderic Wou read the entire manuscript of my dissertation and offered detailed comments. Their advice prompted a decision to rewrite and redo the research for the entire manuscript. I thank each of them for offering me a helping hand when I really needed it.

I based my research for this book largely on primary sources obtained on my trips to mainland China, Taiwan, and the Hoover Institution at Stanford University, as well as materials collected earlier at some of the leading libraries in the United States. Through my fieldwork in Henan alone, I acquired a wealth of unpublished personal notes and diaries, recently compiled local histories (at the county level or even lower), CCP documents, unpublished manuscripts, unpublished or recently published government surveys, government statistics, personal memoirs, gazetteers, interview transcripts, and a variety of other items. Most of these materials were classified as internal information *(neibu)* and therefore could not be taken out of the country. Previously, some had been accessible only to officials in the provincial government. Many others were in the possession of private citizens. For helping me obtain these materials, I thank my dear friends in Henan, many of whom wish to remain anonymous. I also thank Huang Xuelin, Wang Tianjiang, Zheng Yongfu, and Wang Quanying for their friendship and invaluable assistance to my research.

On my visits to Taiwan, I was able to cross-check facts by consulting many documents that would have been unavailable on the mainland, such as the minutes of official meetings held by the Nationalist provincial government. I thank Chen San-Ching, Shen Sung-ch'iao, Shen Huai-yu, and Chen Yung-fa of the Academia Sinica for their gracious hospitality. I am also grateful to the people I met at the Yangmingshan Archive, the National Archive, the GMD History Archive, and the Modern Chinese History Library at the Academia Sinica. Many offered unstinting assistance without even giving me their names.

During the years this book took shape, R. Keith Schoppa has constantly given advice and assistance. Frederic Wakeman encouraged and supported me throughout. To them, I offer my eternal gratitude. Many of my colleagues in the China field have also given help and support: Albert Dien, Joseph Fewsmith, Edward Friedman, Philip Huang, Marilyn A. Levine, William Rowe, Lung-kee Sun, Jeffrey N. Wasserstrom, and Wen-hsin Yeh. Kenneth Pomeranz has provided unflagging encouragement and insightful suggestions, as have William Kirby, the Cambridge Modern China Series editor, and the anonymous readers for the Press. Their professionalism and profound knowledge of China have benefited me immensely. I also thank Mary Child, the Asian Studies editor, and her predecessor, Elizabeth Neal for making it possible for my book to appear on the list of the Modern China Series. Thanks to Robert Furnish and Christine A. T. Dunn for lending their editorial expertise. My gratitude also goes to the Chiang Ching-kuo Foundation, the Pacific Cultural Foundation, and the Center for East Asian Studies of Indiana University at Bloomington for their grants to support the publication of this book.

Last, but certainly not least, I thank my parents and especially my wife, Yang Guangming, to whom this book is dedicated, for her enduring love. I also thank my lovely daughter, Lucie Eda Zhang, for her unerring sense of when to tiptoe past my study, and my two dogs, Hero and Hans. All of them have made my writing a pleasure rather than a chore.

Part I

INTRODUCTION

1

Theoretical Context

ON a hot day in July 1938, shortly after Japanese troops occupied the capital city of Nanjing, Chiang Kai-shek, then the national leader of China, arrived in Wuhan two months before the city fell into the hands of the enemy. As a part of his busy schedule, Chiang had arranged a personal meeting with Bie Tingfang, a local "bully" or "ruffian" from southwestern Henan who had neither political connections outside his native region nor an official position in the Nationalist government.[1] Bie was surprised by Chiang's invitation because such a meeting had never taken place before and certainly not in the time of national emergency. He therefore feared it was a trap set by the officials of Henan, who sought his arrest. But, encouraged by his friends, Bie cautiously entered Wuhan and was warmly received by Chiang. During the meeting, Chiang heaped honors upon his guest. He praised him for his courage in fighting bandits in his home region and his leadership in showing villagers how to improve their lives through economic development. Before the meeting ended, Chiang had offered Bie a medal of honor, proclaimed his home county (Neixiang) to be one of three model counties in China, and placed him in command of the entire militia in Nanyang District (southwestern Henan) – a force of nearly 200,000 men.[2]

Why would a national leader like Chiang Kai-shek court a politically obscure local figure like Bie Tingfang when the Japanese were at the

---

[1] In fact, local officials in Henan had dismissed Bie Tingfang as merely a "bully" or "ruffian."

[2] Neixiang xian wenshi ziliao weiyuan hui, *Neixiang wenshi ziliao: Bie Tingfang shilu* (*Local History of Neixiang County: Special Edition on Bie Tingfang*) (Neixiang: Zhongguo renmin zhengzhi xieshang huiyi, Neixiang xian weiyuan hui, 1985), 63–4; and Chen Shunde et al., *Xianhua wanxi ji* (*Recollections of Southwestern Henan*) (Taipei: Weiqin Chuban She, 1979), 16.

door of the city? The answer lies in dramatic sociopolitical changes in the local society of Henan beginning at the turn of the twentieth century, before the Nationalist government took over the province, which thrust the state into a highly compromised relationship with the local elites. These changes are part of a profound social transformation in the country that originated with individual needs, motives, and actions to meet the challenges of the new century. In other words, these changes were but the tip of an iceberg of a much larger scale of social developments that brought China through its unique path to modernity.[3] Because this transformation evolved from within the society itself, I deem it a genuine self-transformation.

To examine the changes in realms of state and society, scholars of Chinese history have relied on three general approaches, each with its own explanatory capabilities and limitations. The first approach focused on local elites, their personal background, upward mobility, and role in local society. This approach developed from the early notion of an existing "gentry" stratum in Chinese society. Influenced by Max Weber, Wolfram Eberhard first applied the notion of "gentry" to rural elites before the Song dynasty.[4] Later, Hsiao Kung-chuan, Fei Hsiao-t'ung, Chang Chung-li, Ch'u T'ung-tsu, and Franz Michael used the same concept to describe the local elites in the late imperial period.[5] For the Republican period, Susan Mann and Philip Kuhn raise some questions about the notion, but their research still finds it useful in view of the elites' role in assisting the state in local taxation.[6] Subsequently, Prasen-

---

[3] My conception of how the actions of individuals are based on their needs, desires, and perceptions of opportunity came from theoreticians such as Anthony Giddens. See Derek Layder, *Understanding Social Theory* (London: Sage Publications, 1994), 125–50, 207–23. I also owe myself to Ronald S. Burt for the understanding of the dialectic relationship between social change and individual action. See Ronald S. Burt, *Toward a Structural Theory of Action: Network Models of Social Structure, Perception, and Action* (New York: Academic Press, 1982), 9.

[4] Wolfram Eberhard, *Social Mobility in Traditional China* (Leiden: E. J. Brill, 1962).

[5] See Hsiao-t'ung Fei, *China's Gentry: Essays in Rural-Urban Relations* (Chicago: University of Chicago Press, 1953); T'ung-tsu Ch'u, *Local Government in China under the Ch'ing* (Cambridge, MA: Harvard University Press, 1962); Chung-li Chang, *The Chinese Gentry: Studies on Their Role in Nineteenth-Century Chinese Society* (Seattle: University of Washington Press, 1955); Kung-chuan Hsiao, *Rural China: Imperial Control in the Nineteenth Century* (Seattle: University of Washington Press, 1960); and Franz H. Michael, *The Taiping Rebellion; History and Documents*, Margery Anneberg et al., trans. (Seattle: University of Washington Press, 1966–1971).

[6] Philip A. Kuhn and Susan Mann Jones, "Introduction," in *Select Papers from the Center for Far Eastern Studies*, Susan Mann Jones, ed., vol. 3 (Chicago: University of Chicago Press, 1978–79), v–xviii, 100–36, 70–99.

jit Duara's work again demonstrates the local elites acted as brokers between the state and local society in various capacities during the Republican period.[7] This approach has been very useful for understanding the changes in the elite stratum for the imperial period. Since the beginning of the twentieth century, however, the elite stratum as a whole underwent profound change, as a result of which the old system for measuring status, power, and prestige in local communities gradually disappeared. It has become difficult to apply this approach to twentieth-century Chinese society without modification. Many historians, for example, have changed the original term *social mobility* to *elite mobility*.[8]

A second approach was to scrutinize the political dynamics in social mobilization, and to focus, in particular, on the expansion of elite activism. Keith Schoppa has discovered increasing "political differentiation" to be the significant development among the local elites in the core areas of Zhejiang during the early twentieth century.[9] Mary Rankin, William Rowe, and David Strand have further shown that elite activism in the country's commercialized areas and large cities reached a high level of political sophistication in the nineteenth century, and even more so in the early twentieth century. Elites extended their organizational capacity and increased their extrabureaucratic activities, and special interest groups flourished within the cities.[10] This approach is still an analytically powerful tool for identifying which developments in Chinese society contributed significantly to its modern transition. The rise of a highly organized form of elite activism was an integral component of the long-term trend of social mobilization. However, the previous research based on this approach has shown highly organized elite activism was generally restricted to commercialized or urban areas. It therefore conveys the impression that there

---

[7] Prasenjit Duara, *Culture, Power, and the State: Rural North China, 1900–1942* (Stanford: Stanford University Press, 1988).

[8] Joseph W. Esherick and Mary Backus Rankin, eds., *Chinese Local Elites and Patterns of Dominance* (Berkeley: University of California Press, 1990).

[9] R. Keith Schoppa, *Chinese Elites and Political Change: Zhejiang Province in the Early Twentieth Century* (Cambridge, MA: Harvard University Press, 1982).

[10] See Mary Rankin, *Elite Activism and Political Transformation in China: Zhejiang Province, 1965–1911* (Stanford: Stanford University Press, 1986); William T. Rowe, *Hankow: Commerce and Society in a Chinese City* (Stanford: Stanford University Press, 1984); and David Strand, *Rickshaw Beijing: City People and Politics in the 1920s* (Berkeley: University of California Press, 1989).

was a widening gap between urban and rural, and core and peripheral elites.[11]

The third approach was to fathom the impact of state making. Philip Kuhn has discerned a devolution of state power into the hands of local elites – a trend that started in the midst of China's "local militarization" in the eighteenth century.[12] The trend continued through the Self-Government movement of the early twentieth century, and was reversed by the state's aggressive attempt to reassert power over local society during the Republican period.[13] Duara has verified that the goal of state making was shared by Yuan Shikai, the warlords, and the Nationalist government. Judging their efforts to have failed, Duara introduces the concept of "state involution" to describe how their endeavors were jeopardized by the local elites.[14] Perceiving a similar deficiency of state making in the fiscal domain, Susan Mann traces this trend back to 1853, the point at which the Qing government adopted the *lijin* taxes. Mann further notes that the state fashioned many compromises with the local constituencies (namely, the local elites) between the late Qing and the Republican periods.[15] Recently, the state-making model, which relies on a cyclical view of gentry society versus the general dominance of state power, has been questioned by several scholars. By recognizing a dual process of state making and unmaking in coastal areas and the northern hinterland, for instance, Pomeranz suggests going beyond the "simple cyclical scheme" of state making to follow social, economic, and political developments in all directions.[16]

To provide a fresh look at the changes in state and society in China from 1900 to 1937, this study focuses on two regions of Henan, the southwest and the north. Henan is chosen as the locus of my research for two reasons. First, the issues related to state and society in Henan have not been thoroughly addressed. Previous research on this province has either

---

[11] Esherick and Rankin, *Chinese Local Elites*, 339.
[12] Philip Kuhn, *Rebellion and Its Enemies in Late Imperial China: Militarization and Social Structure, 1796–1864* (Cambridge, MA: Harvard University Press, 1970).
[13] Philip Kuhn, "Local Self-government under the Republic: Problems of Control, Autonomy, and Mobilization," in *Conflict and Control in Late Imperial China*, Frederic Wakeman and Carolyn Grant, eds. (Berkeley: University of California Press, 1975).
[14] Duara, *Culture, Power, and the State.*
[15] Susan Mann, *Local Merchants and the Chinese Bureaucracy, 1750–1950* (Stanford: Stanford University Press, 1987).
[16] Kenneth Pomeranz, *The Making of a Hinterland: State, Society, and Economy in Inland North China, 1853–1937* (Berkeley: University of California Press, 1993), 271–6.

centered on communist activities,[17] bandits and secret societies,[18] war-lordism,[19] or late Qing officials and village leaders.[20] This book offers the first serious investigation of the societal transformation in local communities that led to the profound changes in the relationship between the state and society. Second, Henan's location in north-central China allows fruitful comparison with other studies of similar topics. Most previous studies of this nature have focused on southern or southeastern China, but few have concentrated on north-central China. The findings of this research are compared with those of other studies.

Within Henan, the southwest and the north become the target of this investigation because they differ a great deal socially, economically, and topographically. Contrasting the data from these two regions reveals different patterns of social and political developments within the same province. The research focuses on the period between 1900 and 1937 when the local power structure in Henan began to change at the turn of the century. It ends with the Japanese invasion of China in 1937 since the Sino-Japanese War significantly altered the patterns of social change in Henan.[21]

To create a holistic view of the issues related to state and society, I have adopted a synthesis that incorporates the strengths, but circumvents the limitations, of the above-mentioned approaches. Instead of separately examining changes in elite mobility, social mobilization, and state making, as previous research has done, this study treats all three research categories as interrelated aspects of the single self-generating phenomenon of Chinese social transformation, which originated within local society. It begins with the changes observed among individuals, especially local elites, defined broadly here as those who exercised dominance within a local arena through whatever means – a definition that includes not only those powerful community leaders, militia heads, and big

---

[17] See Oderic Y. K. Wou, *Mobilizing the Masses* (Stanford: Stanford University Press, 1994); Ralph Thaxton, *China Turned Rightside Up: Revolutionary Legitimacy in the Peasant World* (New Haven: Yale University Press, 1983); and Ralph Thaxton, *Salt of the Earth* (Berkeley: University of California Press, 1997).

[18] Phil Billingsley, *Bandits in Republican China* (Stanford: Stanford University Press, 1988); and Elizabeth J. Perry, *Rebels and Revolutionaries in North China: 1845–1945* (Stanford: Stanford University Press, 1980).

[19] Oderic Y. K. Wou, *Militarism in Modern China: The Career of Wu P'ei-fu, 1916–39* (Dawson: Australian National University Press, 1978).

[20] See Roger V. Des Forges, *Hsi-liang and the Chinese National Revolution* (New Haven: Yale University Press, 1973); and Peter J. Seybolt, *Throwing the Emperor from his Horse: Portrait of a Village Leader in China, 1923–1995* (Boulder, CO: Westview Press, 1996).

[21] An analysis of developments since the invasion will be treated in a separate study.

landlords but also minor elites such as tax brokers, medicine men, and literary persons.[22] The advantage of using such a broad definition is that it reflects the reality of local society in early twentieth-century China, where the elite stratum had largely expanded to include people from a wide variety of backgrounds and capacities. It then scrutinizes the social and political developments in local society that stemmed from those changes. Finally, it probes the impact of those societal developments upon the relationship between state and society. Within this broader perspective, the reader is able not only to observe the linkage between all the changes in the aspects of individuals, society, and state/society relationship but also to grasp the significance of each change for the larger context of the self-transformation of Chinese society.

The examination starts with the way individuals met the challenges produced by society due to the endogenous and exogenous agents that were acting upon it. It scrutinizes how various members of society exploited the opportunities created by these societal changes in order to maintain, acquire, or enhance personal power, and how the power structure of local Chinese society was transformed by changes in the social environment, as well as by the ambitions, desires, and actions of these individuals.[23] It, therefore, delineates a multidimensional picture of local elites for the early twentieth century. Furthermore, the research focuses on the transformation of the village communities, specifically their power structure, in order to analyze the context of the changes among local elites. From this perspective, it observes not only the upward mobility but also the downward mobility among the elites, against the background of competition for community leadership, a rivalry joined by various new social groups and individuals with diverse personal backgrounds. In this context, the causes for the changes in the elite stratum are shown.

From the perspective of social mobilization, significant institutional developments, a high level of organizational capacity, and political

---

[22] I generally accept Joseph Esherick and Mary Rankin's definition of local elites as "any individuals or families that exercised dominance within a local arena." See Esherick and Rankin, *Chinese Local Elites*, 10.

[23] Here the word *power* is defined in line with both Michel Foucault and Talcott Parsons as one's capability of exercising dominance or obtaining personal goals. See Michel Foucault, *Discipline and Punish: The Birth of the Prison* (New York: Pantheon Books, 1977), 93–6; and Talcott Parsons, *The Structure of Social Action* (New York: Free Press, 1968), 263.

sophistication not only characterized elite activism in the commercialized areas but in the far periphery as well. This investigation explores how the expansion of the sphere of elite activism in the early twentieth century was carried out through the traditional method of personal networking, and how Chinese society was moving toward a differentiated, "disembedded" (Giddens), and "complex" (Parsons) society in the early twentieth century – a development achieved by the combining of traditional and modern elements.[24] It also emphasizes the linkage between the two regions under study, on the premise that social transformation was definitely not confined to the commercialized areas. Momentous developments also transpired in the local power structure of peripheral societies that, in essence, closely resembled those found in the commercialized areas. The change in the periphery also led to extensive political differentiation, although perhaps in different forms, similar to the elite activism often observed in the cities and commercialized areas. Another vital facet of social transformation was the increase of communication, travel, and personal contact in the society at large, which enhanced the sharing of ideas among different elite groups in separate areas, and therefore hastened the narrowing of the gap between them.

As Chinese society marched further into the twentieth century, the process of social transformation became increasingly intertwined with the political process of state making. Because state and society were under the pressures of mutual interpenetration, it has become increasingly difficult to separate research in the two aspects. For instance, one of the main queries of the state-making approach was whether a trend toward state making existed during the Republican period. But whether or not it did, the trend was not determined by the state alone but by developments in society, by the mutual engagement between the state and different social forces competing for the control of society. Therefore, in order to evaluate that trend, one has to first investigate the development of Chinese society, returning to the exact point at which changes in the local power structure began to occur. Based on this mutually transformative relationship between state and society, we are forced to

---

[24] See Anthony Giddens, *Modernity and Self-Identity: Self and Society in the Late Modern Age* (Stanford: Stanford University Press, 1991), 17–18; Talcott Parsons, *The System of Modern Societies* (Englewood Cliffs, NJ: Prentice-Hall, 1971), 71–121; and Talcott Parsons, *Societies: Evolutionary and Comparative Perspective* (Englewood Cliffs, NJ: Prentice-Hall, 1966).

observe state making from a broader perspective, the perspective of social transformation. This study first examines the deliberate efforts by various state authorities to create a strong centralized government according to their self-imposed vision of a "modern state," then shows the success or failure of state making was not solely determined by the endeavors of the state makers but by the results of the transformation in the local power structure as well. Preconditioned by that result, centralization and decentralization became two distinctive patterns in one province. Thus did two patterns arise in the relationship between state and society in China. This multiplicity indicates the processes of social and political transformation in early twentieth-century China were multilinear rather than unilinear.[25]

Finally, this book offers an alternative to the existing models, which are based on the dichotomized view of social change in the Chinese rural community. One such paradigm is G. William Skinner's "open/shut" model for peasant communities. Skinner interpreted the sequential closure and opening of the rural community, during the decline of one dynasty and the rise of the next, as a consequence of developments external to the community.[26] From the perspective of social transformation, we see the seemingly simultaneous "opening" and "closing" of village communities in northern and southwestern Henan in the Republican period were caused by different social and political developments within the peasant communities: the extension of the political arena for the local elites in the north and the localization of elite dominance in the southwest. Furthermore, this societal self-transformation framework permits us to go beyond Joseph Esherick and Mary Rankin's state penetration/elite mobilization paradigm to comprehend each phenomenon of state making and elite activism in the larger analytical scheme of the mutually transformative relationship between state and society.[27] The study also enables us to comprehend the changes in peasant behavior from a broader perspective than Elizabeth Perry's "predatory/protec-

---

[25] See Anthony Giddens, *The Consequences of Modernity* (Stanford: Stanford University Press, 1990); Joel S. Migdal, "The State in Society: An Approach to Struggles for Domination," in *State Power and Social Forces: Domination and Transformation in the Third World*, Joel S. Migdal, Atul Kohli, and Vivienne Shue, eds. (New York: Cambridge University Press, 1994); and Michael Mann, *The Sources of Social Power: The Rise of Classes and Nation-States, 1760–1914* (Cambridge: Cambridge University Press, 1993).

[26] G. William Skinner, "Chinese Peasants and Closed Community: An Open and Shut Case," *Comparative Studies in Society and History* 13, no. 3 (1971): 278–81.

[27] Esherick and Rankin, *Chinese Local Elites*, 342.

tive" theory, which is based on an understanding of their survival strategy.[28] Through this study, for example, we can see the changes in the twentieth-century "ecosystem," the entire social environment, not as threats to the survival of the peasantry but as challenges. To further clarify my conceptualization of social transformation, I offer the following discussion.

SOCIAL TRANSFORMATION AS A CONCEPTUAL FRAMEWORK

The term *social transformation* in my definition is similar to *social change*. But unlike the word *change*, *transformation* implies a process of combining old elements with the new to transform (in the true sense of the word, to create a new form) a society (*Gesellschaft*).[29] Social transformation is an accumulative process – that is, a process in which insignificant changes accumulate quantitatively until they become significant enough to generate qualitative changes in the entire society. The term *social change* fails to impart this richness of meaning. Again, *social transformation* is a much more useful term. It signifies the accumulation of new elements within the historical context of a society while the old elements continue to surface in a new form. I perceive social transformation as not merely an accumulation of changes, but an accumulation that results in the shaping of society into a more complex form of existence.

This ongoing accretion of changes in every aspect of society eventually leads to a higher level of social sophistication, from which individuals are more fully capable of dealing with their environment. Previous Western theories – especially Herbert Spencer's model as well as modernization theory – have used different terminologies and approaches to describe the process, but most of them saw the result of that process was to transform society from simple to complex. For example, Spencer used *structural differentiation* to describe a gradual and accumulative process of social transformation from an "indefinite incoherent homogeneity," characteristic of an informal, simple, and unspecialized society, to a "definite coherent heterogeneity," typifying a formal, complex, and specialized society.[30] Emile Durkheim saw social change as an "evolutionary"

---

[28] Perry, *Rebels and Revolutionaries*.

[29] My understanding of the word *transformation* is generally in agreement with its original meaning as "a thorough and dramatic change in form, outward appearance, character, etc." See Joyce M. Hawkins and Robert Allen, eds., *Oxford Encyclopedic English Dictionary* (Oxford: Clarendon Press, 1991), 1533.

[30] See Herbert Spencer, *Herbert Spencer on Social Evolution: Selected Writings*, J.D.Y. Peel,

process, and believed individual motives for competition have led to the division of labor in Western societies. Division of labor was, in turn, the fundamental force that transformed these societies from a simple "mechanical solidarity" to a complex "organized solidarity."[31] Max Weber believed society evolved by an inexorable process from a simple, more personal form of organization to a complex, impersonal form of bureaucracy. Weber considered capitalism to be the driving force that eventually led society to modernity.[32]

Talcott Parsons also believed society developed through what he called *structural differentiation* – increasing complexity and differentiation, a notion that became the backbone of modernization theory.[33] S. N. Eisenstadt, among the critics of that theory, nevertheless agreed society does not merely transform randomly; it progresses from a simple to a complex form. He used a different term, *social differentiation*, to describe the process.[34] By replacing *differentiation* with *disembeddedness*, Anthony Giddens also recognized society's tendency toward increasing complexity.[35]

Although the concept of society evolving from simple to complex in form has emerged from an understanding of the Western experience, it is also a valuable tool for comprehending the social processes in China from 1900 to 1937. Modern Chinese society might thus be conceived as a progression from its previous traditional stage. However, this progression is not the result of social evolution.[36] Nor should we make any teleological assumptions about the causal relationships between all the

---

ed. (Chicago: University of Chicago Press, 1972), 33–74; Herbert Spencer, *The Principles of Sociology* (New York: D. Appleton and Co., 1876–85); and Herbert Spencer, *The Evolution of Society: Selections from Herbert Spencer's Principles of Sociology*, Robert L. Carneiro, ed. (Chicago: University of Chicago Press, 1974), 1–31, 48–62, 214–15.

[31] See Randall Collins, *Four Sociological Traditions*, rvsd. ed. (New York: Oxford University Press, 1994), 181–93; Anthony Giddens, *Politics, Sociology and Social History: Encounters with Classical and Contemporary Social Thought* (Stanford: Stanford University Press, 1995), 78–115.

[32] See Bryan S. Turner, *Max Weber: From History to Modernity* (London: Routledge, 1993); Giddens, *Politics, Sociology and Social History*, 15–56; Collins, *Sociological Traditions*, 81–92; and Randall Collins and Michael Makowsky, *The Discovery of Society*, 4th ed. (New York: Random House, 1989), 118–40.

[33] See Parsons, *Modern Societies*, 71–121; and Parsons, *System of Modern Societies*.

[34] S. N. Eisenstadt, "Social Differentiation, Integration and Evolution," *American Sociological Review* (June 1954): 376.

[35] Giddens, *Modernity and Self-Identity*, 17–18.

[36] As Stephen Sanderson points out, the notion of progress itself is value ridden. See Stephen K. Sanderson, *Social Transformation: A General Theory of Historical Development* (Cambridge, MA: Basil Blackwell, 1995), 200–3.

major changes in the country and the process of its social transformation. Rather, China's social transformation took place upon the unique set of social conditions that each individual faced.[37]

Furthermore, traditional culture and modern change are treated here not as mutually exclusive, but as interdependent and mutually reinforcing. Modern changes emerge only on the ground of tradition, and tradition can revitalize itself through the modern changes. In this sense, the process of transformation is not a process in which modern elements replace traditional ones, as modernization theory has assumed.[38] Rather, transformation is a marriage of the modern and the traditional.[39]

In addition, I consider the social transformation of China to have been multilinear. My perception resembles Norbert Elias's conceptualization of the multilinear processes of civilization. Elias once suggested the structural changes in society could develop in one of two main directions – either toward increased or decreased differentiation and integration, with the former constituting multilinear development.[40] However, I move beyond Elias to propose that change seemingly in one direction often appears in the guise of change in the opposite direction. In fact, different aspects of society may transform in different directions simultaneously.

This multilinear transformation of Chinese society was triggered by a combination of exogenous and endogenous factors. It is undeniable that external influences shaped Chinese society to some extent, especially

[37] Robert Nisbet, Anthony Giddens, and Michael Mann all criticize evolutionary theory as being teleological; See Robert Nisbet, *Social Change and History: Aspects of the Western Theory of Development* (New York: Oxford University Press, 1969); Mann, *Social Power*, 531–8; Anthony Giddens, *The Constitution of Society* (Berkeley: University of California Press, 1984); and Anthony Giddens, *A Contemporary Critique of Historical Materialism* (Berkeley: University of California Press, 1981).

[38] One of the criticisms of the modernization theory focused on its view of the relationship between tradition and modernity. See Samuel Huntington, "The Change to Change: Modernization, Development, and Politics," in *Comparative Modernization: A Reader*, Cyril E. Black, ed. (New York: Free Press, 1976), 25–61. Responding to this criticism, the scholars associated with the theory adopted a new approach to the development of the Third World countries during the late 1970s. They began to acknowledge that tradition and modernity could coexist in a modern society. See Alvin Y. So, *Social Change and Development: Modernization, Dependency, and World-System Theories* (Newbury Park, CA: Sage Publications, 1990), 116–19.

[39] Here, I totally agree with Michael Gasster. See Michael Gasster, "Reform and Revolution in China's Political Modernization," in *China in Revolution: The First Phase 1900–1913*, Mary C. Wright, ed. (New Haven: Yale University Press, 1968), 82–3.

[40] Norbert Elias, *The Civilizing Process: The Development of Manners*, Edmund Jephcott, trans. (New York: Urizen, 1939), 53–217.

during the early twentieth century. For example, the arrival of the West brought Western technology, introduced the country to the world market, and stimulated economic development in the cities. In this respect, Robert Nisbet's statement holds a great deal of truth for China: "significant change is overwhelmingly the result of . . . factors insepara-ble from external events and intrusion."[41] However, I deem external causes to have been much more important for some parts of the country, such as the coastal areas and large cities like Shanghai, than for the rural areas of Henan. Above all, social transformation in China was a process that started at the level of the individual. External and internal factors merely increased the complexity of the challenges with which those indi-viduals were confronted.

I, therefore, believe the process of social transformation in twentieth-century China originated with individual needs, motives, and actions to meet the societal challenges of the new century. Those challenges were generated by a combination of events, both internal and external, includ-ing the abolition of the examination system, the end of the Qing dynasty, and further commercialization, enhanced by the arrival of foreign tech-nology. All these changes precipitated an alteration in the traditional value system, the opening of new avenues to social advancement (based on personal merit or achievement), and the evolution of new ways of personal networking. All these factors in turn interacted dialectically to shape and reshape individual needs, motives, and actions, thus generat-ing further changes in society.[42]

THE ISSUE OF MODERNITY IN CHINA

A larger issue pertinent to this book is how the process of social trans-formation that occurred locally in rural China contributed to the social transition that occurred throughout the country in the first four decades

---

[41] Nisbet criticizes evolutionary theory because he considers it to imply that all social changes come from within. See Nisbet, *Social Change*, 180.

[42] My conception of how the actions of individuals are based on their needs, desires, and perceptions of opportunity came from theoreticians such as Anthony Giddens. See Derek Layder, *Understanding Social Theory* (London: Sage Publications, 1994), 125–50, 207–23. I also owe myself to Ronald S. Burt for the understanding of the dialectic rela-tionship between social change and individual action. See Ronald S. Burt, *Toward a Structural Theory of Action: Network Models of Social Structure, Perception, and Action* (New York: Academic Press, 1982), 9.

of the twentieth century. This book addresses some basic concerns about modernity as an appropriate concept for studying Chinese society. It is my intention to extend the significance of this study beyond the field of China studies and to make a contribution to the intellectual discourse on the issue of modernity in all non-Western countries.

The question of Chinese modernity always commands the attention of students of Chinese history. Although the words *modern* or *modernity* have been frequently used by many scholars, there have been few successful attempts to provide a set of clear definitions, let alone general agreement on their meanings. This state of scholarship reflects a basic problem: the uncertainty of what constitutes modernity in China. What were its necessary preconditions? What should be the Chinese path to modernity? How do we identify the modern changes in Chinese society? Underlying these questions is the fundamental issue of how to evaluate Chinese modernity within the context of the social, political, and cultural aspects of Chinese society.

As a brief survey shows, most of the earlier studies of Chinese modernity have been dominated by a general assumption that industrialization and capitalist development were prerequisites for modernization, an assumption deeply rooted in the thinking of the Western social theoreticians, including Max Weber, Karl Marx, and many others who were associated with modernization theory.[43] These early studies, therefore, endeavored to uncover the existence, or the lack, of industrialization and the "sprouts of capitalism" in China, in an obvious attempt to find out why China failed to generate modern changes on its own.

Among these previous efforts, Albert Feuerwerker finds China to have experienced merely a "retarded industrialization" before the arrival of the West.[44] Rhoads Murphey perceives the experience of the treaty ports to epitomize the process of China's modernization. According to Murphey, the economic development and political evolution of China – including the emergence of a national market, the inception of a technological revolution in production and transport, and the changes in institutions, organizations, and ideology – were distinct from Westernization: "They were set in train primarily through the presence and

---

[43] See Giddens, *Politics, Sociology and Social History*, 15–56; Collins and Makowsky, *Discovery of Society*, 118–40; and Huntington, "Change to Change," in Comparative Modernization: A reader ed. Cyric E. Black (1976) 30–1. See also discussion in So, *Social Change*, 33.

[44] Albert Feuerwerker, *China's Early Industrialization: Sheng Hsuan-huai and Mandarin Enterprise* (New York: Atheneum, 1970), 1–7.

actions of Westerners in Asia, and are appropriately viewed as Asian responses to Western stimuli."[45]

Mark Elvin concludes the arrival of the West was "the historic contribution" to China that "ease[d] and then br[oke] the high-level equilibrium trap in China," because it opened "the country to the world market in the middle of the nineteenth century, [which] led before long to rapid commercial and industrial growth at the main points of contact. ..."[46] In her study of the emergence of the bourgeois class in China, Marie-Claire Bergère also claims "the opening-up of China by Westerners remains fundamental to the development of China" because only after China had been awakened by the West did modern elements start to appear. Bergère's research demonstrates that after the West arrived, new social groups arose that shared values different from those of the old local elites. The worldview of the new groups included pragmatism, Confucianism, and ideas brought in from the West. As a part of the social transformation of China in the twentieth century, a bourgeois class emerged in the urban areas, especially those in port cities.[47]

This emphasis on the importance of industrialization and capitalist development for Chinese modernity was most evidenced by the appearance of a collection of essays edited by Gilbert Rozman entitled *The Modernization of China*. China, as a relative latecomer to modernity, the contributors argue, could transform itself only by following the pattern of development of those western European countries that had experienced scientific and technological revolutions. The volume also assumes that modernization is one of several "ineluctable examples of social change in human history." Once a country comes in contact with modernity, it will inevitably be drawn onto its path because "all latecomers found that major elements in their social structure were subverted by the enormous appeal and pressure of elements connected with modernization." The book concludes that in order to achieve modernization, China had to overcome many difficulties and structure a plan for the development of capitalism.[48]

---

[45] Rhoads Murphey, "The Treaty Ports and China's Modernization," in *The Chinese City Between Two Worlds*, Mark Elvin and G. William Skinner, eds. (Stanford: Stanford University Press, 1974), 17–19.

[46] Mark Elvin, *The Pattern of the Chinese Past* (Stanford: Stanford University Press, 1973), 315.

[47] Marie-Claire Bergère, *The Golden Age of the Chinese Bourgeoisie: 1911–1937* (New York: Cambridge University Press, 1986), 13.

[48] Gilbert Rozman, ed., *The Modernization of China* (New York: Free Press, 1981), 3–5, 482.

Aiming to break away from the above paradigm, some scholars have made considerable headway in initiating a discussion of "early modern development." Paul Ropp, Lloyd E. Eastman, Susan Naquin, and Evelyn S. Rawski have all used this term to show that China was already on its way to modernization even in the late Ming dynasty, long before the country encountered the West.[49] Ramon Myers and others have also advocated pushing the accepted date for the beginning of modern Chinese history from 1840 to several decades earlier.[50] William Rowe painstakingly compares the similarity of the economy and society in the nineteenth-century city of Wuhan to conditions in cities of western Europe immediately before the Industrial Revolution.[51] Despite the achievements of these scholars, this entire discussion has been criticized for equating the Chinese experience with that of the West.

William Rowe's books have become the target of intense scrutiny during the "public sphere" debate that has arisen in recent years. That debate was triggered by the question of whether there was a public sphere in China during the late nineteenth and early twentieth centuries, similar to that in late seventeenth- and early eighteenth-century western Europe. The debate turned to questions about the validity of the comparison between Chinese history with the Western experience,[52] and considered the existence of a causal relationship between commercialization and modern development.[53] Most criticisms inclined toward the teleological, unilinear, and universalistic assumptions of social change. From this vantage point, the debate raised an important question of how the process of modernity in a society with a non-Western background should be perceived. This debate continues in the field of China studies.

Nevertheless, the debate has touched upon the valid issue of whether a concept such as "modernity," developed from the Western historical context, and thereby inevitably carrying assumptions relevant to Western

---

[49] See Paul Ropp, *Dissent in Early Modern China: Ju-lin Wai-shih and Ch'ing Social Criticism* (Ann Arbor: University of Michigan Press, 1981); Lloyd E. Eastman, *Family, Field, and Ancestors: Constancy and Change in China's Social and Economic History, 1550–1949* (New York: Oxford University Press, 1988), 192–213; and Susan Naquin and Evelyn S. Rawski, *Chinese Society in the Eighteenth Century* (New Haven: Yale University Press, 1987), 232–6.

[50] Naquin and Rawski, *Chinese Society*, 232.

[51] Rowe, *Hankow*.

[52] Frederic Wakeman, "The Civil Society and Public Sphere Debate: Western Reflections on Chinese Political Culture," *Modern China* 19, no. 2 (1993): 113–34.

[53] Philip Huang, "The Paradigmatic Crisis in Chinese Studies," *Modern China* 17, no. 3 (July 1991): 307, 309–12.

societies, can be used to comprehend a non-Western culture. This question is pertinent to this study because not only the notion of *modernity* but also the term *social transformation* have come from the West, as the latter was closely tied to a nineteenth-century view of the evolution of human society in the West. These concepts were adopted by China scholars and have been used to describe China's transition to, or rather its failure to achieve, modernity. Does this mean we should avoid such concepts altogether?

We in the West who study Chinese history face an ultimate dilemma: the entire Western system of discourse about China is bound by Western concepts, terminologies, and analytical constructs. However, to discard that apparatus requires the fabrication of a new system – a solution that is neither practical nor possible. Besides, many of these concepts are analytically powerful, even for other cultures, if used properly and cautiously. The most viable solution, albeit an expedient one, seems to be to use them with full awareness of their limitations and with a sensitivity for the cultural and historical background of Chinese society.

This book, as one effort to resolve this problem, does not provide a final definition for the term *modern* but rather an operational one – a definition that guides both author and readers to search for evidence of the significant changes within Chinese society.[54] Instead of arguing hermeneutically about the literary connotation of the word *modernity*, the facts do and are allowed to speak for themselves. The same criteria most Western theoreticians have used to uncover these evidences are used here. I see this as obligatory, for the entire notion of modernity has come from the West. But, unlike previous scholars, I seek the similarities between Western and Chinese society in the *result* of their modern transformation rather than in the *preconditions* for that transformation or the process itself. I argue that the crucial distinction between Chinese modernity and that of the West lies in the fact Chinese modernity was based neither on industrialization nor on capitalist development. As E. A. Wrigley and Perry Anderson have suggested, a society can achieve

---

[54] According to physicist Bridgman (1927), who invented the term, an *operational definition* is a definition that "tells readers what they can do and what they can look for to bring [the defining process] into their experience." Furthermore, according to Philip Runkel, "the operational definition gives discipline, it reminds researchers not to claim too much for their measures – not to suppose that to grasp a yardstick is to grasp an ultimate reality." See Philip J. Runkel and Margaret Runkel, *A Guide to Usage for Writers and Students in the Social Sciences* (New Jersey: Rowman & Allanheld, 1984), 91.

modernity without industrialization.[55] China is such a case, and I will demonstrate that China took a unique path to modernity. Due to the limited scope of this book, however, I focus primarily on the social aspect of that process, and reveal its impact on the relationship between state and society.

The result of the modern changes in China for the purpose of this study are judged by criteria provided by Talcott Parsons, modernization theorists, and Anthony Giddens. These constitute the operational identification for this investigation. The transition to modernity is a profound process of social transformation. It first appears as a change in a society's system of values. Accompanying that change is a broadening of the avenues of social mobility as society begins to value personal achievement above social rank at birth and family status. Modernity also fosters the expansion of social activities as well as social relations. As a result, interpersonal relationships become impersonal, detached, and indirect. This expansion can result in the multiplication of individuals' social functions, which are no longer confined to their communities and in the highly institutionalized activities created.[56] With these criteria as a yardstick, we now begin our quest for evidence of a modern transformation in Chinese society during the first four decades of the twentieth century.

---

[55] See E. A. Wrigley, "The Process of Modernization and the Industrial Revolution in England," *Journal of Interdisciplinary History* 3 (1972–1973): 225–59; Perry Anderson, *Lineages of the Absolutist State* (London: NLB, 1974); and Perry Anderson, *Passage from Antiquity to Feudalism* (London: NLB, 1977).

[56] See So, *Social Change*, 21–3; Peter Burke, *History and Social Theory* (Ithaca: Cornell University Press, 1992), 132–3; and Giddens, *Modernity and Self-Identity*, 22.

Northern Henan

Hui

Xinxiang

Anyang

Houjia

Shanxi

Xiuwu

Tangyin

Qi

Ji

Shandong

Neixiang

Xichuan

Anhui

Nanzhao

Nanyang

Zhenping

Xinye

Deng

Hubei

Southwestern Henan

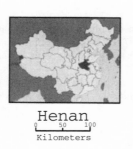

Henan

0   50   100

Kilometers

2

Socioeconomic Setting of Henan

THE early twentieth century was a period of dynamic change in China. That dynamism found expression not only in the political upheavals that turned the old dynasty into new regimes, but also in the various social processes that transformed the country and brought it into the modern era. To investigate these transformative processes, this study will focus primarily on the southwestern and northern regions of Henan. First, however, we shall examine the socioeconomic environment within which these transformations took place.

THE GEOGRAPHY AND MARKETING STRUCTURE OF HENAN

Henan is a densely populated province of 167,000 square kilometers in north-central China. Geographically, the land is uneven in altitude – higher in the western and southeastern sections, lower in the eastern and northeastern regions. The province contains four mountain ranges: the Taihang Mountains at the northwest border between Henan and Shanxi; the Funiu Mountains in the western section; the Tongbai Mountains, which extend from the south to the southeast; and the Dabie Mountains in the far southeast. In the southwest, between the Funiu and Tongbai Mountains, the Nanyang Basin covers 11,900 square kilometers. Almost the entire eastern and northern parts of Henan are flat.

Henan experiences a continental climate characterized by cold winters, hot summers, and four clearly differentiated seasons. The province's harsh weather includes powerful storms in summer, heavy snow in winter, and rainy weather in spring, especially in the mountains. Droughts, floods, and hail storms are frequent.[1]

---

[1] *Henan lishi zhishi*, 1–7; and Chang Jianqiao et al., *Henan sheng dili (Geography of Henan Province)*, Zhongguo dili congshu (Zhengzhou: Henan jiaoyu chuban she, 1985), 15–32, 45–51, 76–81.

Cotton, wheat, beans, and tobacco have traditionally been among the main agricultural products. According to a survey conducted by the Qing government (Ministry of Agriculture, Industry, and Commerce), cotton was grown in nearly half the province in 1910. Zhangde (present Anyang) and Xinxiang, two of the northern counties, were known for cotton growing. Tobacco farming became profitable when the Qing government forbade the growing of opium. In 1904 and 1910, investors from British and American tobacco companies surveyed tobacco farming in Henan. In their report, they estimated the yearly production of the province at between 21,000,000 and 26,000,000 pounds.[2] Nanyang and Deng counties, in the southwest, grew the highest quality tobacco. In the 1920s, however, wheat gradually became an important product as well. John L. Buck surveyed the areas around Xinxiang and Kaifeng between 1921 and 1925 and pronounced northern Henan a part of China's "wheat region" (see Map 2.1).[3] Peanuts and sesame were also grown in most areas. Silk was produced in Nanyang and Zhenping counties in the southwest region. In 1902, for instance, 800 households in the suburbs of the city of Nanyang earned their living through the making and selling of silk. About thirty large stores in the city specialized in the silk business.[4]

G. William Skinner's central-place model offers useful insights into the province's marketing structure. Using such elements as physiographic features (especially the river basins) Skinner divided China into nine macroregions. Henan is mostly a part of the North China macroregion. Only a portion of the province's southwest belongs to the Middle Yangtze macroregion.[5] The locations of market towns that existed before the twentieth century fit very well in Skinner's scheme (see Map 2.2).

The marketing structure of Henan before the turn of the twentieth century was shaped by four major rivers: the Yellow, the Huai, the Hai, and the Yangtze. The Yellow River runs through northern Henan. The Hai River enters northern Henan from Shandong and then forks into

[2] Shen Songqiao, "Jingji zuowu yu jindai Henan nongcun jingji: 1906–1937" (Cash Crops and Peasant Economy in Modern Henan: 1906–1937), in *Jindai Zhongguo nongcun jingji shi lunwen ji* (Taipei: Zhongyang yanjiu yuan jindai shi yanjiu, 1978), 346, 357.

[3] John L. Buck, *Land Utilization in China* (Chicago: University of Chicago Press, 1937), 25; and Han Bangfu et al., *Henan sheng nongcun diaocha* (*Henan Village Survey*) (Shanghai: Shangwu yinshu guan, 1934), 1–2.

[4] Nanyang shi difang shizhi bianchuan weiyuan hui, *Nanyang shizhi* (*Gazetteer of Nanyang City*) (Zhengzhou: Henan renmin chuban she, 1989), 27.

[5] G. William Skinner, "Cities and the Hierarchy of Local Systems," in *The City in Late Imperial China*, G. William Skinner, ed. (Stanford: Stanford University Press, 1977), 281–3; and map in ibid., 214–15.

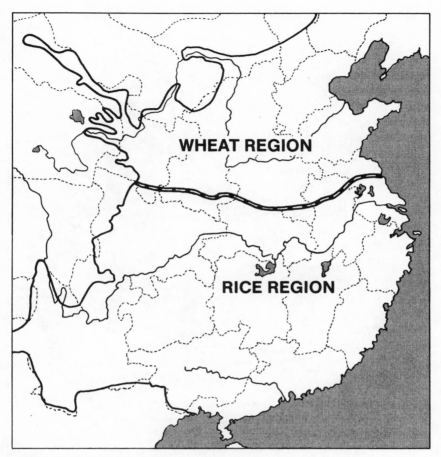

Map 2.1 The Two Main Agricultural Regions of China. *Source:* John Lossing Buck, *Land Utilization in China* (Chicago: University of Chicago Press, 1937), p. 25. Reprinted by permission.

the Wei and the Zhang rivers. The Tang, Bai, and Dan rivers in the southwest corner run into the Yangtze River through the Han basin in Hubei. The Huai River starts in the Tongbai Mountains and flows east across most of the eastern section of the province. The Grand Canal, north of the Yellow River, was built in the Sui dynasty but fell into disuse after 1855, when the Yellow River changed its course into Shandong province. In the eighteenth and nineteenth centuries, rivers and military post roads were the main routes for transportation. Because of their proximity to the roads and rivers, cities such as Kaifeng (formerly called Bianzhou,

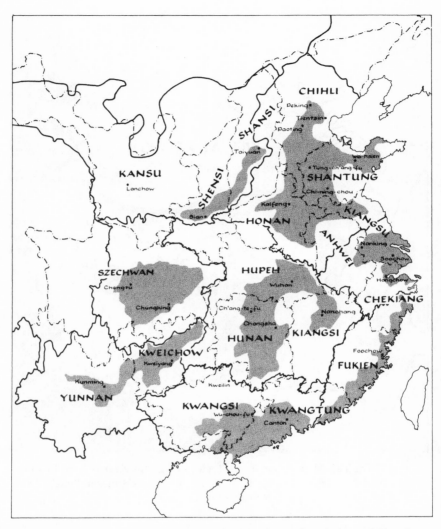

Map 2.2 Physiographic Macroregions in Relation to Provinces and Showing Metropolitan Cities, 1843. *Source: The City in Late Imperial China*, ed. G. William Skinner (Stanford: Stanford University Press, 1977), p. 215. Reprinted by permission.

on the Huiji River) and Luoyang became large metropolitan centers. Smaller cities like Zhuxian, Daokou, Sheqi, Qinghua, Chuwang, and Sanhe were also located on navigable waterways. In northern Henan, for example, the town of Daokou sits at the mouth of the Wei River, which provided the main route for trade between northern Henan and Tianjin through Hebei. Similarly, in southwestern Henan, Sheqi developed into a commercial center because the Tang River made it possible to transport goods to Hankou via the Han River (see Map 2.3).[6]

Changes in the network of rivers before the end of the nineteenth century triggered a decline of the market towns that depended on these waterways for their prosperity. The Tang River in the southwest and the Jialu River in the southeast, for example, gradually became unnavigable because of the accumulation of mud upstream. Commerce in Sheqizhen also declined because the Tang River became less and less navigable. Zhuxianzhen, which had been one of the four busiest small cities in Henan, almost turned into a ghost town.[7]

The most significant changes in Henan's marketing structure, however, were produced by the railroad. By directly linking previously remote areas with many urban centers inside and outside Henan, the railroad remapped the distribution of economic resources in the province and gradually replaced the rivers and military post roads as the chief transportation routes. Located at the intersection of the Jinghan and the Panghai railroads, Zhengzhou gradually emerged as a commercial metropolis the equal of Kaifeng. Through the railroads, other local cities like Luoyang, Zhangde, Xinxiang, and Xuchang joined Kaifeng and Zhengzhou as the principal trading centers in central China. Along the railroads, new market towns also appeared. Luohe, Zhoukou, and Jiaozuo became the most prosperous among the dozen or so newly emerged marketing centers linked to Beijing, Wuhan, and later, Shanghai (after 1927) (see Map 2.4).[8]

Because of the railroads, business in some market towns boomed; others, not located close to railroads, went bust. Zhumadian, for example, had been a wasteland before it grew into a busy market town. But at the same time, commerce in townships like Daokou, Qinghua, Chuwang, and

[6] Chang, *Henan sheng dili*, 84–90; Li Rusong and Cui Xiurong, "Henan gonglu jiaotong gujin (Past and present public road transportation in Henan)," ed. Guo Yingsheng, *Zhongzhou Jingu* (Zhengzhou: Zhongzhou jingu chuban she, 1987): 36; and Lin Furui and Chen Daiguang, *Henan renkou dili (Population Geography in Henan)* (Zhengzhou: Henan sheng kexue yuan dili yanjiu suo, 1981), 128.

[7] Liu Jingxiang et al., eds., *Henan xinzhi (Henan New Gazetteer)*, (Kaifeng: Henan sheng dang'an guan, 1929), 773–9; and Deng Zhiyuan, ed., *Henan shengzhi (Provincial Gazetteer of Henan)* (1925), 32.

[8] Wang Ying, "Tielu ji tielu gongchang zai Henan de xingjian (The Construction of Railroads and Railroad Plants in Henan)," in Yang Yingzhou et al., eds., *Henan sheng difang zhi zhengwen ziliao xuan* (Zhengzhou: Henan sheng difa zhi bianwei zong bianji shi, 1983), 88–90; Qu Mingjing et al., *Henan xianqing (Henan County History)* (Zhengzhou: Henan renmin chuban she, 1990), 63–7; and Lin and Chen, *Renkou dili*, 129.

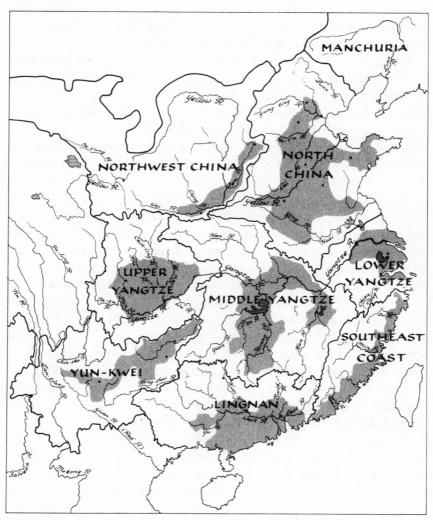

Map 2.3 Physiographic Macroregions of Agrarian China in Relation to Major
Rivers, with Regional Cores Indicated by Shading. *Source: The City in Late
Imperial China*, ed. G. William Skinner (Stanford: Stanford University Press,
1977), p. 214. Reprinted by permission.

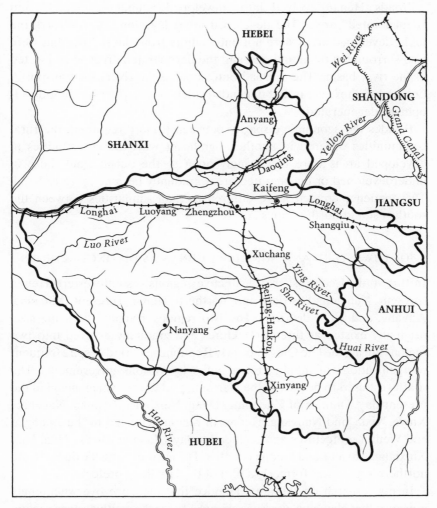

Map 2.4 Henan Rail Transport and Drainage Systems. *Source:* Oderic Y. K. Wou, *Mobilizing the Masses: Building Revolution in Henan* (Stanford: Stanford University Press, 1994), p. 14. Reprinted by permission.

Sanhe drastically declined. Furthermore, there was a slow but steady shift of population toward the new market towns. After the expansion of the railroads, population concentrated along their tracks as well as along rivers.[9]

Oderic Wou insightfully notes that due to the construction of the

[9] Li and Cui, *Henan Renkou dili*, 122, 128; and Deng, *Henan shengzhi*, 32, 48.

railroads, Henan evolved into "developed," "underdeveloped," and "degenerated" areas. The developed areas lay along the railroad; the underdeveloped areas were not only remote from the railroad but were also surrounded by mountains; and the degenerated areas were located in the river basins. The railroad outcompeted the rivers for transportation and so those areas that depended solely on the river for their development degenerated.[10]

Besides the economic disparity between these three areas, the rural communities differed in another significant way: the communities in developed areas were increasingly open to the outside, but those in underdeveloped or degenerated areas gradually became more isolated. This tendency created more differences than similarities between the southwest and north regions.

SOUTHWESTERN AND NORTHERN HENAN AS DISTINCT REGIONS

In this study, I contrast two distinctive regions – southwestern Henan (present Nanyang District) and northern Henan (present Xinxiang, Anyang, and Hebi districts). The two regions, roughly the same size, originally existed as three prefectures and gradually evolved into two regions during the late Qing and early Republican period despite frequent reorganizations of administrative units by various governments. The southwest used to be part of the Nanyang prefecture, which included the present day counties of Zhenping, Deng, Neixiang, Xichuan, Nanzhao, Xinye, Xixia, and Nanyang. The north region belonged to the Zhangde and Weihui prefectures and included today's Tangyin, Ji, Qi, Hua, Hui, Xinxiang, Anyang, and Huojia counties. The current Xiuwu County in the northern region was formerly a part of the Huaiqing prefecture.[11]

In my research on the area, I notice that evidence overwhelmingly indicates that Nanyang was the regional city for the southwestern region. Kaifeng, rather than Wuhan, was the metropolitan city people in southwestern Henan usually considered the higher level marketing center. In northern Henan, Xinxiang and Zhangde were considered the regional cities for the lower and upper portions of the northern region. This

---

[10] Oderic Y. K. Wou, "The Impact of Differential Economic Change on Society in Honan in the 1920s and 1930s" (Unpublished). Most of this paper appears in *Asian Profile* 12, no. 3 (June 1984).

[11] Anyang (Zhangde) and Tangyin counties belonged to Zhangde prefecture. Weihui prefecture included Ji, Xinxiang, Huojia, Qi, Hui, and Hua counties. See Liu, *Henan xinzhi*, 54–8.

feeling of belonging to a region, and not necessarily to a metropolitan city in a macroregion, might seem to contradict every rule of rational choice on which G. William Skinner's macroregion model is based. In fact, people living in what I call a region tend to have a clear sense of its boundaries. Informally, for example, they refer to the southwestern region as Wanxi and the northern region as Yubei. Their activities also are generally confined to the region in which they live. This sense of community among the individuals in a given area might also be influenced by local tradition, habits, and the way people identify themselves with an area.

One way of explaining the differences between the two regions is through the core-periphery paradigm, which employs several criteria to distinguish between the two zones. As his primary criterion for discriminating between core and periphery, Skinner used population density, since it was for him the most reliable indicator of the distribution of economic resources.[12] In my examination of zonal differences between southwestern and northern Henan, I apply Skinner's criterion. According to a population survey compiled by Guan Weilan, northern Henan was generally much more populated than the southwest.[13] And the southwestern counties of Neixiang, Xichun, Zhenping, and Nanzhao were among the least populated counties in Henan. Zhenping County was less populated than most. Population density in Nanyang, Deng, and Xinye counties was at or below the provincial average. In the north region, in contrast, Xinxiang and Anyang counties were among the most populated counties in the entire province, and the population density in Tangyin, Ji, Huojia, and Hua counties was above average. Even the least populated counties in the north were more populated than the most populated counties in the southwest (see Table 2.1).[14]

The relative stage of commercialization in each region also reveals significant differences. In the southwest there was only one local city, Nanyang. There was one central market town in Deng County. In other counties, there was only one intermediate market town and a few stan-

[12] Skinner's other criteria include postal status and the distribution of market schedules. See Skinner, "Local Systems," 282, 347–51. To Skinner's criteria, R. Keith Schoppa has added a financial institution index. See Schoppa, *Chinese Elites*, 176–8.

[13] Guan Weilan, comp., *Zhonghua minguo xingzheng quhua ji tudi renkou tongji biao (Republic of China Administrative District Demarcation and Surveys of Population and Landholding)* (Taipei: Beikai chuban she, 1956), 81–6.

[14] Han Bangfu et al., *Henan sheng nongcun diaocha* (Henan Village Survey) (Shanghai: Shangwu yinshu guan, 1934) and Guan, *Tudi renkou tongji*, 81–6.

Table 2.1. *Population Density by County*

Name of County	Population Density (per square kilometer)	Postal Rank	Name of County	Population Density (per square kilometer)	Postal Rank
Outerperiphery			Innerperiphery (*continued*)		
Lushi	23	3	Queshan	153	2
Luoning	45	3	Yichuan	161	
Neixiang	46	3	Jiyuan	166	3
Song	50		Guangshan	170	3
Fugou	51	3	Taikang	171	3
Jingfu	58		Guangwu	173	
Xiangcheng	59	3	Yiyang	176	3
Shouxiang	60	3	Minquan	183	
Tongbo	60	3	Yanling	183	3
Lingbao	62	3	Dengfeng	184	3
Xichuan	62		Xinye	185	
Shangcheng	64	3	Yanjin	185	3
Shan	66	2	Yangwu	188	3
Yiyang	70	3	Huangchuan	189	
Mianchi	74	2	Lanfeng	193	3
Nanzhao	82	3	Ji	193	
Miyang	98	3			
Between Outerperiphery and Innerperiphery			Between Innerperiphery and Outercore		
			Xi	195	2
Fangchen	109		Yucheng	199	3
Gushi	111	3	Weishi	201	3
Mi	114	3	Qi	204	3
Xinyang	117	2	Xihua	205	3
She	120	3	Nanyang	207	2
Luoshan	120	2	Ye	208	
			Deng	212	2
Innerperiphery			Wuan	213	2
			Baofeng	216	3
Zhongmou	136	3	Yingyang	217	3
Lushan	137	2			
Xinan	138	3	Outercore		
Gong	142	3			
Linru	146		Yuanwu	221	3
Zhenping	147	3	Xiuwu	222	3
Tanghe	149		Boai	222	
Luyi	149	3	Neihuang	227	3
Zhengyang	152	3	Xinzheng	227	2

(*continued*)

Table 2.1. *(continued)*

Name of County	Population Density (per square kilometer)	Postal Rank	Name of County	Population Density (per square kilometer)	Postal Rank
Outercore *(continued)*			Between Outercore and Innercore		
Yu	227	2			
Hui	229	2	Wuzhi	298	
Suiping	235	2	Wuyang	299	
Jia	236	3	Qinyang	301	
Mengjin	237	3	Wen	302	3
Ningling	238	3	Linying	303	2
Lin	249	3	Qi	305	
Xuchang	251		Chenliu	308	3
Huaiyang	253		Fengqiu	309	3
Yanshi	255	3			
Shangqiu	261		Innercore		
Kaifeng	265	1	Meng	315	3
Tangyin	268	3	Yongcheng	320	
Runan	269		Sishui	331	3
Tongxu	279	3	Xiping	345	2
Zheng	280	2	Shangshui	348	3
Zhecheng	285	3	Jun	351	
Weichuan	288	3	Luoyang	352	
Shenqiu	288	3	Huojia	362	3
Hua	290	3	Sui	364	3
Xinchai	291	3	Shangchai	368	3
Changge	292	3	Yancheng	372	2
			Anyang	395	
			Kaocheng	406	3
			Xiayi	526	3
			Xinxiang	575	2

Source: For population density, Guan Weilan, comp., *Zhonghua minguo xingzheng quhua ji tudi renkou tongji biao (Republic of China Administrative District Demarcation and Survey of Population and Landholding)* (Taipei: Beikai chuban she, 1956), 81–6; for postal rank, Toa Dobunkai, comp., *Shina Shôbetsu Zenshi: Henanshô*, 424–34.

dard market towns in each county. Most county seats were locations for both county government and the county's market. In Zhenping County, however, the market was in a little town called Shifushi ("stone-Buddha temple"). In the north, however, there were several local cities and quite a few central market towns. Nearly every county had its own central market town, and all market towns were better developed than their counterparts in the southwest region. Anyang and Xinxiang, two northern local cities, had already developed as centers for banks and money-lenders before 1912.[15] Even Hua County, one of the least commercialized counties in the north, boasted well-organized and prosperous salt businesses, pawn shops, currency exchange services, clothing retailers, grocery stores, and cotton dealers in its central market town.[16] In addition, there were more standard market towns in each northern county than in any of their southwestern counterparts. Tangyin County embraced nine standard market towns in addition to its central market town, Chenguanzhen. Each of these standard market towns was the center of a ward that was named after the township.

Judging by population density and the level of commercialization, northern Henan has been a core area, and the southwest a peripheral area.[17] This categorization is not entirely precise. It is used here only to understand the basic differences in socioeconomic conditions of these regions. Significant anomalies existed within each region. For example, by itself Nanyang County fits into the core category; but the county lies in the center of southwestern Henan, definitely on the periphery.

FOREIGN INTRUSION, COMMERCIALIZATION, AND THE
BANDITRY CRISIS

Two sets of social conditions dominated the two regions during the early twentieth century. Each set of conditions was related to the social, economic, and political changes in the country. As a part of endogenous changes, banditry created an indisputable crisis. Originating in exogenous causes, foreign intrusion engendered conflicts with Chinese traditional values and, at the same time, stimulated agricultural commercialization. Even though some of the conditions were shared by both regions in

---

[15] *Zhonghua renmin gongheguo fensheng ditu ji (Atlas of the People's Republic of China)* (Beijing: Ditu chuban she, 1974); and Toa Dobunkai, comp., *Shina Shobetsu Zenshi: Seko-sho (A Gazetteer of all Provinces of China)*, 13 (Tokyo, 1919), 18.

　　The criteria used in the following description for determining the hierarchy of central places are based on G. William Skinner's system in "Marketing and Social Structure in Rural China," *Journal of Asian Studies* 24 (February 1965): 5–10. See also Skinner, "Local Systems," 285–7.

[16] Wang Puyuan et al., *Chongxiu Huaxian zhi (Gazetteer of Hua County)* (Kaifeng: Kaifeng Xinyu Printing Shop, 1932), 32.

[17] I believe it is more practical for this research to adopt a holistic approach to zonal categorization.

various degrees, the banditry crisis affected the southwest deeply, while foreign intrusion caused a great deal of disturbance in the north. As a result, the social issues that confronted people living in the two regions were very different.

For centuries, banditry had been one of the paramount concerns of the people in Henan, especially in the southwest. According to Phil Billingsley, Henan became China's "cradle of banditry" because bandits had been a part of its socioecology long before the period under discussion. In some parts of western Henan, banditry was a tradition for many poor families; parents encouraged their sons, wives urged their husbands, and brothers inspired other brothers to become bandits.[18]

Southwestern Henan fostered banditry not only because it was an economically backward peripheral zone where life was extremely arduous for ordinary peasants, but also because it was generally neglected by provincial authorities. In his book on the Boxers in Shandong, Joseph Esherick attributes the banditry of western Shandong partly to its location at the borders of Shandong, Jiangsu, and Henan. Like western Shandong, southwestern Henan borders on both Shanxi and Hubei, and was always considered remote from the provincial administration.[19] Bandits throve most heartily at the turn of the century because the Qing government was fully occupied by conflicts between Chinese and foreigners – most of which occurred in less remote areas. Because there were fewer foreigners in southwestern Henan – only a few in Nanyang and Zhenping – and there was no railroad in the area, the provincial government paid even less attention to the region than before. The southwest thus became a refuge for bandits.[20] According to Billingsley, four areas harbored bandits in Henan. One extended from the southeast of Luoyang District to the northwest of Xuchang District. A second was located in the center of present-day Luoyang District. The third was southwestern Henan, and the fourth was the eastern part of the province. For its location in the center of all the subregions, southwestern Henan was considered the "bandit kingdom."[21] Although banditry is a complex social phenomenon associated with a variety of social causes, individual behavior, and personal motivations, the rank and file were mostly gangs

---

[18] Billingsley, *Bandits*, 50.

[19] Joseph W. Esherick, *The Origins of the Boxer Uprising* (Berkeley: University of California Press, 1987), 19.

[20] Zhang Renjun, *Yuzhe huicun (Collection of Imperial Reports)* 55, 1 (Peking, June 4, 1903); *Yongyan shangshu zouyi (Report of the President of the Yongyan Ministry of Foreign Affairs)*, 4 (Beijing, 1904), 45–9.

[21] Billingsley, *Bandits*, 51–3.

of peasants trying to escape misery and starvation.[22] For some gang members, occasional raiding was a part of their survival strategy, a way to supplement their yearly income after farming.[23] Many, adhering to the "green-wood" tradition, left their home villages undisturbed. Yet most "displayed no sense of social consciousness in selecting their victims" and preyed on the rich and the poor in the same "sadistical" manner.[24] As banditry in the southwest reached crisis proportions, life there became insufferable.[25]

While banditry became the key social issue in southwestern Henan, confrontation with foreigners became the major issue in the north. The interests of the foreigners were twofold: religious and economic. The first group of missionaries arrived in Henan in 1843. By 1844 the provincial government designated a district in which the missionaries could build their churches, and soon 2,000 local people had become regular church members. Churches quickly materialized in the north and southwest regions but because of more convenient access to the railroad, a higher concentration developed in the north. Shortly after a church had been erected in Nanyang (1891), the entire Weihui District was opened to the foreign missionaries at their request. Some owned land, hired laborers, and made monetary loans to local people. Sometimes, the missionaries even hired guards and comported themselves like government officials. The missionary activities contributed to the sudden increase in riots in most parts of the province at the end of the Qing. Riots quickly spread to Tangyin, Ji, Hua, Hui, Huojia, Xinxiang, and other northern counties. Only after repeated efforts was the provincial government able to control the antimissionary activity.[26]

---

[22] Ibid., 70–82; Phil Billingsley, "Bandits, Bosses, and Bare Sticks: Beneath the Surface of Local Control in Early Republican China," *Modern China*, no. 3 (July 1981): 235–87; and Stephen C. Averill, "Party, Society and Local Elite in the Jiangxi Communist Movement," *Journal of Asian Studies*, 46, no. 2 (May 1987): 279–98.

[23] Perry, *Rebels and Revolutionaries*, 355–82.

[24] See Billingsley, "Bandits, Bosses, and Bare Sticks," 274–5; and Robert J. Antony, "Peasants, Heroes and Brigands: The Problems of Social Banditry in Early Nineteenth-century South China," *Modern China*, no. 2 (April 1989): 123–48.

[25] Yao Xueying's book contains the best description of the misery bandits have caused the people in southwestern Henan. See Yao Xueyin, *Changye (The Long Night)* (Chongqing, 1945).

[26] Wang Tianjiang, ed., *Henan xinhai geming shishi changbian (Collection of the Historical Records on the Republican Revolution in Henan)*, 1 (Zhengzhou: Henan renmin chuban she, 1986): 75–7; Zhang Aiguo et al., *Huojia xianzhi (Huojia County Gazetteer)*, 9 (Beijing: Sanlian shudian, 1991): 7; *Wuzhi xianzhi (Wuzhi County Gazetteer)*, 2 (Wuzhi: Zhengxie Wuzhixian weiyuan hui, 1984): 10; *Yangwu xianzhi (Yangwu County*

The other group of foreigners to enter Henan at this time, especially in the north, were driven by economic interest. Soon after coal had been discovered in the late nineteenth century, coal mines opened in nearly twenty counties. One, owned by a British mining company called the Fu Company (*fu gongsi*), started business in Xiuwu County in 1893. This concern alone accounted for 40% of all British investment in China at that time. During February and May of 1898, the British coal miners sent an inspection team to survey the prospective site of a new mine. Using red ink, the team marked a map with the site's boundaries according to their understanding (which did not correspond to the original plan laid out in the previous agreement between the British and the local people). In response to the site plan by the British, the local elites in Xiuwu County organized their own inspection team and marked a map with a yellow boundary line. Thus began the so-called "red line/yellow line dispute" between the British and the local inhabitants, which lasted for decades.[27]

Besides the British, the external economic intrusion in general accelerated agricultural commercialization in northern Henan by linking the local agriculture to world markets, and it also destroyed the cottage industries on which many peasants relied to subsidize their income. Railroads played a crucial role in connecting the agricultural economy of Henan to the world commodity market, whose demand for such agricultural products as cotton and tobacco encouraged many peasants to raise these cash crops for quick profit. In the short run, this "dependent commercialization" brought temporary prosperity to the peasants. In the long run, as Philip Huang has judged, this "acceleration" of the process of agricultural commercialization made the peasants much more vulnerable to economic crisis or sudden downturns in the market.[28]

The arising social conditions of the early twentieth century affected

Gazetteer), 3 (Yangwu: Zhengxie Yangwuxian weiyuan hui): 17–18; *Xuchang xianzhi (Xuchang County Gazetteer)*, 4 (Xuchang: Zhengxie Xuchang weiyuan hui): 48; *Tongxu xianzhi (Tongxu County Gazetteer)*, 11 (Tongxu: Zhengxie Tongxuxian weiyuan hui): 28; Wang, *Chongxiu Huaxianzhi*, 20, 19; *Dagong bao* (L'Impartial) (Tianjin), (October 20, 1904): 10, 20; and Wang Tianjiang et al., eds., *Henan dashi ji ziliao congbian: 1840–1918 (Major Events in Henan: 1840–1918)*, (Zhengzhou: Henan renmin chuban she, 1984), 85–6.

27 *Shangwu guanbao* (Shangwu Government News) (Beijing), 3: 11–13; *Zhongguo jindai gongye shi ziliao* (Collection of Materials on Chinese Modern Industry) (Unpublished); *Qingji waijiao shiliao* (*Archives of Relations with Foreign Countries during the Qing*), 132 (Beijing, 1899); and Yang Jingqi et al., eds., *Xiuwu xianzhi* (*Gazetteer of Xiuwu County*), 11 (Xinxiang: Henan renmin chuban she, 1986), 5–7.

28 Philip C. C. Huang, *The Peasant Economy and Social Change in North China* (Stanford: Stanford University Press, 1985), 121–37, 299.

both regions in terms of its social structure to some degree. For example, a high level of absentee landlordism existed in Nanyang County because most substantial landlords, usurers, wealthy merchants, and even government officials moved inside the marketing town to avoid bandits. The persistent banditry crisis also gradually transformed southwestern villages into small units of usually less than thirty-six households that surrounded one household belonging to a big landlord. This social structure evolved over the years because it was most efficient for self-protection against bandit attacks.[29] Thus, a combination of long-term polarization of land ownership and short-term disaster, banditry in particular, caused the decline of living standards and the existence of a paradigm of big landlords versus poor peasants in the southwest.[30]

On the other hand, the impact of foreign intrusion appeared to be less acute than the changes wrought by conditions in the southwest even though railroads quickly changed the economic situation of the peasants in the north. The peasants there were able to take advantage of modern developments and recover from the economic shock that initially accompanied them. As in northern China, the economy of the small peasants in northern Henan was not undermined by the world economy.[31] Instead, the rural community converted itself when the majority of peasants adopted the practice of *tiaojingdicu* (selling fine food grain to buy coarse food grain) – a way of exchanging for a larger quantity of lower quality food with a small amount of fine food that was able to be produced in order to meet the basic needs for food for the family – to survive exogenous shock and to compensate for their losses. Further, in that region, even though there was an underdevelopment of managerial farming and increasing numbers of wage laborers, the number of middle and rich peasants remained constant. In other words, the impact of the foreign economy did not generate a deep polarization of wealth between the landed and landless. Instead of landholdings concentrating in the hands of a few big landlords, as in the southwest, large landholdings

---

[29] Fen Zigang et al., *Nanyang nongcun shehui diaocha baogao (Report from a Village Survey in Nanyang)* (Shanghai: Li ming chuban she, 1934), 21–2, 32–3.

[30] Han, *Nongcun diaocha*, 6. Fen, *Nanyang nongcun*, 12–13. Chen Bozhuang, *Pinghan yanxian nongcun jingji diaocha (Village Survey Along the Peking-Hankou Railroad)* (Shanghai: Zhonghua shuju, 1936), 15–16.

The argument on the decline of peasant living standards in Henan is a modification of Philip Huang's theory used for the peasant in northern China. See Huang, *Peasant Economy*, 299.

[31] Huang, *Peasant Economy*, 70–84.

actually fragmented into smaller ones and thus created a small-peasant economic pattern in the north. This process accelerated especially after 1930.[32]

Because of the persistence of a small-peasant economy in the north, the standard of living among the peasants there was maintained, echoing Ramon Myers's conclusion that the living conditions of small farmers in northern China had not degenerated between 1890 and 1937 because the growing of cash crops provided them with additional income. But Myers's argument can be applied only partially to northern Henan.[33] The other part of the truth is that rural society possesses an excellent potential to successfully accommodate external shocks.

The early twentieth century witnessed monumental changes in the two regions. The existence of different social conditions in the regions ensured that the changes would affect the rural populations of both areas quite differently. That difference would soon become a determining factor for the polarized development in local political structures of southwestern and northern Henan.

[32] Han, *Nongcun diaocha*, 3–11; and Chen, *Pinghan yanxian nongcun*, 15–16.
[33] Ramon H. Myers, *The Chinese Peasant Economy: Agricultural Development in Hopei and Shantung, 1890–1949* (Cambridge, MA: Harvard University Press, 1970), 235–40.

Part II

LOCAL ELITES AND THE TRANSITION OF COMMUNITY POWER

3

Local Society in Transition

A CONSPICUOUS change in the local society of northern Henan during the early twentieth century was the frequent rise and fall of various power groups, usually led by local elites. For various reasons, none of the groups held consistent influence for a long period. Usually within a decade of their ascendance, they either lost appeal to the general population or their influence was eclipsed by the rise of other social forces. This changeable nature of power was one of the important characteristics of the transformation of local society in northern Henan in the early twentieth century. Although it had no fixed pattern, the process was, on the one hand, conditioned by endogenous social circumstances that were in constant flux, triggering the shifting of communal interests, elite self-aggrandizement strategies, and individual ambitions. On the other hand, the transformation was a part of the village community's adjustment to exogenous developments that impacted on the local society. Through this very process, history has chosen its winners and losers. To understand this historical process, let us first explore the changes that occurred in northern Henan – both in the local power structure and among individuals, in particular those who came to wield power – and investigate how their ambitions, desires, and actions led to the evolution of the power structure in the local society.

INSTITUTIONAL DEVELOPMENTS IN THE LATE QING

During the late nineteenth century, the local power structure in northern Henan was dominated by several prominent local elite institutions, namely, the Linked-Village-Association (*lianzhuang hui*), the Bureau of Wagon and Horse (*chema ju*), the Neighborhood Watch Group (*shouwang she*), and, in the market towns, the guilds (*banghui*). At the turn of the twentieth century, considerable changes took place in the structure within and outside these organizations. These changes first appeared as the influence of the Bureau of Wagon and Horse began to wane, continued to take shape as the Boxer movement swept the entire region, and gathered strength with the rise of the chambers of commerce in major market towns, the forming of Self-Government by the Qing initiative, and the appearance of the political organization known as the Revolutionary Alliance (Tongmenhui). In Xiuwu County, these changes coincided with a dispute that broke out between the local people and British mine owners, one that eventually captured the attention of the nation. The power structure of northern Henan had already metamorphosed profoundly before the 1911 Revolution.

During the Taiping Rebellion, the most significant organization at the village level was the Linked-Village-Association. Originally founded by several lower-degree holders as a form of local militia to assist government efforts to combat the rebels, it gradually assumed wider responsibilities in the protection of the community interest. Between 1853 and 1861, for instance, the organization initiated a series of riots in Hui, Xiuwu, Huojia, and Xinxiang counties to protest the government's excessive taxation and the arrival of foreign missionaries. The riots alarmed Qing authorities and were eventually suppressed by government troops, an outcome that created important negative repercussions for the organization. Nevertheless, for the moment the Linked-Village-Association was the most publicly involved organization in the region.[1]

Of a different nature, the Bureau of Wagon and Horse was an equally powerful institution controlled by local elites in every county. Under government sponsorship, this institution was initially designed specifically to accommodate traveling government officials. As they had always been, responsibilities such as the provision of supplies were assumed by the county's wealthier families. The institution was hence unofficially

[1] Xianzhi zongbian shi, "Huojia Li Zhanbiao qiyi" (Li Zhanbiao Uprising in Huojia County), in *Huojia fangzhi bao* (1984): 3; Ren Hongchang, "Huixian lianzhuang hui kangjuan kenbin shimo" (The Experience of Hui County Linked-Village-Association's Resistance to Government Surtax Collection and Burial of Soldiers), in *Huixian wenshi ziliao*, 1 (1990): 6–10; Zhang Boxiu et al., *Henansheng Xiuwuxian xinzhi* (*New Gazetteer of Henan Xiuwu County*) (Taipei: 1983), 12; Zhang Chang, "Fan qing nongmin geming jun: xinxiang lianzhuang hui" (Anti-Qing Peasant Army: Linked-Village-Association in Xinxiang County), in *Xinxiangxian wenshi ziliao (Local History of Xinxiang County)*, 3 (1991): 157–60; and Guo Xisheng, "Xinhai geming qian shinian jian Henan qunzhong zifa douzheng shulue" (Brief Account of the Spontaneous Uprisings of the Henan People in the Decade Before the Republican Revolution), in *Zhongzhou jingu*, ed. Guo Yingsheng (Zhengzhou: Zhongzhou jingu chuban she, 1987): 14.

called the Bureau of Large Households (*dahu ju*). By the end of the nineteenth century, however, the burden on the bureau began to increase as the government was required, in addition to accommodation services, to provide expenses for higher-ranking officials passing through the area. Because these new services were performed by runners for the county government – who demanded compensation from the bureau – the bureau decided to levy its own public surtax to support its mission. Later, the bureau even took on itself the right to increase the tax rate without consulting the elite community. By then, the county government had also become engaged with determining and collecting the surtax, resulting in widespread corruption among government officials and within each bureau. Many leaders of the elite community urged reform of the bureau in their own county. Through these efforts, most reclaimed their rights to collect and control public funds. Thereafter, the bureaus increased their popularity and continued to play a major role in community leadership.[2]

During the same period, smaller organizations also existed in most counties; such associations included the Association for Promoting Young Talent (*juying hui*) and the Association for the Creation of Heroes (*zhuying hui*). As their names indicated, most were formed to accomplish a specific mission – such as to send talented youth to large cities, or even abroad, to pursue higher education. These smaller organizations were usually supported financially by powerful members of the elite community, or even by a single lineage. To the general population of the region they were barely visible.[3]

Also on a smaller scale were the private militia groups organized by different lineages or wealthy individuals to protect their property from bandits. A good example is the Neighborhood Watch Group led by Bao Shibin, then a lower-degree (*lisheng*) holder in Hua County. When the brigandage became intense and widespread, these groups were able to

For a similar analysis of the Linked-Village-Association's role in leading tax resistance, see Yin Gengyun, *Yujun jilue: huifei er (Brief History of the Henan Army: Heterodox Societies II)*, 8a.

[2] Lu Meiyi, "Li Minxiu yu Jixian chemaju" (Li Minxiu and Bureau of Wagon and Horse in Ji County), in *Zhongzhou jingu*, Guo Yingsheng, ed., 4 (1987): 6; Tong Kunhou, "Wang Xiaoting xiansheng nianpu" ("A chronicle of Mr. Wang Xiaoting's life") (Unpublished Manuscript), 14–15; Zou Guyu et al., eds. *Huojia xianzhi (Gazetteer of Huojia County)*, 17 vols. (Kaifeng, 1934): 11; Duan Deren et al., *Henan dashi ji ziliao congbian: 1840–1918 (Chronology of Henan: 1840–1918)* (Kaifeng: Henan Local History Publisher, 1984), 18–20; and Yang, *Xiuwu xianzhi* (1986): 12, 19.

[3] Xiao Guozhen et al., *Xiuwu xianzhi (Gazetteer of Xiuwu County)*, 15 (Kaifeng: 1931): 7–8; and Zhang Honglu, "Zhang Luqing xiansheng zhuan" (Biography of Mr. Zhang Luqing), in *Xiuwu wenshi ziliao* (1987): 46–7.

muster a great deal of support and thus became major political powers in their respective counties. At one time during the banditry crisis the militia dominated the county power arena. On the whole, however, these militia groups were the most unpredictable elements of the local power structure.[4]

In each large market town, the only publicly visible elite institution were the guilds. Guilds were particularly influential in the local cities of Xinxiang, Zhangde, and Xiuwu. Each organization was usually formed among the retailers in the same specialty: the cloth retailers (*pitou*), the Cantonese goods retailers (*guanghuo*), silk goods retailers (*chouduan*), and retailers of imports (*yanghuo*).[5] Their usual functions were similar to what John S. Burgess has listed for the guilds in Beijing of this period: (1) maintaining a monopoly for their members; (2) preventing competition within the same business; and (3) determining prices and wages and otherwise regulating business procedures among its members.[6] In addition to those functions, the guilds in this region were also responsible for processing the government's requirement for the purchase of government bonds among retailers, and for representing the retailers in business inquiries from outside the community. Also guilds often mediated disputes among their own members. Their effectiveness in that role was guaranteed by their ability to impose financial penalties on their members.[7]

Beyond the preceding institutional developments in the elite community, many elite members, as individuals, continued to engage in various community activities that ranged from starting new businesses to founding tutoring schools, from managing community projects to supervising disaster relief programs, and from mediating between neighbors to representing villagers in complaints against officials.[8] These activities helped

[4] Li Ting, "Bao Zhifu" (Ban Shibin), in *Anyang wenshi ziliao* (1989): 34–9.

[5] *Henan xinzhi*, 270.

[6] John S. Burgess, *The Guilds of Peking* (New York: Columbia University Press, 1928), 190–213.

[7] *Henan xinzhi*, 270.

[8] Xiao, *Xiuwu xianzhi*, 9: 47; Zhang Jing, "Anyang xian jiu guanliao dizhu de xingxing sese" (Anecdotes of the Big Landlords in Anyang County), in *Anyang xian wenshi ziliao* (1989): 131–9; Wang, *Chongxiu Huaxian zhi*, 12; Han Bangfu et al., *Xinxiangxian xuzhi* (*Gazetteer of Xinxiang County*) (Kaifeng: 1923), no. 1: 70; Han, *Xinxiangxian xuzhi*, no. 2 (1923): 8–10, 11–13, 14; Han, *Xinxiangxian xuzhi*, no. 5 (1923): 36–7; *Henan wenshi ziliao* (Historical Account of Henan), 15 (Zhengzhou: Henan People's Press, 1984): 107–8, 113; "Huixian Zhi" (Gazetteer of Hui County) (Huixian, Unpublished Manuscript), 1–9; Chen Zifeng et al., *Tangyin xianzhi (Gazetteer of Tangyin County)* (Kaifeng: Henan renmin chuban she, 1987), 382; and Zou, *Huojia xianzhi*, 16 (1934): 15.

those elite members to maintain status and influence in their village communities. Studies by Mary Rankin and Susan Mann have both demonstrated that the power of the local elites expanded during the late
nineteenth century as they were actively involved in a multiplicity of
activities, such as international famine relief, flood control, and (at the
beginning of the twentieth century) assisting tax collection. This general
description of elite activities in China can well be applied to local elites
in Henan.[9]

While changes in the elite community were surfacing in the region, a
dispute erupted between locals and British coal mine owners in the late
1890s in Xiuwu County. Major coal reserves were discovered there
during these years, and two Qing officials from the Imperial Academy,
Wu Shizhao and Chen Enpei, signed a contract allowing the British to
supply equipment, technology, and capital through a company called the
Fu Company to assist the Chinese in the operation of a coal mine. As
soon as the contract was approved by the Qing court, however, the two
Chinese signatories disappeared with handsome payoffs from the
British, leaving the British-controlled Fu Company with exclusive mining
rights. The dispute created many opportunities for local elites to exercise
their leadership of the villagers in the ensuing decades.[10]

CHANGES AT THE TURN OF THE CENTURY

After the turn of the twentieth century, social changes continued to influence the power structure of the region. First, increasing discontent from
within the peasant community against foreigners encouraged the growth
of the Boxer movement. Further, the state persevered in its efforts to
strengthen its involvement in the local society. These changes coincided
with local elites' attempts to take advantage of the opportunities
afforded by the government's new programs in order to preserve their
previous social status.

The twentieth century began with the Qing government's order, in
1901, to disband the Bureau of Wagon and Horse, and while that order
was being carried out, local elites were forming new institutions such as
the Education Associations. But soon the Boxers took center stage on
the local scene. The Boxer movement started as the tension between the
foreigners and the local people began to mount near the end of the nine-

[9] Rankin, *Elite Activism*, 299–309.
[10] Zhang, *Xiuwuxian xinzhi*, 42; and Xiao, *Xiuwu xianzhi*, 1: 5–6.

teenth century. In the following years, the Boxers were responsible for most of the incidents in the region directed against foreigners. Within several years riots had spread to the counties of Tangyin, Ji, Hua, Hui, Huojia, and Xinxiang. During those riots, native churchgoers were forced to denounce the churches publicly and many suffered physical torture and seizure of their property. Response from the elite community toward these incidents varied. While some applauded the effort to reduce foreign influence, others formed militias to prevent the violence from spreading.[11] Along with the Boxers, other "heterodox" sects,[12] some of which were either joined or led by minor elites (the individuals who were influential only at the subcounty level, such as certain lesser-known literary persons and popular medicine men), also expanded their influence through their participation in the antiforeign fever. Such groups included the Circle Dweller (*zaiyuan hui*), the Old Brother Society (*gelao hui*), Nian, and Qingdao Gate (*qingdao men*) based in Anyang County. Because of the rise of the Boxers and other secret societies, the elite community faced serious competition for the leadership of the community.[13]

Shortly after the Boxer Rebellion ended in 1903, the government's initiative to organize the Chamber of Commerce began gradually to take hold in every county.[14] At the outset, the main responsibilities of the chambers of commerce were to settle disputes among their members and to regulate prices in the market. Mary Rankin notes that the chambers of commerce in the commercial area of Zhejiang of the late Qing period were actively involved in various political issues in addition to their usual

[11] Duan, *Henan dashi ji*, 18–20, 85–86; Wang, *Chongxiu Huaxian zhi*, 11; Zou, *Huojia xianzhi*, 3 (1934): 7–10; Chen, *Tangyin xianzhi*, 10, 399; Guo, "Xinhai geming," 14–15; Xiao, *Xiuwu xianzhi*, 8; Henan sheng Jixian zhi zongbianji shi, "Jixian dashi ji" ("Major events in Ji County") (Jixian, Unpublished Manuscript), 21; Dai Lixiu, "Buwei qiangquan weixie bushou jinqian youhuo de dai kai" (Dai Kai: Yield Neither to the Threat of Power Nor to the Temptation of Money), in *Weihui wenshi ziliao*, 2 (1989): 34–6; and Han Bangfu et al., *Xinxiangxian xuzhi*, 2 (1923): 32.

[12] Joseph Esherick has pointed out that the word *heterodox* reflects an official Confucian mind-set toward semireligious sects like the Boxers. See Esherick, *Boxer Uprising*, 38–67. This view was generally held by the educated elites, who had been trained in a Confucian-based system.

[13] Li Jianquan, "Tianmenhui shimo ji" (The Rise and Fall of the Heavenly Gate Society), in *Chongxiu Linxian zhi*, 14 (1932); *Huibao (Reporter)* (Shanghai, May 22, 1907); *Huibao* (June 20, 1905); "Jixian dashi ji," 19–20; and Guo, "Xinhai geming," 15.

[14] *Henan xinhai geming* (1986), 132–3; Wang, *Chongxiu Huaxian zhi*, 12, 32; Chen, *Tangyin xianzhi*, 247, 342; Han, *Xinxiangxian xuzhi*, 1 (1923): 80; Xiao, *Xiuwu xianzhi*, 8; *Henan guanbao (Henan Government News)*, 27, 28 (Kaifeng, 1906): 55–6; and *Henan xinzhi*, 271; "Jixian dashi ji," 22.

economic concerns. They often played a greater role in politics than other elite institutions, such as the Education Association.[15] In this area, the Chambers of Commerce were at least the most noticed, if not the most powerful, elite institutions, especially after the county assemblies had been abolished. They also mediated between their members and the government agencies in such cases as when the members failed to pay the business surtax, *lishui*. For instance, a Henan newspaper, *Gonglun xin bao*, reported in 1909 that about 300 businesses joined the Chamber of Commerce as soon as it was formed. When, later that year, a government agency detained a clothing dealer for failing to pay the *lishui*, the Chamber of Commerce was called upon to gain his release. When it failed in its mission, about 200 businesses renounced their membership to protest the chamber's incompetence. Occasionally, some chambers of commerce even arranged regular meetings for their members to discuss community affairs as well as local or national politics. Before the Qing dynasty ended, the chambers of commerce had already become the most powerful elite institutions in the region, which strengthened the voice of the commercial elites.[16]

After 1908 Self-Government was established according to government decree, leading to further changes in the local power structure. The reactions to the founding of the organizations was at first ambivalent among the local elites. Although some embraced the opportunity to institutionalize their eminent status and dominance through Self-Government, others were wary of the government's actual motives. Subsequently, most local elites came to realize that the occasion could well be used for their advantage. They could procure positions in Self-Government as well as seats in the provincial assemblies. Similar to what John Fincher had also noticed in his study, during the Self-Government movement, many local elites merged into the provincial polity through election.[17] Many, especially certain reform-minded elites, thus turned the organization of Self-Government into a period of competition for power.

While these changes were transpiring a political organization, the Revolutionary Alliance, was inaugurated in Honolulu (1905). News of the organization was brought back mainly by Henan natives studying

[15] Rankin, *Elite Activism*, 209.
[16] *Gonglun xin bao (Public Opinion News)* (Hankou, March 7, 1909); *Henan xinhai geming* (1986), 131; *Henan guanbao (Henan Government News)*, 27, 28 (Kaifeng, 1906): 55–6; and *Dongfang zazhi (Eastern Miscellany)* 2, no. 2, (Shanghai, 1905): 13.
[17] John H. Fincher, *Chinese Democracy: The Self-Government Movement in Local, Provincial and National Politics, 1905–1914* (New York: St. Martin's Press, 1981), 87–122, 244–5.

abroad, although some reports filtered back in letters from relatives and friends in large cities because mail service became available after the turn of the century as post offices appeared in northern Henan between 1903 and 1905. In the beginning, very few people paid attention to the organization. But gradually even some prominent elites were recruited to its political cause. The emergence of Tongmenhui added a political dimension to the elite community.[18]

At the same time, in Xiuwu County, the coal mine dispute (previously mentioned in Chapter 2) continued to heat up. By 1905, through the concerted efforts of local elites, the entire region supported the people of the county in their struggle against the British mine owners. This groundswell of support was enabled by the construction of the Daokou-Qinghua Railroad and by the acquisition of the land for the coal mine by the British, both events fueling the indignation of the Chinese. Adding to that resentment, the government ordered the residents in the mining area off the land already owned by the Fu Company. The order sparked a wave of protests in northern Henan between 1907 and 1909.

Acting as the local spokesmen, local elites in Xiuwu County engaged themselves in the Red Line/Yellow Line controversy – a dispute with the British started in 1904 that centered on the working boundaries of the Fu Company's mine – and filed many petitions to the Qing court. The local elites claimed that according to the previous contract with the British, the mining company was allowed to work only within the territory it had designated on the map. But the British had since redrawn the boundary and stepped outside the previously designated limits. When the dispute was joined by other elites from the rest of the region, the local elites carried their complaint to Beijing. However, the Qing court continued to rule in favor of the British mine owners. Therefore, the local elites organized public protests against the government as well as the British, which forced a temporary suspension of the mine's operation.[19]

In 1910 the controversy took a drastic turn. A leading spokesperson for the Chinese side, Du Yan, a *jinshi*-degree holder, claimed he owned the land supposedly purchased by the British. Due to the claim, the gov-

---

[18] Zou, *Huojia xianzhi*, 3 (1934): 20; Zhang, *Xiuwuxian xinzhi*, 13; Chen, *Tangyin xianzhi*, 10, 695; *Henan xinhai geming* (1986), 325–30; Guo Wenxuan and Qiao Jiabao, "Henan jindai minzhu geming xiangu Guo Zhongkui yishi (Revolutionary Martyr in Modern Henan: The Story of Guo Zhongkui), in *Wenshi ziliao* (*Local History*), vol. 1 (1987), 7–20; Du, "Yu Youren," 72; and Xu, "Guo Zhongwei," 50.

[19] Zhang, *Xiuwuxian xinzhi*, 43, 45; Yang, *Xiuwu xianzhi* (1986), 13, 14.

ernment reopened ownership negotiations. Du joined other delegates to meet with the British mine owners; the meetings were attended by officials from the Ministry of Foreign Affairs and representatives from the British Embassy. The outcome of the new negotiations favored the Chinese, and the dispute temporarily ended with the British agreeing to follow the territorial marking designated by the "yellow line." This local victory not only boosted the morale of the elite community in Xiuwu County but also boosted the popularity of those who had participated in the protest.[20]

Obviously, local society in northern Henan at the beginning of the twentieth century was in constant flux. Change was not only a part of the local power structure itself – a result of power competition and personal efforts to maintain status, power, and influence – but also a part of the village community's response to such external pressures as the presence of missionaries and foreign business interests. During these internal adjustments, each elite community was saturated with a diversity of group and individual interests. Only when nationalistic sentiment against foreign interests galvanized the communities of northern Henan did they display a cohesiveness, a "sense of common engagement in great causes."[21]

SELF-EMPOWERMENT DURING THE 1911 REVOLUTION

The 1911 Revolution brought further changes to northern Henan. It brought opportunity to some and took it from others. The revolution started with the founding of the county assembly, which soon usurped county authority. That was followed by the political strengthening of the chambers of commerce, which enhanced their representation in a wide array of local issues. It culminated in the expansion of private militia groups to meet the emergent need for bandit control in the villages. Of those involved with the perviously mentioned power groups, the revolution made winners. But change did not cease after the revolution, rather it continued in many directions: the influence of the Bureau of Public Funds (*gongkuan ju*) continued to decline; the dispute between the inhabitants in Xiuwu County and the British coal mine owners sprang to life again; and new social elements – such as the workers' union and

---

[20] Zhang, *Xiuwuxian xinzhi*, 45.
[21] Ernest P. Young, *The Presidency of Yuan Shih-K'ai* (Ann Arbor: University of Michigan Press, 1977), 6–14.

the high school student organization – emerged that were associated with the nationalistic movement in the rest of the country. These changes laid the foundation for a major transformation of the local power structure in the mid-1920s.

The first significant change in the elite community during the revolution was the forming of a county assembly in every county. Despite the demise of the Qing government, which had initiated the plan as a part of its preparation for the Constitution in rural areas, the local elites decided to continue the election according to its original schedule. When the assemblies appeared in the region, around 1912, they were recognized widely as the principal voice on community matters ranging from the annual tax rate to the use of public land.[22]

The revolution also witnessed a growing vigor in the chambers of commerce. Since their departure from government sponsorship, the chambers had gained more respect than ever from the people in each county for their financial support of community activities. The organizations gradually expanded their limited representation of the business community to include the general population of market towns, and sometimes even of the county as a whole. Thus the chambers were often major players in local politics.[23]

The chaos exacerbated by the revolution also increased the significance of many self-defense-oriented groups, such as the Neighborhood Watch Group. For instance, the revolution ushered in a sudden escalation of brigandage, although such activity had been reported in Hua and Hui counties in the late Qing, when bandits attacked and even fired cannons at locals.[24] And secret societies garnered much popularity for their role in protecting the villagers from bandits. The following secret societies rose to prominence in the region during this period: the Red Spear in Hua County; the Black Spear, the Yellow Spear, the Heavenly Gate (*tianmen hui*), and Circle Dweller in Huojia County; the Red Spear in Xinxiang County; and the Red Spear and the Heavenly Gate in Tangyin County. These spear groups, which distinguished themselves with different colors, as Oderic Wou has indicated, were all the direct

---

[22] Yang, *Xiuwu xianzhi* (1986), 155; Han, *Xinxiangxian xuzhi*, 1 (1923): 81; and Zou, *Huojia xianzhi*, 3 (1934): 14–16.

[23] Wang, *Chongxiu Huaxian zhi*, 20: 32; Han, *Xinxiangxian xuzhi*, 1 (1923): 80; Zou, *Huojia xianzhi*, 3 (1934): 16; Chen, *Tangyin xianzhi*, 247; and Xiao, *Xiuwu xianzhi*, 45–6.

[24] Wang, *Chongxiu Huaxian zhi*, 20: 9, 10, 38; Han, *Xinxiangxian xuzhi*, 2 (1923): 33; Chen, *Tangyin xianzhi*, 11, 362; and Zou, *Huojia xianzhi*, 7 (1934): 14.

descendants of the Boxers.[25] Depending largely on the residents' need for protection, these groups occasionally achieved county-level status within a few years of their founding.[26]

Confronted with the flourishing vitality of the earlier mentioned power groups, however, some previously influential elite organizations went into precipitous decline. Among them was the Bureau of Public Funds, formerly the Bureau of Wagon and Horse, whose descent was signaled by its shrinking role in the determination of community matters. Similarly, most smaller elite institutions – such as the Education Association, which at the time existed in every county except Ji County – also fell silent because none could compete with the County Assembly for county leadership. Although new groups appeared at the time – such as the Common Folks Association (*pingmin hui*) in Hua County, the Peasant Association in Tangyin County, or the Zhangwei Plantation Society (*zhangwei kenzhi she*) – their influence was narrowly restricted for the same reason.[27]

In Xiuwu County, by contrast, the revolution created more opportunity for local elites. Since the end of the Qing dynasty, the coal mine dispute in that county had been rekindled. Representing the Chinese natives, the local elites in Xiuwu County took center stage. Through networking, they soon gathered many prominent elites from the rest of the region to join their efforts against the British. Some of the elite members in Xiuwu County launched a shipping company to reclaim shipping rights from the British. Others organized regionwide protests to demand the dissolution of the previous agreement between officials of the Qing government and the British mine owners. Through these activities, the local elites increased their communication with those from other counties and thus broadened their influence.[28]

[25] Wou, *Mobilizing the Masses*, 61.

[26] Wang, *Chongxiu Huaxian zhi*, 20: 7; Ibid., 40, 41; Zou, *Huojia xianzhi*, 17 (1934): 10, 14; Chen, *Tangyin xianzhi*, 12, 13, 301, 317, 363, 532, 599; and Han, *Xinxiangxian xuzhi*, 2 (1923): 32–3.

[27] Han, *Xinxiangxian xuzhi*, 1 (1923): 80, 81; Zou, *Huojia xianzhi*, 6 (1934): 42; Xiao, *Xiuwu xianzhi*, 1, 42; Xiao, *Xiuwu xianzhi*, 9: 45–6; *Anyang xianzhi: renwu biao* (*Sequel to the Gazetteer of Anyang County: Personage List*) (Anyang: Minguo), 37–40; *Henan xinzhi*, 444–5; "Jixian dashi ji," 23, 86; Wang, *Chongxiu Huaxian zhi*, 17, 24; Chen, *Tangyin xianzhi*, 342; Hong Jian, "Huanghe gudao shahuang zhong de zhangwei kenzhi she" (Zhangwei Plantation Society in the Wasteland of the Yellow River), in *Weihui wenshi ziliao*, 3 (1991): 79–82; and Liu Shiwu, "Jixian 1927 zhi weicheng bairi" (Hundred-Day Siege of Ji County in 1927), in *Henan wenshi ziliao*, 25 (1988): 41–2.

[28] Xiao, *Xiuwu xianzhi*, 14–15, 18, 117–20.

The initial response to the dispute from Yuan Shikai's government was to urge the local people to adhere to the previous agreement between the Chinese and the British. The postrevolutionary period, therefore, witnessed a new wave of protests in Xiuwu County calling for the cancellation of the agreement. Two prominent members of the elite community, Hu Rulin and Wang Jingfang, were subsequently selected to represent the local community in a series of negotiations with the British mine owners. These negotiations eventually led to a temporary reconciliation between the two sides as the British agreed to share their profits with those leading the protests, in the form of a joint venture called the Zhongyuan Company (*zhongyuan gongsi*). This arrangement, however, soon sparked major conflicts within the elite community because the rest of that group felt betrayed by their leaders. Under the leadership of different elite members, more protests against the mine owners followed in 1914. When the protestors assaulted county officials, an alarmed provincial government immediately dispatched troops to quell the dissension. For the moment, at least, the local elites had been silenced.[29]

The revolution can, therefore, be considered a time of major changes in the local power structure. On one hand, as Lenore Barkan has discovered in her study of Rugao County in northern Jiangsu, the period was marked by the rise of local-elite interest in national and provincial issues. Continuing to act as a link between the state and local society, these local leaders showed great flexibility in adapting to the political changes outside their community.[30] On the other hand, inspired by the opportunities created by the revolution as well as the uncertainty of their future, many local elites struggled continually to stay in the mainstream in order to maintain their prominent position in the village community. Those who could capitalize on opportunities such as the creation of the new institutions and the appearance of new community needs gained much power through the process. Those who lacked foresight and were slow to respond to the opportunities suffered the loss of their influence. In the end, however, all the elite activities ceased by the end of 1914 under the unyielding pressure from Yuan Shikai's ambitious government. For the remainder of the early Republican period, elite activism stopped, then it began to grow again in the mid-1920s.

---

[29] Xiao, *Xiuwu xianzhi*, 11: 15, 16; Zhang, *Xiuwuxian xinzhi*, 47, 48; and *Henan wenshi ziliao*, 15 (1985): 110.

[30] Lenore Barkan, "Patterns of Power: Forty Years of Elite Politics in a Chinese County," in *Chinese Local Elites and Patterns of Dominance*, Joseph W. Esherick and Mary Backus Rankin, eds., 201–3.

THE LOW EBB OF ACTIVISM: THE EARLY REPUBLIC

Even during this slack season of elite activism, new elements continued to emerge in the local society. Between the mid-1910s and mid-1920s, for example, workers and young students began to make their presence felt. The largest group of workers were the 10,000 miners from the British-owned Fu Company, but many others worked at numerous local factories, such as a flour mill in Xinxiang County that employed 200 factory workers. Most important was the growing awareness among these workers of their common interest, demonstrated by the appearance of various workers' unions and other organizations. In Hua County alone there were unions for craftsmen, cooks, textile workers, printers, garment workers, and public-bath employees. The awareness of solidarity often led to strikes for higher pay and better working conditions. The emergence of the workers' unions further broadened the diversity that had already begun in the local power structure.[31]

The young students' participation in national or local politics was also a new phenomenon in the region. At first, through newspapers which became commonly available by the 1910s, students learned about the antecedents of the demonstrations in the large cities during the May Fourth and May Thirtieth Incidents. This knowledge sparked a wave of student activism in the region. In Tangyin and Xiuwu counties, for instance, demonstrations were joined by thousands. Young students from Shanghai mobilized mine workers in Xiuwu County to strike against the British mine owners. The student movement received support from the elite community, including commercial elites, and through that interaction the student movement gradually earned recognition of its importance from the general population.[32]

During this period, many local elites continued to engage in their usual individual activities. Most of those activities, however, focused on leading

[31] Yang, *Xiuwu xianzhi* (1986), 8–9, 14; Han, *Nongcun diaocha*, 99; Wang, *Chongxiu Huaxian zhi*, 31–32; and "Jixian dashi ji," 28.

[32] Zhang, *Xiuwuxian xinzhi*, 13, 40, 49; Zou, *Huojia xianzhi*, 3 (1934): 20; Chen, *Tangyin xianzhi*, 10, 13, 695; Yang, *Xiuwu xianzhi* (1986), 16; *Shen bao* (*Shanghai Newspaper*), (Shanghai, June 3, 1919); *Chen bao* (*Morning Post*) (Peking, August 1919); *Shi bao* (*The Eastern Times*) (Shanghai, June 16, 1919); Pang Shouxin et al., *Wusi yundong zai Henan* (*The May Fourth Movement in Henan*) in Henan difangzhi ziliao congbian, 3 (Zhengzhou: Zhongzhou shuhua she, 1983): 17; *Shanghai minguo ribao* (*Shanghai Republican Daily*) (Shanghai, January 13, 20, 1920); and "Jixian dashi ji," 25.

community efforts against bandits.[33] Banditry, one of the main social crises of the revolutionary era, would eventually contribute to the reemergence of secret societies, one of the principal changes in the local power structure in the mid-1920s.

THE TRANSFORMATION OF LOCAL POLITY IN THE MID-1920S

In the mid-1920s northern Henan saw the most profound transformation in its local power structure. Significant developments during this period were the rise of political parties and the surge of the secret societies to dominance. The former added political dimensions to the elite community, but the latter greatly diminished the influence of the previously powerful elite institutions. These developments began with the increasing militancy of the social activists and with the aid of some minor elites, especially those whose influence did not extend past the village level. By joining secret societies, these activists forced then-leading members of the elite community to share their power. The continuation of the trend finally led to the political parties and secret societies becoming the major political forces on the local scene.

The rise of various groups of social activists was first encouraged by the expansion of public activism in general. The new public organizations differed fundamentally from those founded before the mid-1920s in that they were organized mostly by socially insignificant people. For instance, in Xiuwu County a guild was formed by cooks who were then still little known in the county. A service organization in Tangyin County was created by former army officers to support veterans and their families.[34] The appearance of these organizations, however, created an environment conducive to the emergence of social activists.

An important reason for the social activists to become involved with various political organizations was to increase their visibility in the villages and hence boost their status. Ren Hongxun of Tangyin County was such an activist. While studying at a normal school in Kaifeng, Ren made

---

[33] Zou, *Huojia xianzhi*, 7 (1934): 9, 11; Wang, *Chongxiu Huaxian zhi*, 20: 1; Xiao, *Xiuwu xianzhi*, 7 (1931): 1; Han, *Xinxiangxian xuzhi*, 1 (1923): 62; Han, *Xinxiangxian xuzhi* (1923) 5: 37; and Zhang, "Anyang xian jiu guanliao dizhu de xingxing sese," (Anecdote of the Big Landlords in Anyang County), in *Anyang xian wenshi ziliao* (1989): 55–8.

[34] Yang, *Xiuwu xianzhi* (1986), 16; Hu Wenlan et al., eds., *Yizhan shiqi nongmin yundong (Peasant Movement in Henan During World War I)*, in Zhonggong Henan dangshi ziliao congshu (Zhengzhou: Zhongguo Henansheng dangshi gongzuo weiyuan hui, 1986), 72–3; and Chen, *Tangyin xianzhi*, 595.

the acquaintance of Jiang and Chen, both of whom were involved with the CCP (the Chinese Communist) organization. Under their persuasion, Ren joined the party and then returned home to organize local chapters of the Communist Youth League and the GMD (the Nationalist Party). By doing so, he gained considerable recognition in his home area.[35] In fact, most who introduced the new political parties – the GMD and the CCP – to the region were motivated by the promise of personal gain through political affiliation, by ideological commitment, and, not least, by self-aggrandizement.

The GMD first started in 1924 as a secret organization when a local chapter was founded in Xiuwu County by several modern school graduates from Kaifeng. After several others joined the organization, the founders established several sub-branches, with separate departments for public education, youth activities, welfare of peasants and workers, and internal affairs. The main goal of these departments was to mobilize the peasants around the party's political cause. Like the GMD, the local chapters of the CCP also appeared as underground associations, and were organized by the same people who founded the GMD. For instance, when Ren Hongxun was organizing a local chapter of the GMD, he also organized one for the CCP, after meeting with two CCP members in Kaifeng. He later managed to be in charge of both organizations in Tangyin County. The local chapters of the two parties shared common political agendas before 1927, when the CCP was outlawed by Feng Yuxiang as part of the GMD's declared hostility toward the party.[36]

The county organizers of both political parties had much in common. Many were educated in modern schools and a considerable number studied abroad, or at least in large cities in China. And many in both parties were motivated both by ideology and by an interest in social activism. Yang Jieren typifies the new breed of political organizer. After studying in France and Russia, Yang returned to Henan to become a social activist and CCP party organizer. In 1927 he returned to Hui County to escape GMD persecution. During his stay there he organized peasants into the Association for Resistance against Yuan Shikai's Family, which obstructed the family's collection of rent. At one time, the organization had more than ten thousand members, as well as its own

---

[35] Chen, *Tangyin xianzhi*, 599; "Jixian dashi ji," 27; Yang, *Xiuwu xianzhi* (1986), 16, 228; and Zhang, *Xiuwuxian xinzhi*, 40.

[36] Yang, *Xiuwu xianzhi* (1986), 16, 288; Chen, *Tangyin xianzhi*, 599; Zhang Yucai and Li Xianhua, "Da geming shiqi de qiquan zhongxue" (Qiquan Middle School in the Revolutionary Era), in *Weihui wenshi ziliao*, 3 (1991): 13–18, 317, 599.

militia.[37] At this point, its members' political activity became a way to capitalize on their personal strength to acquire power within the elite community – to promote themselves among other villagers and to maintain their political contacts in the large cities.

The open conflict between the GMD and the CCP, and the subsequent proscription of the CCP by the GMD, did not, however, end the CCP's activities in northern Henan. On the contrary, because many Henanese CCP members returned home to escape persecution, it increased the CCP activities in the region. Gong Yucheng, a native of Anyang County, was such a refugee. Gong had joined the CCP in Shanghai and returned home during the 1927 GMD massacre of CCP members. After his return, he organized a peasant association to lead other villagers. Like Gong, quite a few former CCP members returned to their home counties. Many formed peasant associations to continue their political course. At one point, nearly 25,000 people in Anyang County, 19,000 in Xiuwu County, and 15,000 in Ji County belonged to the peasant associations organized by the returning CCP members after 1927.[38]

As a direct consequence of the sudden increase in CCP activities, tension intensified between the wealthier landlords and the poor peasants. In Jiaozuo County, Liang Guofan was attacked by the peasant association for his role in helping the county government collect surtaxes. Not only was Liang's home vandalized, but his stores were destroyed. The county government brought in troops from Feng Yuxiang's army, stationed nearby, to control the violence. But the soldiers were also assaulted, and Liang was forced to yield to the rioters.[39] Lenore Barkan thus argues for a general surge in political opposition among the peasants against the local elites during the period. When the students, Communists, and Nationalists organized, Barkan suggests, their relentless criticism kept local elites on the defensive.[40] But it is also important to recognize that the tension was the direct result of activities instigated

---

[37] "Jixian dashi ji," 29; Yang, *Xiuwu xianzhi* (1986), 16, 228; Zhang, *Xiuwuxian xinzhi*, 40; Chen, *Tangyin xianzhi*, 317; and Hou Zhiyin et al., eds., *Henan dangshi renwu zhuan (Communist Personages in Henan)*, 4 (Zhengzhou: Henan renmin chuban she, 1989): 33–46.

[38] Xu Binxi, "Nongmin xiehui zai dazhaicun de huodong jiqi youlai" (The Origin and Activities of the Peasant Association in Dazhai Village), in *Anyangxian wenshi ziliao* (1988): 61–3; Hu, *Nongmin yundong*, 83, 89; and "Jixian dashi ji," 29.

[39] Chen Xilian, "1927 de wangchu nongmin kangjuan douzheng" (The 1927 Peasant Tax-resistance Incident at Wangchu Village), in *Jiaozuo xinhuo*, Zhonggong Henan dangshi zhuanti ziliao congshu (Zhengzhou: Zhonggong dangshi chuban she, 1991), 29, 35.

[40] Barkan, "Patterns of Power," 193, 206–8.

by the returnees whose aim was to achieve local dominance in their villages.

During the expansion of social activism, the upsurge of the secret societies had a strong impact in northern Henan. In the mid-1920s, secret societies had gradually become entrenched in local society, receiving growing recognition and support from the general population. One reason is that the growing menace of banditry prompted more villagers to seek protection, often from the secret societies. Furthermore, the constant disturbances and the harsh tax policies from the warlords engendered deep resentment among the peasants, who therefore participated in the secret societies as a "form of resistance."[41] The important questions here are to what degree, and why, were the local elites involved in those secret societies?

Jean Chesneaux has pointed out that secret societies were usually either led or infiltrated by local elites, who used the organizations to enhance their own status.[42] Chesneaux's assertion is certainly applicable to northern Henan. Many elites there were more cautious toward, or even openly despised, secret societies when they appeared in their villages. As the societies' influence increased, the local elites' attitude toward them changed dramatically, for many elites saw therein the opportunity to enhance their own status. This was particularly true for those elites at the lower end of the elite spectrum, such as school teachers and medicine men. Kang Shuqi, a previously little-noticed school teacher from Hui County, typified these minor elites. Through his active role in a local chapter of the Heavenly Gate Society with 200 members, Kang became one of the most well-known figures in his county. Similarly, Wang Xiaosi rose to power in his village in Tangyin County by forming a local chapter of the Blue Gang (*qingbang*).[43]

But the secret societies were yet more complex. A recent study by Oderic Wou shows, for example, that the Red Spear in the mountains of western Henan was largely controlled by local magnates – an amalgam

---

[41] James Scott, "Everyday Forms of Resistance," in *Everyday Forms of Peasant Resistance,* Forrest D. Colburn, ed. (Armonk, NY: M. E. Sharpe, 1989), 3–33. I borrow the term here with full awareness of the difference in Scott's original meaning.

[42] Jean Chesneaux, *Peasant Revolts in China,* 1840–1949 (New York: Norton, 1973), 16–18. See also Jean Chesneaux, ed., *Popular Movements and Secret Societies in China, 1840–1950* (Stanford: Stanford University Press, 1972), passim.

[43] Zhang Zhenzhong, "Xinxiang zaiyuanhui juyi shimo" (The Origin and the Ending of the Circle Dweller Uprising in Xinxiang County), in *Xinxiangxian wenshi ziliao* (1991): 153–6; Wang, *Chongxiu Huaxian zhi,* 20: 7; and Chen, *Tangyin xianzhi,* 532.

of army deserters, bandits, and military strongmen. In the eastern part of the province, however, local elites had exercised considerable authority over that organization through a strict *baojia* (household mutual surveillance) system.[44] Besides the dissimilarities in the societies' style or among their organizers, there were also considerable differences in the activities of such disparate groups as the Red Spear and the Heavenly Gate. Local elites' participation played a major role in the creation of those differences.

To discover the extent of, and reasons for, minor elite participation in secret societies, we must first explore why they were involved with the secret societies in the first place. One reason the Red Spear received much recognition from the general population in northern Henan was certainly related to what Elizabeth Perry calls their "protective" strategy for survival.[45] But Perry's theory can also be applied to those minor elites, who usually had more to lose than the ordinary peasants. This can be confirmed from the writings of well-known CCP leaders Chen Duxiu and Li Dazhao, who reached a similar conclusion after they received reports from the rank-and-file CCP officials in the area that the Red Spear organization was mainly joined or supported by the local elites who were longing for protection from the "predators," both bandits and warlords.[46] Li Dazhao comments that when the magistrate in Tangyin County asked the elite members to disassociate themselves from the Red Spear, they replied they would if the bandits no longer disturbed them, if the government no longer levied exorbitant surtaxes, if various warlord armies no longer threatened them, and if regular taxes were collected in paper currency.[47] From the CCP reports, one can clearly discern that the local elites' primary intention for associating themselves with the secret societies was protection.

Confirming the CCP reports, local history also indicates that protection was the main incentive for minor elites to participate in the Red Spear. Once, in Hua County, the Fengjun (Feng Army) demanded that Zhang Xifu, a village head, pay a fine for the alleged crime of fraternizing with bandits. A friend of his and also an active member of the Red Spear, Li Gaoan, suggested to Zhang that he spend the same amount as

---

[44] Wou, *Mobilizing the Masses*, 60–71.   [45] Perry, *Rebels and Revolutionaries*, 81–8.

[46] Chen Duxiu, "Hongqiang hui yu Zhongguo de nongmin yundong" (Red Spear and the Chinese Peasant Movement), in *Xiangdao* 4, no. 158 (June 16, 1926): 1543–4; and Hu, *Nongmin yundong*, 122.

[47] Li Dazhao, *Li Dazhao xuanji (Selected Works of Li Dazhao)* (Beijing: Renmin chuban she, April 1959), 546.

the penalty to organize a Red Spear group in the county and thus free himself from harassment. Accepting the advice, Zhang gathered all his wealthy friends in the neighborhood to sponsor a local ceremony to which regional Red Spear leaders were invited to help form a local chapter. Within two days, nearly two thousand people had joined the new organization. Zhang and his friends all became leaders of the society. Soon, it spread through the entire county and boasted more than ten thousand members. During the following months, the organization received financial support from the Chamber of Commerce. Many community leaders from the neighboring villages also became friends with the organization, offering advice and financial support. In fact, secret societies such as the Red Spear were primarily dominated by minor elites during the mid-1920s.[48]

The leadership of the Red Spear by minor elites is demonstrated by the following hierarchy. The top leadership was in the hands of the Senior Fellow (*dashixiong*), who held absolute authority over the organization, even the power of life or death over any member. Under the Senior Fellow were his assistants, the Junior Fellows (*ershixiong/sanshixiong*). Below them was the Regiment Commander, who was in charge of the members from one or more counties, and then the Battalion Commander. Under the Battalion Commander were three equal positions: Senior Leaning Mate (*xuezhang*), Company Commander, and Team Leader. The lowest rank of all was the Platoon Leader or the Squad Leader. A Senior Leaning Mate, or his equal, was the leader of a village level unit. Therefore, the organization was actually formed with the village as its basic unit. It is reported that only a highly respected village head could attain a position above Battalion Commander. Those with lower status might become the society's head at the village level.[49]

If protection was the major reason, it was not the only one that compelled many minor elites to join secret societies. At least one more justification, especially for minor elites, was to gain the upper hand in their competition for power. Because this intention was most distinct among those leading the anti-landlord activities of Tianmenhui, I turn now to that organization.

Tianmenhui had existed during the late Qing before it was suppressed

[48] Sun Xiushen et al., "Henan Huaxian hongqiang hui de fazhan yu fumie" (The Rise and Demise of the Red Spear Organization in Henan, Hua County), in *Wenshi ziliao xuanji*, 47 (1967): 66–74; and *Chen bao*, (February 27, 1927).

[49] *Juewu: Minguo ribao* (*Consciousness: Republican Daily*), (Shanghai, December 8, 9, 10, 14, 17, 1928).

by the government. When it resurfaced in the 1920s, it changed its name from the Addition Gate Society (*tianmen hui*) to the Heavenly Gate Society (*tianmen hui*). The organization spread through a branch system, with each branch termed a branch temple (*fentan*). Usually, each branch had two branch leaders, a literary priest (*wenchuan shi*) and a military preacher (*wuchuan shi*), both of whom received orders from the society's headquarters, the Old Temple (*laotan*). Tianmenhui gave its administrative branches such titles as General Affairs, Accounting, Internal Affairs, and Law Enforcement.[50]

The northern Henan chapter of Tianmenhui was established by Han Yuming in 1926. As the child of a poor family, Han was uneducated. Born Han Gen, he and his forty earliest followers changed their names, inserting the character *yu* into the middle. In the beginning, the society was not known to the public, but it earned an immediate reputation for itself and its leader when, in March 1926, it massacred a group of county militiamen sent by the county government to investigate it. The organization later launched an assault on a notorious bandit gang and rescued several villages from them. Both events boosted the society's popularity and its numbers grew rapidly.[51]

Like the Red Spear, the organization led by Han spread to other counties because it advocated resistance to excessive taxation by any government and shielded the people from bandits. When in 1926 Wu Peifu instituted an onerous land tax three times a year, Tianmenhui provided an avenue for organized resistance to the tax. And due to community hostility toward any outside predators – soldiers, bandits, even foreigners – the organization quickly grew into the second largest secret society in the region. And owing to the organization's rapid growth, the site of its headquarters, the village of Youcun, developed into a market town, complete with restaurants and hotels. A year after its emergence, the society already contained several thousand members and covered many counties, including Huojia, Boai, Wuzhi, and Xiuwu.[52]

---

[50] Yang Jingqi et al., eds., *Henan shizhi luncong, 2: Yubei ling hua tang tianmenhui (Heavenly Gate Society in Ling, Hua, and Tang counties of Northern Henan)* (Zhengzhou: Henan renmin chuban she, 1990), 497; Pang Shouxin, "Da geming shiqi de yubei tianmenhui" (Heavenly Gate Society During the Republican Period), in *Henan shizhi ziliao*, 7 (1984): 58; and Li, "Tianmenhui."

[51] Li, "Tianmenhui;" and Pang, "Yubei tianmenhui," 58.

[52] Pang, "Yubei tianmenhui," 58; *Dagong bao*, (May 11, 1927); Zi Zhen, "Fanfeng zhanzheng zhong zhi yubei tianmenhui" (Tianmenhui of Northern Henan during the Anti-Feng Army War), in *Xiangdao zhoubao*, 197 (June 8, 1927): 2164; Guo, "Xinhai

Tianmenhui's slogan reveals the depth of its commitment to oust the big landlords: "exterminate evil, render mutual assistance, fight government soldiers and bandits, resist excessive levying, weed out corrupt officials, and restrain evil gentry." The organization led ordinary peasants in an attack on many wealthier, influential individuals it considered "evil gentry." It not only disavowed its members' previous debts to them, many of whom were landlords, but also demanded contributions, usually in the form of rifles and money, from wealthy families. Those who failed to comply with Tianmenhui's orders often had their houses searched or their family members tortured; some were even executed. In Hui County the organization once ordered a villager from Beizhai to stop selling opium. When he refused, the organization arrested him (and found two rifles in his possession). After his release, when he continued to sell opium, Tianmenhui executed him. In another case, Tianmenhui humiliated a member of the national congress by whipping him repeatedly for allegedly spying and inviting government troops into the county to oppose the organization.[53]

The society's anti-landlord slogan appealed not only to ordinary peasants, who considered joining to renounce their debts, but also to the minor elites who saw the opportunity to aggrandize their own power through participating in the organization against some more influential members of their communities. Cui Zhegang, a lower-degree holder in Hui County not only was responsible for the execution of his wealthier neighbor but also declared himself the county chief.[54] Cui's involvement with Tianmenhui started when he invited the organization's leader in the county to his home village for a martial arts demonstration. Afterward, he brought his entire clan to join the organization and made his home its headquarters for the county. The organization later issued its own currency, set up its own county office, and adopted its own laws. When its membership reached 10,000, the organization attacked the county seat,

geming," 15; and Li Ding, "Huixian tianmenhui de xingshuai" (The Rise and Fall of Heavenly Gate Society in Hui County), in *Huixian wenshi ziliao (Local History of Hui County)*, 1 (1990): 16.

53 Anyangxian Weidangshi ban, "Yijiu erqi nian Anyang qianghui yundong de chubu diaocha" (The General Survey of the 1927 Spear Movement in Anyang County), in *Henan dangshi yanjiu*, 2 (1986): 45; Li, "Huixian tianmenhui," 13–15; Linxian xianwei dang banshi, "Gongchan dang zai yubei tianmenhui de gongzuo" (The Communist Activities in Northern Henan), in *Zhongyuan dadi fa chun hua*, 1 (1991): 22–3; Zi, "Fanfeng zhanzheng," 2164; Pang, "Yubei tianmenhui," 59; and Li, "Tianmenhui."

54 Xuexi wenshi weiyuan hui, *Huixian wenshi ziliao (Local History of Hui County)*, 2 (Huixian: Zhengxie Huixianshi weiyuan hui, 1990): 13–18.

then temporarily controlled by the Fengjun. The battle lasted for nearly half a month, ending in victory for Tianmenhui.

Cui's experience shows that the minor elites joined secret societies as an avenue to establishing dominance in the community. Due largely to the involvement of the minor elites, Tianmenhui and the Red Spear became the dominant power groups in the region. Historical records reveal that by 1926 the popularity of the secret societies had reached its zenith. Throughout the region every village had more than one organization either affiliated with the Red Spear or Tianmenhui. Furthermore, nearly 70% of all adult males in northern Henan were associated in one way or another with one of the societies.[55]

Besides the minor elites, the CCP also saw the importance of infiltrating Tianmenhui – especially in Anyang, Qi, Ji, and Hui counties – in order to inspire a peasant movement against the rich and powerful in the villages. The CCP reorganized some Tianmenhui chapters into Peasant Associations directly controlled by the Communists. In most cases, the CCP promised to supply the organization with rifles and provide military training. But after April 1927 the CCP withdrew its support.[56]

With that popularity, however, came fierce competition for power, conflicts of interest, and factionalism within and among the groups. During one period in Hui County, several different Spear groups fought for dominance of the county. The clash was initiated in Panshanghou Village by Yan Zishen, who led the Red Spear. Nearby, He Tianlong led a society he called the Green Spear. As several other groups sprang up in the county, each with a different color designation, competition for local dominance began. The Broadsword Society (*dadao hui*), also known as the Heart and Soul Society (*yixin hui*), was added to the competition, in opposition to both spear organizations.[57] Eventually, the friction among all three groups created chaos throughout the county.

Factional conflicts also developed within many secret society organizations. In the early 1920s the Red Spear in northern Henan was split between two major factions: the Old Style (*laopai*) faction and the New Style (*xinpai*) faction. Very soon a third group, the Yellow Spear, emerged. On January 10, 1926 the Old Style and New Style groups fought

[55] "Anyang qianghui yundong," 44–5; and Pang, "Yubei tianmenhui," 59.
[56] "Anyang qianghui yundong," 46; and "Gongchan dang zai yubei," 25.
[57] Wang, *Chongxiu Huaxian zhi*, 20: 8; Shi Tongxun, "Huisa rexue xie chunqiu" (Writing History with Warm Blood), in *Zhaoge renwu zhuanlue*, 2, *Qixian wenshi ziliao* (1988): 135–9; and Sun, "Hongqiang hui," 74–8.

a battle at the border between Tangyin and Yingyang counties. The Yellow Spear came to aid the Old Style group, but the combined forces were defeated by the New Style faction.[58]

Obviously, the mid-1920s was a period of major transformation in the local power structure of northern Henan. On the surface, that transformation appeared to consist of the political parties and the secret societies supplanting other elite institutions or power groups at the pinnacle of the local society's power structure. Beneath the surface, however, the internal competition for power (similar to that observed by Keith Schoppa in Zhejiang during the same period) produced constant turmoil among various social forces.[59] On the one hand, these changes turned winners (those who had dominated local society through various elite institutions) into losers; on the other hand, the former winners continued to create conflict, confusion, and chaos in the village community. This situation, as I will discuss in Chapter 8, might have been what prompted Feng Yuxiang to unleash a bloody campaign of suppression against the secret societies.

COPING WITH THE NATIONALIST GOVERNMENT

From the end of 1928, when the Nationalist government took control of Henan, the influence of local elites had diminished until, a year later, almost all their activity outside government channels ground to a halt. The actions of the chambers of commerce that had gained those organizations considerable influence in the business communities during the early Republican period were now restricted by the government. Because of that government intervention, most of the spontaneous elite institutions – such as the Chamber of Commerce, the Education Association, and the Peasant Association – accepted government sponsorship. Although the Nationalist government reinstated Self-Government, as I will discuss in Chapter 7, Self-Government became the vehicle for the government's restraint of local elite activities. For instance, although it had an office in every county, Self-Government attended only to minor duties, such as informing residents of its functions and inspecting to see that foot binding had been stopped. The best explanation of the responsibilities of Self-Government comes from the provincial government's specification, *"chouban quan xian zizhi shiyi"* (taking care of everything

---

[58] *Minguo ribao* (*Republican Daily*), (Shanghai, January 11, 1926).
[59] Schoppa, *Chinese Elites*, 76–7.

that has to do with Self-Government in the county). This charge left Self-Government with virtually no duties or power.[60]

Throughout the 1930s, elite functions were even more severely confined to undertakings that had no possibility of hindering state control of the peasant community. Within such a framework, there was an obvious return of local elites to their traditional roles, such as building modern schools, performing community projects, and organizing relief programs. Although a few prominent elites continued to receive appointments to public office from the government, they were pulled away from the communities that needed their leadership. By the end of the Republican period, elite activism rebounded briefly due to the rise in anti-Japanese sentiment in the region. The entire country was already in the midst of a Japanese invasion, however, before this resurgence of influence was able to turn the situation around.[61] During the Nationalist era, all previous victors in the competition for local power, except for the GMD itself, had been overthrown.

SUMMARY

Local society in northern Henan was transformed during the early twentieth century, and the most obvious changes occurred in its power structure. This process of transformation was closely linked to the long-term social development occurring throughout the country, and that connection encouraged extensive social activity in the region. The expansion of elite activism turned village communities into an open competition for local dominance – a contest joined by many different social forces, and one that finally favored the secret societies.

As I have shown in this chapter, the local society of northern Henan was essentially dominated by several major elite institutions at the end of the nineteenth century. The competition for community leadership, therefore, occurred only within those institutions whose members possessed power and influence in the community largely due to their wealth, status, and prestige. Since the beginning of the twentieth century,

---

[60] Wang, *Chongxiu Huaxian zhi*, 32; "Gexian shehui diaocha" (Social Survey of Every County), in *Xiuwu wenshi ziliao (Local History of Xiuwu County)*, 4 (1988): 78–103; and Xiao, *Xiuwu xianzhi*, 6 (1931): 36, 37.

[61] *Henan wenshi ziliao*, 15 (1985): 124; Ibid., 21: 133–42; and Guo Haichang, "Huiyi *Yubei ribao* (In Memory of *North Henan Daily*), in *Wenshi ziliao (County Gazetteer)*, 1 (1987): 29–38.

several fundamental changes in the country – particularly the intrusion of foreigners and the government's efforts to regain its control of local society – encouraged the competition for community leadership within the local power structure. For the moment, however, the previous power structure remained. On the whole, the elite community continued to provide strong leadership during this turbulent time, especially in the local communities' response to foreigners.

The 1911 Revolution, during which the local elites had assumed authority at the county level, was a brief moment of victory for those individuals. The revolution also intensified the competition for the leadership of the village community among the elites. Such institutions as the county assemblies, chambers of commerce, and Self-Government became their focus. But, in view of the profound social transformation during which it occurred, the revolution had less impact than the increasingly conspicuous new social elements in the area.

In the beginning, these new social elements posed little threat to those who then held local power. But, gradually and surely, they coalesced into several principal social forces – including political parties, workers, modern-school students – to challenge the entire local elite establishment. The increasing activism of these social forces facilitated the expansion of powerful social activities in which all, including the secret societies, participated in their race for dominance.

The existing power structure was thus steadily transformed into a much more open, dynamic, and multidimensional environment. Most notable, the perceivable rules that had previously governed local society lost their validity. For example, social status depended much less on educational degrees, family wealth, or personal prestige. Social interaction proceeded increasingly less according to discernable rules; the end rapidly became the better justification of the means. The former wielders of power thus faced challenges to their positions from all directions, not only among themselves.

The dominance of the secret societies in the late 1920s was due to the involvement of minor elites, those in the lower echelons, many of whom participated in or supported these secret organizations in order to maintain or further acquire their own influence. Given their religious nature, their mutual-assistance mode of organization, and their protective tendency, secret societies were much more appealing to the peasants than such new social activist groups as the CCP. In addition, secret societies became influential in that period because the entire elite community had been weakened.

Above all, the open nature of the region shaped the course of the transformation of local society. My research reveals the region was highly susceptible to outside influence. Most local changes were similar to the social, economic, and political metamorphosis taking place in other areas such as Zhejiang and Jiangsu provinces. The changes in the local society of northern Henan presented village communities with various challenges, even crises. Only those who were able to rise to the occasion and turn these challenges into opportunities emerged, in the eyes of history, as winners. Their actions, in fact, provided the impetus for the region's social transformation.

4

Elite Mobility in a Changing World

THROUGHOUT its history, southwestern Henan has typically been a region of violence and turmoil. Previous studies indicate that such an economically underdeveloped and administratively remote area was often home to large numbers of bandit gangs, as well as secret societies.[1] Although it is abundantly clear that life was dangerous, stressful, and insecure for most inhabitants in similar areas throughout China, comparatively little is known of the societal changes that swept over these peripheral societies, as indeed they did throughout China during the early twentieth century. For example, to what extent were the peripheral areas affected by outside developments? What was the impact of the decline and ultimate fall of the imperial dynasty in those areas? In what ways did local society change as people dealt with the disintegration of the social order? In order to find answers to questions such as these, my research focuses on the developments in village structure that gave rise to a later generation of power holders.

LOCAL SOCIETY IN THE LATE QING

During the early twentieth century, conspicuous changes occurred in elite society in southwestern Henan. Facing rampant banditry, village communities had to recognize and reward upstarts with no previous social status or prestige who were able to deal effectively with a variety

---

[1] See Elizabeth J. Perry, "Social Banditry Revisited: The Case of Bai Lang, a Chinese Brigand," *Modern China* 9 (1983): 355–82; Billingsley, "Bandits, Bosses, and Bare Sticks," 235–87; Billingsley, *Bandits*; Antony, "Peasants, Heroes and Brigands," 123–48; and Stephen C. Averill, "Local Elites and Communist Revolution in the Jiangxi Hill Country," in *Chinese Local Elites and Patterns of Dominance*, Joseph W. Esherick and Mary Backus Rankin, eds., 282–304.

of problems. These individuals came from different personal back-grounds. They included illiterates and modern-school graduates, former administrative personnel, and new-style military cadets. Although their ascent in society was largely due to the pressing social requirements of the banditry crisis – since the existing elite community failed to cope with the crisis, it afforded an opportunity for those with the capacity to assume local leadership – the shift of power in local society was a complicated process that evolved from the struggles between the previous and subsequent power holders.

Before these changes occurred, the elite community in southwestern Henan had been generally dominated by lower-degree holders, owners of small shops, and heads of lineages. Wang Gengxian, for example, was only a *xiucai*-degree holder in Deng County, but he was respected in the neighborhood because as a school teacher he could exert influence on his students and, through them, on their parents. A Zhenping County shop owner named Bi Yufu became chief of Xinmin Township because he was affluent and possessed some education. Since most higher-degree holders and large landholders had already departed the area for various reasons, including a desire for better living conditions, such petty store owners and lower-degree holders wielded a great deal of power in their locales, though their influence often fluctuated from time to time.[2]

Compared with these individuals, the influence of lineage heads tended to be more stable because they were backed by the members of their lineages, which usually numbered from several hundred to a few thousand. Besides owning land, some lineages also operated businesses in the closest market town. Their influence was largely enhanced if they had control of the markets. As reported in the local history, there were nearly twenty lineages in Nanyang County, and together they owned more than 300,000 *mu* (one *mu* equals 0.164 acre) of land, although most was infertile. Most of these lineages ran a number of businesses in the city. Within the city limits were the Gao, Yang, Mi, and Xie lineages. Outside the city were the Wang, Jia, Hu, and Du lineages in the east, the Peng Tai lineage in the north, the Dong lineage in the west, and the Yan lineage in the south. One member of the Gao lineage owned more than

---

[2] Zheng Tu and Qin Jun, "Wang Gengxian zhuanlue" (Biography of Wang Gengxian), in *Nanyang yinglie pu (Revolutionary Martyrs in Nanyang County)*, 1 (1985): 32–5; *Henan wenshi ziliao*, 6 (1981): 153–5; and Wang Guolin, *Zhenpingxian wenshi ziliao: Peng Yuting yishi (Local History of Zhenping County: Peng Yuting Story)* (Zhenping: Zhenpingxian weiyuan hui, 1987), 26–7.

a hundred stores, earning him the nickname Half-City Gao *(gao ban cheng)*. These lineages divided Nanyang County into different territories and contested among themselves for the leadership of the county's elite community. In addition to having economic strength, some lineages produced degree holders, officials, and army officers. Most owned private militias, or at least a few guards.[3]

Just before the dynasty ended, there were a few social organizations in the region. Among them, the Linked-Village-Association in Nanyang County was the most involved in community affairs . Because the organization took upon itself the new role of leading protests against the foreign missionaries around the turn of the century, it remained popular and influential. In 1900, for example, the Linked-Village-Association in Nanyang County led a protest against the French missionaries who were building the Jingang Church in the county. The protest assembled nearly seven thousand people and was supported by the business community in Nanyang City. When the prefect, Fu Fengyang, and the county magistrate, Yuan Fuling, attempted to stop the protest, they · were assaulted by the crowd. After the local police failed to restrain the protesters, a large unit of government troops was brought to the area. But the people continued to defy the government order and even refused to pay for damages to the church. The tension escalated until both sides drew their weapons. Eventually, the officials agreed to negotiate with the leaders of the association and yielded to their terms. Three years after this victory, the association rose again to lead a protest against another church construction project. At that time, several private militia groups also joined the protest. When it was over, the leader of the protest, Wang Zhongsi, enjoyed more popularity than ever. Local history records show that Wang was elected by the elite community of Nanyang to head a newly formed organization, the Neighborhood Watch Association, because of his role in the protest. Because of the association's involvement, the antiforeign movement persisted throughout the region until the Republican Revolution captured the public's attention.[4]

Unlike the Linked-Village-Association, the Chamber of Commerce that appeared in almost every market town beginning in 1906 enjoyed

---

[3] *Nanyang wenshi ziliao*, 2 (Nanyang: Zhengxie Nanyang weiyuan hui, 1986): 20–1.

[4] Nanyang shi difang shizhi bianchuan weiyuan hui, *Nanyang shizhi, (Gazetteer of Nanyang City)* (Zhengzhou: Henan renmin chuban she, 1989): 25–7, 213; Nanyang difang shizhi bianchuan weiyuan hui, *Nanyang xianzhi (Gazetteer of Nanyang County)* (Zhengzhou: Henan renmin chuban she, 1990), 615; and *Nanyangxian wenshi ziliao (Local History of Nanyang County)*, 1 (Nanyang: Wenshi ziliao bianwei hui, 1987): 26.

much less influence in this region than the same organization did in the north. Because the business community in each market town (except in Nanyang City) was usually small, most of the chambers of commerce were actually organized by the wealthy landowners living outside the market. Only in Nanyang City was the Chamber of Commerce formed by a group of guilds that had been organized by different types of business. Every Chamber of Commerce maintained a militia to provide protection for local businesses.[5]

Under the Qing government's initiative, Education Associations appeared in most counties around 1908. Although these associations allowed their leaders the opportunity to address a variety of educational issues, they often suffered from a lack of funds to carry out their missions, since education was not then widely perceived by the elite communities as a pressing concern. Most of the associations, therefore, existed for a short period, or existed in name only.[6]

Overall, institutional development among the local elites in this region was limited. The lack of institutional activism also might have affected the local elites' attitude toward political organization. For example, the Tongmenhui had extremely limited influence in Nanyang City. Its only notable member was a returned student who organized a local chapter in a school, and whose following included only his students.[7]

This paucity of interest in any organized activities was also true of local people's involvement in secret societies, which though prevalent during the late nineteenth century did not flourish in the southwest on the same scale as they had in the rest of the province. As the record shows, the Broadsword Society in Nanyang County and the Secret Teaching Society *(mimi jiao)* in Nanzhao County were very active at one time. But because of a lack of participation or support from the community at large, they were quickly suppressed by the government before they could spread to the entire region.[8]

---

[5] *Nanyang wenshi ziliao*, 5 (1989): 1.
[6] Nanzhaoxian zhibian weihui, "Nanzhao xianzhi: dashi ji" ("Gazetteer of Nanzhao County: major events"), (Nanzhao, Unpublished Manuscript), 26; and Xichuan difangshi bianwei hui, *Xichuan xianzhi (Gazetteer of Xichuan County)* (Zhengzhou: Henan renmin chuban she, 1990), 23.
[7] Ding Yuqing, "Yang Heting zhuanlue" (Biography of Yang Heting), in *Nanyang wenshi ziliao*, 6 (1990): 1; and *Nanyangxian wenshi ziliao*, 1 (1987): 112–3.
[8] *Nanyang shizhi*, 28; "Nanzhao xianzhi: dashi ji," 27; and Nanzhaoxian wenshi ziliao weiyuan hui, *Nanzhao wenshi ziliao (Local History of Nanzhao County)*, 5 (Nanzhao: Zhengxie Henansheng Nanzhaoxian weiyuan hui, 1988): 84–5.

1911 REVOLUTION

The 1911 Revolution roused a certain amount of enthusiasm in the elite community. In Neixiang County, a wealthy and powerful landowner by the name of Yang Shoutian organized a group that called itself the Green and Red Gang *(qinghong bang)* with two of his relatives, Yang Jinggui and Yang Hongyi, and called for an uprising against the county government. The group asked the leaders of the Red Gang *(hong bang)* in Deng County to bring their membership to Neixiang County on February 17, 1912 to assist in the uprising. After the insurgents had caused the county magistrate to flee, Yang Shoutian entered the county seat to release prisoners and distribute silver and food, which had been hoarded by the county government, to the public. But the uprising was soon suppressed by the government.[9]

Shortly thereafter, Yang Heting, a Tongmenhui member and a superintendent of a local high school in Nanyang City, gathered more than a hundred rifles to prepare for a second insurrection. But the plot was soon discovered by the district government, which forced Yang to escape from the city temporarily. Yang returned to the city and persuaded more people to join his effort to overthrow the district government. Under Yang's leadership, this larger group surrounded the county seat and forced the officials to surrender. Immediately after this second uprising, Yang assumed the position of county magistrate.[10]

In Xichuan County, a series of uprisings were also attempted. The first occurred on January 11, 1912, when the Qing dynasty had just bowed out but the region remained under the control of that regime's local officials. As soon as the plot was discovered, the county government arrested and executed 213 people who were involved. Right after this, however, a group of local elites declared the county's independence. The uprising was joined by Liu Binhuan, a Tongmenhui member who had left Neixiang County earlier to join the revolution in Kaifeng and then returned to southwestern Henan to organize uprisings. Together, Liu and other local elites tried to take over the county government. As the former Qing

---

[9] "Neixiang xianzhi: renwu" ("Neixiang local gazetteer: personages"), (Neixiang: Neixiangxian zhizong bianji shi, Unpublished Manuscript), 1–2; "Renwu" *("Personage")* (Unpublished Manuscript), 4–5; "Neixiang xianzhi: dashi ji" ("Neixiang local gazetteer: major events") (Neixiang, Unpublished), 13; and Zhang Dading, "Yang Shoutian" (Yang Shoutian), in *Neixiang yinglie (Revolutionary Martyrs in Neixiang County)* (1985): 10–11.

[10] Ding, "Yang Heting," 1–2; and *Nanyangxian wenshi ziliao*, 1 (1987): 113.

district government sent its troops to Xichuan County to thwart the independence attempt, the troops were intercepted by the Hubei People's
Revolutionary Army. Afterward, the rebels entered Deng County and
expelled the officials from the county. When the insurrection was over,
Wang Tianzong, a former bandit leader who had joined the revolution,
made Liu a county magistrate of Xichuan.[11]

Generally, during the revolutionary period, the local elites throughout
the region assumed control of their communities. In Nanyang County,
for example, the County Assembly, which had been established under
the auspices of the Hubei People's Revolutionary Army when it was temporarily in control of the area, quickly took over the district government
and declared its control of the county. In the city itself, the Chamber of
Commerce immediately formed an organization among the shop owners
to maintain order in the market. In Neixiang County a temporary county
council was organized with twenty-two members to administer the
county.[12]

CHANGES IN THE LOCAL POWER STRUCTURE

But the downfall of the dynasty and the disappearance of a stable government inevitably led to the complete disintegration of social order in
southwestern Henan. As the region was frequently controlled by various
armies and self-proclaimed authorities, banditry emerged as the most
significant cause of the miseries and instability of village life. The situation began to reach a crisis in the village community by the 1910s, pre-
cipitating a transformation of its power structure.

As the threat of brigandage mounted, people built forts (*zhai*) to repel
the bandits, each one a stockaded village surrounded by stone walls. The
first forts appeared in Neixiang County, but they gradually spread
throughout the region. At the outset no one had envisioned the forts
would become the center of power competition among different elite
groups as well as individuals. The following individual histories illustrate
the scope as well as the depth of the changes in the local power structure. These changes initially commenced in Neixiang County. It is to that
location that I now turn.

---

[11] "Neixiang xianzhi: renwu," 7–8.
[12] Xichuanxian zhibian weihui, "Xichuan xianzhi: difang zizhi" ("Gazetteer of Xichuan
County: Self-government") (Xichuan, Unpublished Manuscript [First Draft]), 55;
Nanyang wenshi ziliao, 5 (1989): 2–3; and "Neixiang xianzhi: dashi ji," 13, 15.

Bie Tingfang in Neixiang County

During the mid-1910s in Neixiang County there were about seventy different forts of three different types. The first type was built by individual lineages and was thus called a lineage fort; its leader was the head of the lineage. The second kind was created by a small village, or by several working together, and hence was called a linked-village fort *(lianying zhai)*. The head of such a fort usually hailed from a wealthy family. The so-called mass-built fort *(qunjian zhai)*, the most common type, was constructed under the leadership of locally influential elites (although not necessarily rich landowners), and its members were mostly poor villagers.

The forts' main function was to provide protection from bandits. For that purpose, all forts maintained regular militias that ranged from several dozen to more than a hundred men. The cost of maintaining this permanent force was shared by each household using the fort, except in the mass-built fort, where the guards were volunteers from among the villagers. Villagers returning from the fields at night would leave several of their number on guard as they entered the mass-built fort. Whenever the county was infested with bandits, people stayed in the forts even during the day. The standing militias soon provided aspiring community leaders like Bie Tingfang the opportunity to demonstrate their courage, fighting skills, and ability to command the militia.[13]

Bie Tingfang, the son of a common farmer, was born in 1882 in a small village in Neixiang County. He had very little education, but he was a skilled and brave hunter. In 1911, when Bie had just turned twenty-nine, he was hired by Du Shengtang, the head of Tiger Fort, one of the mass-built forts in the southwest corner of the county. Du chose Bie to lead a small militia group after Du had gathered money from the fort members to purchase several rifles from a Catholic church in Nanyang. The new responsibility for guarding Tiger Fort was the first stepping stone in Bie Tingfang's rise to power.[14]

Bie applied himself diligently in his new job, often sleeping with his rifle and painstakingly raising dogs to watch the fort. His efforts made Tiger Fort the safest in the surrounding area and earned Bie the respect

---

[13] *Bie Tingfang shilu*, 4–5.
[14] *Bie Tingfang shilu*, 10–11; *Zhongyuan wenxian (Henan Local History)* 12, no. 12 (Taipei: Zhongyuan wenxian chuban she, December 25, 1980): 13.

of its members. As Bie's reputation spread, increasing numbers of villagers in the vicinity moved into the fort. Among those who joined were two of Bie's childhood friends (and locally known bullies), Liu Gusan and Yuan Jiangling, who became Bie's bodyguards and assistants. Eventually Bie's popularity compelled Du Shengtang to relinquish his position to Bie.[15]

In 1913 Bie, desiring to expand his influence in the neighborhood, reorganized his militia, then nearly forty strong men, into four units. Then, he requested everyone living seventy to eighty miles around the fort, and between ten and forty years old, to register with his fort and to pay a certain amount for his protection. When Bie's militia swelled to nearly one hundred men, it became a means to intimidate or punish those who resisted the regular collection of protection fees. With the new financial resources now at his disposal, Bie purchased about a hundred rifles from Kaifeng to equip his militia.[16]

As Bie Tingfang's influence began to grow, Monk Dong, the head of the nearby two temples, the Yungai Temple and Tiefo Temple, offered his friendship. Monk Dong lent Bie rifles in exchange for Bie's protecting the temples. As the friendship continued, Monk Dong sometimes allowed his temples to be used for locking up bandit gang members before they were slaughtered by Bie's militiamen. Soon Monk Dong became ill and died, but before his death, Dong sold the temple land to Bie. Instantly, Bie had become a large land-owner.[17]

Even though Bie Tingfang had suddenly risen from poor peasant to rich landlord, his ambition still was not satisfied. By then, he aspired to become one of the most powerful persons in the neighborhood. Toward that goal, he preferred to rely on his militia rather than his wealth. He further bolstered the strength of his militia and launched a series attacks on his neighbors. In February 1915, Bie Tingfang led two dozen militiamen in an assault on Zhaoyang Fort, twenty miles from Tiger Fort, to seize its rifles. In the fighting, Bie's nephew was wounded, and to avoid being recognized as the attacker, Bie dumped his nephew into a raging fire to be killed. After the failed

---

[15] *Bie Tingfang shilu*, 7–10; Qin Jun, "Bie tingfang shengping shilue" (The Life of Bie Tingfang), in *Nanyang shizhi tongxun (Nanyang Historical Newsletter)* (1991): 16; and "Renwu," 32.

[16] Zhang Hexuan, "Wo suo zhidao de Bie Tingfang" (My Knowledge about Bie Tingfang), *Xixia xianzhi (Gazetteer of Xixia County)* (1990): 78–9; and *Bie Tingfang shilu*, 10.

[17] Zhang, "Bie Tingfang," 77–8; and *Bie Tingfang shilu*, 78.

attack, Bie spread the rumor that Zhaoyang Fort had been attacked by bandits.[18]

The failure to break into Zhaoyang Fort did not end Bie's endeavors. However, his target shifted to Shipao Fort (a large fort within only three miles from Tiger Fort), even though the fort's master was his father-in-law, Wang Qianlu. Because it was heavily fortified and well guarded, Bie arranged for one of his militiaman, Wang Minqi, to meet Wang Qianlu and to begin work inside the fort. Wang Minqi was thus able to open the fort gate one night and let in Bie's forces. During the attack, Bie killed Wang Qianlu's entire family, after he had taken every rifle and valuable item from the fort. Having gained control of Shipao Fort, Bie made Liu Gusan its head.[19]

For the first time, Bie Tingfang had tasted victory. That experience merely reinforced his previous conduct. He continued to use intimidation and violence against other influential members of the elite community in the southwest section of the county in order to establish his dominance in that area. Early in 1916, Bie sent an assassin to kill the head of Zhaojia Fort, Zhao Guoding, one of the most influential community leaders in Bie's neighborhood. After Zhao had been liquidated, Bie absorbed his men and rifles into his own militia. A few months later Bie's militia surrounded Du Fort, whose head, Du Yuankai, controlled one of the larger militias in the area, until Du agreed to leave the county for good. As a result of these actions, Bie Tingfang emerged as one of the most powerful individuals in that part of the county.[20]

Bie's violent behavior soon caught the attention of the county government, then under Yuan Shikai's regime. A charge of murder was brought against Bie by the county court, which sent police to arrest him. Bie escaped from jail after his first arrest, but was arrested again within a few days. This time, the county court transferred him to Kaifeng to stand trial in provincial court. Before leaving the county, however, a few community leaders persuaded the county court to try Bie locally. While in court, Du Shengtang, a widely respected neighbor, defended Bie Tingfang's actions as being in self-defense. Nevertheless, the court

---

[18] Qin, "Bie Tingfang," 16; "Renwu," 20; Zhang, "Bie Tingfang," 79; and Xixiaxian zhibian weihui, "Xixia xianzhi: renwu pian" ("Gazetteer of Xixia County: Personage") (Xixia, Unpublished Manuscript), 114.

[19] Qin, "Bie Tingfang," 16; "Renwu", 20, 32; and Bie Binkun, "Youguan zufu Bie Tingfang de huiyi" (Recollections of My Grandfather Bie Tingfang), in *Henan wenshi ziliao*, 33, (1990): 117–18.

[20] *Bie Tingfang shilu*, 13–14.

sentenced Bie to a year in jail for various minor offenses. But Liu Gusan volunteered to serve the term in Bie's place, and Bie was set free.[21] The experience of the trial encouraged Bie's belief that he was above the law. Furthermore, after Yuan Shikai's regime ended, county government itself had become an unstable institution (a situation that continued for years, until the end of the warlord period). It is likely that both Bie's experience and the changes in county government profoundly affected Bie Tingfang's understanding of law and authority – thereafter he disregarded them totally.

After he was released from the county jail, Bie Tingfang clearly became more aggressive than ever in asserting himself in the local power structure. In 1919, Bie began to take on Yuan Baosan, the head of the Bandit Eradication Bureau, a prominent part of the local security establishment supported by the county's entire elite community. Yuan was naturally Bie's next opponent since he was the most influential militia leader in the southwestern section of the county. His head quarters were in Huiche, the market of that area. At the time, Yuan was well connected in the community, providing protection for many wealthy families. In order to compete with Yuan, Bie Tingfang purchased more rifles and machine guns to equip his militia. This move put Yuan on his guard, and he began to plot Bie's assassination. To lure Bie into his trap, Yuan invited him to his home for a family celebration. But Bie was informed of the scheme by a member of Yuan's lineage, Yang Jiesan, and he escaped from Yuan's house in the middle of the banquet. Shortly after this incident, when Yuan was killed during a bandit attack on his fort, Bie lost his opportunity for revenge.[22]

After the death of Yuan Baosan, those who had depended on his protection were forced to pay respect to Bie Tingfang. The residents of Huiche invited Bie and his militia to guard Huiche. At the same time, Bie incorporated Yuan Baosan's militia into his camp and thus boosted his own eight hundred men to a force of two thousand. From then, Bie started to call himself battalion commander *(siling)*, and his militia was thus exalted to a battalion *(mintuan)*.[23]

Taking control of Huiche allowed Bie Tingfang to became a subcounty

[21] Ibid., 16; Qin, "Bie Tingfang," 16; and "Renwu," 32.
[22] Zhang, "Bie Tingfang," 80–81; Bie, "Bie Tingfang," 118–19; and *Henan shizhi ziliao (Local History of Henan)*, 7 (Zhengzhou: Henansheng difang shizhi bianchuan weiyuan hui, 1984): 71.
[23] *Bie Tingfang shilu*, 18–19; and Qin, "Bie Tingfang," 16–17.

elite, but his ambition did not stop there. His next goal was to assume leadership of the entire county, and he set his eyes on Xixiakou, a central market town of Neixiang County. By bribing the head of the town's militia, Zhang Ziyang, Bie was permitted to send two militia units, about two hundred men, into the town. To avoid raising the suspicion of the townspeople, the new units were led by a widely respected resident, Fu Chunxuan, whom Bie had chosen specifically for the task. Bie himself later joined his units in Xixiakou with more militiamen. He settled in the town and started to collect "contributions" from the storeowners in return for protection.[24]

Bie Tingfang's actions elicited different opinions from the members of the elite community, especially those in the Chamber of Commerce, which then controlled the market town. The chairman of the chamber, Nie Guozheng, supported the moves because he felt Bie was more able than others to guarantee the safety of the shopkeepers and their customers, thus stimulating commerce. Others, however, feared Bie's ulterior motives.

After a brief consultation with other community leaders, Nie suggested the magistrate and militia chief of the county, Zhang Hexuan, formally recognize Bie and his militia. Realizing the benefit of placing Bie's militia under his command, Zhang agreed. But to insure Bie's loyalty and cooperation, Zhang initiated a ceremony in which he, Bie Tingfang, Nie Guozheng, and Liu Gusan were sworn to brotherhood. Nie and Zhang then persuaded the county magistrate to name Bie the Chief of Militia in the Second District of the Western Region, thus in a way legitimizing Bie's self-proclaimed status as a local community leader.[25]

Bie Tingfang's quick rise to power aroused the jealousy of Yuan Jiangling who was also a sworn brother, even though he wasn't included in the ceremony with Bie, and the head of the sizable Sanguan Fort. Although Yuan had always supported Bie in the past, he became Bie's competitor for local dominance, especially after Bie's recognition by the county government. Bie resented Yuan's jealousy, and when he heard it rumored that Yuan was criticizing him in front of the county magistrate, Bie had his men kill Yuan in his own home.[26]

[24] *Bie Tingfang shilu*, 19.
[25] *Bie Tingfang shilu*, 19, 20; and Xixiaxian zhibian weihui, *Xixia xianzhi (Gazetteer of Xixia County)* (Xixia: Henan renmin chuban she, 1990), 59.
[26] *Bie Tingfang shilu*, 16–17.

By the beginning of the 1920s, the power structure of Neixiang County had allowed Bie Tingfang to become one of its top militia leaders (along with Nie Guozheng, Luo Jiwu, and Liu Huchen). Each commanded his own militia of more than two thousand men. The head of the county militia, Zhang Hexuan, however, led a unit that contained only eight hundred men. Nevertheless, these troops controlled the county seat, Chenguanzhen (from which they acquired the name Town Faction, *cheng pai*). Inevitably, this obvious imbalance of military and political positions between Zhang Hexuan and the other militia leaders generated considerable controversy for the next five years over the issue of leadership of the county militia – a controversy exacerbated by the intrusion of various state authorities, local officials, and passing armies (see Chapter 7 for details). The conflict finally led to open hostility between Bie Tingfang and Zhang Hexuan.[27]

In 1926, Bie and Zhang quarreled angrily over whether Zhang had the authority to order Bie to move his militia to Nanyang City. To settle the argument, Bie fell back on his usual tactics; he hired Wang Rongguan, a local bully, to assassinate Zhang. Wang was caught in the act by Zhang, who had been warned by one of Wang's friends. Zhang interrogated Wang for days until he confessed that he had been sent by Bie. Because the confession also implicated Zhu Taosheng, an army officer under Wu Peifu who had been sent to Neixiang County to mobilize a local army, Zhu was immediately arrested. As soon as Bie Tingfang heard of Wang's arrest, he led his militia to surround the county seat. But before he arrived at the county seat, Bie took Zhang's family hostage. As war between the two militias loomed, several leaders of the county's elite community intervened. Because these elites enjoyed good relations with both parties, their mediation seemed to have worked – Bie and Zhang acceded to a truce ceremony in Chenghuang Temple. It was agreed that Bie would remain in Neixiang County, but Zhang would leave for Luoyang. According to the agreement, Zhang led his militia out of Neixiang but, suspecting an ambush from Bie, changed his route. Bie calculated that Zhang would smell trouble and change his route; he was thus able to ambush Zhang after all. Zhang narrowly escaped and proceeded to Luoyang alone. With Zhang out of the picture, Bie absorbed his militiamen into his own units. Realizing that competition

---

[27] "Neixiang xianzhi: renwu," 31–2; *Bie Tingfang shilu*, 22–3, 25–6; Qin, "Bie Tingfang," 17; and "Renwu," 58.

with Bie was futile, Nie Guozheng and Fu Chunxuan also surrendered their militia units.[28]

Bie Tingfang was now the ad hoc leader of the county militia, but he was roundly criticized throughout the community. Leading the censure were Zhang Qiaoshu, the Inspector of Education; Hu Gongchen, principal of a normal school; and Qin Bichen, a fort master from the powerful Qin lineage. Bie suppressed the criticism with panache; working with Nie Guozheng and Fu Chunxuan, he had the leaders killed. Bie then blamed the tragedy on bandits and went to mourn the three victims.[29] The deaths of Zhang, Hu, and Qin silenced the opposition immediately, and Bie Tingfang assumed the leadership of the elite community in Neixiang County.

Chen Shunde in Xichuan County

While the above changes were taking place in Neixiang County, a similar trend was underway in Xichuan County, where hitherto there had been only a few small-scale private militia units in 1912 collectively called the Bandit Eradication Bureau. In 1914 some of the groups formed a so-called Self-Defense Militia *(baowei tuan)* after Yuan Shikai ordered private militias in the country be placed under government supervision. Only a few men thus remained in the bureau. Around the county larger militia groups began to emerge, led by Wang Yinghe at Shishiwang, Huang Zhaoyi at Taohe, Li Yongnian at the county seat, Yang Chunzao at Shangji, and Song Zujiao at Songwan. These groups used the payments they collected from the local inhabitants to purchase rifles and supplies and to cover their expenses. Overall, before the end of the 1910s, there wasn't a single militia group large enough to provide sufficient protection to the county. Members of the elite community still sought individuals to organize a militia at the county level. They soon would find their leader in the person of Chen Shunde.[30]

Born in 1901 into a wealthy and highly respected degree holder's family, Chen had attended several high schools and normal schools in Kaifeng and Xinyang, at a time when modern schools were still unavailable in southwest Henan. Having lived in Kaifeng and other large cities, Chen

---

[28] *Bie Tingfang shilu*, 26–33.   [29] Ibid., 44–5.

[30] Xichuan wenshi ziliao yanjiu weiyuan hui, *Xichuan wenshi ziliao (Xichuan Local History)* (Xichuan: Xichuanxian weiyuan hui, 1989), 98–100; and *Xichuan xianzhi* (1990), 25.

had become acquainted with, as well as had personal connections to, influential people of various capacities outside the region. He was, therefore, widely considered to be a well-informed *(jianduo shiguang)* man. In 1920, Chen Shunde was a school principal in Xia County. He received a letter from the villagers of his home county, inviting him to return home to organize a militia to protect them from bandits. Feeling an obligation to his family, friends, and fellow villagers, he returned and was warmly received by his former neighbors. One of them, a wealthy landlord named Wan Nianxin, even sold his land to support a militia, to be led by Chen, that would avenge the loss of his only son to the bandits. Deeply moved by the offer, Chen remained to organize a small group that called itself the Bureau of All Mountain Forts *(quan shanzhai ju)*.

In the beginning, the group contained only about a dozen militiamen and had only seven rifles, six of which were useless. Nevertheless, the bandits in the neighborhood were alarmed. One night they surrounded Chen's house, demanding he disband the militia immediately and threatening to kill his entire family. Chen and his militia calmly resisted the bandits. When they heard gunshots the villagers assembled about sixty men under the leadership of Ren Taisheng, head of the Ren lineage. The bandits withdrew when they saw the armed crowd approaching. Chen and Ren, now fast friends, formed a larger militia group for the protection of several villages in the neighborhood.[31]

Chen Shunde's courage under fire earned him a glowing reputation among the villagers. But this temporary fame was almost wrested away by his father-in-law, Jia Yanling, a wealthy landowner in a nearby village. After Chen had returned home from Kaifeng, Jia asked him to help organize a militia. He even offered Chen a generous salary. But Chen had already agreed to lead a militia for his village. Jia was infuriated by Chen's refusal. Having lost face, Jia filed a complaint with the county government, charging Chen with soliciting bribery. Because the charges came from his father-in-law, they threatened Chen's own reputation. Realizing the possible consequences, Chen avoided open conflict with Jia. Instead, he carefully preserved his father-in-law's dignity (and his own reputation as a righteous man) by bringing him back after he had left home for fear of Chen's retaliation.[32]

---

[31] "Xichuan xianzhi: difang zizhi," 75–6; Chen, *Xianhua wanxi*, 121–4; and Shen Qingbi, *Wanxi Chen Shunde xiansheng zhuan (The Story of Chen Shunde)* (Taipei: Hongdao wenhua shiye chuban she, 1976), 24.

[32] *Zhongyuan wenxian* (1970), 9–10.

In 1920, Chen Shunde's influence began to spread from his neighboring villages to the subcounty ward *(qu)* where his village was located. His first competition for community leadership was with Huan Congshu, a skilled militiaman from the nearby village of Liguanqiao. Both Chen and Huan were being considered by the community for the leadership of a larger militia group then being formed by more than a dozen villages. Fortunately, Huan left Xichuan County voluntarily, having realized that he was in no position to compete with Chen.[33]

By early 1921 Chen Shunde had set his sights on Shangji, a small market town and the center of the northern part of the county. The militia group guarding Shangji was led by Hou Dudu. To compete with Hou, Chen allied himself with Zhang Hongyan, a militia head from the village of Xiwan. Chen soon realized that Hou was a reckless opponent; he had, for example, assassinated a respected neighborhood leader at Shangji. After carefully measuring his own strength against Hou's, Chen realized he was no match for him. He decided to join Hou, then gathering militia groups in the northern part of the county, and wait for the right opportunity to challenge him. In return, Hou offered Chen the position of Assistant Chief of the Local Militia in the Second Ward, under his command.[34]

After his failure to gain control of the militia in Shangji, Chen shifted his attention to the First Ward in order to further his original plan to become the militia leader of the county's northern sector. The ward's largest militia was led by three sons of the Zhou lineage together with two brothers from the Li lineage. After the three sons of Zhou were killed fighting bandits, the Li brothers were in charge of the militia. Having been introduced to the Zhou and Li families, Chen persuaded them to break away from Hou Dudu. Meanwhile, Chen and his aid, Ren Taisheng, forced two wealthy individuals, the most influential in Shangji, to leave town by humiliating them in front of others. Witnesses remember that Chen invited Yu and Hou to a banquet during which Chen asked Ren Taisheng to provoke an argument with Yu. Ren then slapped Yu's face to humiliate him. Seeing that Chen's men were prepared, Yu did not fight back. Although Hou was surprised, he took no action, for Chen was his father-in-law. Chen now moved into Shangji and declared himself leader of the militia of the county's northern sector.

---

[33] *Zhonggong Xichuan xian dangshi ziliao (Chinese Communist Party, Xichuan County Party History Materials)*, 2 (Xichuan: Dangshi ziliao zhengji bianji weiyuan hui, 1987): 250.

[34] "Xichuan xianzhi: difang zizhi," 75–6; and *Xichuan wenshi ziliao* (1989), 104–6, 111.

Faced with Chen Shunde's rising popularity, Hou acknowledged his own defeat.[35]

Caught in a wave of militia formation that swept over the county from 1921 to 1924, the elite community formed a county-level militia. A series of competitions for leadership of the militia attracted several promising candidates, among whom was Li Yongnian, a wealthy landlord known for his earlier success in adopting a mutual assistance system for his village community. After intensive discussions with the leaders of the elite community, the candidates temporarily agreed to merge their own militias to form the Nine-Ward Allied Militia, a joint militia with headquarters in the county seat. Because they could not decide on a permanent leader for the militia, the elite community chose Song Shaowen from Songwan to be the interim chief. Although on the surface, all militia groups in the county were unified under one leadership, each continued to act on its own. And the competition for leadership continued.[36]

The following year, 1924, was critical for Chen Shunde in his rise to power in Xichuan County. Chen perceived himself to be a relative unknown to the people in the county. To bolster his reputation, he bought 120 rifles from Gong County, gave forty to Song Shaowen, and kept the rest for his own men – a deed immediately applauded by the elite community. When Song retired from his position, he recommended Chen Shunde, as he had long planned to do, to head the county militia. Riding a tide of rising popularity, Chen Shunde was immediately confirmed as head of the county militia. From the end of 1924 the county militia led by Chen engaged in a series battles with the large bandit gangs in the adjacent areas. In one battle, the militia defeated the notorious gang leader Zhang Zhanbiao while he was attempting to enter the county seat. The county magistrate deeply appreciated Chen's military prowess and invited him to guard the county government offices. Chen thus became the most influential individual in the county.[37]

Chen now took steps to assure his leadership position in the elite community. Among other strategies, he used the same methods of intimidation he had employed against those who had competed against him for leadership of the county militia (Li Yongnian, Jin Lujiao, Song Lianfang, and Duan Fengxuan). When Li became his most vocal critic, Chen had him killed. Chen's tactics finally forced Duan and Jin to

[35] "Xichuan xianzhi, difang zizhi," 80; and *Xichuan wenshi ziliao* (1989), 107–9.

[36] "Xichuan xianzhi, difang zizhi," 76–7; and *Xichuan wenshi ziliao* (1989), 101–6, 111–12.

[37] "Xichuan xianzhi, difang zizhi," 78, 81; and *Zhongyuan wenxian* (1971), 2–26.

escape to Kaifeng, and terrified Song enough that he hired a full-time bodyguard for his family. Later, in an effort to win over Song, and thus assure his position in the elite community remain unchallenged, Chen arranged for his daughter to marry Song's son and made Song head of the militia of the eighth ward.[38] After that, no one in Xichuan County was able to dispute Chen's absolute authority over the elite community.

In 1926 Chen Shunde's power had already extended to most of Xichuan County. In April 1927 Chen started Self-Government in Xichuan County to replace the authority of the county government. By June the county magistrate had quit his job due to illness. When the National Revolutionary Army entered Xichuan, Chen was the head of the Bureau of Public Funds. The army appointed Chen county magistrate, and in July the provincial government under Feng Yuxiang reappointed him to the same position.[39]

Peng Yuting in Zhenping County

As the elite communities of Neixiang and Xichuan counties were struggling to redefine their leadership, similar contention was stirring in Zhenping County. A man named Peng Yuting arrived home to attend his mother's funeral just as a disagreement broke out in the local elite community over who should lead that county's militia. Peng Yuting, the son of a pharmacy owner, was born in 1883 in the village of Qiji. After attending several local public schools and then two normal schools in Kaifeng, he matriculated at Huiwen University in Beijing, but left in 1913 for lack of financial support. He then returned to Zhenping to teach in a local normal school, where his diligence and talent caught the eye of the school's principal, Yan Jingxuan. When Yan received an appointment from the provincial government in 1919, he recommended Peng to be deputy director of the Printing Department. In 1921, Peng was promoted to chief of the Bureau of Silk Production, and later, still following Yan, he became the supervisor for local transportation in Shanxi province.

[38] Chen Zhiguang, "Chen Shunde yu difang zizhi" (Chen Shunde and Local Self-Government), in *Nanyang shizhi tongxun* (1991), 52; and "Xichuan xianzhi: difang zizhi," 86–7.

[39] "Xichuan xianzhi: difang zizhi," 57; and *Xichuan xian lishi ziliao huibian (Collection of Historical Documents in Xichuan County)* (Xichuan: Xichuan xianzhi zongbianji shi, 1985), 166–7.

When Yan died, Peng attended the funeral and met an army officer named Zhang Zhijiang, with whom he eventually worked, first in the government of Chahaer and then in the Northwest Army. When the Northwest Army disbanded in 1927, Peng visited Liang Zhonghua, a former patron who had supported him financially during his study at the university. In the summer of 1927, Peng received Zhang Zhijiang's recommendation for a job as a senior judge in the National Revolutionary Army's Second Unit, where Zhang himself was the chief judge. Peng was still in this post when he learned of his mother's death in August 1927. Because Peng was educated and had unconventional experiences, most of the county's elites immediately looked upon him favorably.[40]

For someone with such an extraordinary record, the post of county militia leader would normally have been an unacceptably humble office. But in August 1927, as Peng was rushing home to mourn his mother, a group of bandits waylaid him, causing him to miss his mother's funeral. The event aroused his hatred for the bandits and sympathy toward the people of Zhenping. He decided to stay in Zhenping to help organize the villagers against banditry. He borrowed some rifles from a wealthy landlord in Yuanying and used them, as well as militiamen from Yuanying, to arrest several bandit leaders in the area. This brought him immediate fame in his neighborhood, and the chief of Houji Ward offered to relinquish his position for Peng. Soon the elite community of the county also became aware of Peng Yuting's presence. It invited him to head the county's militia. As he accepted the offer, Peng asked Han Fuqu, then governor of Henan, to grant him official confirmation of his title from the provincial government.[41]

In his sudden rise to power, Peng Yuting inescapably encountered jealousy and disapproval from other members of the elite community. The first to air his grievance was Wang Baoshu, a wealthy landowner who had owned a large militia that had merged into the county militia. In order to intimidate Wang, Peng whipped him before a large crowd for smoking

---

[40] Wang, *Peng Yuting*, 11–18; and Li Tengxian, *Peng Yuting yu Zhenping zizhi (Peng Yuting and Self-government in Zhenping County)* (Zhenping: Zhenpingxian difang jianshe cuweihui, 1936), 66–7.

[41] Feng Wengang, "Yuting" ("The story of Peng Yuting") (Unpublished), 63; Qin Jun, "Peng Yuting shilue" ("Stories about Peng Yuting") (Unpublished Manuscript), 3; and Peng Pei, "Lun Peng Yuting difang zizhi" (On Peng Yuting's Self-Government Program at Zhenping County), *Academy Forum of Nandu (Social Science Edition)* 10, no. 1, Yang Mengli et al., eds. (1990): 87.

opium. Wang was forced to leave the county in shame. Although Peng's harsh treatment of Wang Baoshu may have temporarily daunted his detractors, new complaints soon surfaced. In early 1928, when Peng received a report that a degree holder in Jiahe, Lu Guangyuan, was associating with bandits, he saw another opportunity to establish his authority in the elite community. After a brief investigation, Peng's militia arrested Lu and his family. Lu and his three sons were killed without a trial, and the voices against Peng were again temporarily silenced.[42]

But not long thereafter, a serious challenge arrived from Peng's former patron, Bi Yufu. Bi was not only one of the most powerful residents of the county but had also supported Peng financially during his school years. In addition, Bi had his own militia of nearly 300 men. Realizing he risked destroying his reputation by betraying his former patron, Peng decided to intimidate Bi indirectly. Peng saw his opportunity when he discovered a connection between one of Bi's followers, Zhang Shizen, and the leader of a bandit gang. Accompanied by more than 300 militiamen, Peng paid a visit to Bi. In front of Bi, Peng ordered Zhang arrested and summarily executed. No one in the elite community, including Bi Yufu, dared disagree with Peng again.[43]

Ning Xigu in Deng County

When Peng Yuting had recently returned to Zhenping County, a military cadet by the name of Ning Xigu had also arrived in southwestern Henan. A native of Deng County, Ning had been born in 1906 in the village of Ningying, twelve miles south of the county seat. Little is known about his family, childhood, or early education, but it is certain that he eventually enrolled in the Huangpu Military Academy, the most prestigious institution in the country for training military officers at the time.

After graduation, Ning joined the Nationalist Army and rose to the rank of regimental commander during the Northern Expedition. His bravery in battle led Wu Peifu to offer 2,000 to 4,000 *yuan* – a handsome amount of money – for a reward for his capture, dead or alive. For unknown reasons Ning later left the army and returned to southwest Henan. Before Ning appeared in Deng County, his home county, by the end of 1927, a county militia had already been organized by Guo Mingru,

[42] Wang, *Peng Yuting*, 18–19, 31–2.   [43] Ibid., 23–9.

a member of a *jinshi*-degree holder's family. Ning first settled in Zhen-ping County and was introduced by Yang Guixuan, a former friend and a wealthy peasant, to Peng Yuting. In light of Ning's military experience, Peng offered Ning a military instructorship at a training camp set up by Peng. Ning later became dissatisfied with the position and returned to Deng County to become head of the county militia.[44]

To assume that post, Ning realized he would have to confront the incumbent militia leader, Guo Mingru. In broad daylight, Ning marched into Deng County with two brigades of Zhenping militiamen and de-manded that Guo surrender his position. Ning was rejected, but he per-suaded Guo's militiamen to join him. Meanwhile, Ning sent a request to his former instructor at the Baoding Military Academy – Liu Zhi, then military commander of the First Army Division of the Nationalist Army – for confirmation of his self-assumed title of county militia chief. Although Ning's high-handed behavior enraged many members of the elite community in the county, no one was able to challenge him for fear of retaliation.[45]

Local Elites in Nanyang County

Because of its economic, political, and strategic significance for the region, Nanyang City, more than any other area, attracted the attention of state authorities and military strongmen passing through southwest-ern Henan. This notice somehow relieved the need for the county's inhabitants to rely on stockades for protection against bandits. Thus, the kind of political development that the rest of the region experienced was not seen in Nanyang County immediately after the 1911 Revolution. Nevertheless, by the mid-1920s, similar changes had begun to occur as competition for power centered around the establishment of a local militia.

By 1926 a Red Spear chapter had been established in the county. Almost overnight, its membership topped 10,000 and the organization spread to Deng County. Most who joined did so to protect themselves from two threats: bandits and various transient military forces. Because of its protective nature, the organization attacked passing armies, includ-ing that of the CCP. During one battle, the group seized nearly 2,000 rifles

---

[44] Dengzhoushi difang shizong bianshi, "Dengxian zhi: renwu" ("Local history of Deng County: personages"), (Dengxian, Unpublished Manuscript), 34–5.

[45] Wang, *Peng Yuting*, 68–9.

from a CCP army, which caused it to completely disband. Afterwards, both the CCP and GMD penetrated the city and the county in 1927. It has been noted in local history that the CCP even infiltrated the county militia and was very active in the major schools in the city. The GMD was also active in the county.[46]

The local power structure in the late 1920s saw the county generally dominated by the leaders of several militia groups. On the south side of the city, in the area called Liusongying, about 100 villages were under the protection of a militia group with a 100 rifles. The east side of the city was protected by three militia groups. The Lusang Temple Militia, head-quartered in Lusang Temple, offered protection to 150 villages. A second group, the Qingliang Temple Militia, guarded nearly 450 villages with about 200 rifles. The group was known to be active in fighting the bandits but it had also been penetrated by the CCP. The third group, based in Ying Village, had only about a dozen villages under its protection. The largest militia groups in Nanyang County were on the north and north-west sides of the city. The groups claimed to have more than one thousand rifles. Because none of the other militia groups were willing to merge with the groups, a county militia was not formed until much later.[47]

SUMMARY

Until the mid-1920s, southwestern Henan was generally unaffected by the social, economic, political changes that took place outside its borders – the lone exception being another banditry crisis unleashed at the end of the Qing dynasty, as often occurred when the government relaxed its control of the region. Due to the severity of this crisis, however, the people in the area took serious steps to protect themselves. These measures produced "unintended consequences" that led to major developments in the local power structure, which in turn triggered further

---

[46] *Nanyang dangshi renwu zhuan (Biography of Communist Historical Figures in Nanyang County)*, 1, Li Yaojun et al., eds. (Zhengzhou: Henan renmin chuban she, 1987): 51; *Nanyang xianzhi* (1990), 26, 85, 617; Dengxian wenshi ziliao weiyuan hui, *Dengxian wenshi ziliao (Local History of Deng County)*, 2 (Dengxian: Zhengxie Dengxian weiyuan hui, 1985): 32–7; and Sheqixian difang zhizong bianshi, *Sheqi renwu (Personages in Sheqi County)* (Sheqing: Sheqi xian difang zhi zong bian shi, 1986), 3–4.

[47] "Nanyang xianwei daibiao baogao" (Report from the Representatives of CCP Committee of Nanyang County), in *Henan geming lishi wenjian huiji (Collection of Historical Materials on the Revolution in Henan)*, A, no. 8 (CCP Internal Document, Unpublished), 120–1.

transformations in the peripheral society during the early twentieth century.[48]

Two principal measures were used to control banditry: the construction of village forts and the establishment of county militias. In the midst of these activities, a later generation of community leaders began to emerge. These new leaders came from a wide spectrum of personal backgrounds. Ambitious young leaders from humble peasant families, like Bie Tingfang, vied on an equal footing with experienced bureaucrats in the warlord administration, like Peng Yuting. This entire later generation of community leaders rose to power through fierce struggle for power against the former power holders in the elite community, until finally these previous community leaders relinquished their leadership. Their success was largely due to the changes in the community value system; village communities as a whole came to value those who demonstrated their ability to lead the local militia against bandits above those whose status depended largely on a state-conferred degree, family wealth, or the support of a powerful lineage. Upon their emergence, therefore, this later generation of community leaders won popular support as well as the recognition of the elite community.[49]

Another distinctive trait of this new generation of community leaders was their heavy dependence on coercion to obtain and maintain dominance. Although they traveled various paths to power, they all used force, in one form or another, to gain the upper hand in the competition for power. For example, Bie Tingfang's journey to success left a trail of blood as he killed off most of his competitors. Chen Shunde used similar methods, though to a lesser extent, whenever he felt it necessary. Although Peng Yuting did not resort to the same extremes, he used physical punishment as well as public humiliation to control the opposition. In becoming the director of the county militia, Ning Xigu also used coercive measures extensively. In addition, these individuals seemed to share a clear sense that the foundation of power rested in the control of the militia. Their efforts were, therefore, largely focused on assuming the

---

[48] The term comes from Robert Merton; see Jon Elster, "Merton's Functionalist and the Unintended Consequences of Action," in *Robert K. Merton: Consensus and Controversy*, Jon Clark, Celia Modgil, and Sohan Modgil, eds. (London: Falmer Press, 1990), 120–9.

[49] In this sense, the banditry "crisis" fits exactly the meaning of the Chinese word *weiji*, which combines the element of danger with opportunity for the ambitious and able to rise to power. Lowell Dittmer and Samuel S. Kim, "In Search of a Theory of National Identity," in *China's Quest for National Identity*, Lowell Dittmer and Samuel S. Kim, eds. (Ithaca: Cornell University Press, 1993), 4.

directorship of the county militia. As soon as they succeeded, they were declared bona fide community leaders.

The violent behavior of the later generation of community leaders in southwestern Henan certainly added more evidence to the well-grounded perception that the peripheral societies in China were more violent than other areas. Local elites were more likely to command militia units, and so their coercive resources were generally greater than those elites in the core areas.[50] However, the establishment of elite dominance through violence and popular acquiescence to the use of coercive force seemed to indicate the village communities in the region accepted violence as the norm. Or, at least, most of the population believed the individuals who seized community leadership through coercion represented a lesser threat to the communities than did the bandits.

Nevertheless, both the developments in the community value system and the popular acceptance of coercion produced serious consequences. For one thing, a highly concentrated power structure emerged in the local society due to the rise of these community leaders. In each county, essentially one individual now controlled the entire elite community, as well as all the villages. Furthermore, by turning the local militia into their private police force, those leaders not only eliminated crime but effectively stifled all opposition. As I will show in Chapter 6, the perpetuation of this pattern of elite dominance soon ushered in an even more extensive social transformation in southwestern Henan in the ensuing decades.

[50] Esherick and Rankin, *Chinese Local Elites*, 23. This feature of the peripheral society is also noted by G. William Skinner, who suggests that local elites in the peripheral areas usually had short military careers. G. William Skinner, "Mobility Strategies in Late Imperial China: A Regional Systems Analysis," in *Regional Analysis*, 1, Carol A. Smith, ed. (New York: Academic Press, 1976), 355.

Part III

ELITE ACTIVISM AND SOCIAL TRANSFORMATION

5

Society as the Organization of Networks

FEI Xiaotong first used the term *chaxu geju* (differential mode of association) to describe Chinese society. He believed one of the most important features of that society was that it "centered around the individual and was built from networks created from relational ties linking the self with discrete categories of other individuals."[1] Like Fei, many scholars have studied personal networking as one of the important ways people in Chinese society interact with one another.[2] As a part of that mounting interest in Chinese social dynamics, discussion continues on the scope of the personal relations formed within local society. Despite a great deal of excellent research, the general perception persists that most personal ties formed in the villages and standard-marketing communities of imperial China have remained within these boundaries during the early twentieth century.

Before Skinner's study of the marketing system of China appeared, for instance, it had been generally assumed that people in the traditional period usually formed their personal ties within the village community. Skinner challenged that assumption with the notion that the periodic marketing area defined the locus of interpersonal relations, including those of affinal, religious, and local organizations. Changes in the early twentieth century, Skinner proposed, only caused the local community

---

[1] Hsiao-tung Fei, *From the Soil, the Foundations of Chinese Society*: Translation of Fei Xiaotong's Xiangtu Zhongguo, with an introduction and epilogue, Gary G. Hamilton and Wang Zheng, trans. (Berkeley: University of California Press, 1992), 24, 70.

[2] See Robert Hymes, *Statesmen and Gentlemen: The Elite of Fu-chou, Chiang-hsi, in Northern and Southern Sung* (Cambridge: Cambridge University Press, 1986), 82–136; Naquin and Rawski, *Chinese Society*, 51–4; Esherick and Rankin, *Chinese Local Elites*, conclusion; and Mayfair Mei-hui Yang, *Gifts, Favors, and Banquets: The Art of Social Relationship in China* (Ithaca: Cornell University Press, 1994), 287–311.

to shrink, again making the village the place for individuals to maintain relations.[3]

A few years later, Skinner modified his earlier view by offering a model of the open and closed peasant community. According to that theory, both the integrated marketing system and the insular village community were spheres of personal interconnection, but at different times. During the decline of a dynasty or the fall of a regime, the community would close up in the following sequence: normative closure, economic closure, and coercive closure. These progressive states corresponded to the external developments that led to the dwindling of political opportunities, the diminution of economic opportunities, and, finally, the breakdown of social order. During such periods of social closure, most people formed relations only within their insular village communities. However, once these conditions were reversed – at the beginning of a new dynasty, after order was restored and the opportunities reappeared – the sequence was reversed and the villages would open up. Personal relations would then extend to the appropriate standard-marketing community.[4]

Revisions of Skinner's view have come from different perspectives, but most have focused on the physical parameter by which personal relations were usually extended. For example, Author Wolf feels that standard-marketing communities were not necessarily the only arenas in which personal relations were forged. He argues that sometimes various interests could motivate any group of people to extend their relations outside the limits of the marketing area.[5] Philip Kuhn brings two modes of social interconnections to our attention, the "nested-concentric mode" and the "tinker-peddler mode." While in the former most villagers formed relationships through the routes of the marketing system that differed from the commercial-administrative arrangement, the routes they followed resembled the paths tinkers and peddlers traveled from village to village.[6] Reemphasizing the village, Philip Huang argues that "even in the 1930s, all but the most highly commercialized villages of the North China plain were still relatively insular communities." Before the full-scale commercialization of the twentieth century, most villages had very little contact with outsiders.[7]

---

[3] Skinner, "Marketing" (1965): 211–27; and Skinner, "Marketing" (1964): 40–3.

[4] Skinner, "Closed Community," 278–81.

[5] Arthur P. Wolf, Introduction to *Religion and Ritual in Chinese Society*, Arthur P. Wolf, ed. (Stanford: Stanford University Press, 1974), 5–6.

[6] Kuhn, *Rebellion and Its Enemies*, vi–vii.   [7] Huang, *Peasant Economy*, 219.

To highlight the role of human agency, Prasenjit Duara points out that personal networks in local society worked not through any particular system or structure but rather in a "subject-centered universe of power." That universe, which Duara terms the "cultural nexus of power," was composed of people and social groupings, not of geographic zones or a particular hierarchical system. Within that nexus of power, not only did all the groups differ from each other, but they also all interlocked through informal personal ties that centered around the village communities, through market towns, or outside the marketing system. The early twentieth century brought with it changes that caused the reshuffling of the "points of coordination" within the nexus, as well as the rise and subsequent decline of the significance of the village as the center of the networks.[8]

The present study offers a look at the changes in the scope and internal mechanism of personal networking during the early twentieth century. As I intend to show, one of the important changes of that period was the expansion of the scope of personal relations to an "indefinite tract of time-space."[9] This development took place among certain members of the elite strata in northern Henan. Although the initial motivation of those local elites to create an elite network was to maintain their previous social status and influence in their home areas, their efforts led to the expansion of their social network from the local level to the national level, an amplification that also became a part of their effort to penetrate the state. In return, the undertakings of those former local elites enabled them to alter the course of political development in Henan through their manipulation of the influence of the national leader, Yuan Shikai.

THE EARLY YEARS OF THE LITERARY SOCIETY

By the late nineteenth century, as I have shown in Chapter 3, Ji County, like the rest of Henan province, was undergoing radical social changes. Within the local power configuration several elite associations predominated: the Linked-Village-Association, the Bureau of Wagon and Horse, and the Neighborhood Watch Group. Gradually, however, a literary society rose to prominence in the county. Comprising a number of influential individuals, this organization became the axis of an elite network whose influence encompassed the entire region.

---

[8] Duara, *Culture, Power, and the State*, 15–16, 20–3, 26–41.
[9] Giddens, *Modernity and Self-Identity*, 18.

The literary society was created by three degree holders: Wang Xitong, Li Minxiu, and Gao Youxia. Wang and Li had been close friends since they met in 1879; Gao was a mutual friend of Wang and Li. The three had long shared the idea of creating a literary society. In 1883 Wang and Li, with two of their friends, He Lanfen and Wang Ying, had initiated a literary club called the Society of Literature. But due to lack of enthusiasm from other members of the elite community the organization remained inactive. Two years later, after Wang Xitong had left to accept a teaching position in Kaifeng, the association was dissolved. Despite their club's failure, however, Wang and Li clung to their idea, and their correspondence was filled with discussions of the subject. As soon as Wang returned home, in 1889, he again organized a full-fledged literary society, calling it the Society for Classical Learning *(jingzheng shushe)*. Both Li Minxiu and Gao Youxia joined Wang in his endeavor. Acknowledging Wang Xitong and Li Minxiu's literary accomplishment in the elite community, some lower-degree holders began to pay attention to their literary society. Soon a number of literary men had joined the group.[10]

The first membership meeting was held at Li Minxiu's home in 1897. It was decided that each member would submit four *taels* of silver as his annual dues. Li Minxiu contributed his entire earnings from the Bureau of Wagon and Horse – nearly 100 *taels* of silver – for the purchase of books. With that fund, Wang Xitong later was able to bring back more than 100 books from Beijing, including volumes of history and the classics, as well as translations of Western writers. At the first meeting it was also decided that the members would gather once a month at the home of either Li Minxiu, Wang Xitong, or Gao Youxia for regular discussions of their readings. Li Minxiu and Wang Xitong were to be responsible for reading every member's study notes and offering criticism.[11]

As the society grew, Li Minxiu, Wang Xitong, and Gao Youxia gained more influence outside their local community, especially after gaining the support of prominent individuals in other counties. Through the society's other members, Li Minxiu and Wang Xitong became acquainted with

[10] Tong, "Wang Xiaoting," 6–10; and "Jixian dashi ji," 20.
[11] Gen Yuru, "Ningzuo dashi buzuo da guan de Li Minxiu" (Li Minxiu: A Person Pursuing Important Matters rather than Important Positions), in *Xinxiang wenshi ziliao*, 4 (1990): 88; Hu Shaofen and Gen Yuru, "Yidai qiru Li Minxiu xiansheng" (Li Minxiu: A Senior Scholar of Our Generation), in *Henan wenshi ziliao*, 5 (1987): 31; and Li Yishan, "Jixian jingzheng shushe jiqi tushuguan de gaishu" (General Information about the Society for Classic Learning and the Library in Ji County), in *Jixian wenshi ziliao*, 1 (1988): 33.

Wang Anlan, a *jinshi*-degree holder in Xinxiang County, who later became one of the central figures in the network that was about to take shape. Wang had been a member (*shujishi*) of the Imperial Academy and was given the degree of Second-Class Compiler and Corrector (*bianxiu*) for his achievement in an examination held by a special commission with the palace. For reasons unknown, Wang Anlan returned to Xinxiang to stay. Also through the society's discussion sessions, Wang Xitong became friends with Gao Maocai, another renown scholar in Xinxiang County, who occasionally joined the meetings. Wang's younger brother married Gao's daughter. Initiated by the older brother, the union was to serve as a "form of social connection" for both Wang Xitong and Gao Maocai.[12]

The growing literary society also began to attract new members from Xinxiang, Yanjin, Hua, and Lin counties. The society's leaders, realizing the need for a permanent facility, asked Wang Anlan for assistance. Wang solicited his cohorts, including Shi Xiaozhou of Hui County and Li Xingro of Yanjin County, to petition the district government for funding. When the requisition was approved, a house was acquired that would serve as the society's home. To the founders of the literary society, the process of obtaining the petition was as gratifying as receiving the funding. The society was able to persuade those who had participated to become members; its leadership was thus expanded to include Wang Anlan, Shi Xiaozhou, Li Xingro, and Guo Yiqin. The change in leadership solidified the society's stature in the region. Consequently, even more people from adjacent counties applied for membership. At this point, the society's leaders adopted a set of requirements for membership, among which were proficiency in reading the classics and recommendation by eminent members of the elite community – prerequisites intended to bar anyone of lower social status.[13]

By the end of the nineteenth century, an elite network had arisen that revolved around the literary society. Among its members were many prominent citizens of Gong, Hua, Hui, Qi, Xinxiang, Yuanyang, and Yu counties. Through the society's seasonal gatherings and monthly sessions,

---

[12] Tong, "Wang Xiaoting," 12–13, 16; and Wang Xitong, "Yan yu ping zong" ("My life in Henan and Hebei") (unpublished diary), 27.

Timothy Brook has argued that marriage was a "powerful form of social connection" for the gentry in traditional China. See Timothy Brook, "Family Continuity and Cultural Hegemony: The Gentry of Ningbo, 1368–1911," in *Chinese Local Elites and Patterns of Dominance*, Joseph W. Esherick and Mary Backus Rankin, eds., 27–50.

[13] Li, "Jingzheng shushe," 34.

which were sometimes visited by people from outside the region, the leaders of the society were able to extend their network of personal relations to the elite community in Kaifeng.[14]

The development of the network so far fits very well with the same pattern of networking that Timothy Brook has discovered among gentry members in Ningbo during the traditional period. Brook has shown that cultural pursuits such as reading the classics and writing poems "were organized through the networks of elite society, and mastering cultural skills was necessary for those who sought access to those networks." Therefore, "literary accomplishment was a key basis for signaling status and forming groups among the elites."[15]

The evolution of the literary society from its inception to its emergence as an elite network followed the traditional steps associated with the forming of personal networks: engaging in reading the classics, establishing marriage affinity between members' families, and cooperating to submit petitions to the government. Above all, the very existence of the literary society placed its members in what sociologist Alfred Schutz considers "a face-to-face situation," in which "the partners are constantly revising and enlarging their knowledge of the other." This face-to-face contact among individuals, according to Schutz, was crucial in enabling them to form close social relations.[16]

LOCAL TIES AND LOCAL POWER

Near the turn of the twentieth century, as it gradually gained momentum, the literary society became one of the major elite establishments in Ji County. The key members of the society exerted substantial influence on community affairs at the county level. Its members' voices came to be heard throughout the county, and soon, the region. An example is Li Minxiu's nomination of Wang Xitong to head the Bureau of Wagon and Horse. Wang and Li had been intimate friends since childhood; their joint operation of the literary society only solidified their friendship and mutual trust. By the end of 1898, Li Minxiu had recommended Wang Xitong to temporarily replace him as director of the bureau during a leave of absence.[17]

---

[14] Gen, "Ningzuo dashi," 89; and Li, "Jingzheng shushe," 35.

[15] Brook, "Family Continuity," 40–3.

[16] Alfred Schutz, *The Phenomenology of the Social World*, George Walsh and Frederick Lehnert, trans. (Evanston, IL: Northwestern University Press, 1967), 219.

[17] Tong, "Wang Xiaoting," 14–15.

Li's departure arose from bickering that had begun a few years earlier, when Li had conceived a plan to prevent certain community leaders from interfering with the bureau's affairs. In order to implement his plan, Li had sought the endorsement of the governor of Henan, Liu Shutang. Of the eight individual agendas on Li's proposal to the governor, three were particularly sensitive: that the bureau alone be responsible for the collection of a surtax to provide for such functions as the hosting of government officials passing through the region, that the head of county government be excluded from participation in the bureau's regular functions, and that salaries for the bureau's staff be trimmed. The proposal was sanctioned by the governor and was later introduced to the entire province. However, it infringed upon the personal interests of certain individuals, who in their anger spread the rumor that Li would control the bureau for his own benefit. As a result, Li was compelled to leave the bureau.[18]

Wang Xitong perceived Li's departure as an opportunity to demonstrate his ability to assume leadership of the elite community. In his attempt to do so, Wang Xitong sought a great deal of assistance from his friends in the literary society. Once, for instance, the bureau urgently needed to transport rice to relieve famine on the other side of the Yellow River. When several owners of horses and wagons refused their help, Wang convinced his wealthy friends to allow him to use their horses and wagons in lieu of their annual contribution to the bureau's surtax. His handling of the matter brought him immediate fame in the county. To uphold that reputation, Wang Xitong deliberately relinquished his position after he accomplished the mission. Upon leaving the bureau, he declined his salary, thus conferring on himself general recognition as a man of virtue.[19]

In addition to serving as advocates for one another, members of the network, in the course of their official assignments, introduced one another to government officials above the district level. The first of these contacts was Wang Anlan's friendship with two officials in the Qing court, Zheng Fumeng and Ma Jisheng – a junior metropolitan censor *(jishizhong)* and a second-class compiler and corrector, both natives of northern Henan. Through their relationship, in January 1900 Zheng and Ma put Wang in charge of apportioning relief goods in Jiyuan County,

---

[18] Lu Meiyi, "Li Minxiu yu jixian chemaju" (Li Minxiu and the Bureau of Wagon and Horse in Ji County), in Zhongzhou Jingu, vol. 4, ed. Guo Yingsheng (Zhengzhou: Zhongzhou jingu chuban she, 1987): 7–8; and Hu and Gen, "Yidai qiru," 32.

[19] Tong, "Wang Xiaoting," 14–16.

an assignment he carried out with the help of his friends in the literary society: Li Minxiu, Wang Xitong, Shi Xiaozhou, Wang Xitao, and Xia Jichuan. Thereafter, the district chief chose Wang Anlan, Li Minxiu, and Wang Xitao to carry out a similar project for the entire region. The three enlisted many of their friends from the literary society to assist in distributing relief items in Neihuang and Anyang counties in Zhangde prefecture, Ji and Hui counties in Weihui prefecture, and Xiuwu County in Huaiqing prefecture. For their efforts, the literary society earned the considerable gratitude of the district government.[20]

Mary Rankin's study indicates that by the late nineteenth century the local elites in Zhejiang had extended their activities to the macroregional level, especially to Shanghai, through their personal networks.[21] Similarly, the network under scrutiny in the present study also became a vehicle by which its participants were able to elevate their status and influence in the early twentieth century. By joining the network, an individual could, on the strength of personal relationships alone, draw upon many resources. The discernible benefit from the network seemed to inspire the leaders of the literary society to extend their influence in the region through networking.

GAINING REGIONAL STATUS

The leaders of the literary society next extended their personal ties to the officials in the district government. In so doing, they reasoned, they would be recognized as the sole representatives of the elite communities for the entire region. And by attaining that status, these individuals would extend their social activities to the regional level.

The Boxer Rebellion of 1900 provided the opportunity they desired. At the rebellion's onset, the leaders were invited by the district chief *(daotai)*, Cen Churong, through Wang Anlan's recommendation, to consider the organizing of a regional militia. A meeting for this purpose on August 7 was attended by Wang Xitong, Li Minxiu, Wang Anlan, Shi Xiaozhou, and Wang Xinquan, the only person who did not yet belong to the network of friends. During the meeting, each person was given the opportunity to express his opinion, while the county magistrate from Wuzhi took minutes. In addition, according to plan, local communities of each county would be responsible for supplying food and monetary compensation to the militia. The government officials

[20] Ibid., 15–17.   [21] Rankin, *Elite Activism*, 137–42.

would cooperate with community leaders to collect a supplemental land tax to fund these expenses. The participants at the meeting decided to set up a regional headquarters for the militia, the Bureau of Defense Preparation *(choufang ju)*, under which was one branch office and two militia battalions in each prefecture. Cen himself was to be titular head of the militia, but the militia would be run by the members of the elite community. Those participating in the meeting offered Cen the opportunity to formulate the militia and later be in charge of it. Chen Kuilong, the governor of Henan, soon approved the plan and it was carried out immediately.[22]

During the meeting, Wang Xitong also advised Cen to post a warning against the Boxers. Wang's suggestion was well appreciated by Cen, who entreated Wang to personally sign the warning. Through their participation in the meeting and their subsequent work in developing the militia, Wang Anlan, Wang Xitong, Li Minxiu, and Shi Xiaozhou became well acquainted with Cen, a friendship that enabled these gentry members to gain regional status, through which they were able to influence many of the decisions by officials in the district government.[23]

Through their constant giving of advice, the key members of the society gradually implanted a sense of trust in the minds of district officials, as illustrated by the following examples. Cen chose Wang Xitong to be a lecturer at the School for Practical Knowledge *(zhi yong jing she)*. After Wang declined the position, Li Minxiu received the appointment. Cen then invited Wang to be the head lecturer at the school. After Wang again declined, Li Minxiu was promoted to the position. Cen's decision was based solely on his friendship with the two individuals.[24]

On another occasion, Wang Xitong, Li Minxiu, and Wang Junlan, another celebrated scholar in the region, decided to expand the literary society by appending a new school, the School for the Original Script of the Classics *(jing zheng shu she)*. Coincidentally, as the plan was being conceived, the Bureau of Defense Preparation was dissolved. The three saw the chance to use the funds from the bureau to support their school projects. They approached Cen, who approved the transfer of six hundred *taels* of silver for the acquisition of two houses at the West Gate of Ji County. He also set aside supplementary funds for the school's routine expenses. When the school opened it was staffed exclusively by

---

[22] Tong, "Wang Xiaoting," 17.   [23] Ibid., 18.
[24] Gen, "Ningzuo dashi," 94; Hu and Gen, "Yidai qiru," 35; and Tong, "Wang Xiaoting," 20.

members of the literary society that included Wang Xitong, Li Minxiu, Shi Xiaozhou, Xia Ziding, and Cui Xiuling.[25]

In return for such favors, the literary society came to the aid of district officials whenever necessary. In 1902, when Cen was under scrutiny by the Qing court for his leniency toward the Boxers, the key members of the network – Wang Xitong, Li Minxiu, and Wang Anlan – immediately mobilized the elite communities in the entire region to plead for his innocence. Due to their efforts, the court halted its investigation.[26] After the event, the leading members of the literary society began to demand more recognition from district (as well as local) officials – not only because they realized the magnitude of their influence in the region but also because they had developed a clear sense of their indispensability to the officials.

This realization originated in a change in their attitude toward the officials. For instance, when the district chief, Zhu, had just arrived in northern Henan to succeed Cen in 1902, Wang Xitong resigned his position at the School for Practical Knowledge (which was sponsored by the district government) in protest over Zhu's neglecting to pay him a formal visit. Although Zhu had left his business card with Wang after his visit with Li Minxiu, Wang nevertheless felt insulted. A few months later, a similar incident occurred with the arrival of Ji County's new magistrate, Xiao Qing. Without comprehending Wang Xitong's status in the elite community, the new magistrate sent a message to Wang, asking for a meeting in his office, instead of paying Wang a personal visit. Feeling insulted, Wang refused to meet Xiao and also quit working for the Sanfeng Coal Company, a position he had assumed at the invitation of the former county magistrate. To reconcile Wang and Xiao, Li Minxiu and other members of the literary society convinced Xiao to visit Wang personally; after that the two became friends.[27]

The arrogance among the leaders of the literary society continued to mount, and they used such insolent gestures to command from the new officials the attention they deemed proper. By March 1906 they had finally procured the regional status they sought, as signified by their invitation by the prefect *(taishou)*, Zhai Shaowen, on February 1, 1905 to the annual ceremony for the deceased "village notables" *(xiangxian)* as representatives of the communities from the entire region. Thereafter, they were invited annually as representatives of the local communities of their

---

[25] Tong, "Wang Xiaoting," 21.   [26] Ibid., 22.
[27] Ibid., 21, 25; and Wang, "Yan yu ping zong," 10–11.

prefect. The custom continued for some time, regardless of who became prefect, indicating the continuing recognition of these gentry members as the representatives of the communities in northern Henan. When Hua Zaiyun replaced Zhai Shaowen as the new prefect, he continued with the tradition of holding a memorial ceremony for the deceased village gentry. Again, those on his list of invitations were Wang Jingbo, Xia Ziding, Li Minxiu, Gao Youxia, and Wang Xitong. In addition, Wang Xitong was offered the position of general manager for a local coal mine in Yu County because he was the only one capable of dealing with its officials.[28]

Attainment of influence within their region was vital to the career advancement of the network's leaders. They achieved that influence through relying on personal networking and demanding recognition from government officials. Having thus achieved regional status, the leaders were ready to further their political interests as well as various personal ambitions.

APPROACHING A HIGHER LEVEL

In view of their successes on the local and regional levels, the network's leaders had the opportunity to use personal channels to acquaint themselves with officials at the next level of government: the provincial government or Qing court. In the ensuing years, they consistently paid visits to targeted officials. Through these undertakings, they entered a larger scale of activism at the provincial level.

In 1906 Li Minxiu and Wang Xitong arrived at Kaifeng to meet with Yu, a *daotai* in the provincial government. Through Yu's introduction, Wang Xitong met with Hu, an official of the same rank, several months later. On November 7 Wang Xitong went again to Kaifeng to visit Yu and Hu. Through them, he also met the Commis-sioner of Education. In the same period, Wang Xitong twice traveled to Beijing to visit former Yu County magistrate Cao Dongyin, then a Counselor of Ministry of Rites *(libu canyi)* in the Qing court. Finding him absent both times, Wang finally wrote a note criticizing Cao for neglecting him after he was promoted. The criticism angered Cao, who ended the friendship.[29]

The overall networking efforts with provincial officials nevertheless resulted in increased political clout for the group of individuals currently

[28] Wang, "Yan yu ping zong," 3–4, 12–14, 23.   [29] Ibid., 5, 14–15, 16–17.

under study. Through an occurrence in Yu County in April 1906, even they soon realized this new status. Several hundred local people, ignoring the county government, had been mining coal without permission. Those heading the group claimed to belong to the families of powerful officials in the Qing court. After the case was reported to the prefectural government, the prefect, Chen Fuqing, sent troops to disperse the crowd. The troops exchanged gunfire with the crowd, and people on both sides were wounded. The prefect, under public pressure to halt the free mining attempts, nonetheless feared that further police action could inflame the court officials whose relatives were leading the riots. The prefect consulted Wang Xitong, who asked an acquaintance in the provincial government to inquire into the background of the self-proclaimed relatives of the court. As soon as he was notified that these people were not related to any official, he informed the prefect, who had them arrested. Wang's connection with provincial officials thus helped him gain the respect and gratitude of the prefect.[30]

These individuals received other benefits from their relationship with provincial officials, however. First, they received many appointments from the provincial government. In September 1906, for example, the government founded the Office of the Commissioner of Education. The administration designated Li Minxiu its chief counselor *(yishen)*, and appointed Wang Xitong, Wang Anlan, Shi Xiaozhou, and Zhang Zhongfu to its staff. Second, these essentially literary men were able to influence many decisions of the provincial government on matters pertaining to their local communities, their personal interests, and the welfare of their friends. For instance, in late March 1907 Wang Xitong persuaded the provincial government to abandon its plan to take over the Three Peaks Coal Mine. He also convinced them to employ Western mining technology. Finally, through their relationship with provincial officials, these gentry members strengthened their positions in their elite communities. For example, they became the members of an ad hoc committee of the Association of Mining Affairs, whose mission was to express to the Qing court the entire region's grievances against the British.[31]

---

[30] Ibid., 14–15.

[31] Tong, "Wang Xiaoting," 28, 31; Wang, "Yan yu ping zong," 16–18, 23; and Gen Yuru, "Aiguo minzhu shiye jia Wang Xitong" (Patriotic and Democratic Industrialist Wang Xitong), in *Jixian wenshi ziliao*, 1 (1988): 23.

SURVIVING THE CRISIS

Although the influence of the leaders of the literary society continued to increase, it also earned the jealousy of the neighbors in their home county residence. These feelings soon intensified until they threatened the reputation and safety of the families of Wang Xitong and Li Minxiu. In order to preserve their influence in their village it was imperative they solve this crisis, which began with a single incident symptomatic of the tension that already existed between those excluded by the literary society and its leaders.

The incident occurred in late January 1907, during a community festival for the Bixia Goddess *(bixia yuanjun)*, a fertility deity, at the Three Immortals Temple *(san xian miao)* in Ji County, where the families of Wang Xitong and Li Minxiu lived while they were away from home. According to local custom, a worship service was held every year in front of the temple. During this particular ceremony, while watching a performance, students from the school headed by Wang Xitong and Li Minxiu unintentionally knocked over a statue of the goddess. The villagers attending the ceremony demanded that the students be punished. When the angry crowd realized they were students of Wang and Li, they stormed the school and the houses of the teachers' families.[32]

Most villagers involved in the incident were lower-degree holders who had suffered various privations as the literary society gained influence. Because the literary society promoted, among other things, new learning, it attracted mostly young students to its schools. Previously, many villagers had earned a living by tutoring students in the local schools. But with the influx of younger students, these tutors lost their livelihood. Furthermore, Wang and Li had been known for opposing the idle worship of deities such as the Bixia Goddess. The villagers were thus eager to blame the school for sending its students to create the "accident"; the fact they resorted to violence against Wang Xitong and Li Minxiu was no surprise.

Wang Xitong and Li Minxiu learned of the incident through a letter from their relatives and returned quickly to resolve the crisis. They met with the prefect, Hua Zaiyun, and the county magistrate, Ye Dongbing, who stated their desire to penalize the rioters. The two officials solicited the opinions of Li and Wang, and both repudiated the idea of punish-

---

[32] "Jixian zhi: renwu" ("Gazetteer of Ji County: Personages") (Ji County, Unpublished Manuscript), 1; and Tong, "Wang Xiaoting," 30.

ment. In fact, they blamed themselves, for being unable to serve their community adequately. When they learned of Li and Wang's response to the officials, the villagers who had participated in the disturbance were deeply moved.[33]

Wang and Li's handling of the crisis thus helped them to establish a benevolent reputation among the villagers. Meanwhile, the incident also gained the sympathy of many prominent natives from other parts of the region, and allowed Wang and Li to bring new members into the network. After the crisis, in early March 1907, Wang Yinchuan, an influential scholar in Xinxiang County, wrote to Wang Xitong and Li Minxiu conveying his support for their endeavors in the literary society. Wang Xitong and Li Minxiu developed an enduring friendship with Wang Yinchuan through that correspondence.[34]

Timothy Brook has suggested that "the key to the dominance" of the local elites in traditional China was "their interaction with each other ... they were consistently forming and reforming ties, building networks that favored men of equal status and disadvantaged lesser gentry and nongentry. Friendship, marriage, political commitment, and cultural pursuits all furnished opportunities for the elite to associate with one another."[35] In this case, the crisis merely created another opportunity for Wang Xitong and Li Minxiu to interact with people like Wang Yinchuan and to extend their network of relations.

Overall, the crisis allowed Wang Xitong and Li Minxiu to strengthen their ties with their community, while extending their contacts to more prominent members of elite communities throughout the region. Their handling of its conclusion also demonstrated their skill in dealing with any challenge to their influence in the community – a skill necessary for maintaining power in the ever-changing local power structure.

TRANSREGIONAL ACTIVISM

At this point, the influence of the leaders of the literary society had peaked in the region. Setting their sights on the network of power at the provincial level, these local elites next launched a variety of transregional activities that centered around Kaifeng. They began to zealously represent the region's elite communities in provincial politics in order to safeguard native interests from foreign exploitation.

---

[33] Wang, "Yan yu ping zong," 17; and Tong, "Wang Xiaoting," 30.
[34] Wang, "Yan yu ping zong," 23.   [35] Brook, "Family Continuity," 39.

Begun as a set of deliberations that focused on the strategy against British coal mining, the discussions led the local elites to debate the issue of the ownership of the Luyang-Tongbo Railroad, which echoed the self-ownership movement in many parts of the country. In midst of the movement, a series of conventions were organized by Li Minxiu, Wang Anlan, Zhang Luqing, Zhang Zongfu, Yang Fengjiu, and Zhang Panmin between April 1907 and December 1907. These meetings were attended by several officials including the governor, several prefects, and a few magistrates. Through them the leaders of the literary society extended their relations with various prominent individuals, such as Zhu, the former northern Henan district chief, then Lieutenant-Governor of Henan, who later became a patron of the elite network. The organizers were also able to befriend Liu Shaoyan, the senior counselor in the Ministry of Rites; Yuan Keding, the son of Yuan Shikai and then the secretary at the Ministry of Trade; and Wang Zutong, a preeminent individual from the north region. Through Yuan Keding, the network would soon reach Yuan Shikai. After this series of meetings, representatives from different regions jointly petitioned the Qing court for permission to build a railroad owned solely by Chinese. As a result of the meetings, a Public Office for Railroad Construction was formed, which elected Liu Shaoyan its general manager. These local elites' involvement with officials of the Qing court not only legitimized their activities but also made them a liaison between the people of the region and the court.[36] Meanwhile, Wang Xitong, Li Minxiu, and other members of the network continued to negotiate mining rights with British mine owners. On February 9, 1909, Wang left for Kaifeng to join Li Minxiu for meetings with officials of the Mining Committee on the dispute between the native people and the British Fu Company. In early May 1909 Wang Xitong and Li Minxiu attended similar meetings with Ge Chengxiu, Du Junyan, and Hu Shiqing, three representatives from other parts of the region. Through these contacts, Wang Xitong and Li Minxiu established more personal ties with other representatives, including officials native to Henan working at the Qing court. In June 1909 Wang, Ge Chengxiu, Du Junyan, and Hu Shiqing, all of whom were part of the regional network, represented the people of northern Henan in negotiations with the British Fu Company. While in Beijing, however, these four visited all

---

[36] Wang, "Yan yu ping zong," 27–30; Tong, "Wang Xiaoting," 31–2; and Zhang Luqing, "Shuangliu laoren nianpu" (Biography of Zhang Luqing), in *Xiuwu wenshi ziliao*, 5 (1989): 11.

the Qing officials who were Henan natives – Ding Xunqing, Yang Shaoquan, Wei Xingwu, Chen Shantong, Gu Yu, Pei Yunshan, and Liu Shaoyan.[37]

In another attempt to extend their contacts, Wang Xitong, Liu Shishan, Liu Zhenhua, and Chu Weijing also participated in a project to transform a local tutoring school into a provincial center for modern education. They changed its name from the School of Enlightenment *(mingdao shuyuan)* to the Public School of the Central Plain *(zhongzhou gongxue)*, and, through the introduction of Wang Xitong's son, they invited prominent scholars from Kaifeng, including Liu Xueya and Chu Zixiang, to share in its planning. This project gave Wang Xitong and Li Minxiu reasons to visit several well-known scholars outside the region and some officials in the Qing court. On April 24, 1907 Wang traveled to Beijing to meet with Xiu, an official in the Ministry of Education. Later, Wang and Li both visited Lin Yaohan, a superintendent of the School of Law and Administration for the Five Provinces, who was known to many modern-school graduates in Henan. A few months later, the two met with Commissioner Kong.[38]

As a consequence of his recently extended sphere of influence and prestige, Wang Xitong was elected chairman of the board of the Association for the Fostering of Public Education *(quanxue suo)*, a county-level organization under the authority of the Commissioner of Education. Likewise, in February 1908 Shi Xiaozhou was designated by the Qing court as Secretary of the Supreme Court of Justice. In May 1909, Wang Xitong was offered the position of Provincial Inspector of Education by the provincial government. Wang decided to assume the last position but refused to accept a salary. Before he could travel to the provincial government to accept the appointment, however, he became enmeshed in negotiations with the British Fu Company, and seeing that his responsibility lay there, decided to decline the position.[39]

Although the key members of the literary society were already able to dominate affairs at the provincial level, they nevertheless continued to extend their network beyond that level whenever the chance arose. Therefore, when the opportunity to meet with Yuan Shikai presented itself, they seized it immediately.

---

[37] Wang, "Yan yu ping zong," 43–5; and Tong, "Wang Xiaoting," 35–6.
[38] Wang, "Yan yu ping zong," 23–4, 25; Tong, "Wang Xiaoting," 31–3.
[39] Wang, "Yan yu ping zong," 25–6, 29, 44; and Tong, "Wang Xiaoting," 32–3.

MEETING YUAN SHIKAI

Shortly after the imperial examination was abolished (1905), many of the literary society's members were disseminated to places outside the region to pursue various interests. Faced with this drastic change, the leaders of the society began to look for ways to sustain the strength of their social network. The meeting between Yuan Shikai and two prominent members of the elite network, Wang Xitong and Li Minxiu, provided such an opportunity.

The meeting took place shortly after Yuan Shikai was forced out of the Qing court by Prince Jun on January 2, 1909 and he returned to his family residence on Mashi Street of Chengguanzhen in Ji County. Having learned of Yuan's return, Wang Zutong wrote to Wang Xitong and Li Minxiu on January 25, urging them to pay Yuan a visit. Realizing Yuan was still very influential in the country and could easily return to power if the political atmosphere shifted, the two followed Wang Zutong's advice. They soon discovered, however, that Yuan would permit no visitors. Wang and Li then asked Zhi Lanfen, a friend who had served in Yuan's army and who still was close to him, to arrange a meeting.[40]

During the meeting at Yuan's residence in early February, Wang and Li explained their scheme for the economic development of the region. They also offered suggestions on how to control powerful lineages (e.g., through reliance on disciplinary, but not antagonistic, policies). Their ideas apparently aroused Yuan's interest, for thereafter he sought their company as friends. A few days later, Yuan Shikai invited certain prominent residents of the region to participate in his programs for the economic development of the country. Four among these leaders were members of the elite network. On Wang Zutong's recommendation, Yuan Shikai asked Wang Xitong to head the economic programs.[41]

It had actually been Wang Zutong's idea to use local people to carry out Yuan Shikai's programs. In July 1909, after Wang Zutong met Yuan

---

[40] Yin Quanhai, "Yuan Shikai keju zhangde de yinzhong" (The Unknown Reason for Yuan Shikai's Sojourn at Zhangde), in *Zhongzhou jingu*, 5, Wang Guoquan et al., eds. (1989): 53–4; Tong, "Wang Xiaoting," 34; Wang, "Yan yu ping zong," 38–9; and Zhang Suiqing, "Henan qingquan gonghe bu duli de neimu" (The Inside Story of the Pro-Republic-Versus-Independence Petition in Henan), in *Henan wenshi ziliao*, 7 (1982): 122–3.

[41] Zhang, "Henan qingquan gonghe," 122–3; Gen Yuru, "Yuan Shikai zai weihui" (Yuan Shikai's sojourn at Ji County), in *Jixian wenshi ziliao* (*Local History of Ji County*), vol. 1 (Ji County: Zhengxie Henansheng Jixian Weiyuanhui, 1988): 15–16; and Tong, "Wang Xiaoting," 15–16, 34.

Shikai in Hui County, where Yuan had just moved his family, the two considered a way to implement Yuan Shikai's plan for the national development of agriculture, industry, and trade *(ban shiye)*. Yuan asked Wang to recommend someone to take charge of his projects, which had already been operating as businesses (e.g., a water company in Beijing; the coal mine at Kaiping in Luanzhou, halfway between Mukden and Beijing; and a cement plant in Tangshan of Zhili). Wang Zutong recommended Wang Xitong. At Yuan's request, Wang Zutong wrote several letters to Wang Xitong, urging him to work for Yuan.[42]

Wang Xitong carefully weighed the advantages and disadvantages of the proposal. His fear of inadequacy as a manager was outweighed by the opportunity to establish a close relationship with such a potentially powerful ally. Wang Xitong also sought the opinions of his friends. Some, like Ge Chengxiu, urged Wang to associate with Yuan regardless of his managerial capability. Others, like Du Junyan, expressed doubts about the benefits of assuming a close relationship with Yuan; judged by his present status, Yuan was out of power. A number of friends, like Hu Shiqing, remained silent. After considering the counsel of all his friends, and after a brief consultation with his mother, Wang Xitong finally decided to accept Yuan Shikai's invitation. That decision proved to be the turning point not only of his career but of the elite network of which he was a key member. In late July 1909, having decided to accept Yuan Shikai's invitation, Wang went to visit Yuan at Zhangde, where Yuan had just moved his family. Upon Yuan's request, Wang stayed at Yuan's residence for the following few days to discuss China's economic development and salvation. This meeting was the turning point in Wang's relationship with Yuan Shikai. During the conversation, Yuan told Wang that Zhou Xuexi, a personal friend of Yuan's, had formerly been in charge of the economic development projects. But because Zhou had been appointed a provincial judge by the Qing court, the economic projects had been left unfinished. Yuan insisted that Wang assume responsibility for the projects abandoned by Zhou, and Wang agreed.[43]

Recent research on patron-client interactions offers much insight into relationships, such as the one the group in this study entered into with Yuan Shikai. The patron-client relationship can be characterized by the

---

[42] Wang, "Yan yu ping zong," 45–6; Tong, "Wang Xiaoting," 36–7; and Gen, "Yuan Shikai," 15–16.
[43] Wang, "Yan yu ping zong," 45–7; and Tong, "Wang Xiaoting," 36–7.

following elements: the relationship is voluntary; reciprocity is the key; and resources are exchanged, though on unequal terms.[44]

From the beginning, the relationship between Yuan Shikai and his Henan native friends was voluntary, based on an unspoken sense of reciprocity. From the perspective of Yuan's followers, their contribution to the relationship was substantiated through their complete devotion to Yuan's political career. Once, when Yuan Shikai needed assistance for a silver mining project, he asked Wang Xitong for assistance. Wang gathered his friends, thus demonstrating his commitment to Yuan. In return, these former local notables were able to take advantage of Yuan Shikai's influence to become associated with many officials, prominent scholars, even military officers, outside Henan. For example, through Yuan Shikai, Wang Xitong and Li Minxiu made the acquaintance of Zhou Jizhi, then one of the managers of the water company in Beijing.[45]

Zhou had been a lower-degree holder from Shandong. He received his university education in the United States, and, between 1896 and 1908, served as a representative of the Qing government in America. Zhou and Yuan Shikai knew each other through their mutual acquaintance, Liang Shiyi, a scholar who had excelled in a specially arranged national examination for economic talent while Yuan was still the Grant Councilor and Minister of Foreign Affairs at the Qing court. Yuan recruited Liang into his camp and later, through Liang, he met Zhou,[46] forging a relationship that was soon to help Wang Xitong and Li Minxiu in the realization of their political ambitions.[47]

A few months later, Wang Xitong had a chance to make the acquaintance of another follower of Yuan Shikai, Yan Fansun, then vice-president of the Ministry of Education, who also held the rank of the Second Class Compiler for the National Academy *(hanlin yuan bianxiu)*, the highest-ranking degree among the *jinshi*-degree holders. Yan became a personal friend of Yuan Shikai after he was promoted by Yuan to the

---

[44] See Eric R. Wolf, "Kinship, Friendship, and Patron-Client Relations in Complex Societies," A.S.A. Monographs, no. 9, in *The Social Anthropology of Complex Societies*, Michael Banton, ed. (London: Tavistock Publications, 1969), 16–17; James Scott, "Patron-Client Politics and Political Change in Southeast Asia," *American Political Science Review* 66 (1972): 93–5; and S. N. Eisenstadt and Louis Roniger, "Patron-Client Relations as a Model of Structuring Social Exchange," *Comparative Studies in Society and History* 22 (1980): 49–50.

[45] Wang, "Yan yu ping zong," 49–56, 79–80.   [46] Young, *Yuan Shih-K'ai*, 66–8.

[47] Gen, "Aiguo minzhu shiye jia," 24–5; Tong, "Wang Xiaoting," 37; and Wang, "Yan yu ping zong," 48.

post of director of the Committee on Educational Affairs in Zhili, while Yuan was the governor-general of Zhili. When Yuan Shikai was removed from office, only Yan had remained loyal to him. Yan had even requested the Qing court to sack him along with Yuan, a request later rebuffed by the court. Wang Xitong met Yan at a meeting arranged by Yuan Keding. Their subsequent friendship led to sworn brotherhood.[48]

Through his work for Yuan Shikai, Wang Xitong also came to know Yuan's family – especially Yuan Keding and Yuan's cousin, Zhang Zhenfang. Wang became a frequent visitor of Yuan's family. In his early letters, Yuan Keding had addressed Wang as *xiansheng* ("teacher" or "Sir"). As they became closer, Wang asked Yuan to call him *xiongzhang* ("brother") instead, and the two became sworn brothers. This intimacy with Yuan Shikai's family sealed Wang's personal relationship with Yuan Shikai. During Yuan Keding's illness in April 1910, for example, Wang Xitong kept him constant company. Wang had known Zhang since the latter was an editor for the journal *History of Salt Law*, a position he left in July 1910 to work for Yuan Shikai. It was only after Wang had assumed a close relationship with Yuan Shikai that his friendship with Zhang had begun to develop.[49]

Through working for Yuan Shikai, therefore, the key members of the literary society were able to join his network of personal alliances and became a part of a much larger set of relations that all revolved around the leader. The society was thus transformed into a network that achieved far greater political influence in the country than it had ever intended. As the end of the final dynasty approached, these literary men seemed to be more eager than ever to take advantage of their unique relationship with Yuan to express their own political views in the national capital and to expand their influence throughout Henan province.

THE RISE OF YUAN SHIKAI

A major event in China in 1911 provided the literary elites with a glimpse of the profits from their investment. As the Republican Revolution was clearing the path for Yuan's return to power, his followers foresaw the ample benefits soon to come their way through their personal relations with Yuan, and they redoubled their efforts in his service. For his part, Yuan Shikai, because of his uncertain future as well as the precarious

[48] Wang, "Yan yu ping zong," 51–2, 54–5.
[49] Tong, "Wang Xiaoting," 38; and Wang, "Yan yu ping zong," 54–5, 57–60.

political situation of the country, became increasingly attentive to the advice of friends from his native Henan, to the exclusion of the counsel of others. This situation fostered a feeling of mutual trust between Yuan and his protégés.

On October 10, 1911 the gunfire of the Wuchang Uprising echoed across the nation. A few days later, the Qing court appointed Yuan Shikai governor of Hunan Province and requested him to take office immediately in order to subdue the revolutionaries in that province. Upon hearing the news of Yuan's appointment, those around him calculated that he should wait until the political situation had cleared up to accept any offer from the court. His advisers saw the revolution was the best opportunity for Yuan to regain his previous political power. As Wang Xitong maintained, if Yuan accepted the governorship immediately, he could easily crush the revolutionaries, since the rebellion was in its infancy. In that case, Yuan himself would probably be in personal danger because Prince Jun would again try to limit his power. Yuan Shikai thus declined the court's offer despite repeated urges from Prince Jun.[50]

However, while he was still residing at Zhangde, Yuan Shikai was approached by the chief of the Ministry of War, Yin Wulou. At first, Yuan turned down Yin's visit, claiming a "leg ailment." Yin forced his way to Yuan's bed, where in private conversation Yuan announced his acceptance of the court's appointment. On October 30, 1911, he left Zhangde for Hunan to command government troops against the revolutionaries.[51]

By November 1, 1911, after several provinces had proclaimed independence, Yuan Shikai was designated premier by the Qing court, and he immediately formed his cabinet. As he quickly rose in power, Yuan Shikai became increasingly wary of the country's political situation. He once directed Wang Xitong to help him contact the revolutionaries in the south. On November 27, 1911, when his army was crossing to the south of the Yangtze River to attack the revolutionaries, Yuan heeded Wang Xitong's advice to stop the troops. When Yuan Shikai's general, Feng Guozhang, became commander of the troops garrisoned in Beijing to control the capital, Yuan Shikai called upon

---

[50] Zhang, "Henan qingquan gonghe bu duli de neimu" (The Inside Story of Pro-Republic-Versus-Independence Petition in Henan), in *Henan wenshi ziliao*, 7 (1982): 122–3; Tong, "Wang Xiaoting," 40; and Wang, "Yan yu ping zong," 51–2, 81–2.

[51] Tong, "Wang Xiaoting," 40; and Wang, "Yan yu ping zong," 82.

Wang Zutong to assist Zhang Zhenfang in managing supplies for Feng's army.[52]

Yuan Shikai's personal friends were at times exposed to personal danger because of their close association with such an important political figure. In early November 1911, for example, Wang Xitong was recovering from dysentery at Yuan Shikai's residence. Suddenly, out of his hatred for Yuan, Wu Luzhen, a division commander of the Qing army, ordered his soldiers to attack Yuan Shikai's family. The soldiers defied the order and killed the officer instead. After the incident, Wang Xitong reckoned that had the soldiers carried out the order his life would have been in jeopardy. Learning of such incidents Wang Xitong's first son attempted to convince Wang to leave Yuan's residence, but Wang, through his commitment to Yuan, insisted on remaining. When Yuan Shikai heard of the incident and of Wang Xitong's refusal to move out of Zhangde, he was deeply moved and began to trust Wang even more than ever.[53]

That trust was soon tested when the loyalty of those like Wang Xitong was disputed by one of Yuan Shikai's circle of relations. On December 22, 1911, after Prince Jun had abdicated the regency, Yuan's position in the Qing court became indissoluble, and the issue of his presidency became quite real. At the time, two views existed in Yuan's camp: one favored the reinstalling of a native Chinese (Han) government, the other, a Manchurian dynasty. Because Yuan Keding advocated the former plan, he was opposed by those endorsing the latter. At this same time, Yuan Keding obtained a loan of several *taels* of silver – to pay for his rent in Beijing and daily expenses – through the company Wang Xitong was supervising. A rumor was promptly spread that Wang Xitong was plotting with Yuan Keding against Yuan Shikai, news that alienated many of Wang Xitong's close friends. Wang Xitong's relationship with Yuan Shikai nevertheless persevered.[54]

To this point, the personal relationship between Yuan Shikai and his friends from his native Henan had been based on a sense of mutual commitment and trust, a relationship initially derived from ties to their birthplace. Within that relationship, those friends continued to regard Yuan's

---

[52] Wang, "Yan yu ping zong," 84–7; Tong, "Wang Xiaoting," 41–3; and Zheng Yongfu, "Yuan Shikai cehua Henan gonghe bu duli chouju shimo" (Yuan Shikai's Scheme for the Founding of a Republic Instead of the Independence of Henan), in *Zhongzhou jingu*, 2, Guo Yingsheng, ed. (1986): 61–2.

[53] Tong, "Wang Xiaoting," 41; and Wang, "Yan yu ping zong," 83.

[54] Wang, "Yan yu ping zong," 85; and Tong, "Wang Xiaoting," 42.

desire to become president of the new republic as their own mission. In return, Yuan Shikai offered his political power to assist his followers in realizing their plans to control the political development of their native province.

THE MOVEMENT "FOR REPUBLIC, AGAINST INDEPENDENCE"

By the end of 1911, Yuan Shikai had become an indispensable intermediary between the revolutionaries and the Qing court. Upon realizing this, Yuan's native friends began to ponder how they could further his attainment of absolute control of the Beijing government – and, of course, use their relationship with Yuan to influence the course of political development in Henan. In Henan, they fashioned a political campaign later known as the movement "For Republic, Against Independence" *(gonghe bu duli).*[55]

The movement was conceived in a discussion between Wang Xitong, Li Minxiu, and Wang Zutong, during which Wang Xitong proposed that Henan declare its independence from Beijing. Li Minxiu and Wang Zutong argued that once the province became independent, law and order would be difficult to maintain since any self-proclaimed revolutionary could assume authority. After deliberations with other friends, the group decided on a provincewide campaign to urge the Qing court to accept the creation of a new republic – a campaign whose actual motive was to urge the Qing court to transfer more power to Yuan Shikai. Once in agreement, the movement's organizers dispatched representatives to the newspapers in Shanghai to publicize their idea, which they had formulated as "For Republic, Against Independence." Hu Shiqing, Wang Bosha, Liu Furo, and Zhang Zhongfu were sent to other provinces to promote the movement.[56]

On December 29, 1912 Wang Xitong received a telegram from Yuan requesting a meeting in Beijing immediately. During that meeting, the two first discussed Yuan's delicate relationship with the Qing court. Wang suggested that Yuan not trust the court, citing the anecdotal relationship between the Han emperor and Han Xin. Wang underscored the fact that once the Han emperor became emperor he tried to remove Han Xin from the court. On hearing this, Yuan Shikai expressed his

[55] Li, "Jingzheng shushe," 35.
[56] Wang, "Yan yu ping zong," 87; Tong, "Wang Xiaoting," 42–3; and Zhang, "Henan qingquan gonghe," 122–3.

repugnance for the Qing court and aired his proposition to urge each province to declare independence and to pressure the regent into abdication. Yuan then admonished Wang to spread his idea among various elite groups in Henan to initiate a bottom-up movement. Wang, however, presented his own plan of "For Republic, Against Independence." The trouble with Yuan's plan, he said, was that after the Qing government was overthrown, the independent provinces would be difficult to control. After deliberating, Yuan Shikai accepted Wang Xitong's plan.[57]

Having reached a consensus, Yuan Shikai and his native friends committed to action wholeheartedly. As the initial step, Yuan Shikai asked Wang to assume the governorship of Henan, in order to take charge of the movement. Since he had never intended to hold public office, Wang declined, but he recommended Wang Zutong for the job. Yuan immediately sent for Wang Zutong, but by that time, the latter had just begun to manage the administrative office of Zhang Zhenfang, the new governor of Zhili, and was reluctant to leave. After persuasion from several of Wang's friends, Wang accepted Yuan's offer but asked Yuan to keep the present governor, Qi Zhengyan, and allow him to serve as lieutenant-governor. Yuan Shikai agreed.[58]

Once Wang Zutong had assumed his new position, the group of Henan natives launched a full-scale campaign to achieve their political goal. On January 3, 1912, while Yuan Shikai was moving closer toward fulfillment of his scheme to force the Qing regent to abdicate and to assume the presidency after the resignation of Sun Yat-sen, several of his personal friends – including Wang Zutong, Fang Ganzhou, Wang Xitong, and Zhang Zhongfu – traveled to Zhangde to meet with Yuan Keding. Together they cajoled the troops in Henan to join their petition for the Qing court to found a republic.[59]

A few days later, Wang Xitong and Wang Zutong appeared at the office of Governor Qi Zhengyan, who had already learned of their visit from Yuan Shikai's telegram. Because the message had identified them only as celebrated gentry members from the province, however, Qi suspected that they were connected to the revolutionaries. He therefore ordered his bodyguards to stay on alert while the visitors approached.

---

[57] Wang, "Yan yu ping zong," 86–8; Tong, "Wang Xiaoting," 43–4; and Zheng, "Yuan Shikai," 61–2.

[58] Wang, "Yan yu ping zong," 86–8; and Tong, "Wang Xiaoting," 43–4.

[59] Tong, "Wang Xiaoting," 45; and Wang, "Yan yu ping zong," 88.

Qi was relieved to see Wang Xitong and Wang Zutong, reckoning that they had been sent by Yuan Shikai. The two visitors disclosed the plan for the petition, and Qi agreed to present it to the Qing court on their behalf.[60]

The campaign gathered momentum throughout the province. On February 4, 1912, Wang Xitong assembled all his friends in Kaifeng to hear the presentation of the petition statement, after which, they began to marshal all elite groups in the province to legally file the petition. Two days later, Wang Zutong was formally appointed lieutenant-governor by Yuan Shikai. A few days after the petition appeared in every major provincial newspaper, Governor Qi presented it to the Qing court. Eventually, about ten days after the Kaifeng meeting, the court announced the creation of a new republic, with Yuan Shikai to act as its provisional president.[61]

In their handling of the "For Republic, Against Independence" movement – from its conception to the final filing of the petition – for the first time those literary men displayed their astounding capacity to mobilize a political campaign at the provincial level. Their triumph depended on their personal relationship with Yuan Shikai at the national level and their close association with other elite groups at the local level. Both of these connections were crucial to allow them to maneuver freely in provincial politics.

LINKING THE NETWORKS

When Yuan Shikai became the provisional president of the Republic, his personal friends instantly gained tremendous political clout. They maintained direct access to Yuan Shikai, the most powerful political figure in the country, and some of them even assumed high offices in the national government. Gradually, they recognized their unrivaled position as intermediaries between Yuan Shikai and members of their own network as well as different political groups throughout the country.[62]

After Yuan Shikai assumed the provisional presidency, a series of political events occurred around him. Yuan first invited Sun Yat-sen and Huang Xin to the capital to ease their suspicions about his ambition. He then instigated the assassination plot that killed Song Jiaoren (Sung

---

[60] Wang, "Yan yu ping zong," 88.   [61] Ibid., 88–9.
[62] Wang, "Minguo xianren" ("Man of leisure during the republic"), (Unpublished Diary), 2–4.

Chiao-jen).[63] By July 1913, Yuan's army had crushed the opposition from the six southern provinces that declared independence after Yuan dissolved Parliament over disagreement about Yuan's reorganization loan from the Five-Power Banking Consortium, an event that came to be known as the Second Republican Revolution. After these events, on October 6, 1913, the two houses of Parliament held a presidential election, under Yuan's close supervision, to confirm Yuan as president of the republic. At this point, Yuan's dream of emperorship had finally commenced.

Gradually, Yuan Shikai became the center of the attention of many disparate political groups. For his part, Yuan needed to keep abreast of the political situation in all parts of the country. Thus Yuan's native friends found themselves in the indispensable position of liaison, of controlling access to Yuan Shikai. Such an individual was Wang Xitong, who was approached in mid-March 1912 by two representatives of the Weiwu army to arrange a meeting with Yuan Shikai. Because both officers had been schoolmates in Japan of Wang's son, Wang Zeban, they asked him to introduce them to Wang Xitong, who would in turn introduce them to Yuan Shikai. Wang Xitong agreed to the arrangement, and on March 22, 1912 he learned that the commander of the Hu army, Liu Jiyan (whom Wang Zeban was then working for) also expressed his desire to meet with Yuan Shikai. Sensing great political advantage for Yuan, Wang Xitong also introduced Liu to Yuan, after which Liu's army supported Yuan.[64]

Thereafter, the gamut of people who visited Wang Xitong expanded to include army officers, political figures, representatives of various social groups, and acquaintances from his childhood. These people all knew that Yuan received everyone being brought to him by Wang Xitong. Wang Xitong's position of influencing those who were seeking his assistance enabled him to further his own political agenda and those of his cohorts.[65]

Shortly before Yuan Shikai became president of the republic, a delegation led by Cai Yuanpei (Ts'ai Yuan-p'ei), then Minister of Education, arrived in Beijing to persuade Yuan Shikai to remove the capital to

---

[63] Although it has never been certain, it has generally been assumed, in light of events surrounding the deed, that Yuan Shikai was the mastermind behind the assassination of Song Jiaoren. See Immanuel C. Hsu, *The Rise of Modern China*, 4th ed. (New York: Oxford University Press, 1990), 477–8.

[64] Wang, "Minguo xianren," 4–5.   [65] Ibid., 4–5.

Nanjing. The delegation planned to gain access to Yuan Shikai through Zen Kelou, a friend of Wang Xitong and Yuan Keding. As soon as Zen appeared in Beijing, he visited Wang Xitong and asked him to arrange a meeting for Cai. Having heard the delegation's objective, Wang gave several reasons for his disapproval. If Yuan Shikai moved to the south of the country, he would no longer be able to control the riots in the north. Furthermore, the new government needed to maintain close contact with the foreign embassies in Beijing. Zen was convinced by Wang's arguments, and persuaded the delegation to abandon their idea. Wang learned of their decision a few days later.[66]

Yuan Shikai also delegated Li Minxiu and Wang Xitong, in their ongoing role as liaison, to travel throughout Henan, Tianjin, and Beijing, passing messages to various people within Yuan's personal networks and persuading them to serve Yuan in different capacities. Occasionally they returned to Beijing to report the responses of these individuals to Yuan. During the missions, Yuan Shikai instructed Wang Xitong to convince Zhou Jizhi to accept an appointment as Minister of Finance. Wang Xitong was also sent by Yuan Shikai to persuade Zhao Bingjun to accept the posts of Acting Premier and Minister of Internal Affairs in Yuan's government.[67]

Acting as a liaison allowed individuals like Wang Xitong to achieve several goals at the same time. They could serve their patron unconditionally while establishing valuable personal contacts with those who sought an audience with Yuan Shikai. This unique role allowed the ambitious to acquire influence among different political forces in the country.

THE POWER OF LIAISON

As an exemplar of the classic tie between client and patron, the relationship between Yuan Shikai and his native friends was voluntary and mutually beneficial. To Yuan Shikai, the contributions from his clients were substantiated in their devoted service, which included offering advice, working for his projects, and linking Yuan to his personal networks. Regardless of how "asymmetrical" this relation can be for those on the other end of the relationship, its greatest value lay in access to their powerful patron, through which they gained status, prestige, and

---

[66] Ibid., 4; and Tong, "Wang Xiaoting," 46–7.   [67] Wang, "Minguo xianren," 9–10.

influence over others – what Pierre Bourdieu has called "symbolic capital."[68]

Such capital can only be measured when those who possess it interact with others. On March 23, 1912, Qi Yaolin resigned as governor of Henan in frustration over the arrangement decreed by Yuan Shikai that Wang Zutong and Li Minxiu control most of his administrative affairs. Qi wired his resignation to Yuan Shikai and petitioned Wang Xitong for his help in persuading Yuan to agree with his action. When Wang asked Qi to remain in his position, Qi handed his post to Wang Zutong. Wang Zutong, however, declined. Seeing Qi's determination, Wang Xitong finally convinced Yuan Shikai to replace Qi with Zhang Zhenfang. Through the entire episode, Wang Xitong was treated as if he were higher in official status than Governor Qi.[69]

In other cases as well, Wang Xitong was accorded by local officials the courtesy and respect usually reserved for higher administrative officials. When Wang Xitong visited his own home on January 16, 1913, the county magistrate called on him. Informed that the magistrate had used his family contribution as a way to persuade other villagers to pay for the dues collected by the Bureau of Public Funds, Wang demanded that the magistrate halt the practice. Later, Wang's proposal to nullify the bureau and the dues altogether astounded the magistrate and his friends Zhang Zhenfang and Wang Zutong, who were then heading the provincial government. Wang Xitong had already surpassed a member of the regional elite in status.[70]

The sheer power individuals like Wang Xitong achieved merely by being close associates of Yuan Shikai is illustrated by Wang's securing the release of his friend Wang Shujiao from the provincial police. The two had become acquainted when Wang Xitong was being tutored by Wang Shujiao's grandfather. Wang Shujiao was also an acquaintance of Li Minxiu, who once recommended him to the chief of the Board of the Interior, Zhang Fentai, for the position of magistrate of Xiangfu (today's Kaifeng County). On October 1, 1913 Wang Shujiao was detained for

---

[68] Joseph Esherick and Mary Rankin have also suggested that patron-client relations between individuals of lower social status and those of higher status were "unquestionably asymmetrical." See Esherick and Rankin, *Chinese Local Elites*, Conclusion.

Pierre Bourdieu, *Outline of a Theory of Practice*, 1, Jack Goody, ed., Richard Nice, trans., Cambridge Studies in Social Anthropology (Cambridge: Cambridge University Press, 1977), 171–82.

[69] Wang, "Minguo xianren," 5–6; and Tong, "Wang Xiaoting," 47.

[70] Wang, "Minguo xianren," 12.

allegedly conspiring to overthrow Yuan Shikai's government – a plot known in the province as the Yanzi Gu conspiracy. Despite the seriousness of the crime, Wang Xitong boldly proclaimed Wang Shujiao's innocence to both Yuan Shikai and Zhang Zhenfang and pleaded for the prisoner's release. Although Zhang hesitated, Wang mobilized his friends to petition Yuan, and Wang Shujiao was finally set free.[71]

According to Bourdieu, symbolic capital – respect, esteem, and prestige – can be transferred into tangible gains.[72] Prasenjit Duara's research also shows that such capital, embodied in the concept of face *(mianzi)*, was a vital element of local elites' dominance in the Chinese village.[73] In the present case, such impalpable resources as prestige and respect could also be transferred into political appointments, personal favors, and various benefits for friends, home communities, and family members.

In Republican China, one way of sustaining one's political influence was to trade symbolic capital to acquire official positions for one's close friends. After Qi Yaolin had resigned his position as governor of Henan, for instance, Yuan Shikai was informed by his personal advisers that the elite communities in Henan would accept no replacement who was unfamiliar to them. Meanwhile, Wang Xitong also informed Yuan not to trust anyone with whom he was not in a close relationship. Eventually, Yuan appointed his cousin Zhang Zhenfang. As soon as Zhang assumed the governorship, Wang Xitong recommended Li Minxiu for lieutenant-governor as well as Chief of Education, and Li received both posts simultaneously. Ironically, Wang declined when immediately thereafter Zhang Zhenfang offered him the directorship of the Department of Agriculture, Industry, and Trade *(shiye si)* in his provincial administration.[74]

Although Wang Xitong's repeated refusal of official appointments seems to contradict his political ambitions, it actually stems from the same calculation.[75] Wang reasoned he would benefit far more from being next to Yuan Shikai than by assuming an official post that would limit his influence within a small scale. Because, after he assumed an official position

---

[71] Tong, "Wang Xiaoting," 49–50.   [72] Bourdieu, *Theory of Practice*, 171–82.

[73] Prasenjit Duara, "Elites and the Structures of Authority in the Villages of North China, 1900–1949," in *Chinese Local Elites and Patterns of Dominance*, Joseph W. Esherick and Mary Backus Rankin, eds., 261–81.

[74] Wang, "Minguo xianren," 5–6, 11; Tong, "Wang Xiaoting," 47; and Gen, "Ningzuo dashi," 87.

[75] My interpretation of Wang's intention is based on the recent theory that perceives human action to be purposive and goal oriented. Although some researchers disagree

away from Beijing, he could no longer have direct access to Yuan, which was essential to remain influential in the national government.

With his wide range of capabilities, which mostly derived from his close relationship to Yuan, Wang Xitong then acted as a patron himself, for the benefit of his locality, friends, and family. By writing to the central government's Board of War, he helped the Bureau of Township Security in Weihui prefecture (a militia organization run by the local elites) to obtain a permit for purchasing rifles. In January 1914 Wang wrote to Zhang Zhenfang in order to assist his younger brother, then a county magistrate in Luoyang County, to gain the release of a friend from prison.[76]

Wang Xitong also exercised his influence to advance the interests of his family. He asked his friend Wang Yuebo, a newspaper editor in Shanghai, to collaborate with his son in Henan in starting a newspaper called *Freedom Herald (da ziyou bao)*. In exchange, Wang Xitong promised Wang Yuebo a private meeting with Yuan Shikai. The promise of such a meeting also persuaded *juren*-degree holder Yu Youren to lend a hand to the son's newspaper. And through Wang's networking, his younger brother received an appointment as the magistrate of Yu County, after which Wang helped him purchase rifles to equip the county militia.[77]

By exploiting prestige and personal influence, a well-connected person like Wang Xitong could eventually reap far more tangible benefits than by any other means, even the use of wealth. Like economic capital, symbolic capital can be transferred to other forms of material interest. Unlike wealth, however, symbolic capital is not exhausted after it has been spent – the very process of transference creates a new cycle in which the benefactors continue to accumulate capital from their beneficiaries.

CREATING A NATIONAL NETWORK

Having far exceeded their initial goal, the members of the literary society perceived that a condition was ripe to extend their network to all those sons of Henan who had attained high position or status anywhere in

over the issue of how a human being acts as "agent" in society (cf. the debate between E. P. Thompson and Perry Anderson), there is a consensus among social scientists that human actions derive from purposeful calculation, although the actions often create unintended consequences. For details on Thompson/Anderson, see Anthony Giddens, *Social Theory and Modern Sociology* (Stanford: Stanford University Press, 1987), 203–24.
[76] Wang, "Minguo xianren," 9–10, 19.   [77] Ibid., 6, 9.

China. Thus, although the nationwide collection they planned, the Central Plain Historical Book Collection, had the ostensible objective of gathering rare books either about Henan or by Henanese writers, its true mission was to establish contacts with its prominent native sons. When the center was inaugurated in Beijing in 1914, Li Minxiu became its first director. The center was immediately endorsed by Xu Shichang, a close friend of Yuan Shikai,[78] then Secretary of State, and Tian Wenlie, then military governor of Henan, and shortly attracted the attention of many eminent Henanese natives, especially those sojourning in Beijing.[79]

In the ensuing months, the institution served as a locus for a large network of Henan natives throughout the country. Through its pretext of book collection it maintained regular communications with Xu Shichang, Tian Wenlie, and Zhao Ti, soon to become military governor of Henan after the accession of Tian Wenlie to the governorship of the province. Meanwhile, the organization gathered a group of provincially renowned intellectuals – including Jing Junqi, Yang Linge, Xu Shihen, and Zhang Jiame – to work for its mission, and thus brought them close to its founders. The organization also formed a club for students from Henan then studying in Beijing. Some of them, young talents like Ji Wenfu, would eventually become key figures in the provincial politics of their home province.[80]

Following a similar strategy at the provincial level, the center sent students to each county during their summer vacations. Their mission was to initiate contacts with community leaders, extending the organizers' influence to every corner of the province. Many local notables – like Zhang Zhongfu from Nanyang County, Liu Cuixuan from Xinchai County, and Jing Junqi from Shangqiu County – were thus brought into the network.[81]

In sum, the center, by emphasizing the sharing of common origins, helped promote a sense of "imaginary community" among many indi-

---

[78] According to Ernest Young, Xu Shichang was originally a scholar from Hunan, a *jinshi*-degree holder. He was one of two people who had the longest association with Yuan Shikai. Because Yuan had brought him to Beijing during Yuan's presidency, Xu was given important official positions and became a powerful figure in Chinese political history. See Young, *Yuan Shih-K'ai*, 65–6.

[79] Lu, "Li Minxiu," 38; and "Jixian zhi: renwu," 2.   [80] Gen, "Ningzuo dashi," 87–8, 97.

[81] Jing Junqi, "Xueyuan hansou yiwang" (Jing Junqi's Autobiography) in *Henan wenshi ziliao*, 35 (Zhengzhou: Henan wenshi ziliao weiyuan hui, 1990): 19, 46–7; and Zhang Songtao, "Zhang Zhongfu shengping nianpu" (Zhang Zhongfu's Chronology), in *Nanyang wenshi ziliao*, 3 (1987): 4.

viduals in the country who belonged to the same native origins.[82] The impact for the creation of such a center on the province would not be fathomed for decades. For the time, the center's organizers had placed themselves at the axis of a large sphere of influential individuals throughout the country.

TEMPORARY SETBACK

By the end of 1913, the influence of our protagonists had reached its peak, and was about to suffer a temporary setback. This roadblock, at first related to Yuan Shikai's intentions, was aggravated by controversy over a newspaper with which Wang Xitong was associated. These literary men quickly renewed their efforts to strengthen their relations with Yuan Shikai through every possible channel.

On January 1, 1914 the new government system initiated by the presidency of Yuan Shikai was formally introduced to the entire country. According to Yuan's scheme, Parliament had been dissolved and the country was moving toward dictatorship. Despite dissent by friends, Yuan proceeded with his agenda, which included orders to terminate such county institutions as the County Assembly, Self-Government, Peasant Association, and the Bureau for Public Funds. Just before the order was issued, Wang Xitong expressed his dissatisfaction with the new system, but Yuan Shikai refused to listen.[83]

Partially as a result of these actions, Yuan Shikai's popularity began to wane, in some cases causing followers to resign their positions. On January 17, 1914, for example, Wang Zutong left his post as lieutenant-governor of Henan under the pretext of illness. Exactly four months later, Zhang Zhenfang relinquished his governorship. When Wang Xitong asked Zhang Zhenfang the reason for his resignation, Zhang cited the difficulty of dealing with bandits, especially the group led by Bai Lang. Wang Xitong promptly recommended to Yuan that Tian Wenlie replace Zhang. Tian had been a scholar, a civil official, and later

---

[82] See Benedict Anderson, *Imagined Communities: Reflections on the Origin and Spread of Nationalism* (London: Verso, 1983), 15. Anderson explores the same concept in the 1991 edition. Here, although I am not discussing nationalism or indirect relationships among modern people, the concept is also useful. Once relationships among a group of people extend beyond the scope of face-to-face contact, they may still be bound by an imaginary corporate identity – either a sense of community or a large social network.

[83] Wang, "Minguo xianren," 18–19.

a brigade general in the Qing government. Wang Xitong had always respected Tian's talents and therefore had recommended him many times to Yuan Shikai after the latter had become president. On May 25, 1914 Tian became the Henan Provincial Chief of Civil Affairs.[84]

As these events were occurring, Wang Xitong's second son was embroiled in a political controversy surrounding his newspaper. On July 25, 1914 the *Freedom Herald* was closed by the provincial authorities for its radical opinions. Wang Xitong approached the government agency supposedly handling the matter, but was informed that Duan Qirui, then commander-in-chief of the army, was responsible for the closing. Finally, Wang discovered that Xu Shuzheng, deputy commander of the army, had masterminded the entire incident. He had acted from the conviction that the newspaper contradicted the Constitutional Compact, a document based on the revision of the 1912 constitution that provided the legal underpinning for Yuan Shikai to be the de facto monarch of China. To rescue the newspaper, Wang Xitong asked his son to compile a list of essays endorsing the new constitution to be presented to Yuan Shikai as evidence against Xu. Wang Xitong also sought the help of Zhang Zhenfang. Finally, Wang Zeban was released, but the paper's days were numbered.[85]

Throughout this ordeal, Wang Xitong and his cohorts began to apprehend the resentment that had been growing among officials in the Beijing administration toward the group's influence on Yuan Shikai's administrative decisions. They, therefore, intensified their efforts in three areas: consolidating their personal relationship with Yuan Shikai, persuading their influential friends to remain in their high positions, and avoiding future controversy at all costs.

Wang Xitong and his cohorts, seeking to reinforce personal ties with Yuan Shikai through every possible means, became more enthusiastic than ever to advance his projects. On June 13, 1915 Yuan asked Zhou Jizhi to designate funds to establish the Tonghui Company. He also asked Wang Xitong to head another business, later named the Hengfeng Company, whose purpose was to cultivate and reclaim land and to establish commercial banks. During his birthday celebration, Wang discussed these projects with many of his friends. The group finally resolved to form the Tonghui Company for establishing commercial banks and to fund the Hengfeng Company for land cultivation and reclamation. Two days after the meeting, a few high-ranking officials also joined the operation,

---

[84] Ibid., 19–20.　　[85] Ibid., 22–3.

including Wu Junzhui, then garrison commander of Gansu and Liaoning, and Zhang Zuolin, then lieutenant-general of the 27th Division of the garrison forces at Mukden. They were invited by Wang Xitong's friends. Soon, the group had gathered sufficient funds for Yuan Shikai's projects.[86]

Wang's group also launched a crusade of persuasion aimed at all their relations holding high office. On January 4, 1915, for example, with the permission of Yuan Shikai, Wang Xitong persuaded Zhou Jizhi to resume his position as Minister of Finance. Zhou had left the post earlier due to his disagreement with Yuan Shikai over the securing of a "reorganization loan" from the Five-Power Banking Consortium composed of Britain, France, Germany, Russia, and Japan. Because he was in the position of managing the loan, Zhou was a natural target for the rising national suspicion of corruption – a feeling that included even Yuan Shikai. To avoid controversy, Zhou left his position, but Wang Xitong and his friends needed Zhou to stay in office in order to maintain their influence in the central government. After two months of persuasion by Wang, Zhou resumed his former position.[87]

The group also attempted to place Zhao Ti in the central government. On February 10, 1915 Zhou Jizhi and Wang Xitong met with Zhao Ti, a former general in the Army of Henan *(Henan jiangjun)*. While in Beijing, Zhao met with Wang Xitong who later recommended Zhao to Yuan Shikai. Yuan then appointed Zhao Inspector General for Customs. Unfortunately, Zhao declined the offer in order to mourn his deceased parents.[88]

To avoid any future controversy, Wang Xitong and Li Minxiu closed Wang Zeban's newspaper, for two ostensible reasons. First, it had already published many articles criticizing Yuan Shikai's government after Yuan had begun to negotiate with the Japanese on their Twenty-one Demands. It had thus aroused suspicions even within Yuan Shikai's camp. Second, the newspaper was no longer able to sell stocks or raise funds. In truth, Wang and Li feared the newspaper would threaten the relationship between Wang and Yuan because it already had a reputation for criticizing Yuan.[89]

By striving in the three directions, therefore, Wang Xitong and Li Minxiu survived the temporary impediment to their ambitions. And at the same time, they proved to their home communities that they could

---

[86] Ibid., 28–30, 32.   [87] Ibid., 27–8.   [88] Ibid., 28–9.   [89] Ibid., 32–3.

respond to a crisis. But the foundation of their influence was soon to be shaken.

THE MONARCHY DEBATE

When Yuan Shikai announced his plan to pursue the emperorship, the division of opinion among those of his inner circle gradually widened into a wider question of loyalty. More seriously, the debate put Wang Xitong at the focal point of criticism and threatened to destroy the personal ties between Wang and his patron. In August 1915, Wang Xitong expressed to Zhang Zhenfang his disapproval of the mission of the Peace-Preparation Society to install Yuan Shikai as the emperor of China, fearing the plan would be perceived by the Chinese people as an occasion to raise taxes. Subsequently, Wang also approached Yan Fansun, a close friend of Yuan Keding, with the intention that Yan would help him persuade Yuan Keding, and through Yuan Keding eventually convince Yuan Shikai to abandon the plan.[90]

In October debate arose among those close to Yuan Shikai over the feasibility of Yuan pursuing the emperorship. During the discussions, Li Minxiu warned Wang Xitong to be prudent when airing his views, since most who openly criticized Yuan wound up in jail. Zhang Ziwen added that because of his disagreement with the plan he had been placed under police surveillance in Shaanxi and had to move to Beijing to avoid Yuan's suspicion. Wang Xitong responded to these warnings by proclaiming his confidence in his close relationship with Yuan. After the exchange, increasing numbers within Yuan's circle began to question Wang Xitong's loyalty. Wang Zutong even considered Wang Xitong's actions treasonous. In the end, Yuan was able to see past Wang's criticism and the friendship between the two prevailed. As a sign of his trust, Yuan made Wang a member of the National People's Representative Assembly. On October 30, 1915 Wang Xitong received a certificate for his appointment to the National People's Representative Assembly. During the meeting, when Yuan Shikai asked him if he was pleased to be a member, Wang was deeply moved. To him Yuan's question indicated that he did not mind Wang's criticism of Yuan's plan to become the emperor of China.[91]

By the time the debate over Wang Xitong's loyalty had subsided, the

---

[90] Ibid., 34–5. [91] Ibid., 35–7.

preparation for Yuan Shikai to become emperor was already underway, as the National People's Representative Assembly received many petitions from the country urging Yuan to assume the emperorship. To prepare for the ceremony, the central government requested every province to assume huge debts. On December 11, 1915 the assembly voted to establish a monarchy in China. On December 13, the assembly welcomed the new emperor, Yuan Shikai, at Xinhua Gate.[92]

Now that Wang Xitong could no longer express his disagreement with Yuan's designs for a monarchy, he spent most of his time attending the National People's Representative Assembly or attending to his duties at his three businesses: the Beijing Water Company, the Qixin Cement Company, and the Tonghui Company. However, on January 30, 1916 with his close friends Yan Zhongyuan, Zhou Lizhi, and Zhou Shizhi he visited Zhou Jizhi, who was also known for opposing Yuan Shikai's plan. It was thus perceived by those around Yuan Shikai that Wang still clung to his early opposition to the monarchy plan.[93]

While the disagreement toward Yuan Shikai's being an emperor continued, on March 25, 1916 the Beijing government announced its decision to abolish the monarchy and to restore the former republic. On May 1, 1916 Yuan Shikai sent for Wang Xitong for the first private meeting since Yuan disclosed his plan. During the meeting, Yuan Shikai assured Wang again of his trust, and so ended the monarchy debate. Although the relationship between Yuan Shikai and Wang Xitong survived the debate over monarchy, the dissension had created permanent rifts among the members of Yuan's inner circle. Eventually, these differences would take their toll on the strength of a system weakened by the death of Yuan Shikai.[94]

DECLINE OF THE NETWORK

The elite network relied mostly on Yuan Shikai for its influence, and it suffered a major blow when Yuan died. But even before that event shocked its members, there had already been signs that the network's strength was ebbing as Yuan Shikai's national popularity waned – as evidenced by the internal strife in Yuan's inner circle during the monarchy debate. Shortly before Yuan's death, in June 1916, the political climate in China had begun to turn hostile toward all of Yuan's followers. Since Wang Xitong's last meeting with Yuan Shikai in March 1916 he, along

[92] Ibid., 38–9.   [93] Ibid., 60–2.   [94] Ibid., 63–6.

with his cronies Zhang Zhenfang and Wang Zutong, had avoided a return to Beijing for fear that a rapid political change could bring them harm. On May 16, 1916 Wang Zutong abdicated the governorship of Guangxi after the garrison commander, Lu Rongting, and his troops declared the independence of the province.[95]

Realizing that their golden era had ended, many of Yuan Shikai's protégés resumed their business interests but avoided any involvement in politics. Li Minxiu, for example, declined an offer to work for then president Li Yuanhong, an offer that came from Li's uncle, Li Rongsheng, who was then Li Yuanhong's secretary. The death knell for the network's influence sounded when Zhang Zhenfang was arrested by Duan Qirui for attempting to reinstate the Manchu emperor. On March 1, 1917 Zhang Xun, military governor of Anhui province came to Beijing to request the restoration of the last Manchu emperor, Pu Yi. During his attempt, Zhang Xun appointed Zhang Zhenfang chief of the Ministry of Finance. Zhang Zhenfang was arrested when the plot was crushed under the attack of Duan Qirui and Cao Kun's army. The members of the network tried to rescue Zhang using tactics they had relied on for years. They not only called on their many acquaintances in the Beijing government but also tried to have Zhang moved from prison to a hospital, claiming he was ill. This time, however, when all their efforts failed, they realized that their influence had finally vanished.[96]

Since then and well into the 1920s and 1930s, with a few isolated exceptions, none of these people were able to regain their former influence, although most were still accorded some respect in their home communities. They withdrew completely from national politics and engaged in scholarly pursuits at home or, occasionally, at the provincial level. Meanwhile, Li Minxiu, Wang Kuisan, Zhao Qing, Xu Shihen, and three other scholars formed the Henan-Luoyang Society of Learning *(Heluo xueshe)* to continue the mission of rare book collection.[97]

SUMMARY

One of the significant changes in the local society of northern Henan during the early twentieth century was the broadening of the scope of

---

[95] Ibid., 65–8.   [96] Gen, "Ningzuo dashi," 87.

[97] Liang Guichen, "Zhongzhou mingru Li Minxiu" (Li Minxiu: Renowned Scholar in Henan), in *Xinxiang wenshi ziliao*, 4 (1990): 97–8; and Zheng Bomin, "Li minxiu xiansheng liangsan shi" (Anecdotes about Li Minxiu), in *Weihui wenshi ziliao*, 3 (1991): 8–9.

personal relations among the local elites.[98] Directly after the turn of the century those elites resorted to personal networking in order to preserve their previous status as community leaders and to enhance their influence in the region. Their endeavors led to an expansion of their personal network from within their village communities to outside the region, enabling them to exert political influence at the provincial level.

At the start of this change, the first decade of the twentieth century, the local power structure was undergoing major recasting. That restructuring, as I have shown in Chapter 3, provided abundant opportunities for some to increase their dominance in their communities but caused others to fear the loss of their previous positions as community leaders. Taking advantage of the opportunities, as well as feeling pressures from various societal changes, such as the abolition of the imperial examination system, individuals like Wang Xitong and Li Minxiu chose to rely on personal networking, the traditional technique for self-aggrandizement, to gain wider recognition from officials and other members of elite communities around the region.[99] These ambitious people began by turning the literary society, an institution previously organized to further Chinese classical learning, into a nucleus for their regional network, and then launched a major effort to reach out to administrative officials, including those at the district level, to attain the status of regional community leaders. From this point on, the literary society began to pursue a dual mission. On one hand, it continued to provide its members a place for the dialogue on classical discourse and political legitimation. On the other hand, it had become a communication center through which its members could mobilize among themselves in a concerted effort to gain political clout in their competition for regional influence. With these objectives, the literary society resembled similar literary schools or elite institutions that were widespread in Ming-Qing China – institutions that served

---

[98] Giddens remarks, " 'Society' is of course an ambiguous notion, referring both to 'social association' in a generic way and to a distinct system of social relations." Giddens, *Consequences of Modernity*, 12.

[99] David Strand has suggested that the abolition of the examination system made the measurement of social status difficult because of its constant state of flux. David Strand, "Mediation, Representation, and Repression: Local Elites in 1920s Beijing," in *Chinese Local Elites and Patterns of Dominance*, Joseph W. Esherick and Mary Backus Rankin, eds., 219–21.

the dual functions of pursuing classical learning and sustaining the status of members of the gentry.[100]

While these activities succeeded admirably, however, considerable changes began to appear in the scope of the members' personal relations. Within a few years the network they had created expanded from one that initially covered only nearby counties to a grid whose lines extended far beyond the region. Two antecedents contributed to that expansion. First, as more and more people joined the network, it eventually extended even beyond the region and the key members who had connected themselves to Yuan Shikai through ties to a common birthplace. Thus, the elite network was absorbed by a much larger circle of relations revolving around Yuan that included numerous political figures, army officials, and eminent social activists throughout the country. Second, the local elites themselves were drawn into their own undertakings in the spheres of business management, education, and provincial politics, all outside northern Henan. As a result of these changes, the scope of affiliation of these literary men could no longer be confined to their "traditional settings,"[101] the villages, the marketing community, and even the region.

Accompanying the previously mentioned changes was a shift in the way the personal network operated. The closeness of person-to-person contact, which had been essential to the existence of the elite network, gradually disappeared. Instead, most relations were maintained by mail, telegraph, and occasional long-distance visits, now made possible by train travel. Once the elite network was assimilated by Yuan's network, its key members became the links to many "social circles" revolving around Yuan, stretching in many directions and involving numerous distinctive personal interests.[102] They were then tied into a much more complex system of reciprocal relationships, which, at the same time, involved many people who came from all directions, were all linked together by

---

[100] Benjamin A. Elman, *Classicism, Politics, and Kinship: The Ch'ang-chou School of New Text Confucianism in Late Imperial China* (Berkeley: University of California Press, 1990), 1–15, 74–85, 257–306.

[101] Giddens, *Modernity and Self-Identity*, 22.

[102] According to C. Kadushin, within a large network there can be several social circles; moreover each individual can be involved with several circles and serve as a link between those circles. See C. Kadushin, "Power, Influence and Social Circles: A New Methodology for Studying Opinion Makers," *American Sociological Review* 33 (1968): 685–98. See also, C. Kadushin, "The Friends and Supporters of Psychotherapy: On Social Circles in Urban Life," *American Sociological Review* 31 (1966): 786–802.

political ambitions, and were part of many other "exchange networks" of their own.[103] By maneuvering among these relations, these literary men were able to turn their position as doorkeepers for Yuan Shikai into political power.[104]

Above all, the networking activities of the individuals in this study had profound social impact. To comprehend that effect, I refer to Michael Mann's recent theory on the development of the modern state in Europe. Mann suggests that while the modern state was actively attempting to penetrate society with law and administration, the state itself was also subject to the penetration efforts of various social forces. When such interpenetration occurs, the state will eventually become the representative of the "citizens' internal sense of community," while society will become a nation-state.[105] As the present study reveals, the actions of the protagonists doubtless constituted what Mann would consider a societal effort to penetrate the state. Although in the beginning, that effort was aimed at the local administrations, it became highly focused on the central government, once the former local elites had glimpsed the opportunity for influencing the national government after meeting Yuan Shikai. They succeeded in their endeavor by assisting Yuan's return to power and serving him as personal advisers.

Based on these facts, I suggest we recognize the local elites' effort to penetrate the state as one of the major developments of the period – a development that profoundly influenced the changes in national polity as well as local society. As I have shown, this effort resulted, at the very least, in the following developments in the country. At the national level, such an effort made it possible for the state, under Yuan Shikai, to represent the elites' interests, allowing the "continuing social dominance

---

[103] Richard Emerson has recently pioneered the combining of social exchange theory with network analysis. Since Emerson, many scholars have followed this approach. Among them are Toshio Yamagishi, "An Exchange Theoretical Approach to Network Positions," in *Social Exchange Theory*, Karen S. Cook, ed. (Beverly Hills: Sage Publications, 1987), 149–69; and Peter Marsden, "Elements of Interactor Dependence," in *Social Exchange Theory*, Karen S. Cook, ed., 130–48.

[104] My understanding of how the local elites gained power by maneuvering among these exchange relations is based on Karen Cook's notion. According to Richard M. Emerson, power derives from interpersonal exchange relations; it "emerges from the patterns of exchange relations or the way actors are linked to one another through access to resources. Social structure, then, is conceived as a series of interconnected positions in an exchange network." Quoted in Karen Cook et al., "Exchange Theory: A Blueprint for Structure and Process," in *Frontiers of Social Theory: The New Syntheses*, George Ritzer, ed. (New York: Columbia University Press, 1990), 165.

[105] Mann, *Social Power*, 56–7.

of the gentry class" during his regime.[106] But due to the instability of the state itself, the elites' effort in the end failed. At the local level, it diverted the able leaders of elite society from county and regional arenas, which resulted in the lack of coherent community leadership in the region. This latter development in many ways weakened local society, especially its ability to deal with the state (as we will see in Chapter 8).

---

[106] Ernest Young suggests that two of the three most important features of the society under Yuan Shikai's rule were: "the continuing social dominance of the gentry class, even as it modified somewhat its shape and cultural content; and the politicization of the unofficial elites of the gentry and wealthy merchants." Young, *Yuan Shih-K'ai*, 25.

6

Local Identity, Localism, and Crisis of Legitimacy

THE pattern of dominance for the local elites in areas similar to southwestern Henan is mostly understood to be coercive: a small group of strongmen maintained dictatorial control of their locale by relying on a strong military following.[1] These strongmen were often perceived as politically conservative, slow to adapt to modern changes, and generally warlord-like. Unlike their counterparts in the cities or commercialized areas, they normally lacked organizational skills and displayed little capacity for sponsoring institutionalized activism.

According to Keith Schoppa, the members of the local oligarchy in the counties of Zhejiang's inner and outer periphery during the Republican period were generally conservative, politically apathetic, and slow to develop modern-style voluntary associations and professional institutions *(fatuan)*. Many of its members came from the strong lineages or "newly risen families" who controlled local society. Sometimes, the oligarchy also comprised secret society members, bandits, students, and Self-Government elites, or included members of the gentry and merchants, who had strong ties with the prominent families.[2]

Johanna Meskill's study indicates during the late imperial period local elites in the frontier region of Taiwan performed various community activities, such as sponsoring shrines, managing relief programs, and patronizing people within their communities. These activities were mostly aimed at promoting the elite's personal wealth and preying on their rivals. These local elites held their power by controlling an armed

---

[1] According to Joseph Esherick and Mary Rankin, "peripheries tended to be more violent and disorderly. Elites were more likely to command militia units, and their coercive resources were generally greater than those of the elites in the core." See Esherick and Rankin, *Chinese Local Elites*, 23.

[2] Schoppa, *Chinese Elites*, 115–41, 116–17, 132.

retinue. The strongmen were neither exploiters nor outsiders preying on the local society. They were "knights-errant" who depended on the local community as a power base from which they drew support and in return shared its wealth.[3]

In his work on the hill country of Jiangxi, Stephen Averill has delineated a diversified and complex elite society that existed at the time of the communist movement, a "multitiered collection of people" – large landholders, merchants, and heads of powerful lineages in the upper stratum; school teachers, village elders, and militia captains in the lower stratum. Powerful upper elites often used a militia from their own lineage against other lineages or acted as intermediaries between the community and the government, while some lower elites supported communist efforts to mobilize the peasantry. Many members of elite society engaged in factional conflict and inter-elite strife. Often they were joined by bandits, secret societies, and sworn brotherhoods.[4]

Edward McCord describes how the newly emerged elites of the Liu family of Xingyi County in Guizhou became enthusiastically involved in various community activities in the late nineteenth and early twentieth centuries. These activities included particularly educational reforms, through which the new elites enhanced the family's reputation and fostered their relationship with the elite members at the provincial and national level, after they had achieved prominence through military strength. Through these ventures, the head of the family became a regional warlord.[5]

In this chapter, however, I will demonstrate that although a similar pattern existed in southwestern Henan during the Republican period, it resulted from three concurrent developments in the local society: the emergence of what I have called a Self-Government movement, the reconstruction of a local identity among the newly risen members of the local elite, and the rise of localism in the village communities. In midst of these developments, this latter generation of community leaders demonstrated considerable organizational capacity as well as flexibility in accepting and implementing new methods for mobilizing the villagers. These characteristics indicate that highly institutionalized elite activism

[3] Johanna Meskill, *A Chinese Family: The Lins of Wu-feng, Taiwan, 1729–1895* (Princeton: Princeton University Press, 1979), 88–9, 102, 260.

[4] Averill, "Party, Society and Local Elite," 282–304.

[5] Edward McCord, "Local Military Power and Elite Formation: The Liu Family of Xingyi County, Guizhou," in *Chinese Local Elites and Patterns of Dominance*, Joseph W. Esherick and Mary Backus Rankin, eds., 162–90.

was no longer the exclusive domain of the cities or commercialized areas.

THE FOUNDING OF SELF-GOVERNMENT

By the end of the 1920s, competition for the leadership of the county militia had ended in four counties: Neixiang, Zhenping, Xichuan, and Deng. New leaders of the elite communities in those counties had emerged: Bie Tingfang, Chen Shunde, Peng Yuting, and Ning Xigu. Despite their dissimilar backgrounds, they shared a common trait: their experiences, skills, and personal networks had all contributed to their leadership over their county's militia. Each had climbed the ladder of upward mobility with capability, courage, and, most important, the determination to reach the top of the local power structure at all costs.

But to gain power is one thing; to maintain it is yet another. As such community leaders understood, although violence had been very useful, perhaps necessary, in their struggle with their opponents, they could not rely solely on that means to maintain their dominance. Therefore, they jointly created a collective alliance of the local elites in the four counties. Through that organization these individuals hoped to maintain, even maximize, their control of the village communities – from resource mobilization to legal sanctions – vis-à-vis state authority. The founding of local Self-Government *(difang zizhi)* was thus at the core of a movement they created, a movement I have termed Self-Government.

The term *local self-government* is translated from the Chinese *difang zizhi*. I realize the term has a different connotation in English than it does in Chinese. However, since other scholars studying modern China have used it extensively, it can be assumed that it will be acceptable in my discourse. Therefore, in this book *local Self-Government* refers only to the autonomous governing body organized by the local elites in southwestern Henan during the early twentieth century. It has nothing to do with either the local Self-Government system set up by the Qing court or the Self-Government movement as we have seen it in the West.[6] In addition, it needs to be noted that the Self-Government movement as practiced in the four counties was very different from the Self-Government that existed during the 1900s (and off and on during the early republic) by elites in some cities, notably Shanghai. It was also different from the use of the idea by various militarists to justify their

---

[6] Jones, ed., *Select Papers*; and Kuhn, "Local Self-Government."

control of some provinces. I use the term to characterize the four-county system mostly because that is the term the organizers used.

The movement commenced formally when Four-County Local Self-Government was inaugurated, at a time when the spirit of "self-government" was still lingering around the country from the late Qing initiative of 1908. The more recent movement was inaugurated at a meeting convened in Neixiang County on September 27, 1930, after several months of consultation among the four leaders, Bie Tingfang, Chen Shunde, Peng Yuting, and Ning Xigu. The remainder of the meeting's participants all held positions in the militias of each of the four counties. They included Liu Gusan (Neixiang County), Wang Decen (Neixiang County), and Lei Yunting (Deng County).[7] During the meeting, Peng Yuting not only presented his blueprint for the new organization, but also introduced the participants to programs already in existence: the village program in Hebei, Ting County, organized by Zhu Jiansan and Zhu's son, Zhu Diegang, as well as the Institute of Village Government at Baiquan in Hui County. Although most participants (especially Bie Tingfang) did not understand much of the programs and ideas being discussed, they all found the concept of self-government *(zizhi)* attractive.[8]

The participants eventually established a collective leadership organ for southwestern Henan, through Self-Government, whereby Bie, Chen, Peng, and Ning were to share joint responsibility for creating or changing policy. In the end, the assembly elected Bie Tingfang commander-in-chief of the four-county militia, and everyone in attendance received a position in the new organization. The meeting promised the beginning of a new era in southwestern Henan, an era during which the Self-Government program would dominate people's lives and its leaders would become the de facto authorities of the region.[9]

The indisputable architect of Self-Government was Peng Yuting. A close investigation, however, will reveal a great affinity between his idea and the Institute of Village Government *(baiquan cunzhi xueyuan)* in Hui County. And this institute, in turn, was a product of a so-called rural reconstruction movement in the country.

---

[7] "Xichuan xianzhi: renwu" ("Gazetteer of Xichuan County: Personages") (Xichuan, Unpublished Manuscript), 50, 86; Chen, *Xianhua wanxi*, 6; *Zhenping wenshi ziliao (Local History of Zhenping County)* (Zhenping: Zhengxie Zhenpingxian weiyuan hui), 9–10; Li, *Peng Yuting*, 71–2; and "Renwu," 21–2.

[8] *Bie Tingfang shilu*, 101–2.

[9] "Xichuan xianzhi: difang zizhi," 86; "Renwu," 21–2; and *Bie Tingfang shilu*, 102.

The rural reconstruction movement surfaced in China during the 1920s, and was popularized by renowned scholars like Liang Shuming and Tao Xingzhi who advocated the creation of a new society in China, starting with the rural areas, in which village schools would educate peasants in Confucian morals, traditional values, and modern agricultural techniques. Many of these urban intellectuals had been educated in the Western fashion and had little personal experience with rural life. But they began to pay attention to rural developments and tried to address the "peasant problem" *(nongmin wenti)*. Both Tao Xingzhi and Liang Shuming put their theories into practice. During the 1920s, Tao organized the Xiaozhuang Experimental Rural Normal School outside Nanjing. In June 1931, Liang founded the Shandong Rural Reconstruction Institute in Zouping County, Shandong.

The roots of the rural reconstruction movement trace back to Ting County, Hebei province, during the end of the Qing, with the enthusiastic involvement of a community leader by the name of Mi Qiansan. After Mi and his Japanese-educated son formed a "village government group" *(cunzhi pai)* in Beijing to advocate village reform, Liang Shuming became interested in the movement. Then, an American-educated scholar, Yan Yangqu, chose Ting County as the site of his Mass Education Association, an experimental model for the rural reconstruction program. As the movement grew, a Columbia University graduate, Tao Xingzhi, brought the experiment to a place called Xiaozhuang in Nanjing. Tao's school in Xiaozhuang inspired Liang Shuming to become active with the Shandong Rural Reconstruction Institute in Shandong. All these experimental schools shared an appreciation of the importance of educating peasants in the skills necessary to deal with their economic problems and, eventually, to solve their political problems. One model in Ting County particularly impressed Peng Yuting because it incorporated education and efforts to promote public morals with its program for local security.[10]

Before Peng Yuting returned to Zhenping County early in 1927, he established the Institute of Village Government with several of his friends, including Liang Zhonghua and Wang Bincheng. Actually, Peng had the plan in mind for some time. After discussing it with his sworn brother, Liang Zhonghua, a former classmate at Beijing's Huiwen University, Peng brought the idea to Han Fuqu, then governor of Henan

---

[10] Philip Kuhn, "The Development of Local Government," in *The Cambridge History of China: Republican China 1912–1949, Part 2*, vol. 13, Denis Twitchett and John K. Fairbank, eds. (Cambridge: Cambridge University Press, 1986), 353–60.

under Feng Yuxiang. While Han wanted Peng to assume the position of Chief Commander of the Southern Henan Militia, Peng refused the offer. Instead, he proposed his plan to Han. When he learned that Liang Shuming was passing through Kaifeng just at that time, Peng Yuting asked him to join with his friends in discussing the founding of a school for rural reconstruction. The idea finally won Han's support, and he authorized Peng to establish a school for training cadres to carry out such a village-level self-development plan. Han promised funding for the school and suggested that it be erected at Baiquan in Hui County. The school came under Han's direct authority and received full sponsorship from Marshal Feng Yuxiang.[11]

It was nearly two years after the Nationalist government took control of Henan before the institute finally enrolled students. But because Han Fuqu remained the chairman of the provincial government, a position equivalent to governor, the institute continued to receive his support. In August 1929, the institute named Peng Yuting its president, Liang Zhonghua vice-president, Liang Shuming superintendent, and Wang Bincheng headmaster. The school included departments for Rural Education, Rural Organization, and Rural Security. The curriculum was geared to train village school teachers, *baojia* chiefs, and security personnel. Later, a department for the training of village heads was added.[12]

When Peng Yuting left Zhenping County temporarily to become the institute's first president, he was more convinced than ever that he had found a solution to the social problems, chaos, and misery caused by warlordism and banditry. He decided to bring the solution back to his home community one day. The opportunity to do this arose only a few days after Peng had served as president of the Institute of Village Government, when he learned that a gang of 6,000 bandits, led by Deng Baigu, had invaded the Zhenping county seat, publicly executed the magistrate, and kidnapped or killed 12,000 innocent people. Even in a region continually overwhelmed by roving brigands, the scale and brutality of the attack were unprecedented, and Peng returned to Zhenping County immediately to organize a community response.[13]

As soon as he arrived, Peng's uncle was kidnapped and subsequently

---

[11] *Huixian wenshi ziliao*, 2 (1991): 63; Li, *Peng Yuting*, 69; Wu Yangfu, "Henan cunzhi xueyuan he Zhenping zizhi" (The Institute of Village Government in Henan and Self-Government in Zhenping), in *Henan wenshi ziliao (Henan Local History)*, 29 (1989): 123–4; Wang, *Peng Yuting yishi*, 60–2; and Qin, "Peng Yuting," 3–4.

[12] Li, *Peng Yuting*, 69–70; and Wu, "Henan cunzhi xueyuan," 123–4.

[13] *Bie Tingfang shilu*, 101; and Chen, *Xianhua wanxi*, 21–2.

killed by a group of bandits. Peng's friend Chen Shunde attended the uncle's burial service, where he told Peng he was organizing the people in Xichuan County under the banner of Self-Government to control the banditry problem. Peng's interest was piqued. He wrote to Chen a few days later, citing the current incident in Zhenping as justification for the formation of a centralized regional leadership in southwestern Henan that would allow the joint deployment of militia from all four counties to defend against bandits. Realizing the advantages of such an organization both for helping people in his county and for maintaining his own personal power, Chen decided to lobby other community leaders on Peng's behalf. He began by sending Peng's letter to Bie Tingfang.[14]

Bie Tingfang's initial response to Chen Shunde's overture was not at all encouraging. Bie told Chen during a personal meeting that he would join Chen in his Self-Government campaign. He would not, however, join with Ning Xigu and Peng Yuting because, he said, a four-county alliance would cause the Nationalist Army in the area to suspect antigovernment intentions. But Chen persuaded Bie that, in order to succeed, Self-Government would require the participation of the other two counties. Bie thus took part in the meeting that inaugurated Four-County Local Self-Government.[15]

Immediately thereafter, on October 13, 1930, Ning Xigu was ambushed and killed by his opponents in a longstanding but recently intensified power struggle in Deng County, during which he had taken power away from certain individuals, including magistrate Kan Baozhen. Peng Yuting and Bie Tingfang immediately filled the vacuum left by the removal of Deng County's leading power figure. Ning's death thus had little effect on the process of political development in southwestern Henan.[16]

The Self-Government movement in southwestern Henan can be linked to the rural reconstruction movement throughout the country.[17] The basic ideas of the rural reconstruction advocates – especially from the earlier program model in Ting County, Hebei – found their way into Peng Yuting's design for the various Self-Government programs. In order to understand this linkage, we shall now turn to the Self-Government programs.

---

[14] "Xichuan xianzhi: difang zizhi," 57, 85; Wang, *Peng Yuting yishi*, 76–7; and Qin, "Peng Yuting," 4.
[15] "Xichuan xianzhi: difang zizhi," 85.
[16] Wang, *Peng Yuting yishi*, 66–7; and Feng, "Peng Yuting," 65.
[17] Wang, *Peng Yuting yishi*, 61.

PROGRAMS OF SELF-GOVERNMENT

Elizabeth Perry has theorized that Chinese peasants employed a variety of strategies to cope with poor living conditions, limited food production, and perils from the world outside their communities. Most prominent among these methods were the predatory and the protective strategies. In the former, a peasant relied on the deprivation of others to enhance his own interest. The latter strategy consisted entirely of defensive countermeasures. The predatory strategy led to collective violence, and the protective strategy produced opportunities for the mobilization of the peasants by the elites.[18]

If one views the founding of Self-Government by the local elites – and the willingness of the villagers to follow the leaders of that movement – as a part of the protective strategy of the village communities in southwestern Henan against the "dangers in the environment" brought about by warlord governments, various armies, and, especially, the bandits, one may find that the key to the design of the various Self-Government programs was to allow its leaders to effectively mobilize the peasants as well as the local resources for their own purposes. Through these programs, the leaders of the movement achieved their goal by satisfying the three prerequisites specified by Roy Hofheinz for building a successful elite organization in the peasant community: linking their goals with their capacity to provide sufficient incentives to the peasants, communicating effectively with the members of the local community, and attracting a group of committed individuals to work for the cause.[19]

Before the organization's structure was delineated, a few general guidelines for its activities were adopted. These guidelines were summarized as the Ten Agreements and the Five Methods. The Ten Agreements were: (1) each peasant would receive military training and become a member of the militia; (2) the four counties would be subject to one command; (3) the entire area would organize unified support for the needy; (4) each neighborhood would provide both food and arms for its militiamen; (5) each county would reorganize its militia; (6) each county would perform a land survey; (7) the entire area would establish schools for public education; (8) the four counties would establish health clinics; (9) the four counties would establish local assemblies; and (10) Self-

---

[18] Perry, *Rebels and Revolutionaries*, 48–95.
[19] Roy Hofheinz, *The Broken Wave: The Chinese Communist Peasant Movement, 1922–1928* (Cambridge, MA: Harvard University Press, 1977), 108–9.

Government was to promote practical attitudes. The Five Methods were: (1) not to tolerate bandits; (2) not to allow false accusations; (3) not to allow interference in judicial procedures; (4) not to waste public funds; and (5) to listen to the needs of the people. In addition to these methods, the local elites also adopted measures such as land surveys, militia expansion, and public financial support for the militia. They were determined to mobilize local resources, both human and financial, for their own goals.[20]

According to the guidelines, Self-Government formed committees such as the Committee for Household Registration, the Committee for the Surveying of Land, the Committee for Taxation, and the Committee for the Mediation of Disputes. The committees were designed with the specific purpose of replacing the corresponding local government agencies. For example, the Committee for the Mediation of Disputes was intended to function exactly like the county court. The significant difference was that it could reconcile a neighborhood dispute within a few days, whereas it would take at least half a year for a county court to settle a case. County court investigations often met with uncooperative community leaders, but Self-Government was virtually guaranteed public cooperation. Once the committees were established, Self-Government warned the people not to deal with the county government. The committees thus became the de facto authorities on neighborhood disputes in southwestern Henan.[21]

Besides forming the committees, Self-Government adopted a series of measures to force the peasants to join its organization. As its leaders, especially Peng Yuting, understood, the essence of the Self-Government movement was to be able to mobilize the people. Without a successful program that allowed Peng and his cohorts to organize villagers, the Self-Government organization would differ little from the Red Spear and other self-defense groups that had existed in the region, all of which had perished within a short period. Peng used the following analogy to highlight the importance of organization: "If one uses silk to make cloth, he is organizing the silk thread. If one then makes that material into a piece of clothing, he is conducting training. If a large group of people does not organize or undergo training, that group is just like a thread

---

[20] Jin Yingwu, "Xichuanxian sanzi banfa tiyao" (Summary of the Three-self Method from Xichuan County), *Xichuan wenshi ziliao (Xichuan Local History)* (1989): 6–24; *Zhenping wenshi ziliao*, 49–50; and "Xichuan xianzhi: difang zizhi," 86.

[21] *Zhenping zizhi gaikuang (Self-Government in Zhenping)* (Zhenping, 1933), 30; and *Zhenping wenshi ziliao*, 54–6.

(i.e., easily broken)." Therefore, Self-Government undertook a major effort to organize the peasants into a form they felt would best free the villagers from banditry and poverty.[22] At the core of that organization – Self-Government – was an amalgam of *baojia* structure and militia organization.

As Philip Kuhn has commented, the *baojia* system was developed before the Wang Anshi reforms of the Song dynasty by the villagers in Henan, near Kaifeng, in order to protect themselves from bandits. But once it was adopted by the Ming reform legislation, the *baojia* was used by the dynasty as a system to exert total control over the country. Self-Government used the *baojia* system for exactly the same purpose the Ming emperor had, as a means of control as well as of self-defense.[23]

In 1931, in order to achieve this dual purpose, Self-Government required each individual, including infants and the infirm, to be registered with the organization. The registration included animals, weapons, and other personal properties. After that, the households were arranged into the decimal units of the *baojia* and were supervised by both *bao* and *jia* chiefs. In each ward, the so-called Linked-Bao Director *(lianbao zhuren)* supervised the *bao*s and *jia*s, and reported regularly to the Self-Government headquarters. Once each household was tied to a *bao*, it was responsible for the deeds of its neighbors. If a neighbor violated any Self-Government regulation, the households of an entire *bao* would be punished.[24]

The *baojia* thus became the foundation of a security system similar to that organized by the local elites throughout the country in the late Qing as part of a phenomenon Philip Kuhn has described as local militarization. Kuhn suggests that in south and central China, communities were bound together through personal networks. Within the *baojia* system, each village was bound to neighboring villages in a hierarchical order. In that networking structure, simplex units, each containing a single village, combined to form such complex structures as the extended-multiplex unit, which contained a hundred or more villages.[25]

Peng Yuting perceived this security system to be the foundation for Self-Government: "Without the system of defense *(ziwei)*, there would

[22] *Zhenping zizhi gaikuang*, 186; and Jin, "Sanzi banfa," 6.
[23] Kuhn, *Rebellion and Its Enemies*, 33.
[24] *Bie Tingfang shilu*, 113–5; and Qin, "Bie Tingfang," 17–18.
[25] Kuhn, *Rebellion and Its Enemies*, 65–76; the similarity of the militia organization in southwestern Henan is discussed in Li, *Peng Yuting*, 237.

be no Self-Government *(zizhi)*." Self-Government required that all adults, both men and women, ages eighteen to forty-five, register for the local militia. This broad-based recruitment was called Combining Farming and Military Training *(bing nong he yi)*. Villages were reorganized into militia units according to the *baojia* system. Militia members were divided into two groups: regulars worked in the factories set up by Self-Government; reserves remained farmers during the farming seasons in spring and fall. Those not eligible for either group were placed in a support group for the regulars. While training, each militia member received a salary from Self-Government; members of the support group did not. Both the regular militia and the farming team were organized into *baojia* units.[26]

As soon as Self-Government was established, Bie Tingfang reorganized his militia in Neixiang County. He divided the militia, composed of males between eighteen and forty-five, into nine regiments, which he considered the regular units. A security unit was created for those too old (over forty-five) to serve as regular militiamen. Only the regular units carried rifles, and their main function was to fight bandits or any other enemies (as determined by Self-Government). The security unit, whose members carried only knives or sticks, mainly helped maintain public security by thwarting infiltration by bandits, although it could also assist the regular unit to fight against bandits.[27]

In addition to the regular and security units, Bie also created the following specialized groups. The Able-Bodied Men *(zhuangding dui)* contained those between eighteen and thirty-five who were not chosen by the regular or reserve units. The Able-Bodied Men's Training Unit supplied militiamen for the regular and reserve units. The Able-Bodied Patrol *(zhuangding xuncha dui)* safeguarded the neighborhoods. The Messengers delivered messages between militia units. The Pickets *(jiucha dui)*, whose members were between the ages of fifty-five and sixty-five, monitored the neighborhood to prevent infiltration by bandits. Under Self-Government, all adults thus participated in maintaining the security of the village.[28]

Once the framework of the militia was established, all its members

---

[26] *Zhenping zizhi gaikuang*, 147, 178; Wang Binzhi, "Zhenping xiangcun gongzuo baogao" (Report of Zhenping County Village Work), in *Xiangcun gongzuo taolun huibian: xiangcun jianshe shiyan (Collection of the Discussions on Village Work: Rural Construction Experiment)*, 2 (1937): 210–11; and *Bie Tingfang shilu*, 82–3.

[27] *Zhenping zizhi gaikuang*, 158; and Wang, "Zhenping xiangcun," 211–12.

[28] *Bie Tingfang shilu*, 81–2, 86–7.

underwent military training specifically designed for different categories: those between eighteen and thirty years of age, people from wealthy families, those before eighteen and after thirty, and so forth. All those with physical disabilities were exempt from the training, but everyone who was qualified had to participate; no one could hire a substitute. Each training session lasted four months – usually longer during the slack farming season. After the training, the militiamen returned home to lead their normal lives. Records note that between 1933 and 1935, in Neixiang County alone, Self-Government trained 20,000 militiamen for the regular units and 11,000 militiamen for the reserve units.[29]

In this way, on the one hand, the peasants under Self-Government had become what Peng Yuting considered to be the ideal combination of full soldier, student, worker, and farmer. In other words, they had become "militarized ordinary people" *(wu zhuang qilai de laobaixing)*, everyday people who had been armed, organized, trained, and were capable of self-defense. They were "locally trained, self-reliant, invincible" men who were capable of fighting the bandits as well as working in the fields. On the other hand, however, as Peng Yuting and other leaders of Self-Government clearly understood, this very measure could allow them to exercise a military style of control over the villagers. Since within the organization, every adult was a member of the militia as well as of Self-Government, the leaders of Self-Government were able to apply military rules to every villager and thus demand their absolute cooperation and obedience. Through the complex design of the militia, the four counties in southwestern Henan were totally militarized.[30]

This state of militarization, however, differed from that among the local elites in south and central China during the late Qing, as studied by Philip Kuhn. Under Self-Government, the militia was designed as a system of local control, to include everyone in the village community, and not only for the purposes of maintaining local order. Most villagers assumed a dual identity as farmers as well as militiamen who remained

[29] Li, *Peng Yuting*, 232–3, 239–41; and Chen Chuanhai, "Bie Tingfang yu wanxi difang zizhi" (Bie Tingfang and Self-Government in Southwestern Henan), *Academy Forum of Nandu (Social Science Edition)* 10, no. 1., Yang Mengli et al., eds. (1990): 94.

[30] *Zhenping zizhi gaikuang*, 226, 263; Li, *Peng Yuting*, 220; Wang Shifan, "Zhonghua minguo ershi nian Xichuanxian difang zizhi gongzuo baogao" (Outline of Local Self-government Three-year Planning during the Twentieth-fourth Year of the Chinese Republic), *Xichuan wenshi ziliao (Xichuan Local History)* (1989): 70; Wang, "Zhenping xiangcun," 210–12, 233–4.

connected to their civil life. Unlike the gentry-established militia in Qing *baojia* systems, which were only temporarily effective, the militarization of southwestern Henan gave the leaders of Self-Government absolute control over local society.[31]

Essentially for the same reason it had adopted *baojia* and instituted a complex structure for the militia, Self-Government also introduced a series of programs for political indoctrination. These programs, which were conducted by the schools that had been created by Self-Government, lent new meaning to the old Chinese expression *zheng jiao he yi*. Roughly translated as the "Combination of Administrative Control with Political Teaching," this slogan was used by the Self-Government founders to assert their influence.[32]

To administer the indoctrination program, the branch office of Self-Government in each ward contained a department responsible for propaganda whose duties were: (1) to educate the public about the resolutions and policies of Self-Government; (2) to educate people about what should be encouraged and discouraged in the local community; (3) to train local functionaries and educate the public; (4) to train militiamen; (5) to advise Self-Government officers at the village, town, ward, and neighborhood levels on the fulfillment of their Self-Government duties; (6) to supervise the accomplishments of Self-Government at village and town levels; (7) to recognize outstanding members of Self-Government in the village or town; (8) to report the needs or suffering of the villagers; (9) to conduct village surveys; (10) to promote cultural activities; (11) to compile any Self-Government publications; and, finally, (12) to perform any other duties related to propaganda. Paramount among their responsibilities, the propaganda officers had the duty to inspect other officers, as well as the villages, and report the results to the county headquarters of Self-Government.[33]

Since the focus of the program was instruction, Self-Government combined or restructured the existing schools in the four counties according to its needs. The Southwestern Henan Village Normal School *(wanxi xiangcun shifan xueyuan)*, located on the site of a former temple and, therefore, commonly known as Tianmingsi Normal School, was the most important of all. Peng Yuting served as principal and Bie Tingfang became a member of its board of directors.[34]

---

[31] For a comparison to the local militarization in the late Qing, refer to Kuhn, *Rebellion and Its Enemies*, 14.

[32] Li, *Peng Yuting*, 206–8.   [33] Ibid., 201–2, 204–5.   [34] Chen, *Xianhua wanxi*, 30–1.

The chief mission of the Southwestern Henan Village Normal School was to train Self-Government functionaries. The curriculum was thus designed solely to familiarize students with Self-Government's policies and principles. During the training sessions, trainees also received publications describing the programs and structure of Self-Government. The school produced three categories of functionaries: community service personnel, Self-Government officers, and village heads. Classes were geared to the specific needs of each category. For example, the instruction of community service personnel aspired to such goals as the following: (1) to convince them of the significance of the Self-Government program; (2) to familiarize them with social, political, and economic conditions in their villages and to teach them to solve problems; and (3) to instruct them in practical skills such as math, military skills, and conducting surveys.[35]

Like the functionaries just described, every militiaman had to go through a similar education process to understand the significance of Self-Government and the reasons for following its leadership. The entire curriculum for militiamen was designed to convince them that all Self-Government programs were imperative for protecting themselves against bandits and for rescuing themselves from poverty. To ensure that the students were following the instructions, the schools required them to write diaries in which they examined their own thoughts. Students' daily entries were routinely reviewed by their instructors.[36]

The instructors were carefully chosen by Self-Government, primarily from among graduates of the Village Normal School. Once they began to teach, their thoughts and behavior were closely scrutinized by school officials. One time a teacher, in contradiction of Self-Government dogma, criticized a Confucian idea. He was immediately reported to Self-Government headquarters, which issued a stern and speedy reprimand against him.[37]

The Self-Government schools also offered students instruction in literacy and agricultural skills. Textbooks compiled by the schools covered a variety of subjects, from tree planting to cooking methods. But students were also taught to follow traditional ethics. For those who did not have

---

[35] Li, *Peng Yuting*, 202–4.

[36] *Wei Xichuanxian difang zizhi sannian jihua gaiyao (Three-Year Plan of Self-government in Xinchuan County)*, Archive at the Xichuan Public Security Bureau, 38, Archive No: Dewei juan, wenlin 1 (Xichuan: Archival Office of the District Government); and *Bie Tingfang shilu*, 134.

[37] *Bie Tingfang shilu*, 134–5.

the opportunity to attend one of the schools, Self-Government set up programs outside the classroom. Group sessions held in the neighborhoods familiarized villagers with the idea of Self-Government, Confucian ethics, and military skills. As a part of the effort to educate the entire spectrum of society, public libraries were also established.[38]

The *baojia* and the organization of the militia enabled the leaders of Self-Government to control the villagers' bodies. The schools and other educational programs permitted domination of their minds. Together, these programs may have laid a solid foundation for the creation of a safe community, but they also isolated those communities from the outside world and allowed the newly emerged local elites to exert control over local resources.

Before we examine how the Self-Government leaders mobilized local resources for their own purposes, let us first examine the sphere of law and punishment crucial to maintaining the safety of the area, which was after all the main goal of Self-Government – or at least so the movement claimed. As history shows, the leaders of Self-Government fully understood the importance of enforcing law and order in the village community, not only for the safety of the area but also in order to maintain their dominance. Through many rather austere measures, these individuals hoped to secure the four counties from banditry and, more importantly, turn many previously violent or unruly villagers into "docile bodies" willing to follow the regulations of Self-Government.[39]

Among the wide array of security measures to prevent bandits from attacking, or even infiltrating the area, Self-Government issued five different passes to people traveling through the area. Passes were even issued to peddlers, relatives of local inhabitants, and beggars. Those who were traveling without a pass were immediately detained for questioning. This system had at least two major consequences. First, the four counties became a tightly secured area, free from bandits. Second, due to the restrictions on travel, the area became isolated; for years, the people

---

[38] Ibid., 133, 135; and *Zhenping wenshi ziliao*, 57–9.
[39] Michel Foucault, quoted in Anthony Giddens. Giddens adds, "Foucault himself seemed to accept something of a similar view in his earlier writings, seeing modern social life as intrinsically bound up with the rise of 'disciplinary power,' characteristic of the prison and the asylum, but also of other organizations, such as business firms, schools or hospitals. Disciplinary power supposedly produced 'docile bodies,' controlled and regulated in their activities rather than able spontaneously to act on the prompting of desire." See Anthony Giddens, *The Transformation of Intimacy: Sexuality, Love and Eroticism in Modern Societies* (Stanford: Stanford University Press, 1992), 18–19.

living in the four counties were kept completely ignorant of changes outside the region. Most of them had not even heard of the Nationalist government until it moved the provincial administration into southwestern Henan to escape Japanese attack.[40]

Self-Government also fashioned its own regulations concerning the conduct of the people. It forbade foot binding, gambling, the smoking and selling of opium, alcoholism, stealing, selling children, and keeping concubines – all practices that formerly had been common in the area. Later, Self-Government also forbade gambling during festivals. Those who violated the rules were severely punished, regardless of their status or family background. Before Self-Government was founded, 40% of the population in Neixiang County smoked opium. Opium farming had produced the largest income in the county. In 1931, Self-Government forbade opium farming and smoking. Those who violated the regulation were publicly whipped or even executed. Subsequently, the prohibition was extended to cigarette smoking. When Bie Tingfang's own son-in-law was unable to quit smoking opium, Bie had him publicly executed to demonstrate that the "moral standards of the community" *(gongzhong liyi)* had to be observed at all costs.[41]

Certainly, under this regime of extensive regulation, and especially the threat of severe punishment, the four counties of southwestern Henan became far safer and more efficient than they had been at the beginning of the twentieth century. Banditry gradually diminished; the crime rate sank to its lowest point since the late Qing; taxes were always collected on time; and public service was performed by every adult in the community. Moreover, tight community control also meant secret societies and even literary societies that flourished elsewhere were relatively inactive in the four counties.[42]

Treated as worse than criminals, the Communists were rigidly constrained by Self-Government's security measures. In 1933, the CCP plotted to take over Xichuan County, including stealing rifles from the militia headquarters – a coup attempt later known as the Red Temple Uprising *(hongmiao baodong)*. Before the coup could be carried out,

---

[40] Jin, "Sanzi banfa," 6–24.

[41] *Bie Tingfang shilu*, 117–26, 121–2; *Zhenping wenshi ziliao*, 57–9; Bie, "Bie Tingfang," 124–5; and Chen, *Xianhua wanxi*, 12–13.

[42] Wang, "Xichuanxian difang zizhi gongzuo baogao" (Outline of Local Self-government Three-year Planning during the Twentieth-fourth Year of the Chinese Republic), *Xichuan wenshi ziliao (Xichuan Local History)* (1989): 70–7; and *Zhenping wenshi ziliao*, 10–12.

however, it was discovered by Self-Government. The organization acted promptly; the county militia was dispatched to surround the plotters at the Red Temple, and several were executed. After that, CCP activists either disappeared or went underground.[43]

Even more important for the maintenance of local control than Self-Government's rule of law was the mobilization of resources by its leaders. When it came to power, Self-Government undertook a comprehensive survey of all land in the four counties. By the mid-1930s it used the *baojia* system to complete the survey, which in turn allowed a simple determination of the amount of tax each household was required to pay to the organization (instead of to the county government). Because a land survey had not be done on such a large scale for many years, the previous records were fraught with mistakes. They no longer reflected reality, and many details had purposefully been concealed. The present survey corrected the problem. In Neixiang County alone about two hundred people received training in survey skills and were then sent into the villages to train others. Eventually, more than ten thousand citizens of the county were involved in the effort. During the survey, teams of investigators categorized parcels of land by size and features. Accuracy and reliability were a high priority. Bie Tingfang even insisted on checking for himself the amount of land reported by certain wealthy landlords; in nearly every case, he found the survey team to be in error.[44]

After the land survey, Self-Government set up a Deed Management Bureau to manage the transfer of land ownership. A surtax was collected on every land transfer and most of the funds were kept by Self-Government to finance its programs. Self-Government also imposed its own tax on each household, in addition to the government levies. At the same time, it completely eliminated the practice of *tanpai* – an extreme form of tax collection used by the warlords to coerce huge payments from all the villagers – and replaced it with the new "accumulative tax ratio method" *(leijing shuilü)*, a graduated tax based on the amount of land owned. Those who owned from one to five *qing* of land paid 1% of the fixed tax amount for each *qing* of land. Those who owned between five and ten *qing* of land paid 2% of the fixed amount for each *qing*. Thereafter, for each tenfold increase in area owned, the tax rate increased 1% for each *qing* of land. It is important to remember that this

---

[43] *Nanyang dangshi renwu zhuan*, 1 (1987): 98–9, 103.
[44] Jin, "Sanzi banfa," 15–18; and *Bie Tingfang shilu*, 108–13.

method was applied only to the taxes collected for Self-Government, not to the government tax quota.[45]

Furthermore, Self-Government also abolished the common practice of using brokers; it forbade anyone from adding fees or surcharges to taxes. Those who attempted to act as brokers between Self-Government and the villagers were harshly punished. This regulation also extended to middlemen, who frequently plied their trade in the market town. According to the regulation, a middleman's commission was limited to only 3% of the total transaction, as opposed to the 20% or more he had formerly collected.[46]

This access to local economic resources gave Self-Government the chance to develop the four-county area economically through many community projects. The first large-scale project, the River and Land Transformation Program, was realized in the mid-1930s. As part of that venture, Bie Tingfang sent people to Tongbo County to learn how to construct dams. He then supervised the creation of several dams in Neixiang County, turning more than three thousand *mu* of wetland into cultivable soil.[47]

In addition to the River and Land Transformation Program, each household was responsible for planting a certain number of trees along roads, around dams, and in many public areas. This was deemed by Self-Government as significant as the River and Land Transformation project. Self-Government delegated the Linked-Bao Director to supervise the tree planting and punish any individual failing to meet his or her quota.[48]

Furthermore, Self-Government mobilized villagers to build numerous public roads, and to maintain them routinely. During the project, the villagers not only provided labor but also were responsible for their own personal needs. The project soon included the installation of a telephone system, connecting each county with the city of Nanyang. Later, a station was constructed to generate electricity for the area.[49]

In another economic development strategy, Self-Government promoted local trade and village industry. They created factories, encouraged silk production in Zhenping, and protected business in the markets. Records show that Bie Tingfang was involved in establishing a con-

---

[45] Li, *Peng Yuting*, 256; Wang, "Zhenping xiangcun," 189–90; and *Bie Tingfang shilu*, 113.
[46] *Zhenping zizhi gaikuang*, 44.
[47] *Bie Tingfang shilu*, 126–8; and Bie, "Bie Tingfang," 123–4.
[48] *Bie Tingfang shilu*, 129–30.   [49] Ibid., 132–3; and Jin, "Sanzi banfa," 20–1.

nection between the four-county area and the business community in Shanghai. His efforts produced outlets for local products to be sold in Shanghai and other cities, and some local goods became known throughout the country.[50]

In addition to the above efforts, Self-Government promoted public hygiene, a famine relief program, and community welfare. In 1930, the region's first public health clinic was established in Neixiang County with four resident physicians. In 1931, classes in the four counties trained the region's first group of doctors in Western and Chinese medicine. Self-Government also arranged for the storage of grain in preparation for the famine season, and its relief plan saved many lives.[51]

In sum, the unique power machine called Self-Government, created by the recently emerged community leaders in southwestern Henan to exert their dominance over village communities, also wrought significant changes – social, economic, and political – in the area. These changes altered the lives of the villagers in every possible aspect. Why then were the villagers willing to follow these individuals? How did the Self-Government leaders justify their control of the villagers? Most important, what psychology motivated the leaders of Self-Government to launch the movement in the first place? To answer these questions, I now turn to the issues of legitimacy and the formation of a local identity vis-à-vis state authority among the local elites during the Republican period.

A CRISIS IN LEGITIMACY

Guy S. Alitto has suggested that one of the important changes in local rural society since the downfall of the Qing dynasty was one of perception: local elites no longer believed that their authority derived, as per Chinese tradition, from the concept of the "Son of Heaven"; rather they perceived their legitimacy to originate with "the people." Alitto argues that this shift was caused by the dissolution of the "centralized institutional structure" of the government at the national level and the resulting societal disarray at the local level.[52] What Alitto has noticed is an important phenomenon, the phenomenon of the crisis of legitimacy

---

[50] *Zhenping wenshi ziliao*, 52–4; and *Bie Tingfang shilu*, 140–3.

[51] *Bie Tingfang shilu*, 146–9; and Li, *Peng Yuting*, 261–2.

[52] See Guy S. Alitto, "Rural Elites in Transition: China's Cultural Crisis and the Problem of Legitimacy," in *Select Papers from the Center for Far Eastern Studies*, 3, 1978–9, Susan

that surfaced in the Republican period. But what was the nature of that crisis? How did the absence of a centralized state authority cause the crisis? Furthermore, why did this profound nationwide crisis give rise to the Self-Government movement in southwestern Henan? To find the answers to these questions, we must seek the connection between a crisis of legitimacy and the formation of local identity among the local elites under discussion. Let us begin with the very concept of self-government *(zizhi)*.

As those familiar with the late Qing and Republican period are aware, the term *self-government* initially came from England, where it was used for local organization. A similar form of organization was adopted by Japan in 1888 to galvanize public support as well as participation in the state effort to modernize the nation. The idea of self-government was introduced to China by Westerners like the American missionary, Elijah C. Bridgman, and was quickly espoused as the solution to many societal ills by prominent scholars and officials, among them Feng Guifeng, Zhang Qian, Kang Youwei, and Liang Qichao. In 1908 the Empress Dowager, yielding to increasing pressure from many reform-minded officials and individuals within and outside the government, adopted a program of self-government. The Qing government intended to use that institution to restrict the local elites' activities by circumscribing their responsibilities.[53] As Philip Kuhn has pointed out, under the late Qing initiative, "local self-government" *(difang zizhi)* was never intended to be anything but the "complement to *guanzhi* (rule by officials)."[54]

During the Republican period, Feng Yuxiang and the Nationalist government both meant to reinstate self-government in the local community and to use it as a form of local control (see Chapter 7 for details). However, when the name Self-Government was adopted by its organizers, it definitely bore a different set of connotations, which actually were

---

Mann Jones, ed., 218–63. Though Alitto's wording may sound similar to Joseph Levenson's earlier comment about Chinese intellectuals having experienced a transformation in their conceptualization of China – from *tianxia* (the world) to *guojia* (the nation), after the country was opened to the West – he was discussing an entirely different phenomenon. Alitto refers to the alteration of local elites' understanding of the source of their legitimacy after the downfall of the Qing dynasty. See Joseph Levenson, *Confucian China and Its Modern Fate: The Problem of Intellectual Continuity* (Berkeley: University of California Press, 1958), 98–116.

[53] Sheng Huaiyu, "Qingmo difang zizhi sixiang de shuru," 159–82. See also Philip Kuhn "Local Self-Government Under the Republic" in *Conflict and Control in Late Imperial China*, Frederic Wakeman and Carolyn Grant, eds. (1975): 268–80.

[54] Kuhn, *Rebellion and Its Enemies*, 216.

much closer to the original meaning of the term *difang zizhi*, which can be translated either as "autonomy" or "popular rule." The following stories illustrate their understanding.

Wang Wenzhi, a participant in Self-Government once explained the term in this way. "*Difang*," he said, "implies local versus state, whereas *zizhi* means for a person to manage his own affairs." In other words, Wang clarified, *difang zizhi* means "local people managing their own matters by themselves." Here his interpretation of *difang zizhi* was close to "autonomy." This interpretation echoes some of Peng Yuting's writings and speeches. In a letter to Chen Shunde, before he returned to Zhenping, Peng suggested that self-government be established in southwestern Henan as the solution to the societal problems there. There could be many forms of self-government, he said, but its prime purpose in southwestern Henan should be for the local community to achieve autonomy from warlord regimes and roving gangs of bandits by developing the capacity to defend itself. In his later speeches, Peng also claimed that people must choose between government and self-government. "If you want self-government, you have to oppose the government's running of the local society *(dadao guanzhi)*."[55]

Meanwhile, however, *difang zizhi* was also interpreted to mean "popular rule." Some of Self-Government's documents, for example, make it clear that the goal of Self-Government was to allow local people to participate in this institution for local governance, and, therefore, its officials should be chosen from among the local people. The same spirit also appeared in Peng Yuting's diary, which states the idea of Self-Government was the combination of the two elements for self-governing: autonomy and popular rule. The best way to save China was through first political, then educational, and finally economic channels. The political channel would "mobilize the people" *(zuzhi minzhong)* against both the warlord government and the evil gentry (he meant those who used to lead the previous elite establishments). "I believe," Peng said, "the principle of self-government *(zizhi)* was to undermine the control [of local society] by both the government *(dadao guanzhi)* and the gentry *(shenzhi)*."[56]

---

[55] Wang Wenzhi, "Wanxi de difang zizhi" (Self-Government in Southwestern Henan), in *Xichuanxian lishi ziliao huibian*, 196; Chen, *Xianhua wanxi*, 21–2; and Qin, "Peng Yuting," 6.

[56] Jin, "Sanzi banfa," 6–7; Wang, *Peng Yuting yishi*, 105–6; and Peng Yuting, "Peng Yuting riji size" (Four Pieces of Peng Yuting's Diary), in *Henan wenshi ziliao (Henan Local History)*, 33 (1990): 117.

As suggested by this evidence, the founders of Self-Government espoused both possible meanings of the term *difang zizhi*. The ambiguity that existed in its translation also intimates the complex intertwining of the two main ideas that defined the goal of the Self-Government movement. To fully comprehend the nature of that movement, we must first examine each of those concepts separately.

Autonomy was one of the motivating forces, and it became a principal slogan of the movement because, during the entire Republican period, the people of southwestern Henan no longer recognized any government or regime as possessing legitimate authority. This phenomenon belongs to a category of political crisis that Jürgen Habermas calls "legitimation crisis." Habermas divides political crisis in modern society (capitalist society) into two parts: rationality crisis and legitimation crisis. The rationality crisis is an economic crisis that arises when a capitalist state fails to steer the economic system. But the legitimation crisis is one of identity. Political systems require an input of mass loyalty, and when the state's legitimizing system can no longer maintain that loyalty, a legitimation crisis occurs.[57] Habermas defines legitimacy by concentrating on the word *recognition*. In other words, legitimacy comes from people's recognition of the righteousness of any political order: "Legitimacy means that there are good arguments for a political order's claim to be recognized as right and just; a legitimate order deserves recognition. Legitimacy means a political order's worthiness to be recognized."[58] This conceptualization of legitimacy is consistent with R. M. Merelman's earlier conviction that legitimacy is established in modern society when the population under state domination reaches the belief that "the structures, procedures, actions, decisions, policies, officials, or political leaders of a state possess the quality of rightness, of appropriateness, of the morally good, and ought to be recognized in virtue of this quality."[59]

Habermas's notion of legitimation crisis is very useful. One only needs to look at the main philosophy of the Self-Government movement,

---

[57] Jürgen Habermas, *Legitimation Crisis*, Thomas McCarthy, trans. (Boston: Beacon Press, 1975), 46–8.

[58] See Jürgen Habermas, *Communication and the Evolution of Society*, Thomas McCarthy, trans. (Boston: Beacon Press, 1976), 178–80; David Held, "Crisis Tendencies, Legitimation and the State," in *Habermas Critical Debates*, John B. Thompson and David Held, eds. (Cambridge, MA: M. I. T. Press, 1982), 182.

[59] R. M. Merelman, "Learning and Legitimacy," *American Political Science Review* 60 (1966): 548.

embodied in the so-called Three-Self Principles *(sanzi zhuyi)*, to realize that the movement's founders refused to recognize either the
warlord regimes or the Nationalist government as legitimate authorities.
The Three-Self Principles were self-defense, self-government, and self-
reliance. As the movement's founders always maintained, the provincial
authorities had never paid attention to southwestern Henan when the
area needed their protection from bandits. Therefore, none of them,
including the Nationalist government, was trustworthy, and should
never be allowed to exercise any authority. The textbooks used in the
Southwestern Henan Village Normal School, books compiled by the
leaders of Self-Government, indicated the rationale for organizing Self-
Government under the Three-Self Principles was simply that the warlord
regimes and their armies had precipitated the miseries of the local
people. These so-called governments and their militaries were in reality
bandits. The Three-Self Principles were meant to deal with the three
outside forces plaguing the people: the bandits, the bandit-like warlord
armies, and corrupt government officials.[60]

Once they rejected all state authorities, the newly risen local elites
beheld Self-Government not as an illegitimate institution, but rather as
an avenue for self-salvation, even after a centralized state, restored by
the Nationalist government, had repeatedly declared Self-Government
to be illegitimate since its inception. As Peng emphasized, the people in
Zhenping County could not rely on the government – any government
– to bring them a better life or to change society. They had to help themselves. Peng asserted that his program of self-government would bring
both self-salvation *(zijiu)* and national salvation *(jiuguo)*. Peng Yuting
argued that, since the warlord governments and their banditlike armies
could not save or protect people, the local people should not depend
on them. The peasants' only hope for salvation was self-salvation. Peng
frequently used three terms – "localism" *(difang zhuyi)*, "self-salvation"
(zijiu zhuyi), and "local revolution" *(difang geming)* – to define his idea
of self-government, whose purpose, he claimed, was self-salvation. In his
words, local revolution was the combination of the localized version of
national revolution *(guomin geming)*, nationalism *(minzu zhuyi)*, and
democracy *(minquan zhuyi)*, that were advocated by Sun Yat-sen in the
Three People's Principles. Sun failed to accomplish his goal of national
revolution because he was out of touch with peasants at the village level.

---

[60] *Wei Xichuanxian difang zizhi*; Chen, *Xianhua wanxi*, 6, 162–4; *Bie Tingfang shilu*, 104–5;
and *Zhenping zizhi gaikuang*, 194, 204–5, 256.

According to Peng Yuting, an ideal society, such as that Sun Yat-sen aimed to achieve through the Three People's Principles, was to be achieved by Self-Government in southwestern Henan by the application of the following tenets: "No Need to Close the Door at Night, No One Pockets What They Find on the Road, No Village Files Lawsuits, and Every Household Has a Surplus of Food."[61]

Peng Yuting further explained that self-defense, the local equivalent of nationalism *(minzu zhuyi)*, was targeted primarily at bandits because they posed the most urgent threat to the lives of the people in southwestern Henan. Self-Government was the local equivalent of democracy *(minquan zhuyi)* because it not only taught the people to govern themselves but also allowed them to elect their own local officials, such as *baojia* head and ward chief. Sun Yat-sen's democratic ideal could never have reached southwestern Henan if not for the creation of Self-Government. For many years, government officials had cloaked themselves in slogans such as democracy in order to aggrandize themselves and to fool the people. If the people truly desired democracy, their only course was to overthrow the government *(guanzhi)* and pursue autonomy. In addition, self-reliance, the local equivalent of national revolution, was the only way of upholding the Principle of the People's livelihood *(minsheng zhuyi)* because the most practical method of creating a society based on the equal distribution of wealth was to create wealth among the people. In southwestern Henan there was no capital to start with, and thus no need to restrict the accumulation of capital. Therefore, the Three-Self Principles was the only practical version of Sun Yat-sen's Three People's Principles.[62]

The leaders of the Self-Government movement also argued that, in order to further legitimize their movement, salvation on a national level had to begin in the local communities. In the epitaph for twenty-eight militiamen who died battling bandits, Peng Yuting wrote the only way to save the country was to save the local community. In a similar aphorism, Peng also wrote that before one can save his country one has to save his village first. On various occasions, the Self-Government leaders argued that localism, self-salvation, and local revolution had to start at the village level because most of the Chinese people were peasants living in villages. Past regimes, Chen Shunde claimed, relied only on movement from the top down; there was no movement from the bottom up. But

---

[61] *Zhenping zizhi gaikuang*, 194, 204–5.
[62] *Peng Yuting jiangyan ji (Speeches of Peng Yuting)* (Zhenping, 1933), 88–92; *Zhenping wenshi ziliao*, 11.

such movement, based on elevating the quality of people's lives, was the key to prosperity for the entire country. Furthermore, a Self-Government document stated, "In China, the closer one gets to the bottom of society, the more poorly organized the political institutions are, and the more fractured the society is." Therefore, the leaders of Self-Government believed that through that movement the people of southwestern Henan would not only save themselves but also contribute to national salvation.[63]

This evidence points in only one direction: the rise of the Self-Government movement was the result of a profound crisis of legitimacy in the local society. That crisis surfaced when the leaders of the movement no longer identified with the warlord regimes or the Nationalist government. Instead, they began to find the source of their legitimacy within their local communities – in other words, with the people. The yearning for local autonomy was only a superficial indication that such a change had taken place.[64] In this sense, Habermas is right to suggest that "a legitimation crisis is an identity crisis." It is a motivational crisis in which the existing political system has failed to shape the desire of the people to identify themselves with the system.[65] To further comprehend the nature of this particular crisis of legitimacy, we must understand why the changes in the local elites' political identification occurred. I, therefore, turn to the issue of local identity, its nature, and on what conditions it is formed.

THE ISSUE OF LOCAL IDENTITY

Local identity is basically a sense of belonging to a local community. Benedict Anderson argues the development of nationalism depends a great deal on the print media because nations largely exist in the collective imaginations of their citizens.[66] Following Anderson, Craig Calhoun has suggested that the present indirect relationships between people were formed through a feeling of being part of an imagined whole.[67] This notion of "imagined community" is highly useful because

---

[63] *Zhenping wenshi ziliao*, 63; Wang, "Difang zizhi," 1991; *Peng Yuting jiangyan ji*, 252; Chen, *Xianhua wanxi*, 21, 39; and *Zhenpingxian zizhi gaikuang (Self-government in Zhenping County)* (Beijing: Jingcheng chuban she, 1923), 226.

[64] Feng, "Peng Yuting," 65; and Chen, *Xianhua wanxi*, 43–50, 60, 155–6.

[65] Habermas, *Communication*, 182–3. [66] Anderson, *Imagined Communities*, 15.

[67] Craig Calhoun, "Indirect Relationship and Imagined Communities: Large-Scale Integration and the Transformation of Everyday Life," in *Social Theory for a Changing Society*, Pierre Bourdieu and James S. Coleman, eds. (Boulder, CO: Westview Press, 1991), 95–121.

it tells us that local identity in southwestern Henan was based on an imagined "communion" among those within the area controlled by Self-Government. Why then did the Self-Government leaders chose to identify with this community and not with other kinds of communities? For answers, we may look at the nature of community identity as it was manifested in China.

Two decades ago, Frederic Wakeman pointed out the volatile nature of community identity in China, although he did not use the term *community identity* directly. In his study of the Sanyuanli incident in Guangdong during the Opium War, Wakeman states that for Chinese peasants, identity could be broken down into many components. The word *xenophobia* conveys one of those facets: the uniting of peasants against any strangers from outside the province. Wakeman presents an example showing that the people of Guangdong treated soldiers from Hunan in quite the same way as they treated the British. He therefore concludes that, during the Sanyuanli incident, the peasants in Guangdong were not acting out of nationalism but rather from a combination of antigovernment sentiment, xenophobia, and urbanocentrism (the defense of the city of Guangdong). For those peasants, Wakeman says, "there are too many other particular localities: village, siblings, land, or even dialect."[68]

Another feature of community identity is its ad hoc nature. In her study of the native-place associations in Shanghai between 1853 and 1937, Bryna Goodman notes that identities are not exclusive. People often identify with more than one community (locality, region, nation, kin group, gender, etc.) at the same time, many of which are imagined. Moreover, community identity is often formed for a particular purpose. Goodman's evidence reveals that the native-place associations, as well as native-place identity, were created not as the response to demographic changes in the city but rather to serve a political or economic purpose.[69]

A community identity can also be misleading. Emily Honig realized the so-called Subeiren (people from north of the Yangtze River) is a questionable designation of identity that was used by those not in that group to characterize Subei people as inferior "Others." Not only was it difficult to determine the territory of Subei (north of the Yangtze River),

---

[68] Frederic Wakeman, *Strangers at the Gate: Social Disorder in South China, 1839–1861* (Berkeley: University of California Press, 1966), 56–8.

[69] Bryna Goodman, *Native Place, City, and Nation: Regional Networks and Identities in Shanghai, 1853–1937* (Berkeley: University of California Press, 1995), 308.

but even those who were considered by others to be Subei people perceived their own identity quite differently. They usually identified with the many different subareas of their origins within the general area of what was considered Subei.[70]

Further adding to the complexity of the issue of identity is the instability of any identity itself. In Prasenjit Duara's words, "Individuals and groups in both modern and agrarian societies identify simultaneously with several communities, all of which are imagined. These identifications are historically changeable and often conflicted internally and with each other. . . . people historically identified with different representations of communities, and when these identifications became politicized, they came to resemble what is called modern 'national identities.'"[71] Duara questions the use of the expression *identity* at all, arguing that it somehow implies "a prior, primordial self that identifies with a social or cultural representation." According to Duara, "the self is constituted neither primordially nor monolithically but within a network of changing and often conflicting representations. For example, nationalism or national identity is one of many changeable, interchangeable, conflicted, or harmonious identifications that were all within the 'representational networks.'"[72]

In general agreement with these analyses, I emphasize the following points. First, while a group of individuals may identify simultaneously with a number of imagined communities, they also have the potential, for various reasons, to withdraw from identifying with any of those communities. An identity with a more narrowly defined region or local community usually becomes more prominent among a group of people when they have withdrawn from identifying with the larger community of a nation. The formation of a strong local identity among the recently emerged local elites in southwestern Henan is such an example.

Duara suggests that communities have either "soft boundaries" or "hard boundaries," depending largely on whether the individuals identify themselves as a community that shares cultural practices with other groups. If a group does not prevent itself from sharing some elements of

---

[70] See Emily Honig, *Creating Chinese Ethnicity: Subei People in Shanghai, 1850–1980* (New Haven: Yale University Press, 1992), 77–91; and Emily Honig, "Migrant Culture in Shanghai: In Search of a Subei Identity," in *Shanghai Sojourners,* Wen-hsin Yeh and Frederic Wakeman Jr., eds. (Berkeley: University of California, Institute of East Asian Studies, 1992), 239–65.

[71] Prasenjit Duara, *Rescuing History from the Nation: Questioning Narratives of Modern China* (Chicago: University of Chicago Press, 1995), 54.

[72] Duara, *Rescuing History*, 7–8.

its culture with other groups, its community is surrounded by a soft boundary. Culturally closed communities, on the other hand, form hard boundaries. An incipient nationality emerges, Duara argues, when the perceived boundaries of a community are transformed from soft to hard. When such closure occurs, the group tends to "develop an intolerance and suspicion toward the adoption of the other's practices and strive to distinguish, in some way or the other, practices that they share. In this sense, communities with hard boundaries will emphasize the differences between them."[73] In the case of southwestern Henan, this process occurred in the political rather than the cultural context, and with the issues of legitimacy, state, and authority as its reference. The leaders of Self-Government certainly were not disassociating themselves from the general cultural mores of the country. Rather, they chose to disconnect from the political identity of a large community, the nation.

Second, each process of identification takes place in a situational context, and is circumstantial. Circumstances create the condition for a group of individuals to withdraw themselves from other community identities – whether that move is politically, economically, or socially oriented.[74] Circumstances in southwestern Henan, in particular the lack of a centralized state, prevented the development of a national identity. We may understand this absence of a national identity with the help of Ernest Gellner's theory on nationalism.

According to Gellner, the existence of a centralized state was the necessary condition for people to identify with a community greater than their own. It seems that "nationalism emerges only in milieux in which the existence of the state is already very much taken for granted. The existence of politically centralized units, and of a moral-political climate in which such centralized units are taken for granted and are treated as normative, is a necessary though by no means a sufficient condition of nationalism." Gellner further comments that culture became the source of political legitimacy only in the age of nationalism, as only then did a situation arise in which the "well-educationally sanctioned" and "unified" culture was identified by the people within the same political unit.[75] From Gellner's arguments it is quite clear that one of the pre-

---

[73] Ibid., 65–9.

[74] As Ernest Gellner has argued, will alone cannot produce a community identity, as it can a national identity. See Ernest Gellner, *Nations and Nationalism* (Ithaca: Cornell University Press, 1983), 53–4.

[75] Gellner, *Nations and Nationalism*, 4, 53–5.

requisite conditions for the formation of a national identity is not culture but the existence of a centralized state. In southwestern Henan, that condition was definitely absent. Instead, the entire Republican period witnessed what might be considered by Alessandro Passerin d'Entreves to be a stateless condition.[76] This circumstance alone was responsible for supporting the emergence of a local identity, as opposed to a national identity. Other causes, such as the area's geographical remoteness and cultural and political isolation, may have contributed to that development but definitely were secondary.

Finally, the two aspects of community identity just discussed are responsible for its third characteristic, its *pro hac vice* nature. As things and events are in a state of constant flux, so community identities come and go, and therefore appear to be volatile, ad hoc, and sometimes misleading to observers. Only when the situation or circumstance that gave rise to a particular community identity continues to exist does that identity become an enduring phenomenon.

As I will show in Chapter 8, the stateless condition that persisted in southwestern Henan, even after the Nationalist government had restored a centralized state throughout China, was the main reason a local identity remained. That condition was used to continuously justify the dominance of the local elites, as well as to perpetuate the "blaming game" they conducted against the Nationalist government.[77] When the Sino-Japanese War erupted and the government had successfully presented the image of itself as a centralized state to the local elites (see Chapter 8), circumstances no longer favored the formation of a local identity over a national identity. Only then did the local elites begin to identify with the nation and embrace the Nationalist government as the legitimate authority.

THE PHENOMENON OF LOCALISM

Like *local identity*, the term *localism* has been never been clearly defined. But basing our understanding on the previous discussion, I come to

---

[76] Alessandro Passerin d'Entreves, *The Notion of the State* (London: Oxford University Press, 1967), Introduction.

[77] Hobsbawm indicates that a community identity is sometimes used by one group to blame another. In this way, Hobsbawm says, national identity has become a device for defining communities and also for identifying those who are responsible for the ills of the people in those communities. See E. J. Hobsbawm, *Nations and Nationalism Since 1780: Programme, Myth, Reality* (Cambridge: Cambridge University Press, 1990), 174.

comprehend localism as a feeling or sentiment, a blind commitment or loyalty to a particular community on the part of the individual members who have identified with that community. I define this community as local because it is usually, but not necessarily, much smaller than other communities with which it is in contact, such as provincial or national spheres. And like local identity, localism is an ad hoc phenomenon that can serve different purposes. For example, Frederic Wakeman has insightfully suggested in his study of the Qing massacre of the Han Chinese at Jiangyin City that localism could be set against nationalism, although the commitment to one's native soil, which was an import-ant component of the localism, could also form the basis of modern nationalism.[78]

One can easily imagine how the autonomous spirit of Self-Government gave rise to strong localistic feelings among the later gen-eration of community leaders in southwestern Henan. And evidence from the area supports that deduction. For instance, a main feature of Self-Government is its exclusive use of local people to operate local organizations, where they served in every capacity, even as officers. Although, occasionally, intellectuals or individuals with specific skills unavailable in the local community were brought into the area to teach at the Southwestern Henan Village Normal School. In Zhenping County all of the nearly 500 officers and other functionaries were natives of the county. In Xichuan County, Chen Shunde insisted that all the *lianbao* (an administrative system similar to *baojia*) heads and militia officials be graduates of the Southwestern Henan Village Normal School. In Nei-xiang County, Bie Tingfang also employed only those who had received their training in local schools. This insistence on local schooling became a rule for Self-Government functionaries.[79]

Not only did Self-Government leaders have a profound suspicion of adults educated outside their area, they also opposed the idea of young people leaving the community to be educated elsewhere. Bie Tingfang once rebuffed a scholar, recently returned from his studies in France, who was applying for a job with Self-Government: "No matter which school you graduated from in England or France, if you left this place as a

---

[78] Frederic Wakeman, "Localism and Loyalism During the Ch'ing conquest of Kiangnan: The Tragedy of Chiang-Yin," in *Conflict and Control in Late Imperial China*, Frederic Wakeman and Carolyn Grant, eds. (Berkeley: University of California Press, 1975), 85.

[79] Li, *Peng Yuting*, 209–10; "Xichuan xianzhi: difang zizhi," 90; Wang, "Xichuanxian difang zizhi," 69; and *Bie Tingfang shilu*, 133–4.

donkey, you will remain a donkey when you return. If you do not attend the Tianmensi Normal School that I created, you will not even be appointed a *jia* chief." In fact, Bie Tingfang discouraged students from attending schools anywhere else. He recalled with bitterness those young people who had left the region to attend schools in Kaifeng or other cities outside the region, and then had allied themselves with the Communists.[80]

Also in the spirit of localism, Self-Government forbade the selling of commodities or manufactured goods from outside the area. A 1931 directive from Bie Tingfang expressly prohibited the sale, purchase, or use of any "foreign product" – a term stipulated to mean anything not made locally, even including cloth made in Zhengzhou or Kaifeng. With equal ardor, Self-Government promoted pride in belonging to the local community. In the local schools, teachers and texts alike continually taught students to be proud of their local heritage. Pushing localism to its limit, Self-Government even designed a school anthem, a militia anthem, a Bandit Eradication Song, and a Stop Lawsuits/Up with Self-Government Song. All reinforced the localistic doctrine that south-western Henan is a paradise on earth and Self-Government provides the ideal home.[81]

The construction of a local identity and the rise of localism were the keys to the particular attitude the leaders of Self-Government adopted toward the people of other communities and to the nation as a whole. That attitude dominated their dealings with state officials. And it thus deeply affected the relationship between the state and local society.

FROM ELITE DOMINATION TO POPULAR PARTICIPATION

As mentioned earlier, the local elites in southwestern Henan embraced both interpretations of the term *self-government*: "autonomy" and "popular rule." Due largely to this dual perception, the Self-Government movement fostered the transition from absolute elite dominance to some degree of popular participation. Even though this effort to create change was not sufficient to alter the overall nature of the organization, it is still noteworthy.

When Four-County Self-Government was established, its leaders had

---

[80] "Renwu," 22; *Bie Tingfang shilu*, 136–7; and Qin, "Bie Tingfang," 17.
[81] Jin, "Sanzi banfa," 20; Bie, "Bie Tingfang," 125; *Bie tingfang shilu*, 123–6; "Xixia xianzhi: renwu pian," 118; and Li, *Peng Yuting*, 74–5.

no doubt that the organization would be the vehicle for their dominance. Therefore, from the top to the bottom, all its officers came from either the organization's followers, the wealthy, or educated members of the elite community.[82] A survey of the organization's administrative hierarchy confirms this.

The highest authority in each county was the County Administrative Council. Below that was the Self-Government Administrative Office. Each ward contained an office for the Committee for Dispute Mediation, the administrative branch of Self-Government, and the Three-in-One Self-Government Committee (for household registration, land survey, and taxation). According to the bylaws of Self-Government, the members of the County Administrative Council were chosen among the ward chiefs and the Self-Government personnel in the county. Of the five members of the Committee for Dispute Mediation, three were chosen by the County Administrative Council. The other two were selected by the director of the committee from among the members of other Self-Government offices. In fact, all officers for the entire Self-Government organization were selected either from the Self-Government offices or the members of the elite community. The method of officer selection was predominantly by the leaders or the senior officers of Self-Government.[83]

Many contemporaries thus considered Self-Government an elite-dominated institution. The chairman of the Henan Provincial Government commented at the time that the movement relied on only a few community leaders. Without these individuals, there was no Self-Government; they were the only authority. The four-county area was not run by law *(fa zhi)* but by an oligarchy of local elites *(ren zhi)*. On the other hand, southwestern Henan was governed by the local elites *(sheng zhi)* and not by the people *(min zhi)*. Another participant of the movement, Wang Wenzhi, echoed that opinion, claiming Self-Government was "dominated" by a coterie of elites *(tong zhi)* rather than people governing themselves *(renmin zizhi)*.[84]

Beginning in 1931, however, Self-Government started to pay attention to the winning of public support through the expansion of popular par-

---

[82] Li, *Peng Yuting*, 191; and "Neixiang xianzhi: renwu," 172–3.

[83] *Zhenping zizhi gaikuang*, 4; Li, *Peng Yuting*, 192; and Wang, "Zhenping xiangcun," 180–1.

[84] Li Zonghuang, "Wanxi difang zizhi pingjia" (Assessment of the Self-Government Movement in Southwestern Henan), in Chen, *Xianhua wanxi*, 238–9; and Wang, "Difang zizhi," 196.

ticipation in the lower level of administration of its organization, owing to the open-minded leader Peng Yuting. Peng discerned the true source of legitimacy: "the center of gravity of today's society is no longer in the upper level, among the elites, but at the lower level, among the ordinary people." He differentiated himself from those whom he called "local bullies and evil gentry" – his description for leaders who had lost their power during the previous changes in the local power structure – arguing these individuals abused their connections to the government agents and exploited ordinary people by acting as power brokers. Peng saw the expansion of popular participation as the only way of maintaining the organization's influence.[85]

In accord with Peng Yuting's concept, Self-Government in Zhenping County altered the selection process for its ward committee members. By the end of 1931, of the twenty-five officers in the Self-Government office of each ward (including the chief officers of the Committee for Dispute Mediation, the Self-Government Administrative Office, and the Three-in-One Self-Government Committee), Peng allowed all except the directors and assistant directors to be elected from among village-level Self-Government functionaries. This procedure permitted some young people from humble families to become committee members, although Self-Government continued to be dominated by those newly risen local community leaders.[86]

Soon, the reorganizing effort was in full swing. The chief officers of the Self-Government Administrative Offices in each county were allowed to serve only one year before submitting to the reselection process. In the beginning, the Self-Government officers nominated three candidates for each available position, with the winner finally selected by the headquarters of Four-County Self-Government. But later, an election for these posts was held among the village heads, school teachers, and primary school graduates over the age of sixteen. Although the administrative offices still nominated its three candidates for each position, the election considerably broadened popular participation in Self-Government.[87]

In November 1932 the same endeavor continued with the revision of the organization's bylaws. According to the new rules, the Self-Government Council of each county would comprise thirty-five members, more than half of them to be elected by people who met the

---

[85] *Zhenping zizhi gaikuang*, 252; and Li, *Peng Yuting*, 120, 251.
[86] *Zhenping zizhi gaikuang*, 22.   [87] Ibid., 14; and Li, *Peng Yuting*, 195–6.

following qualifications: village and town chiefs, functionaries of Self-Government Administrative Offices, primary school teachers, and primary school graduates over the age of twenty. The criteria for candidacy were also changed. A person had to be twenty-five years or older; be a primary school graduate; have been educated in the local Self-Government schools; have served in the Self-Government Administrative Office (branch office) for one year; and have made a noticeable contribution to the local community. Although the election still favored the educated, respected members of the elite community, or other locally influential individuals, it nevertheless ended the former practice of internal selection of officers.

Half of the chief officer's positions in the Self-Government Administrative Offices were thus subject to election by voters who met the same qualifications as those who chose the Self-Government Council members. Also, all village or town chiefs were elected by villagers, again giving those of humble origin the chance to become officers, at the ward level, of the Self-Government Administrative Office and the Self-Government Council. In Zhenping County, for instance, more than two-thirds of the council members were young people who had been educated at local schools. Even the selection of village and town chiefs was subject to change. Qualification for voters was broadened to include those who had lived in the village or town for more than one year and were at least twenty years old. In effect, now every adult had the right to vote for village or town chief.[88]

On March 25, 1933, while Self-Government was infusing itself with new blood, Peng Yuting was suffocated by two wealthy Zhenping residents who had bribed his bodyguards. As in the case of Ning Xigu, the assassination climaxed a power struggle between Peng and other local power figures. Peng had made enemies when he assumed control of the Zhenping militia, causing some heads of large families to lose their influence. After Peng became a leader of Self-Government, he continued to intimidate once-respected people in the county. This important loss in the leadership of Self-Government, however, did not impede the organization's progress. On the contrary, it accelerated the concentration of power in the hands of Bie Tingfang and Chen Shunde. Upon hearing of Peng's death, Bie and Chen immediately took control of Zhenping until, years later, they found a satisfactory successor for Peng.[89]

[88] Li, *Peng Yuting*, 196–201.
[89] Chen, *Xianhua wanxi*, 26–7; *Zhenping wenshi ziliao*, 74–5; and Li, *Peng Yuting*, 77–8.

The death of Peng Yuting did not end the development already underway. Instead, the public election of officials continued to the end of the Republican period. During that time, as we can well imagine, Self-Government was gradually transformed (except at the highest levels of its leadership) into an organization that was being served by many young, educated, ambitious people from the community.[90] The transformation of Self-Government had been in progress since its inception and was consistent with what its leaders, especially Peng Yuting, understood to be the source of its legitimacy during the Republican period. It also reflected the effects of the crisis of legitimacy that had caused the leaders of the Self-Government movement to expand their base of dominance by allowing some popular participation in the lower-level administration of its institution. Moreover, this development proved to be a significant step toward winning greater public support for Self-Government.

SELF-GOVERNMENT IN NANZHAO

Outside the four-county area, the Self-Government movement was disseminated to Nanzhao County by Li Yiwen, a leader of the elite community there. In 1929 Li, then chief of the County Education Bureau, learned about the concept of self-government when he visited Peng Yuting and his friends Luo Zhuoru, Wu Liquan, Yang Yishan, and Wang Fushan in Zhenping County. Excited by the idea, Li returned to Nanzhao County to initiate Self-Government there.

The response from the elite community was mixed, but generally supportive. By the end of the year, Li had decided to consolidate the local elites in the four counties to form a single Self-Government unit. His plan was immediately supported by Peng Yuting, who promised to help Li to establish Self-Government offices for militia training, local trade, and water control. Soon, however, opposition surfaced within the elite community, particularly from the powerful Yang Family. To suppress the opposition of that lineage, Li called in Peng Yuting's militia to attack Yang's village. When one of the family's heads, Yang San, was killed, the entire lineage surrendered. After the incident, however, the Yang Family filed a complaint with the provincial government of the time, targeting the attention of Liu Zhi, the chairman of the Nationalist provincial gov-

---

[90] Chen, *Xianhua wanxi*, 30.

ernment. Liu dispatched government troops to Nanzhao to arrest Li, and Li was forced to leave the county.[91]

In 1931, Li Yiwen returned to Nanzhao County to restore Self-Government. His undertaking was supported by Wang Ligang, an influential community leader who headed a large militia. Among his efforts, Li initiated a survey to reset the tax rate on local land in order to collect surcharges for Self-Government. The Yang Family again rose up to resist Li. They took their grievance to the provincial government's chairman, Liu Zhi, who issued an order to the Nationalist troops stationed in Nanyang City to drive Li out of Nanzhao County. After the troops arrived at Nanzhao, Li escaped to Neixiang County, and thus ended the second attempt to establish the Self-Government movement in the county.[92]

In 1932 Peng Yuting led a group of militiamen into Nanzhao County in another bid to restore Self-Government. As soon as he arrived, he arrested the secretary general of the county government office and the chairman of the Chamber of Commerce, an influential community leader who supported the Yang Family despite their alleged corruption and abuse of power. After interrogation, both officials were publicly beaten. Peng's actions terrified those members of the elite community who had refused to cooperate with Li. Directly after the incident, Peng convened all the county officials, including the magistrate, and directed them to rearrange the county government to accommodate the requirements of Self-Government. Some county functionaries were reassigned to positions in Self-Government offices to expedite their operation. The county magistrate not only followed the order but also instructed his subordinate to cooperate with Li Yiwen.[93]

After the death of Peng Yuting, Self-Government in Nanzhao was supervised by Bie Tingfang, who sometimes led militiamen into the county to bolster the support of Li Yiwen. In October 1933, Bie Tingfang called for a meeting in Nanzhao County of all local elites in order to

[91] Nanzhaoxian zhibian weihui, "Nanzhao xianzhi" ("Gazetteer of Nanzhao County") (Nanzhao, Unpublished Manuscript), 20–1, 28–9, 38; and Zhou Qibang, "Wo suo jingli de Nanzhao zizhi yundong" (My Experience with the Nanzhao Self-government Movement), in *Henan wenshi ziliao (Historical Account of Henan)*, 14 (1983): 34–43.

[92] "Nanzhao xianzhi," 40; and Zhou, "Nanzhao zizhi," 40–3.

[93] Nanzhaoxian wenshi ziliao weiyuan hui, *Nanzhao wenshi ziliao (Local History of Nanzhao County)*, 3 (Nanzhao: Zhengxie Henansheng Nanzhaoxian weiyuan hui, 1988): 93–4; and Zhou, "Nanzhao zizhi," 38.

incorporate Nanzhao County into the Self-Government program of the four counties.[94] Li Yiwen organized the Nanzhao County Executive Committee to assist the incorporation effort in the county. The committee replaced the county government agencies in the same way the Four-County Self-Government had in the four counties. The movement was backed by more than 7,000 regular militiamen. Until 1938 Nanzhao County remained a part of the Self-Government movement in southwestern Henan.[95]

SUMMARY

As my study of the region shows, the pattern of local elite dominance in southwestern Henan was similar in its coercive nature to that found in other peripheral locations, but was quite distinctive in the organized form of elite activism that created it. Within their sphere of activities, the newly risen local elites displayed an immense capacity to institutionalize their dominance of the area. Indeed, their behavior differed substantially from the accepted portrait of peripheral elites elsewhere.

Schoppa finds that local elites in both the "inner-peripheral" and "outer-peripheral" zones of Zhejiang were slow to develop new-style voluntary organizations, independent of state power, for maintaining their dominance. Instead, the local elites in these areas commonly tried to stay in power by securing employment in local government offices and associating with powerful and currently serving county magistrates. The established power structures of the oligarchic elite in these areas frequently persisted largely intact and unaffected by outside influences, at least until the late 1920s.[96] The local elites in Meskill's study of Taiwan also appear to have been weak in forming social links and using organization to obtain their goals. Despite the cohesive ties between the military strongmen and their followings, there was little local-level organization working to expand the horizon of their dictatorial control.[97]

Local elites in Guizhou and Jiangxi were quite sophisticated in adopting new strategies and conducting various activities to enhance their

---

[94] *Feng yu zheng cheng (History of Revolutionary Movements in Nanzhao County)* (Zhengzhou: Henan renmin chuban she, 1991), 54–5; and Zhou, "Nanzhao zizhi," 14 (1983): 40–1.

[95] *Nanzhao wenshi ziliao*, 4 (1989): 2–8, 14–16, 28–9, 64–6; and *Feng yu zheng cheng, (History of Revolutionary Movements in Nanzhao County)* (Zhengzhou: Henan renmin chuban she, 1991), 10–12, 55–8.

[96] Schoppa, *Chinese Elites*, 118, 134, 115–41.   [97] Meskill, *Chinese Family*, 88–9.

family wealth and influence. Some Jiangxi elites became deeply involved in the embryonic Communist-led revolutionary movement, for example. In addition, in southern Jiangxi between 1934 and 1937, local elites took advantage of the reform efforts of the Nationalist government to enhance their own interests. They were involved with state-sponsored rural rehabilitation programs (through which they controlled the *baojia* system), introduced ideological indoctrination in schools, and staffed various government agencies.[98]

By comparison, however, the later generation of community leaders in southwestern Henan were not only willing to accept new ideas from outside, but also eager to incorporate those ideas into their own agendas. Under the influence of external ideas, these community leaders formulated their own institution, Self-Government, which exclusively represented their political interests against those of the state as well as any other social groups, including political parties and secret societies. A closer look at the design of Self-Government reveals that its organizers gained impressive organizational skills and a deep understanding of methods for political mobilization, the mechanisms of grassroots organization, and the basic structure of a modern bureaucracy.

At the beginning of the Self-Government movement, its founders had stated its principles and specified its goals and procedures. During the implementation of the blueprint for the Self-Government programs, these individuals combined the traditional method for security maintenance and community control, the *baojia* system, with the modern style of education for the purpose of political indoctrination to ensure that every citizen in the area was not only under their control but also fully cooperative. And for the mobilization of resources and the maintenance of public order, these self-assured elites created bureaucratic institutions that were quite complex, even by modern standards. Furthermore, these individuals also took gradual though limited steps in the direction of broadening popular participation in the management of their organization.

All these characteristics suggest the political development of southwestern Henan was similar to that observed in the cities or the commercialized areas, as measured by the "increase in the political interdependency and complexity of elites, their associations and institu-

---

[98] McCord, "Local Military Power," 162–90; Averill, "Party, Society and Local Elite," 282–304; and Stephen Averill, "The New Life in Action: The Nationalist Government in South Jiangxi, 1934–37," *China Quarterly*, no. 88 (December 1981): 622–7.

tions."[99] They also imply that, in terms of the political sophistication of elite activism, the boundaries between the core and periphery, urban and rural, city and countryside were blurring in China. The barriers once created by social, economic, and geographic conditions could not stop the flow of ideas, particularly the highly sophisticated undertakings of the elites.

While recognizing the narrowing gap between the core and periphery in regard to the political sophistication among the local elites, however, one should also be aware of the distinctive manner in which southwestern Henan responded to external stimuli. Obviously, exposure to outside influences did not lead to the opening of the area, although the regular channel of communication between the founders of Self-Government and their outside contacts remained throughout the period. On the contrary, that exposure facilitated the trend of localization, a trend characterized by the local elites concentrating on the utilization of local political and military resources – such as popular support, alliance among themselves, and militia organization – to establish exclusive control of the area.[100] As I demonstrated in Chapter 4, this trend had already evolved within the local society itself and became obvious long before the founding of Self-Government, as the leadership of the community was becoming concentrated. And it continued in the changes among the local elites, namely, in the Self-Government movement, the formation of

---

[99] Schoppa, *Chinese Elites*, 6. Schoppa offers the following definition of political development: "Political development in general occurs in a social system, defined as a unit of components (for example, individuals, groups, institutions, local political units) linked over time. The level of development refers to the interdependency and complexity of a system's components at any point in time. At its simplest, the process of political development is the transition from primary to composite and complex political structures and phenomena. Around primary kin, patron-client, and brokerage relationships evolve more differentiated and institutionalized structures. This evolution does not mean the displacement or diminution of the primary by the complex. In Zhejiang, primary phenomena remained dominant features amid increased sociopolitical variety and differentiation."

[100] Robert Hymes's study indicates that in Fuzhou County of Jiangxi, the local elites not only localized their personal network, including marriage ties, but also focused on local activism instead of seeking office at the national level. The major components of their local activism were local defense against banditry, social welfare, and maintenance of community religious life through the building of temples. Hymes, *Statesmen and Gentlemen*. I use the term *localization* differently from Hymes. Here it describes the isolation of southwestern Henan and the exclusive nature of local elite dominance in that region, which completely neutralized the influence of the state authorities and any other social groups, such as secret societies or the large-scale political parties we usually see in other areas.

a local identity, and the rise of localism. The establishment of Self-Government, based on ideas related to the Rural Reconstruction Movement, only hastened the trend.

It is, therefore, imperative to view the trend toward localization as one of the major developments in Chinese society during the Republican period. As Schoppa and Duara have both argued, provincialism and nationalism were the two coexisting entities in Chinese political discourse during the first quarter of the twentieth century.[101] Along with provincialism and nationalism, as I will argue, localism became a part of political discourse in China in the second quarter of the twentieth century. As the preceding case strongly suggests, it was the formation of local identity as well as the emergence of localism among the local elites that was at the heart of a deep crisis of legitimacy in southwestern Henan. Based only on that identification crisis, the behavior of those local community leaders during the Self-Government movement was not only self-legitimized but self-justified.

---

[101] Keith Schoppa, "Province and Nation: The Chekiang Provincial Autonomy Movement, 1917–1927," *Journal of Asian Studies* 36, no. 4 (1977): 661–74; and Duara, *Rescuing History*, 178–9.

Part IV

MODERN STATE MAKING AND THE INTERACTION BETWEEN STATE AND SOCIETY

7

State Making during the Republican Period

TO ascertain Chinese state-making endeavors during the Republican period, the prevailing studies have predominantly centered on the vertical mode, the top-to-bottom process, of state penetration, accentuating the state's imposition of its authority down to the level of local society. Leading those researchers, Philip Kuhn discerns a similarity of intrusiveness among the administrations of Yuan Shikai, the warlords, and the Nationalist government. He perceives one continuous trend in state making since the late Qing and throughout the Republican period.[1] Prasenjit Duara posits that although these state entities had striven to gain control of local society, their course was derailed by the local elites, who had taken advantage of the opportunity to aggrandize their wealth and power. Thus, Duara maintains, the state's ventures in creating and reorganizing local government bureaucracy only resulted in the opposite of their original goal – to control local society – owing to the very existence of entrepreneurial state brokers whom the state was unable to control. These efforts actually accelerated the devolution of state power into the hands of the local elites.[2]

Dissenting with this view, however, Keith Schoppa, Elizabeth Perry, and Stephen MacKinnon postulate a strengthening of both state and society in core areas.[3] Kathryn Bernhardt has ascertained that the influence of the Republican state was greatly enhanced, as exemplified by increasing government pressure on land-

---

[1] Kuhn, "Local Self-Government."

[2] Duara, *Culture, Power, and the State*, 73–7, 255–6.

[3] Schoppa, *Chinese Elites*, 5–8, 186–7; Elizabeth Perry, "Collective Violence in China, 1880–1980," in *Theory and Society* 13, no. 3 (1984): 427–54; and Stephen R. MacKinnon, *Power and Politics in Late Imperial China: Yuan Shi-kai in Beijing and Tianjin, 1901–1908* (Berkeley: University of California Press, 1980), 6–11, 219–24.

lords.[4] Kenneth Pomeranz's research demonstrates the simultaneous strengthening of the early Republican state in the coastal areas and its withdrawal from the inland areas.[5]

One subject that has not received sufficient attention in previous scholarship is the horizontal facet, the center-to-periphery process, of state making. Although some of the aforementioned studies have focused on both highly commercialized and noncommercialized areas, there is still insufficient information about the interactions between the state and local society in the peripheral areas, due largely to the scarcity of previously attainable materials. To deal with the broad issue of state making, the present research intends to shed some light on the general question of whether, and how, the Republican states – including those of Yuan Shikai, the warlords, Feng Yuxiang, the Nationalist government, and various lower-level political and military entities – attempted to create a modern state.[6] I will examine both vertical and horizontal processes of state making during the period, including the following two dimensions: the Republican regimes' attempts to extend their administrative control to rural society, and the state's expansion into the fiscal domain. But before I begin my examination, I shall first define the entity of what we call the state.

A DEFINITION OF STATE

The definition of "state" has continually varied in the Western literature of the social sciences. According to a Marxist theoretician, a state is a "concentrated and organized means of legitimate class domination."[7] It is not only a class-based and unitary apparatus but also is very much determined by its modes of economic production. In this sense, the Western states were the governing apparatus that reflected capitalist interests.[8] From the pluralist view, however, a state is a cohesive politi-

---

[4] Kathryn Bernhardt, *Rents, Taxes, and Peasant Resistance* (Stanford: Stanford University Press, 1992), 230–2.

[5] Pomeranz, *Making of a Hinterland*, 271–6.

[6] I believe that modern state making is a deliberate effort on the part of state entities, and therefore differs fundamentally from social transformation, which does not result from premeditated actions.

[7] M. Zeitlin et al., "On Classes, Class Conflict, and the State: An Introductory Note," in *Classes, Class Conflict and the State: Empirical Studies in Class Analysis*, M. Zeitlin, ed. (Cambridge, MA: Winthrop, 1980), 15.

[8] N. Poulantzas, *Political Power and Social Classes* (London: New Left Books, 1973); and R. Miliband, *The State in Capitalist Society* (New York: Basic Books, 1969).

cal organ that represents the interests of individual citizens, or various interest groups.[9] As a part of the inevitable modernization process, therefore, the state shifted its power from "kings to the people."[10] In addition, according to the "elitist," or the "statist" approach, the state is "a set of administrative, policing, and military organizations headed and more or less well co-ordinated by an executive authority."[11]

A generally accepted notion of the state by those studying China is Charles Tilly's definition of the state as "an organization, controlling the principal means of coercion within a given territory, which is differentiated from other organizations operating in the same territory, autonomous, centralized and formally coordinated."[12] But problems arise when this definition is applied to the early Republican period, especially from the local perspective, when such an identifiable state entity was absent. Although the warlords and other military strongmen all proclaimed themselves to be the legitimate authorities, none of their administrations fell into the category of "autonomous, centralized and formally coordinated" political organization by which Tilly identified the early modern European state. Recently, Michael Mann has suggested the state is not a unitary but rather a "polymorphous" entity. Such an entity contains many different local-regional identities and classes, as well as sectional identities. Mann's definition seems to be most apt for early Republican China.[13]

To borrow Mann's notion of the state, I have identified the following governing entities in Henan. The first list covers the provincial authority established by Yuan Shikai, various warlords, and the Nationalist government. The list gives the names of the governor, the military governor, and the duration of each administration (see Table A.1 in the Appendix). When looking at the list, however, one must guard against the notion that whoever established a provincial government was in control of the entire province. This is untrue in many cases. For example, not only was the regional authority in southwestern Henan sometimes not affili-

---

[9] R. A. Dahl, *Polyarchy* (New Haven: Yale University Press, 1977); and S. M. Lipset, *Political Man* (London: Mercury Books, 1959).

[10] R. Bendix, *Kings or People: Power and the Mandate to Rule* (Berkeley: University of California Press, 1978), title.

[11] Theda Skocpol, *States and Social Revolutions: A Comparative Analysis of France, Russia, and China* (New York: Cambridge University Press, 1979), 27, 29–30.

[12] Charles Tilly, ed., *The Formation of National States in Western Europe* (Princeton: Princeton University Press, 1975), 70, 638.

[13] Mann, *Social Power*, 723–39.

ated with the provincial authority, but even within the region the governing entity often differed from one county to the next (see Tables A.2, A.3, and A.4 in Appendix). This suggests the state was a fluid and transitory entity that varied from time to time and from place to place before the Nationalist government came to power. Therefore, my definition of state for the early Republican period includes any political or military power who established authority over the northern and southwestern regions of Henan. With this definition in mind, I will now begin my investigation of how each Republican state attempted state making in northern and southwestern Henan.

NORTHERN HENAN

The Expansion of Administrative Control

An indispensable component of state making is the expansion of the state's bureaucratic control to the local level.[14] In order to achieve that control, the governments of states in the Republican period had to reinstate their authority in the peasant community through the strengthening of their local administrations and the installation of systems for the supervision of local society. To reach these goals, some state authorities created elaborate local government organs; others relied on their military and police forces. At this point, I will investigate all state involvement in northern Henan and assess the authorities' ability to achieve supervision, intervention, and bureaucratic control of local society.

The Early Republican Period. After the demise of the Qing dynasty, Yuan Shikai was the first to attempt to create a powerful state by organizing at the local level. His primary focus was the restoration of county administration. As soon as Sun Yat-sen relinquished his presidency to Yuan on February 13, 1912, the governor of Henan, Qi Yaolin, reinstated the authority of the county magistrate by following a directive from Yuan to resume government administration in every county. According to

---

[14] According to Charles Tilly there are three major paradigms for the theories of state making: the developmental, the functional, and the historical. Although each approaches the issue differently, they all recognize field administration (or bureaucratization) to be an essential component of the state-making process in order for the state to achieve its main goals: mobilizing resources, maintaining public order, and coordinating collective efforts. See Tilly, *Formation of National States*, 604–32.

180

Yuan's guideline, most local officials from the previous regime retained their positions, and the former structure of the local administration was left intact. The first responsibilities of the county administration were to establish subcounty wards. It also closely supervised both the operation of each ward and the actions of its functionaries.[15] After Yuan Shikai's withdrawal from constitutionalism in 1915, the subcounty wards were the lowest formal unit of government.[16]

Under Yuan Shikai's regime, the provincial administration also paid substantial attention to strengthening the county police and to taking control of the elite-led militia. By 1914 a police unit had been formed in every county in accordance with instructions from above.[17] As Stephen R. MacKinnon has pointed out in his study of Zhili, this proceeding was the continuation of Yuan Shikai's previous endeavor to institute a strong police apparatus at the local level.[18] At the same time, the government also attempted to take control of private militias. Also, according to the directive from Yuan Shikai, the county magistrates merged the militia groups into a large unit under their control. Despite protest from the elite community, the mergers were consummated shortly after the order from above was received.[19] Keith Schoppa has suggested the same measure, applied by Yuan Shikai's administration in Zhejiang, enhanced county government's capacity for police control in the core zone. In northern Henan, a similar result occurred.[20]

In 1914, Yuan abolished the county assembly so as to enhance the county government's influence in the rural community,[21] because just as the county assemblies in Zhejiang, they had become so powerful that even the county government had to yield to their decisions.[22] Yuan's order was carried out under the intense supervision of the provincial authority, and like the consolidation of the county militias, it was executed quickly, despite considerable opposition from the elite community.[23] Yuan's measure, however, as Lenore Barkan has observed in her

[15] Yang, *Xiuwu xianzhi* (1986), 14; Xinxiang xianzhi bianchuan weiyuan hui, *Xinxiang xianzhi (Local Gazetteer of Xinxiang County)* (Xinxiang: Shenghuo, Dushu, Xinzhi Sanlian Shudian, 1991), 326; and Chen, *Tangyin xianzhi*, 328.

[16] Duara, *Culture, Power, and the State*, 61.

[17] Yang, *Xiuwu xianzhi* (1986), 208; and Zou, *Huojia xianzhi*, 7 (1934): 14.

[18] MacKinnon, *Power and Politics*, 139–43, 150–63.

[19] Chen, *Tangyin xianzhi*, 348, 362; and Zhang, *Huojia xianzhi* (1991), 17.

[20] Schoppa, *Chinese Elites*, 79.

[21] *Xinxiang xianzhi* (1991), 326; and Yang, *Xiuwu xianzhi* (1986), 155.

[22] Schoppa, *Chinese Elites*, 78.

[23] Yang, *Xiuwu xianzhi* (1986), 155.

study of Jiangsu, may have diverted the political ambitions of many local elites from the county assembly to other activities, often commercially oriented, especially in the years to come.[24]

Another target of administrative control was elite institutions such as the Chamber of Commerce, an organization formed under government sponsorship at the end of the Qing, but which became independent from government authority during the 1911 Revolution. Before the end of the dynasty, the chambers of commerce in every county energetically engaged in various pursuits within the local community, representing more than their economic interests. They were among the most noticeable, if not the most powerful, institutions in every county after the county assemblies had been eradicated. Having realized their political potential, the administration ordered their leadership to be transferred to elites who would cooperate with the county authority, and government sponsorship was resumed.[25]

Yuan Shikai's vigorous state-making efforts were not limited to the strengthening of local bureaucracy, subcounty wards, and county police. His intervention also extended to control of the county assembly, local militia, and other elite institutions. Through these efforts Yuan's authority over local government was enhanced, and the influence of the local elites was greatly diminished. As Edward McCord notes, in Hubei and Hunan the government under Yuan Shikai was very successful in its effort to centralize bureaucracy at the provincial level. As the present study shows, this consolidation also occurred within the local administration in northern Henan, which became highly responsive to the provincial authority.[26]

In contrast to that of Yuan Shikai, the Beijing administrations of Li Yuanhong, Feng Guozhang, Xu Shichang, Huang Fu, and Duan Qirui approached state making quite differently. They concentrated primarily on reinforcing county police and restraining the activities of private militia organizations in order to minimize noncompliance of the rural population and maximize state control of the area. When Tian Wenlie was governor of Henan, in 1918 he ordered a local security force to be organized under the supervision of local magistrates. Acting on that

[24] Barkan, "Patterns of Power," 203–6.
[25] *Xinxiang xianzhi* (1991), 326; Xiao, *Xiuwu xianzhi*, 9 (1931): 45–6; and Han, *Xinxiang-xian xuzhi*, 1 (1923): 80.
[26] Edward McCord, *The Power of the Gun: The Emergence of Modern Chinese Warlordism* (Berkeley: University of California Press, 1993), 161–204.

directive, magistrates organized county security units in every county, and abolished the Neighborhood Watch Groups.[27]

An identical strategy was adopted by Feng Yuxiang, then military governor of Henan appointed by Xu Shichang. In May 1922, for instance, Feng Yuxiang issued a guideline for the provincial government in which he gave the order to reorganize the local militia in Henan in order to maintain public order. From the beginning of 1926, Feng reasserted his desire to reorganize the local security force. Following his order, county police headquarters were founded in every county.[28] According to James Sheridan, Feng's outline of administrative goals also included the investigation and arrest of corrupt officials.[29]

Similarly, when Wu Peifu was in Henan in March 1926, his initial inclination was to reorganize the county police to fight bandits. As soon as Wu returned to Henan, he ordered the reorganization of the county police. Once the banditry was curtailed, Wu quickly shifted his focus to the expansion of local administration. To each county government he added new bureaus for finance, education, and construction, while giving the county police more responsibility for tax collection.[30] Meanwhile, during Wu's stay in Henan, Zhili, and Shandong in 1924, according to Oderic Wou, he filled the provincial and county official positions in Henan with many of his relatives and subordinates.[31] Wu's endeavors were cut short, however, by his defeat at the hands of Chiang Kai-shek.

As soon as Feng established his authority over Henan (by late 1927), he renamed the county government *zhengfu* (meaning simply "government") and coined the term *xianzhang* ("chief of the county") for the county magistrate. Although these changes seem trivial, they indicate Feng's determination to clothe his government in a modern image. Subsequently, he embarked on a comprehensive reform of county government by streamlining the remaining departments and adding new ones that focused on security, education, water conservation, public funds, and

[27] Wang, *Chongxiu Huaxian zhi*, 20: 9, 38, 55; and Chen, *Tangyin xianzhi*, 11, 362.

[28] Guo Xuyin and Chen Xingtang, *Aiguo jiangjun Feng Yuxiang (Patriot General Feng Yuxiang)* (Zhengzhou: Henan renmin chuban she, 1987), 49; *Xinxiang xianzhi* (1991), 16; Yang, *Xiuwu xianzhi* (1986), 208; Wang, *Chongxiu Huaxian zhi*, no. 55; and Zou, *Huojia xianzhi*, 3 (1934): 16.

[29] James Sheridan, *Chinese Warlord: The Career of Feng Yu-hsiang* (Stanford: Stanford University Press, 1966), 112–15.

[30] Xiao, *Xiuwu xianzhi*, 7 (1931): 41–2; Chen, *Tangyin xianzhi*, 348; and Yang, *Xiuwu xianzhi* (1986), 179.

[31] Wou, *Militarism*, 58–62.

taxation. Having devised the Bureau of Public Security to replace the county police, Feng also reinstalled a county court and authorized the county magistrate to act as an interim judge before permanent magistrates were designated by the high court.[32] These steps were clearly aimed at maximizing state supervision at the local level.

To further his state-making effort, Feng Yuxiang attempted to subjugate the private militia groups under his authority. He orchestrated the formation of the Henan Provincial Militia, under which every individual militia group was consolidated into a single large unit called the People's Defense Militia. The local militia in northern Henan was reorganized into the People's Self-Defense Militia. Militiamen were not only required to wear the same uniforms, but also were to follow Feng's orders, especially on when to use weapons.[33]

Furthermore, Feng was distrustful of local elite institutions. During his governance, the county governments received a number of specified instructions to curb the activities of such organizations as the Chamber of Commerce and the Bureau of Finance, two of the elite institutions remaining in the region. The chambers of commerce in some counties were thus converted into committees of local commerce, subject to the authority of the county governments.[34]

Feng also decided to establish subcounty wards. He then ordered the county governments to select and train ward chiefs, drawing only from graduates of specially created schools that bore the name School for Political Education. There were no exemptions from the training process. Feng even conceived a plan to use self-government to achieve control over local society, and thus ordered every county to form preparatory committees for self-government. It was reported in local gazetteers that in Xiuwu County there were self-government offices in every *li* (one for every ten households).[35]

Feng Yuxiang envisioned the creation of a truly modern state, whose central government was more powerful than any previous regime. In that

---

[32] Xiao, *Xiuwu xianzhi*, 7 (1931): 42, 328; Chen, *Tangyin xianzhi*, 328; Zhang, *Huojia xianzhi* (1991), 183; and Yang, *Xiuwu xianzhi* (1986), 179.

[33] Chen, *Tangyin xianzhi*, 362, 598; Yang, *Xiuwu xianzhi* (1986), 208; Zou, *Huojia xianzhi*, 7 (1934): 14; Han Desan, "Henan mintuan jun de yanbian" (Transformation of the Provincial Militia in Henan), in *Henan wenshi ziliao (Henan Local History)*, 27 (1988): 89–93; Zou, *Huojia xianzhi*, 3 (1934): 14–16; Wang, *Chongxiu Huaxian zhi*, 56; and Xiao, *Xiuwu xianzhi*, 7 (1931): 1–2, 47.

[34] Wang, *Chongxiu Huaxian zhi*, 32; and Zou, *Huojia xianzhi*, 6 (1934): 2.

[35] Xiao, *Xiuwu xianzhi*, 6 (1931): 37.

regard his regime surpassed even that of Yuan Shikai in such areas as the modernization of local administration and the use of political training to familiarize local functionaries with his state-making ideas. Feng might have planned a campaign against official corruption like the one he tried when he was military governor of Henan.[36] In his memoirs Feng Yuxiang shares his guidelines for his rule in Henan. One of its points was to establish an honest government.[37] But because war between him and Chiang Kai-shek broke out in May 1929, Feng's plans ended prematurely.

The Nanjing Decade. The Nationalist government launched a full-scale modernization of county government as soon as it took power in Henan. As its first step, in June 1929 the central government inaugurated district headquarters to carefully supervise all operations below the provincial level.[38] Simultaneously, the government added elaborate offices for various functions according to its County Organization Law issued in September 1929. These offices reported directly to the respective division in the provincial administration, thus relieving the county magistrate of the authority to appoint the chief of each office.

Between 1928 and 1930, for instance, the Nationalist government created the following offices for each county government. Its program began with two departments. The first contained offices for civil administration, education, construction projects, the judiciary, the secretary of the county government office, the official seal, the GMD organization, and a police force responsible for making arrests, enforcing tax payment, and delivering government documents. The second department included offices for national tax collection, government bonds, currency administration, and government spending. This department also had separate offices for the administration of land and head taxes, miscellaneous surtaxes, and delivery of collected taxes to the next higher level of government. Later, the government also added offices for banking, hygiene, famine relief, accounting, coordination of community projects, and the Self-Government surtax. Just before 1930, the government established separate bureaus for finance, construction, education, and police.[39]

---

[36] Chen Yaoxin, "Henan de quzhang renmian" (The Appointment of Ward Chief in Henan), in *Henan wenshi ziliao (Historical Account of Henan)*, 33 (1990): 180.

[37] Feng Yuxiang, *Wo de shenghuo (My Life)* (Bowen shuju, 1974), 726.

[38] *Wunian lai Henan zhengzhi zong baogao: caizheng (General Report of the Last Five-Years of Political Affairs in Henan: Finance)* (Kaifeng: Henan sheng zhengfu mishu chu, October 1935), 2; *Xinxiang xianzhi* (1991), 326.

[39] *Nanyang xianzhi* (1990), 119; *Nanyang shizhi*, 269; and *Xixia xianzhi* (1990), 414.

Guided by Sun Yat-sen's ideal of forming local organization as a way to prepare for a constitution for the nation, and by Yan Xishan's model for Shanxi, the government strove to use Self-Government to bring local elites into its political system and to promote their interest in the government's programs. For instance, a 1932 provincial government report recommended that Self-Government first be organized under the leadership of the Nationalist party, with leadership gradually transferred to the people. The report also called for the honoring of local culture and traditions. One of the primary aims of Self-Government was the eradication of government corruption. According to another government report, the Self-Government program not only included such measures as household registration, community security, disaster relief, public education, and economic development, but, more importantly, also emphasized the respecting of the public's legal rights, a measure aimed at winning increased public support for the regime.[40] Under the name of "political tutelage," Self-Government became an imperative component of a national campaign to politicize the rural population for the support of its regime. Self-Government was thus seen as an alternative means for both local control and mobilization.

Fei Xiaotong has suggested that Self-Government was initiated in order to help local government better administer such functions as those delineated in the Law Governing the Organization of the District, promulgated by the Nationalist government on June 5, 1929: census taking, land survey, public works, education, self-defense, physical training, public health, water regulation, forest preservation, industrial and commercial improvement, food storage and regulation, protection of plantations and fisheries, prohibition of illegal fishing, cooperation on community projects, public relief, public enterprise, and financial control. In August 1932, however, the main mission of Self-Government was redefined to serve the Nationalist government's military campaign against the Communists, after the Headquarters of the Punitive Campaign against the Communists in central China issued a decree

---

[40] "Henan sheng zhengfu mishu chu geke gongzuo gaiyao" (General Report on the Works in the Secretary Office of the Henan Provincial Government), *Henan zhengzhi yuekan (Monthly Report of Political Affairs in Henan)* 2, no. 9 (August 1932) (Kaifeng: Henan sheng zhengfu bianyichu chuban): 2–3; and Henan sheng minzheng ting, "Henan sheng minzheng ting ershi yi nian wu yue fen xingzheng baogao" (Administrative Report of May 1932 on the Civil Administration of the Henan Provincial Government), *Henan minzheng yuekan* (1932): 76.

to organize the people in central China according to the *baojia* system.[41]

Although a main mission of Self-Government doubtless was to help relieve the burden of local government in managing the functions listed by Fei, its most important function was to achieve local control by the Nationalist government. Philip Kuhn has pointed out that once the previous system for local control was rendered obsolete by modern changes, the only alternative for the Nationalist government – besides facing the same problem in peasant society that occurred during the Qing dynasty – was either to bureaucratize the government down to the lowest level of society or to involve local elites with its political system in a new way.[42] My argument, that the Nationalist government intended to reach both ends specified by Kuhn with one form of local organization, will be explained in the next chapter. There I will discuss how Self-Government was designed to allow for close supervision of the local community.

In order to prepare functionaries for Self-Government, in 1932 the government selected many educated young people to attend specially designed schools. In the beginning, some officials who used to serve under Feng Yuxiang's regime were also included in this program, but they were replaced shortly afterward. After an initial trial of the program, however, problems arose, especially when administrative guidelines conflicted with local realities. Besides, the central government soon discovered that many lower-level Self-Government officers shared the presumption that they were entitled to use their positions for personal benefit. Despite the efforts of the Nationalist government, the Self-Government program accomplished only a fraction of its goals. Discussions among state officials indicate a failure to understand the program's importance as a means to strengthen the Nationalist state. The government, therefore, decided in 1933 to shelve Self-Government momentarily, and a year later it proceeded to bureaucratize it under county government.[43] Thus, an institution that Sun Yat-sen had consid-

---

[41] Hsiao-tung Fei, *Peasant Life in China: A Field Study of Country Life in the Yangtze Valley* (London: Routledge & Kegan, 1939), 109–16.

[42] Kuhn, "Local Self-Government," 281–3.

[43] "Yi yue lai zhi minzheng" (Monthly Report from the Civil Administration), *Henan zhengzhi yuekan (Monthly Report of Political Affairs in Henan)* 2, no. 3 (1932): 2; Chen, "Quzhang renmian," 180; and "Henan sheng zhuanyuan fenshu huiyi an" (Minutes of the Henan Provincial Government, Special Commissioner's Office), 2, National Archives (1939): Archival no. 28-10-18: 12.

ered a means of achieving national integration and democracy became another form of bureaucratic control.[44]

Under bureaucratization, the Self-Government system was defined by the term *xiang-zhen-lu-lin* (village-town-lane-neighborhood), which suggests the amalgamation of all the control mechanisms of the subcounty ward, the household registration, and the *baojia*. According to the County Organizational Law, the government, beginning in late 1928, established the ward as the next unit below the county. A ward contained from ten to fifty townships. Below the ward was the village *(xiang)*, usually 100 to 250 households, and the town *(zhen)*. Beneath village and town units were the lane *(lu)*, usually a twenty-five-household unit, and the neighborhood *(lin)*, five households or fewer.[45] According to the initial plan, elections were held for the representatives of each unit, from the lowest to the highest level of the system. This election was conceived for the close supervision of the rural communities.[46] Indeed, through the system, the state positioned itself to assume close contact with all levels of local society. Meanwhile, Duara has pointed out in his study of Shandong that the government did try to bring the village community closer to the state in order to empower the community to perform the tasks of nation building and tax levying. I agree with Duara that the space between the state and the local society was narrowed through the implementation of the system under discussion.[47]

By 1932, the government decided to change the system of self-government to a *baojia* system in order to intensify neighborhood surveillance *(lianbao)* and household policing *(hujing)*. In 1935 the government rearranged the *bao* units to fit them into the natural boundary of villages and townships for better surveillance. The responsibility of household policing was then assigned to the neighborhood militia that had been formed in every ward. According to the provincial government report there was also a consistent plan for household registration around 1932. The government trained people for that task, which was carried out

---

[44] *The National Government's Outline of National Reconstruction*, promulgated in April 1924, explained that Self-Government was a form of mobilization to pave the way for the arrival of constitutionalism. However, the actual program of Self-Government established by the Nationalist government was quite different from Sun's ideal. See Kuhn, "Local Self-Government," 283.

[45] Henan sheng minzheng ting, "Shicha Qixian zhengzhi baogao" (Report on the Political Situation in Qi County), *Henan minzheng yuekan* (Kaifeng: Henan sheng zhengfu chuban she, 1932), 105.

[46] Kuhn, "Local Government," 345–52.

[47] Duara, *Culture, Power, and the State*, 63–4.

under specific guidelines.[48] With these changes, the traditional *baojia* system allowed the state to supervise the rural community much more effectively than it had the earlier dynasties, such as the Southern Song.[49] Under the Nationalist government, the state extended local administration to include the household police, whose main purpose was the control of local affairs rather than the maintenance of security.[50]

The Nationalist government also had an agenda for the local militia quite different from those of the previous regimes. As soon as the government had completed its rearrangement of the *baojia*, it severely restricted the activities of local militia to prevent them from being used by the local elites against the government. As chairman of the provincial government, Liu Zhi gave a speech at the first provincial conference of the militia organization in which he stated that the militia had been used against the government by local elites. Liu's speech clearly indicates the government's position opposing the use of the militia by local elities against itself.[51] Earlier, in late 1929, the Nationalist government had already requested that every male adult between the ages of twenty and forty undergo military training and participate in the militia. The order also called for the organization of local militia groups controlled by local elites into a county militia called the Regiment of Local Defense *(difang baowei tuan)*, whose sole headquarters was to be the county government.[52] By 1930, the government further affirmed its authority over all militia groups by sending an officer to each district to command them.

In 1930 the provincial government issued new regulations for the reorganization of the local militia, which had been in the hands of local elites who were using them to exercise power in their own communities. The

---

[48] "Shicha Qixian zhengzhi baogao" (June 1932), 105; Ibid. (May 1932), 71; "Jixian dashi ji," 33; Zhang, *Huojia xianzhi* (1991), 75; *Xinxiang xianzhi* (1991), 328–9; and Zou, *Huojia xianzhi*, 7 (1934): 15.

[49] Brian E. McKnight, *Village and Bureaucracy in Southern Sung China* (Chicago: University of Chicago Press, 1971), 38–94; and *Wunian lai Henan zhengzhi zong baogao (General Report of the Last Five-Years of Political Affairs in Henan)* (Kaifeng: Henan sheng zhengfu mishuchu, October 1935), 22.

[50] *Wu nian lai Henan zhengzhi*, 22.

[51] *Henan quansheng baojia yundong huiyi congkan (Minutes from the Henan Provincial Conference on the Baojia Movement)* (Kaifeng: Henan sheng zhengfu chuban she, October 1, 1931), 15.

[52] *Xichuan wenshi ziliao* (1989), 112.

The same phenomenon was also noticed in Ting County in northern China, pointing to a comprehensive national policy. See Sidney Gamble, *Ting Hsien: A North China Rural Community* (Berkeley: University of California Press, 1954), 135.

ultimate aim of the regulations was the control of these militia. In 1931, after the reorganization, the provincial government divided the province into ten districts and appointed a militia commander for each. Once the militias were fully taken over by the government, they were prohibited from leaving their native county without a specific order, even for such suitable reasons as chasing bandits – a measure probably designed to prevent local militias from engaging in antigovernment activity.[53]

In 1932 the government reorganized the militia groups so that each was linked to the provincial headquarters through a "joint defense" *(lianfang)* program. Although initially a few county natives who had "previously contributed significantly to the maintaining of public order" were appointed heads of militias, the government shortly declared that only the county magistrate should command a militia. Once authority over the militias had been rigidly defined, the government restricted the number of firearms allowed for each militia unit.[54] The state had thus completely tightened its control over local militias in this region between 1930 and 1933. As early as the end of 1931, travelers to Henan, such as the freelance writer Zhao Chen, concluded that the Nationalist government had nearly gained full control of the local militia. But by the end of 1933, the Nationalist government had definitely assumed full control of the local militia.[55]

Actually, the reclamation of state authority over local militias was only a fraction of what the Nationalist government aspired to accomplish. Its ultimate goal was to transform these private groups into a military resource for the government and to permanently eradicate their potential menace to the regime. While the reorganization was underway, the provincial government reevaluated the performance of the native militia officers who then occupied many secondary positions. One crucial criterion of the review was cooperation with state authority; those found uncooperative were summarily dismissed.[56]

Furthermore, in 1931 the provincial government sponsored the first provincial conference of local militias. During the conference, it was

---

[53] *Wunian lai Henan zhengzhi*, 1; *Baojia yundong huiyi congkan*, 12.

[54] *Henan sheng zhengfu gongbao (Henan Provincial Government Communique)*, 470 (Kaifeng: Henan Provincial Government, 1932), 2; *Wu nian lai Henan zhengzhi: caizheng*, 2.

[55] Chen, *Nongcun Xianzhuang*, 2. Quoted in Shen Songqiao, "Difang jingying yu guojia quanli: minguo shiqide Wanxi zizhi, 1930–1943" (Local Elites and State Power: Wanxi Self-Government during the Republican Period, 1930–1943), in *Zhongyang yanjiu yuan jindai shi yanjiu suo jikan*, 21 (1992): 388.

[56] *Baojia yundong huiyi congkan*, 11.

resolved that every militiaman undergo indoctrination of the GMD. Regardless of objections from rank-and-file militiamen, the political education program was implemented and the training process was closely administered by officials sent from the provincial government. Militiamen were also required to undergo more intensified military training; both areas of education and training were intended to prepare them for threats from abroad and from the Communists. The provincial government in 1932 ordered the county government to reorganize and to take full command of the local militia. After the order was received, the county government was given the responsibility of retraining the militia according to government requirements. Local elites resisted the retraining out of a concern that the militiamen would then have to follow the orders of the government, not those of the local elites. The final transition from local militia into military resource came in 1935. The government changed the name of the militia organizations to the Candidates for Conscription, designating them the reserve force for the Nationalist army. The county magistrate was again commissioned to be the commanding officer of the militia of each county unit. These measures asserted state control over the local military.[57]

Gerald M. Britan and Ronald Cohen maintain that a modern bureaucracy must "achieve rational efficiency through well-defined formal structures. Each bureaucracy administers its official's duties through an explicit hierarchical system. Specified roles and statuses divide necessary work into orderly spheres of professional competence."[58] To create such a modern bureaucracy, the Nationalist government also focused on two essential weaknesses within local government: inefficiency and corruption. To be sure, an important feature of the modern bureaucracy was professionalization, but the Nationalist government did not comprehend the need for professionalization until, confronted by the inefficiency of its local governments, it began to understand (but then only to a limited degree) that efficiency was the "power of bureaucracy."[59] That vague comprehension led to the establishment of governmental procedures and the training of administrative personnel. In 1932 the government

---

[57] *Baojia yundong huiyi congkan*, 10; *Zhengfu gongbao*, 371 (1932): 3; "Mishu chu geke gongzuo gaiyao," 23; and *Wunian lai Henan zhengzhi: caizheng*, 4–9.

[58] Gerald M. Britan and Ronald Cohen, "Toward an Anthropology of Formal Organizations," in *Hierarchy and Society*, Gerald M. Britan and Ronald Cohen, eds. (Philadelphia: Institute for the Study of Human Issues, 1980), 14.

[59] Thomas Metzger, *The Internal Organization of Ching Bureaucracy: Legal, Normative, and Communication Aspects* (Cambridge, MA: Harvard University Press, 1973), 2.

granted permission for the public election of the subcounty ward chief. After each election, the provincial government was to carefully screen every electee before confirming him. After confirmation, ward chiefs would be trained intensively to familiarize them with the government's procedures and political doctrine. The same process was later adopted for the *baojia* head.[60]

As an additional step, the government reviewed the performance of all local officials above ward level. Although the method was similar to that employed during the late Qing (according to John Watt, the method included a wide array of items), it also incorporated a survey of public opinion of each official.[61] The review's criteria included administrative performance, police work, evaluation of ward chief, prohibition of drug production and opium smoking, relief projects, public hygiene, and the reversal of foot binding. In 1932 the provincial government decided to publicly post the results of the annual official review. This move not only gave the provincial administration the advantage of supervising the county officials but also secured the support of the general population. After each review, usually conducted quarterly, the county officials were divided into four divisions, according to their performance. Those who received the lowest ratings either received a warning or were dismissed. Although the review eventually became a formality, initially it promoted efficiency.[62]

As for corruption in local government, Barrington Moore has noted that the impediment for any preindustrial state to maintain a large bureaucracy was its inability to pay the salaries of its functionaries. During the imperial period, the Chinese answer to that difficult problem was to turn a blind eye to more or less open corruption.[63] Previous studies have verified that the Qing government's permission for the collection of "customary fees" by the local officials – fees from which the local government derived the bulk of revenue – led to nationwide corruption during that dynasty,[64] and helped foster a political culture con-

---

[60] *Wunian lai Henan zhengzhi*, 17, 20, 43–4; "Yi yue lai zhi minzheng," 6, no. 7 (April 1936): 2; Zou, *Huojia xianzhi*, 6 (1934): 2; Xiao, *Xiuwu xianzhi*, 6 (1931): 37; and Han, *Nongcun diaocha*, 72–3.

[61] John Watt, *The District Magistrate in Late Imperial China* (New York: Columbia University Press, 1972), 169–84.

[62] "Xingzheng baogao," 70, 72; *Wunian lai Henan zhengzhi*, 1–24; and "Yi yue lai zhi minzheng," 2, no. 3 (March 1932): 3–4.

[63] Barrington Moore Jr., *Social Origins of Dictatorship and Democracy* (Boston: Beacon Press, 1966), 172.

[64] Ch'u, *Local Government*, 28–9, 196–7.

ducive to corruption during the Republican period.[65] Aware of the problem, the Nationalist government prompted officials to report one another for corruption or misconduct. Once they had received a series of complaints against a high-ranking official, the provincial government would send an investigator. Because of the complaints of ward chiefs, county magistrates were often the targets of such investigations. In 1936 the provincial administration even allowed local officials to report incidents of wrongdoing by mail. According to a 1936 administrative report of the secretary office of the provincial government, about six hundred cases were filed every month by the people in Henan. Among them, several dozens were filed against the county magistrates. Those cases were handled by the provincial government itself.[66]

The Nationalist state, through numerous pivotal advances in the bureaucratic aspect of state making, was well on its way to becoming a modern state. Such was the progress of the Republican state in northern Henan, in which each state entity attempted, to some degree, to create a powerful state bureaucracy at the local level – and most, especially the Nationalist government, succeeded. But how did these successes in the bureaucratic aspect of state making affect the ability of the Republican state to increase its financial resources?

The Expansion of Fiscal Control

If the control of local resources is a cardinal goal of any state during its making, the state makers in the Republican period encountered several significant obstacles to its attainment.[67] The first stemmed from the tension between the revenue-seeking state and the tax-paying villagers. Under the Qing government's aggressive search for revenues during its late phase of state building, taxes multiplied dramatically in the form of miscellaneous surcharges, particularly the *mujuan* (nonstatutory surcharges), levied at twice the statutory rate so the government could honor foreign debts and finance modern projects. This burdensome taxation – in comparison with the relatively light taxes during most of the

---

[65] Eastman, *The Abortive Revolution: China under Nationalist Rule, 1927–1937* (Cambridge, MA: Harvard University Press, 1990), 296–303.

[66] "Mishu chu geke gongzuo gaiyao," 99; and "Henan sheng mishu chu zuijin gongzuo gaikuang" (Report on the Secretary Office of the Henan Provincial Government), *Henan zhengzhi (Political Affairs in Henan)* 6, no. 7 (1936): 2, 4.

[67] Arthur Smith argues that tax levying is the foremost goal of any state. See Arthur H. Smith, *Village Life in China* (New York: Fleming H. Revell, 1899), 228.

Ming and early Qing dynasties – generated tension between the government and the taxpayers in rural areas.[68] The financial burden did not abate when the dynasty ceased to exist, however. During the ensuing political disarray, in which various political contenders competed for the mandate of the country, it again fell most heavily on the peasantry, increasing antigovernment sentiment. During the Republican period, therefore, the state makers faced a dilemma: the state needed more revenue to finance its state-building projects and military efforts, but raising those funds risked magnifying tension within the local society and, in the end, hampered the state's endeavors at that level.

The second obstacle to the control of local resources was that, since the late Qing, the provincial and county finances remained continuously undifferentiated, which, in addition to the confusion it engendered, served as a constant source of contention between the two levels of administration as they vied for a share of state revenue.[69] Ramon Myers's data from Hebei and Shandong indicate that during the late Qing most of the revenues that usually came from the land tax were turned over to the provincial finance office.[70] As the competition for revenue escalated at the end of the dynasty, the state lost nearly most of its share of vital financial resources to the local government, which retained them for such administrative expenses as official salaries and maintaining police. This constant rivalry between the central authority and local government for the control of revenues, especially from the land tax, the custom tax, the gabelle, and the *lijin* tax – all regular sources of income for the state – continued during the early Republican period.[71]

The major barrier to total state control of local resources was the local elite community's involvement in taxation. During the tax increases of

---

[68] Hilary J. Beattie's study of Tongzheng County of Anhui demonstrates that the land taxes were not high during the Ming dynasty. See Hilary J. Beattie, *Land and Lineage in China: A Study of T'ung-Ch'eng County, Anhwei, in the Ming and Ch'ing Dynasties* (Cambridge: Cambridge University Press, 1979), 67. Before the Taiping Rebellion, the tax structure under the Qing government was similar to that of the late Ming and the land-tax burden was also light due to relatively low government spending. See Yeh-chien Wang, *Land Taxation in Imperial China, 1750–1911* (Cambridge, MA: Harvard University Press, 1973), 8–12, 49–61, 129–33.

[69] See Philip A. Kuhn, "Local Taxation and Finance in Republican China," in *Select Papers from the Center for Far Eastern Studies*, 3, Susan Mann Jones, ed. (1978–79): 113–31; and Duara, *Culture, Power, and the State*, 77–85.

[70] Myers, *Peasant Economy*, 85–6.

[71] Hsi-sheng Ch'i, *Warlord Politics in China, 1916–1928* (Stanford: Stanford University Press, 1976), 154–5.

the late Qing, many of these powerful citizens had acted as tax farmers, passing land and household information to the county government and then helping to collect taxes. The elites not only affixed more financial burdens to the rural population, but also consistently took part in negotiations over tax rates on behalf of the local community against the state. Both activities hampered the state's ability to tax local communities.[72] To overcome these barriers, aside from dealing with the local elites (since this section deals with state expansion in the fiscal domain, the issue will be discussed in Chapter 8), the state needed a modern fiscal system to regulate revenue collection, to supervise the local government on taxation, and to maintain its access to other local resources. To attain these goals was one of the greatest challenges to any state government of the Republican period.

The Early Republican Period. At the beginning of Yuan Shikai's era, the primary goal of the central government was to augment its revenue through a surtax on land *(mujuan)*. The entire tax rates escalated immediately after Yuan Shikai became the provisional president of the Republic of China. As a result, the land tax nearly doubled.[73] A year later, the Department of Treasury of the provincial government not only proclaimed another tax increase, but introduced a new tax on silk.[74] Increases in the land surtax proceeded well into 1915, and within a year, the rate in some areas had even tripled as the government added *mujuan.*[75]

Accompanying the collection of land surtax, in 1913 the new governor, Zhang Zhenfang, inaugurated a stamp duty,[76] and instructed local officials to collect taxes from the Manchurian families that fit the following criteria: (1) families that were dying out; (2) families that had paid their agents for their services by giving them land subject to negligible rent; (3) families whose land had been confiscated because family members had been convicted of crime.[77] When the central government eradicated Self-Government in 1914, it had intended to circumscribe the

---

[72] Huang, *Peasant Economy*, 286–7; and Duara, *Culture, Power, and the State*, 73–7.

[73] Wang Tianjiang, "Henan lishi: zhongpian, xihua de beiju" ("History of Henan: part two, the tragedy of westernization") (Unpublished Manuscript).

[74] Xiao, *Xiuwu xianzhi*, 9 (1931): 42; and Han, *Xinxiangxian xuzhi*, 2 (1923): 18.

[75] Wang, "Henan lishi."

[76] Yang, *Xiuwu xianzhi* (1986), 14; Han, *Xinxiangxian xuzhi*, 1 (1923): 18; and Zou, *Huojia xianzhi*, 6 (1934): 4.

[77] The same measure was taken in North China. See Gamble, *Ting Hsien*, 170–3.

local elite community's involvement in taxation while strengthening its own grip.[78]

In addition to its taxation measures, Yuan Shikai's government also strove to mitigate the financial strain from foreign and domestic loans by distributing paper notes. With no silver reserve behind them, the notes devalued rapidly against coins and abruptly threw the monetary system into turmoil.[79] And in 1915 the government converted the payment for the *diding* (head and land tax) from silver to silver *yuan* in order to compensate for revenues lost due to the discontinuance of the leap month; the diminishing quality of silver; and inflation.[80] Although both procedures brought the government some immediate relief in terms of revenue, they hastened the erosion of public confidence in the government's fiscal policy.

Despite the substantial success of Yuan Shikai's efforts to minimize local elites' involvement in taxation, they had been aimed only at gaining immediate access to local resources. There was, therefore, little evidence of any desire by the state to reinstate a traditional fiscal system after it had been dissolved with the dynasty. Nor was there any sign that any fiscal system would be created to meet modern needs.

The end of the Yuan Shikai era marked the inception of a period of warlordism in China, during which taxes continued to increase, and at a faster pace than before. In the late 1910s the tax rate was still at the level set by Yuan Shikai's government. Increases had occurred on only two occasions, once in 1916 when governor Zhao Ti, serving Li Yuanhong's Beijing government, raised the rate of the gabelle, and the other when the provincial government under Feng Guozhang changed the payment of *diding* and *caoliang* (water-transported grain) taxes from silver to silver coin. But between 1916 and 1920, when Henan was under the various authorities of Li Yuanhong, Feng Guozhang, and Xu Shichang, the *diding* increased by 50%.[81] This was only a prelude to a trend of exhaustive taxation in the ensuing decade.

A harbinger of this trend was the collection of taxes by the local government in advance, a result of the insecure tenure of state authority. In

---

[78] Kuhn, "Local Taxation," 121.

   For an example of the central government's efforts, see Yang, *Xiuwu xianzhi* (1986), 14.

[79] Jerome Ch'en, *Yuan Shih-k'ai* (Stanford: Stanford University Press, 1972), 180–4.

[80] Zhao Boyan, "Minguo shiqi de Henan sheng tianfu gaikuang" (General Situation of Land Taxation in Henan Province during the Republican Period), in *Henan shizhi ziliao*, 5 (1984): 73.

[81] Wang, "Henan lishi."

1919 some county governments collected taxes for the subsequent years in advance, and the practice was soon widespread, especially after 1921.[82] In the 1920s, northern Henan experienced a rapid increase in taxes, due not only to advance collection but also to the creation of many new tax categories and the introduction of various surcharges by different authorities. To enforce the collection of taxes in general, the government founded a Bureau of Household Surveys in every county to assess household and land-holding taxes.[83] In the cities, collection stations for *lijin* taxes also multiplied. A contemporary local history report shows there were nearly 120 stations in Henan for the collection of the *lijin* tax.[84]

Not only did tax rates escalate, the frequency of collection also increased. In 1920, when Henan was governed by Xu Shichang, Zhao Ti originated a plan for collecting famine relief funds. He collected 3,500,000 *yuan* within a short time. In the same year, the government a lso added a subsidy tax *(buzhu juan)*. Although most of these surtaxes were initially conceived ad hoc, they became permanent fixtures and eventually their actual amount far exceeded the total amount of the regular taxes that were usually collected in the three categories of state, province, and county during the Republican period.[85] The surtax phenomenon was symptomatic of the collapse of the state fiscal system at the local level.

When Feng Yuxiang became the military governor of Henan in May 1922 he had no intention of altering the trend of taxation; his preeminent interest was to secure financial resources to sustain his troops. According to James Sheridan, during the few months when Feng's troops were staying in Henan, Feng received no financial support from the central government. He was obliged to collect all the funds himself. Not until the fall of 1922 did the central government promise Feng a monthly remittance of 200,000 *yuan* from the revenue of Henan to cover the expenses of his army. However, for a ten-month period Feng received a total of only 160,000 *yuan* from the central government.[86] With the objective of securing financial resources for his troops in mind, he required local officials to disclose the amount of tax being collected and demanded that county governments submit their expenditures for his

---

[82] Ibid.
[83] Xiao, *Xiuwu xianzhi*, 6 (1931): 37.
[84] Wang, "Henan lishi." See also, Wou, *Militarism*, 75.
[85] Chen, *Tangyin xianzhi*, 513; Zhang, *Huojia xianzhi* (1991), 426; and *Nanyang shizhi*, 590.
[86] Sheridan, *Chinese Warlord*, 126.

supervision.[87] Feng also attempted to stabilize the depreciation of the silver coin, which was debasing the value of all funds being collected throughout the country.[88]

A few months later, when Feng left Henan, more taxes were heaped upon the people of northern Henan under the administrations of Li Yuanhong, Duan Qirui, and Wu Peifu. During that time, the land tax also increased precipitously, sometimes doubling within two years. According to a Japanese survey conducted by Amano Motonosuke, the land tax increased dramatically in Shandong during the 1920s. In 1925, for instance, the index point had risen to 268 from a baseline of 100 in 1902. Two years later the index point jumped to 468. I believe the citizens of Henan would have experienced similar severe taxation during this period.[89] Tax resistance against the provincial authorities escalated concomitantly. One of the most serious incidents transpired when Wu Peifu was in control of the region, during which the Red Spear summoned a large number of followers from Ji, Qi, Hua, and Hui counties against Wu's troops. Even such open defiance was not sufficient to convince the authorities to diminish their excessive taxation.[90]

As soon as Feng Yuxiang had returned to power in Henan in 1927, his administration began to tackle the problem of unreasonable levying. In the beginning, it set a cap on the total amount of surtax to be collected by the local government – an amount equal to the land tax. But shortly thereafter, the administration continued to impose numerous surtaxes that ultimately totaled nearly thirty times the amount of the land tax, for Feng desperately needed funds to support his troops. Therefore, it is reasonable for James Sheridan to blame Feng Yuxiang's overtaxation for the famine in Henan, one of several provinces that suffered from that disaster. Sheridan argues the famine in Henan stemmed not from a scarcity of food it was able to produce but from the shortage of money from the peasants to pay for it – a shortage brought about primarily by Feng's excessive levying.[91]

Thus far, the exhaustive taxation under various warlord governments had clearly been motivated by financial desperation. Impelled by similar considerations, local governments employed similar methods to augment

[87] Guo and Chen, *Feng Yuxiang*, 49.   [88] Sheridan, *Chinese Warlord*, 113–15.

[89] Myers, *Peasant Economy*, 264.

[90] Henan sheng jixian zhi zong bianji shi, "Jixian shehui zhi" ("Social history of Ji County"), (Jixian, Unpublished Manuscript), 85.

[91] Sheridan, *Chinese Warlord*, 247–9.

their revenues. Their actions, of course, merely exacerbated the oppressive taxation.

The Nanjing Decade. When it came to power, the Nationalist government faced a financial predicament. It had depleted its funds during its military campaign against the warlords and needed revenues to finance its modernization programs as well as to keep up with the expansion of its bureaucracy. In addition, previous regimes had almost totally exhausted local resources. At the beginning of its administration, the Nationalist government's basic concern was similar to that of its predecessors: to increase its revenues. It did nothing to avert further deterioration of the fiscal condition in the countryside. After the Ministry of Finance, which was created to expand provincial control of local finance, combined *diding* and *caoliang* taxes into a single category *(dingcao)* in 1929, a vast increase of taxes ensued, initiated by both central and local administrations.[92] Confusion and conflict thus arose between the two offices: the finance bureaus, established by the ministries of Interior and Finance in 1928, and the county finance offices.[93]

In the ensuing years, the growth of government revenues and expenditures, especially those of its local administration, continued. Ramon H. Myers's study of Hebei and Shandong shows that most of the new taxes took the form of *tankuan* (tax appropriations), which were used to cover the salary of local officials during the expansion of county government and for the expenses of county police and militia. But expenditures for education and economic development were reduced.[94] Myers's finding could well apply to northern Henan. In early 1929 for example, the Nationalist government had imposed various surtaxes to every household, including the Educational Fee, the Public Security Fee, the Law Enforcement Officers Fee, and the Militia Fee. But eventually, most of the funds collected were spent for the police and militia instead of education.[95]

This increase also affected commercial taxes. In 1931 the central government created a new category called *yingye shui* (business tax) to replace the *lijin* tax as an effort to increase its collection of business taxes. The application of the new tax was more uniform and less corrupt than

[92] *Henan xinzhi*, 307; and Ch'i, *Warlord Politics*, 175.
[93] Kuhn, "Local Taxation," 120–4.   [94] Myers, *Peasant Economy*, 62–6.
[95] Zou, *Huojia xianzhi*, 5 (1934): 14–16.

that of the *lijin*.[96] These government undertakings perpetuated the tension between the state and the rural population, similar to the situation Sidney Gamble notes in 1928 in Ting County of Hebei Province, when the Nationalist government rearranged the previous tax program, abolishing some taxes but eventually adding more.[97]

Having gradually comprehended the problem, the Nationalist government first focused on the reduction of taxes. In 1930 it announced that it would collect only 70% of the land tax and concede the remaining 30% as a rebate of advance taxes collected during earlier regimes. Therefore, the government reduced 30% of rent in northern Henan. The government also terminated several surtaxes.[98] Despite occasional financial squeezes by the government troops – in 1931 one division of the army collected several million *yuan* from Anyang County without going through provincial or local government channels – the general population in several counties took these moves as gestures of good faith.[99]

The government's efforts at tax abatement continued in 1932. By then, it had begun to adopt a fiscal policy that was not only more stable but more responsive to people's needs than its policies of the early years. The government lowered taxes during natural disasters, and it allowed the continuation of the traditional method for land measurement when the new method proved impractical. Meanwhile, the provincial government began to carefully observe the county administration of taxation. In a number of cases, it ordered the county government to abolish unauthorized levies. Occasionally, it sent inspectors to examine the taxation procedures of the local administration. In addition, it issued orders to each of the county governments, compelling them to comply with proper procedures, to rely on tax collection agencies instead of tax farmers, and to report the amount of land tax being collected. All these measures by the provincial government produced little effect; the county administrations continued their usual practices. The government also increased pressure on rich landowners. Only those who registered their deeds with the government were recognized as legitimate owners – a policy devised

[96] *Wunian lai Henan zhengzhi: caizheng*, 22.

[97] Gamble, *Ting Hsien*, 167–9.

[98] *Wunian lai Henan zhengzhi: caizheng*, 8–15, 19; *Zhengfu gongbao*, 310 (1932): 3; "Mishu chu geke gongzuo gaiyao," 2, no. 10 (1932): 5; and *Wunian lai shizheng tongji: caizheng*, (1935), 30–8, Material no. 25.

[99] Qing Guitai et al., *Henan sheng Anyang xianzhi (Gazetteer of Anyang County in Henan)* (Anyang: Anyang wenxian bianji weiyuan hui, 1933), 1126.

not only to ensure personal ownership rights, but also to redistribute the tax responsibility among landowners.[100] As Kathryn Bernhart has noted for northern Zhejiang, during the GMD era the government started a campaign that succeeded to some degree in limiting rent increases.[101] In northern Henan, the emphasis of the Nationalist government effort seems to have been on restricting landlords from making usurious loans to tenants. In addition, the county governments were instructed to severely punish those who resisted taxation.[102]

Despite these efforts to ease the tension between government and the majority of the population, the trend of exhaustive taxation continued. Even with the restraint placed on the county government and the retraction of a number of surtaxes, *tanpai* persisted into 1933. As Tables 7.1 and 7.2 show, the number of surtaxes and their rates were still staggering. Within a few months, for instance, people in one county had to come up with more than 10,000 *yuan*, for fees ranging from a national salvation program to administrative expenses for ward offices. Most surtaxes, however, were exclusively for the expenses of the local government (see Tables 7.1 and 7.2).[103]

To further restrain the county government from excessive levying, the Nationalist government adopted standard accounting procedures in 1934 and began to train accountants, which it planned to then install in the administration of the various counties. In order to streamline the procedures for regular taxation, the government converted the form of payment of *dingcao* taxes into silver *yuan* and adopted a new name for the land tax *(tianfu)*. In 1935, the government placed a cap on the amount of surtax allowed on grains (less than 25% of the total amount of annual tax), and it abolished certain other surtaxes. Finally, a specific order was issued to control the *tanpai*.[104]

As soon as these measures began to take effect, however, the provincial government observed, not surprisingly, a steep decrease in revenues.

---

[100] "Mishu chu geke gongzuo gaiyao," 5–6, 9; *Zhengfu gongbao*, 417 (1932): 1; "Yi yue lai zhi minzheng," 4, no. 6 (June 1933): 2; *Wunian lai Henan zhengzhi: caizheng*, 22; and "Xingzheng baogao," (May 1932), 71.

[101] Bernhardt, *Rents, Taxes, and Peasant Resistance*, 161–88.

[102] "Mishu chu geke gongzuo gaiyao," 2; and "Yi yue lai zhi caizheng" (Finance of the Past Month), *Henan zhengzhi yuekan (Monthly Report of Political Affairs in Henan)* 4, no. 12 (1934): 1.

[103] Han, *Nongcun diaocha*, 79–82.

[104] *Wunian lai Henan zhengzhi: caizheng*, 16, 19, 44–5; and Xuexi wenshi weiyuan hui, *Weihui wenshi ziliao (Weihui Local History)*, 3 (Weihui: Zhengxie Henan weihui, 1991): 48–9.

Table 7.1. Tanpai *in Xinxiang County, Ward 1 (January–April, 1933)*

Local security training fee:	2,400
Local security administration expenses:	300
Instruction fee:	1,400
Ward militia expenses:	2,300
Ward office administration expenses:	1,800
"National salvation" contribution:	2,500
Anti-bandit campaign award:	300
Communication expenses:	108
	TOTAL 11,108 *yuan*

Source: Han Bangfu et al., *Henan sheng nongcun diaocha* (Henan Village Survey) (Shanghai: Shangwu yinshu guan, 1934), 79.

It immediately suspected tax evasion, and launched a provincewide land survey to delineate the tax obligation of each landowner. The government then charged the *bao* chief with the enforcement of tax collection and the reporting of those who delayed or refused payment. A conference of county magistrates discussed ways to multiply revenues without resorting to additional surcharges and decided to streamline procedures for the collection of land and sales taxes. The participants also agreed to allow the accounting officers sent by the provincial government to supervise county finances.[105] Shortly thereafter, however, the Nationalist government transferred all responsibility for county finances to the county administration.[106]

In the end, all these methods netted the Nationalist government increased revenues, and so the *tanpai* was allowed to continue into the late 1930s. The combined rate of the new surtaxes ultimately exceeded ten times the rate of the previous ones (see Table 7.3).[107]

Lloyd E. Eastman generally considers *tanpai* to have been harmful to the relationship between the Nationalist government and the peasants. He argues it created a real burden on the peasants and, moreover, that most of the *tanpai* were illegal, since they had not been officially

---

[105] *Zhengfu gongbao*, 150 (1931): 6; Ibid., 186: 3; "Fenshu huiyi an" (Nanjing, 1939), Archival no. 28-10-18, 11, 26; and *Wunian lai Henan zhengzhi: caizheng*, 47–9.

[106] Kuhn, "Local Taxation," 125–30.

[107] Han, *Nongcun diaocha*, 79, 80.

Table 7.2. Tanpai *in Dashi Village, Hui County (January–July, 1933)*

January	
Ward office	
Temporary administration fee:	32.0
Local security fee:	30.4
February	
Meat-processing tax:	2.29
Rice surtax:	72.00
Seedling fee:	3.64
House maintenance fee:	4.55
February 24	
Printing surtax:	2.00
Self-Government administration expenses:	2.00
Flag fee:	0.90
March	
Ward primary school tax:	16.20
Construction fee:	60.32
Public primary school fee:	0.38
March 3	
Primary school fee:	28.39
Truck and wagon fee:	34.1
May	
Bandits clearing and related matters fee:	4.13
Local security uniform fee:	3.22
Meat-processing fee:	3.22
Seedling fee:	3.64
Airplane surtax:	16.15
May 30	
Military trainee salary:	16.15
June	
Local security expenses:	16.15
Ward office administration fee:	12.16
June 6	
Military trainee salary:	0.70
July 5	
Printing tax:	2.00
	TOTAL 366.69 *yuan*

Source: Han Bangfu et al., *Henan sheng nongcun diaocha* (Henan Village Survey) (Shanghai: Shangwu yinshu guan, 1934), 80–2.

Table 7.3. Tanpai *in Baiquan Village, Hui County (1930)*

Military expenses (collected by the Treasury Department):	95.50
Food fee:	11.04
Public relations fee:	85.80
Wheat quota fee:	96.275
Local military expenses:	98.00
Firewood fee:	14.35
Saddle fee:	20.00
Autumn fee:	22.00
Protection (from bandits) fee:	29.00
Conscription substitute expenses:	309.00
Messenger fee:	83.00
Postal fee:	30.00
Wheat tax:	62.70
Ward office administration expenses:	45.56
Bandit clearing campaign fee:	80.00
"Military personnel" contribution:	48.00
Medicine fee:	55.00
Printing tax:	5.50
Printing of paper currency fee:	19.40
Tobacco tax:	108.00
Additional printing tax:	11.91
Animal-related transaction fee:	254.00
Transportation fee:	304.00
Transportation-related fee:	10.50
Drivers fee:	82.20
Wheat shipment fee:	39.22
Other:	592.716
	TOTAL 2,612.671 *yuan*

Source: Han Bangfu et al., *Henan sheng nongcun diaocha* (Henan Village Survey) (Shanghai: Shangwu yinshu guan, 1934), 79–80.

approved by the higher authorities. Given the situation as Lloyd E. Eastman has described it, I believe the peasants would not have conceived the tax increases as reasonable. They resented any kind of tax increase, especially when the local government used *tanpai* to heap numerous miscellaneous surtaxes on the people in the countryside.[108] This growing resentment certainly contributed to the continuous

---

[108] Lloyd E. Eastman, *Seeds of Destruction: Nationalist China in War and Revolution, 1937–1949* (Stanford: Stanford University Press, 1984), 45–6, 54–9.

tension between the Nationalist state and the peasants during the late 1930s.

The Nationalist government was initially triumphant both in its competition with local government for revenues and in its crusade to prevent rich landlords from further exploiting the peasants. The former efforts expanded its revenues, whereas the latter helped assuage the animosity with which the majority of the peasantry had regarded it. However, the government lacked a total commitment for modernizing its fiscal system. When experiencing financial straits it had resorted, like its predecessors, to excessive taxation. It might have won the battle over control of local resources against both local government and local elites, but the Nationalist government lost the war whose prize was the support of the rural population. In this same period, the Republican state fared quite differently in the southwestern region, as we shall see.

SOUTHWESTERN HENAN

The Expansion of Administrative Control

The Early Republican Period. At the beginning of the Republican period, southwestern Henan was under the dominion of various regional authorities, such as the army named *luefenyongjun*.[109] As soon as Yuan Shikai's influence had extended to the region, his provincial administration instantly assigned new county magistrates and set out to reorganize the county governments. Under its efforts, the county governments underwent radical changes not only in the titles but in the organization of their administrative offices. Following this reorganization, the county governments resumed their operations, but, given such unfavorable conditions as remoteness from the provincial authority, they generally lacked the power to carry out orders from above.[110]

In March 1913 an initiative from the central government on rearranging the administrative system began to be implemented in Henan. According to the initiative, the former Nanyang prefecture *(fu)* was turned into a county, Nanzhao County was placed under a different district, and Xichuan was changed from an independent subprefecture into a regular county. Following that, on January 22, 1913 the provincial gov-

---

[109] See the chronology of Nanyang, Neixiang, and Xichuan counties in the Appendix (Tables A.2, A.3, A.4).

[110] "Nanzhao xianzhi," 28; *Nanyang shizhi*, 269, 320; "Neixiang xianzhi: dashi ji," 14; and *Xichuan xianzhi* (1990), 61.

ernment designated a Commissioner of Nanyang Regional Security. Though the principal obligation of the commissioner was to maintain security, he became the de facto highest authority in the region.[111]

The paramount concern for the general population in southwestern Henan at that time was safety against banditry. The authorities, however, were primarily concerned with the rapid spread of violence – many individuals owned firearms and militia groups controlled by the local elite community had proliferated. In February 1912, immediately after the end of the Qing dynasty, for example, a county security force of approximately one hundred militiamen was being organized in Nanyang County by *luefenyongjun*.[112] When local military expansion persisted the government stepped in to control it.

As soon as the Commissioner of Regional Security arrived in Nanyang in 1913, he formed the Central Bureau for Bandit Suppression, with the unmistakable intent of subjugating all private militia groups in the region under his authority. According to his initial orders, the duty of the militia was confined to gathering privately owned firearms and assisting government endeavors against banditry. A year later, the provincial government authorized the formation of a security unit, the Regiment of Local Defense, in each county. Its apparent objective was to consolidate all private militias into a government-sponsored organization over which the county magistrate had direct authority.[113]

Having achieved modest success in controlling the local militia, the government turned its attention to such elite institutions as the county assembly. Unlike its attitude toward the county assemblies in northern Henan, however, the provincial authority was ambivalent toward the assemblies created under various transient military powers. Although the presence of these organizations might generate a challenge to the county authority, they could also render assistance to the government (e.g., by coordinating community efforts). Therefore, the county assemblies were reinstated in April 1912, a month after the military governor, Zhang Zhenfang, had terminated them. Finally, by January 1914, an order from the central government abolished all county assemblies throughout the country.[114]

---

[111] "Nanzhao xianzhi," 28; *Nanyang xianzhi* (1990), 119; *Xichuan xianzhi* (1990), 24; and *Nanyang shizhi*, 29.

[112] *Nanyang xianzhi* (1990), 167; and *Nanyang shizhi*, 324.

[113] *Xichuan wenshi ziliao* (1989), 110; and *Xichuan xianzhi* (1990), 17, 471.

[114] *Nanyang xianzhi* (1990), 23, 270; and *Nanyang shizhi*, 28.

While flip-flopping on the county assemblies, the provincial government was nevertheless consistent in dealing with other private elite institutions, including the Education Promotion Office. In most counties, this office was ordered closed soon after the county assemblies were, indicating that the administration's determination to restrain the activities of the local elites had never wavered. Only in Neixiang County, where the office remained open, did the provincial government assign a county education commissioner.[115]

Compared to the progress achieved in northern Henan, the state under Yuan Shikai had limited success in the southwest. Although, the results were respectable if the area's social, political, and geographic conditions were taken into account. The regime's steadfast endeavors in resuming its authority and eradicating the potential challenges to its power were rewarded with some degree of influence over local activities.

After Yuan Shikai's regime ended and the government allowed its attention to wander from the region, southwestern Henan gradually separated itself from the provincial authority. Bureaucratic changes in the latter part of the early Republican period thus became sporadic and were usually originated by the local authorities or various small-scale military strongmen passing through the region. These few changes included renaming the county government, patronizing some elite organizations, and rearranging subcounty wards. Even with such limited undertakings, most provincial administrations of the period desired to use the region's private militia organizations in their campaign against banditry. For instance, in 1917, because the provincial authority under Feng Guozhang was unable to provide sufficient troops for security in the southwest, the military governor, Zhao Ti, ordered each county to form a county security force called the Security Patrol Group. Moreover, each of the four wards of Nanyang County had a division of the security patrol. In 1921 the security patrol was changed to a county police force, called successively the Government Military Police, the Self-Defense Militia, and the Local Militia Defense Bureau.[116]

In 1922, when Feng Yuxiang assumed the governorship of Henan under Xu Shichang's Beijing administration, he was able to exercise limited authority over the region, instituting a few new departments for each county administration. In Nanyang County these included depart-

---

[115] "Neixiang xianzhi: dashi ji," 17.
[116] *Nanyang shizhi*, 30–1, 324; *Xixia xianzhi* (1990), 19, 59; and *Nanyang xianzhi* (1990), 167.

ments of education, finance, and interior. However, Feng's influence was short-lived since a regional military force, the *Yujun* (Yu Army), occupied the area. Subsequent changes in the administration of the counties were most likely the accomplishment of the *Yujun* rather than of Feng's administration.[117]

After 1922 various military authorities attempted to use the military resources of southwestern Henan against other political powers. An example of this anomalous pattern occurred a year after Ma Zhimin's move into Nanyang, when he sent his son to Neixiang, Xichuan, and Zhenping counties to collect privately owned rifles for his army, under the pretext of reorganizing the private militias. When the Nationalist Revolutionary Army passed through Neixiang later that year, it delegated one of its officers and a native of the county, Zhu Taosheng, to create an army regiment from among the private militias. By early spring 1926 a division commander of *Zhensong jun*, Zang Zhigong, occupied the region. His subordinate, Zhang Zongfen, Regional Security Commander of Southwestern Henan, also sought to merge the county militia of Neixiang into the army.[118] Although these military authorities all wanted to capitalize on the military resources of southwestern Henan, they demonstrated no interest in establishing a bureaucracy of their own.

In 1926 Henan fell under the dominion of Wu Peifu. Unlike most previous state authorities, Wu was able to make bureaucratic changes in the county administration of this region. Besides modifying the names of the departments of county government and the official title of the magistrate, Wu also regrouped the subcounty wards in some counties, strengthened the county police, and formulated new departments for the security bureau.[119] After he had vowed allegiance to the Nationalist government, Feng Yuxiang returned to Henan in June 1927. Still warring against other military powers, Feng failed to keep southwestern Henan in his attention. In contrast to his accomplishments in the north, Feng's attainments in the southwest were limited to making a few appointments and changing the name of the county government.[120]

The Nanjing Decade. The Nationalist government fared no better when it moved into the region in December 1928. Although it was able to effect

---

[117] "Nanzhao xianzhi," 33–4; *Nanyang xianzhi* (1990), 25; *Nanyang shizhi*, 31; and "Neixiang xianzhi: dashi ji," 20–1.

[118] "Neixiang xianzhi: dashi ji," 20–2.

[119] *Xixia xianzhi* (1990), 21, 26, 61; and *Nanyang xianzhi* (1990), 133.

[120] *Xichuan xianzhi* (1990), 27; and "Neixiang xianzhi: dashi ji," 23.

a few bureaucratic changes similar to those that had occurred in northern Henan, most were in Nanyang County. In 1932 Nanyang County was designated to be the sixth administrative district. The county government became an administration parallel with the administrative district office, whose chief also served as the county magistrate. The office encompassed branch offices for civil administration, judiciary, finance, education and construction, and police. A survey conducted by Nationalist officials indicates the county administration and county judiciary office had been combined before the Nationalist government took over. The government anticipated the problems stemming from this overlapping – for example, that certain rich and powerful landowners were able to influence the county officials and thus interfere with decisions of the county court during a legal dispute – and in 1930 decided to separate the two offices.

In autumn 1931 a preparatory county court was established in Nanyang City. Formally registered in 1933 as the Nanyang County Court, it was expanded to a National District Court in 1935. And in 1930 the provincial government set up police bureaus in Nanyang City. In October 1932, a police headquarters was established in Nanyang County. The police chief was also appointed by the county magistrate. In the district, however, there emerged a new organization, a part of the secret service, the Liaison Office for the Central Military Academies. But it was led by Liu Zhi as a chapter of the Society of Loyalty *(zhongyihui)*, as it was known in the rest of the country.[121]

Before the government took full control of the southwest, it had little authority over the private militia groups in the region. But in 1928 it attempted to take control of the militia organization in Nanyang County by creating a county militia unit. Under the new organization, one militia group was established for each ward. Below the ward level, there was a militia group for each village. All groups fell under the authority of the county militia. In 1929, a command headquarters was established in the county, and in 1931, the local militias were placed under the command of the provincial militia headquarters. The county unit commanding officer was selected by the county magistrate, but his appointment had to be confirmed by the provincial government.

While the local militia in Nanyang County was being reorganized, the provincial government was not able to touch the private militias in south-

---

[121] *Nanyang xianzhi* (1990), 28, 119, 133; *Nanyang shizhi*, 33, 269; and *Henan zhengzhi yuekan (Monthly Report of Political Affairs in Henan)* 2, no. 12 (Kaifeng: Henan sheng zhengfu bianyichu chuban, January 1933): 3.

western Henan. In Neixiang County, for instance, after the provincial government failed to control Bie's large militia by 1934, it had to keep it as an independent unit that remained under the leadership of the local elites. However, in 1937, the situation had completely changed. By then, the government was able to separate the police bureau and county government, thus diffusing the concentration of local power. The police bureau was directly under the order of the provincial police head-quarters. There was a police bureau in each county.[122] The reason for this drastic change in the local power structure will be explained in Chapter 8.

Even though its influence was limited in most parts of the region, the government still tried to implement its local surveillance system. At first, it sought to introduce the program of Self-Government to the region, but in this effort it succeeded only in Nanyang County. In 1932, Liu Zhenhua's eleventh division of the Nationalist Army moved into Nanyang County. Liu had been sent by the Nationalist government to take charge of public security in Henan, Shaanxi, and Hubei provinces. Liu divided Nanyang County into ten self-governing wards and established ward offices for each. He then replaced Self-Government with the ward-village-lane-neighborhood system. In 1933, the provincial government issued an order abolishing any previous regulations or instructions for its Self-Government program. The government decided instead to focus on finalizing the *baojia*. These actions indicate the government's primary concern was local security and, of course, the control of the area. Soon the ward-village-lane-neighborhood system had been established in almost every corner of the region, facilitated by the willingness of the local elite community to support it (since they realized they could use it for their own purposes).[123] In the end, the system ironically became a vehicle through which local elites strengthened the domination of their villages and prevented penetration by the state, a phenomenon that will be discussed in detail in Chapter 8.

Above all, like most of its predecessors, the Nationalist government accomplished little bureaucratic expansion in most parts of southwestern Henan. The main cause for this failure to penetrate the region was closely tied to the political developments there, especially among the local elites.

---

[122] *Nanyang xianzhi* (1990), 119, 133, 167; and *Nanyang shizhi*, 269, 324.

[123] *Xichuan xianzhi* (1990), 28–9, 61, 411; *Nanyang xianzhi* (1990), 28; *Nanyang shizhi*, 33–4; *Zhengzhi yuekan* 2, no. 12 (January 1933): 2–3; and "Nanzhao xianzhi," 42.

The Expansion of Fiscal Control

Before we address the influence of local elites in the region, let us continue our examination of the government's state-making efforts in southwestern Henan in the fiscal domain, a component of the end that administrative expansion was to serve in this region.[124]

The Early Republican Period. In this region the provincial administration under Yuan Shikai reclaimed its authority over taxation as soon as its influence could extend to southwestern Henan. In December 1913, shortly after its regional officials arrived at Nanyang City, Yuan's administration began to collect stamp duties. And over the next two years, it affixed an additional amount to the land surtax for each household. However, these were the only efforts to increase revenue that the administration could pursue in this region because it had very limited control of the region's administration, which generally ignored its fiscal policies.[125]

After Yuan Shikai's regime ended, taxation in southwestern Henan was plunged into turmoil. Because the warlords passing through the region shifted their financial burden to the shoulders of the people, the total amount of taxes increased at alarming speed during this period. According to Liu Zhi, the former chairman of the provincial government, the total expenditure of the army in Henan increased nearly five-fold between 1912 and 1923. In the next two years, that amount again quadrupled. Southwestern Henan had to share the financial burden of these expenditures.[126] Its population had to contend not only with a frequently staggering tax burden but also with confusion over the methods of collection.

In January 1925 a unit of soldiers from Wu Peifu's army named *zhensongjun*, under the command of Zhang Zhigong, engaged troops of the Nationalist Revolutionary Army led by the Nanyang Region Security Commander, Ma Zhimin. After seven days of ferocious fighting, a truce was reached. But at the negotiating table, Zhang demanded 90,000 *yuan* from Xichuan County, where the battle had taken place. A few days later,

---

[124] According to Max Weber, the ancient Chinese bureaucracy, unlike that in the West, took its form from its system of public taxation. See Max Weber, *Max Weber on Capitalism, Bureaucracy and Religion: A Selection of Texts*, Stanislav Andreski, ed., Stanislav Andreski, trans. (London: George Allen & Unwin, 1983), 71.

[125] *Nanyang shizhi*, 29; and *Xixia xianzhi* (1990), 18, 24.

[126] Liu Zhi, *Wo de huiyi (Personal Memoirs)* (Taipei: Self-printed, 1966), 121.

as he left the county, Zhang insisted on an additional payment of 200,000 *yuan*. A few months later, other troops from Zhili retreated into Xichuan County, having been defeated by Feng Yuxiang's army. On their retreat, they were joined by a bandit gang proclaiming itself the Henan People's Guard Army *(weiminyujun)*. When they arrived, there were also demands by the army for supplies.[127]

Such roving military bands often resorted to coercive force or looting to obtain their payments. When Duan Qirui's army occupied Henan in 1925, it used force to collect its own excessive levies. To survive, many people were forced to either become bandits or join the army. In 1926, when the *jianguoyujun* was in Nanyang, its commander, Fan Zhongxiu, simply confiscated the holdings of several private banks. In Neixiang County in 1927 the troops of various warlords collected food, supplies, and payments for military expenses at gunpoint. In 1928, as Yue Weijun's Second Group Army was in Zhenping County, its soldiers forced the people to pay 800,000 *yuan* for its provisions. In the following years, a group of Feng Yuxiang's soldiers led by Shi Yousan used the same method to seize at least 200,000 *yuan* on one occasion and 500,000 *yuan* on another. Even after some of these warlords had established their governments in Kaifeng, their troops continued to act on their own, collecting ad hoc taxes as if they were bandits.[128]

Furthermore, the county governments that existed now and then along with the changing provincial authority also collected their own taxes, mostly from opium cultivation and silk production, for these operations were more remunerative than the cultivation of grain. As Hsi-sheng Ch'i has pointed out, the opium tax was an important source of revenue for the state during the early Republican period. Actually, Yuan Shikai had banned the cultivation of opium. After his death the central government allowed production to resume because it was tempted by the large potential income. During the 1920s, most militarists also relied on the opium tax to supplement their revenue.[129] The evidence from southwestern Henan can well support Ch'i's assertion. In Neixiang County 80% of the

---

[127] *Xichuan xianzhi* (1990), 26; and "Neixiang xianzhi: dashi ji," 21.

[128] *Nanyang xianzhi* (1990), 412; *Shuntian shibao (Peking Times)*, (March 5, 1925); "Neixiang xianzhi: dashi ji," 23; Xinzheng yuan nongcun fuxing weiyuan hui, *Henan sheng nongcun diaocha (Henan Village Survey)* (Shanghai: Shangwu yinshu guan, 1934), 78; and *Nanyang shizhi*, 32.

[129] Ch'i, *Warlord Politics*, 163–5. For Wu Peifu's opium taxation in Henan, see Wou, *Militarism*, 76–7.

land was used to grow opium in 1921, and the county government sent police to assist in the taxation of the resulting revenue.[130]

Another source of financial confusion came from the variety of paper currencies used in the region. Since the end of the Qing, different notes had been issued by the branch offices of the government banks, as well as other private banks. In 1913 Yuan Shikai's government released its own currency. The new paper currency was widely used in the market towns, alongside other currencies.[131] Between 1913 and 1923, other currencies were circulated by such diverse sources as the local business community and the Roman Catholic Church, in additional to those already issued by the Hubei government banks, the military government in Sichuan, the Bank of China, and the Bank of Communications controlled by Sun Yat-sen's Guangzhou government.

As our data show, the most popular, and most commonly used, currency in the early 1920s was issued by the Henan Province Bank of Agriculture and Industry. By the late 1920s, the prevailing currency in the regional market was the one jointly issued by the Bank of China and the Bank of Communications. As a countermeasure, the local business community started to issue its own currency in 1928. Usually, these currency notes were more widely accepted than those issued by any government. In 1935, the provincial government finally forbade the issuing of currency by business associations. Local businesses boycotted the Nationalist government's effort to standardize its currency.[132]

When Wu Peifu instituted the Henan Provincial Bank as one of four banks he established in the country, he founded a branch office in Nanyang City.[133] He also issued new paper currency, in addition to proffering loans to local businesses and offering an exchange service between paper currency and silver or gold (paper currency was used by the public until 1927, when the bank failed).[134] In 1927 Feng Yuxing printed one million *yuan* worth of military notes with stone blocks. The currency was used by Feng's troops to pay for daily necessities.[135]

---

[130] "Neixiang xianzhi: dashi ji," 16, 18; and *Xixia xianzhi* (1990), 18.

[131] *Nanyang xianzhi* (1990), 413; and "Nanzhao xianzhi," 29.

[132] *Nanyang xianzhi* (1990), 413; "Nanzhao xianzhi," 36; "Neixiang xianzhi: dashi ji," 25; *Zhengzhi yuekan* 2, no. 12 (January 1933): 3; and *Nanyang shizhi*, 32.

[133] The other three banks were the Railroad Bank at Loyang (October 1923), the China Industrial Bank at Hankou (May 1924), and the Zhuan Kuan Bank in Henan (created between 1923 and 1925). See Wou, *Militarism*, 72–3.

[134] *Nanyang xianzhi* (1990), 413, 415.

[135] Ch'i, *Warlord Politics*, 162.

The primary reason for the warlords to issue paper currency was to further squeeze the population in Henan for local resources.[136] Since the currencies were never backed by credit, nor did they retain their usefulness after the warlords left the area, their issuing could only degrade the living conditions of the ordinary people and increase friction between the warlords and the local inhabitants. As in the northern region, financial desperation had driven various provincial authorities and militaries to rely on thorough methods of revenue collection. But collection methods appeared to be even more devastating in the southwest because local resources had already been depleted due to the harsh agricultural conditions. In fact, during the early Republican period, tax collection in peripheral areas wreaked total disaster on their population.

The Nanjing Decade. As the Nationalist government was endeavoring to impose a fiscal system from the top down, it encountered a number of obstacles in the southwest. First, many local resources had already been drained by numerous authorities and troops. Second, widespread public animosity opposed any government fiscal policy. Third, local elites had already taken advantage of this public sentiment to appropriate local resources. In the early 1930s, the Nationalist government ventured to collect tax in the southwest with the assistance of county police. But immediate strong opposition compelled it to transfer this duty to local elites, who thereafter negotiated tax rates. This situation continued until the provincial government was moved to the region during the Sino-Japanese War. Only in Nanyang City and Nanzhao County did the government assume limited authority over taxation. It established several tax agencies in the former and conducted land surveys in the latter.[137]

Notwithstanding its failure to control taxation, the government took steps to standardize the currency. On November 4, 1935, it issued new paper currency through the country's four major banks: the Central Bank of China, the Bank of China, the Bank of Communications, and the Farmers' Bank of China. The government also prohibited the use of any local currency. It further ordered the public to use the new currency (called *fabi*), but the old currency, the silver dollar, remained in wide circulation in the region until the early 1940s.[138]

---

[136] Ch'i, *Warlord Politics*, 161–2.
[137] *Nanyang shizhi*, 34, 589–90.
[138] "Neixiang xianzhi: dashi ji," 33; *Xixia xianzhi* (1990), 24; and *Nanyang xianzhi* (1990), 29, 415.

In conclusion, although it met resistance from the general population, the major obstacle to the expansion of the Nationalist government's revenues in southwestern Henan was competition from local elites for control of local resources. This profound problem was met by every state maker during the Republican period. To further comprehend the way state making was affected by social transformation, we shall examine in the next chapter how state makers of the Republican period dealt with the local elites.

SUMMARY

In the early twentieth century the Chinese states struggled to strengthen themselves. That struggle, in both vertical and horizontal directions, took place not only in the administrative but also the fiscal theaters of state making. Among their endeavors, the creation of powerful states was evidently a goal shared by Yuan Shikai, the warlords, Feng Yuxiang, and the Nationalist government. From this vantage point, one may argue for a definite trend toward state making during the Republican period.

Within that trend, however, one should not neglect the considerable differences among the separate regions as well as among the individual endeavors of each state. In administrative affairs, for instance, one will notice the trend to be highly visible in northern Henan during most of the Republican period but barely noticeable in the southwest after Yuan Shikai's regime, and even during the periods of Feng Yuxiang and the Nationalist government. By concentrating on a different aspect of state making, however, one may arrive at a different conclusion. The states under Yuan Shikai, Feng Yuxiang, and the Nationalist government were able to continuously maintain a high level of political, military, and even police control in the north by eliminating any possible resistance from the local elites. Although, at the beginning of each regime, the local elites there displayed greater potential for appropriating the authority of the local government, their influence was drastically reduced under the state-making efforts of each regime, no matter how short-lived, ad hoc, or driven by fiscal desperation any of these regimes were. Just the opposite occurred in the southwest, where the local elites were not only able to mobilize among themselves during the Republican period but also to force the state to retreat from the region. Mounting evidence confirms these two distinctive effects of greatly differing environments on attempted state making.

This then raises the important question of whether a generalization

215

about state making in Republican China is historically plausible. There is an apparent danger of falling into the trap of oversimplification when such a generalization is based on the observation of a single locale, without paying sufficient attention to diversities in different locales. Obviously, for the Henan case, two distinctive, regionally defined trends of state making seem more plausible than a single, unevenly distributed trend.[139]

---

[139] Kenneth Pomeranz also argues for the existence of two separate processes – "state making and unmaking" – during the Republican period. He further suggests these two processes were operating in all directions and everywhere at the same, which makes it rather difficult for us to find any pattern. Pomeranz, *Making of a Hinterland*.

8

State and Society in Mutual Engagement

ONE way of assessing the success of state making is to gauge the efficacy of the state's penetration of the local society. But that success depends largely on the state's ability to meet the challenges from the society it is penetrating. As Joel Migdal claims, the success of state making should be measured by the state's ability to regulate social relations and to make people behave the way it wants them to.[1] According to Samuel P. Huntington, the most important political distinction among countries lies not in their forms of government but in the degree to which they are able to govern.[2] In other words, state making involves not only bureaucratic extension and fiscal expansion, but more importantly, engagement with various social forces competing against the state for dominance over society.[3] To understand the delicacy as well as the dynamism of this relationship between the state and society for Republican China, I now move beyond the examination of state efforts in bureaucratic and fiscal expansion to explore how the Republican states dealt with various social forces during this period of state making.

LOCAL CONTROL AND MODERN STATE MAKING

A vital concern of the Chinese state since the late Ming until the end of the Qing was local control, the control of the local society. For centuries, local elites had been competing with the local government for authority over their own village communities and local resources. The state gen-

[1] Joel S. Migdal, *Strong Societies and Weak States: State-Society Relations and State Capabilities in the Third World* (Princeton: Princeton University Press, 1988), 4.
[2] Samuel Huntington, *Political Order in Changing Societies* (New Haven: Yale University Press, 1977), 1.
[3] Migdal, *Strong Societies*, 10–41.

erally had the upper hand in this struggle in the beginning of the dynasties, but its grip on local affairs tended to weaken at the end of each dynasty. One important reason for this breakdown of centralized authority was population growth always outpaced the expansion of state bureaucracy.[4] According to Ho Ping-ti, the population of China increased from 175 million to 430 million between 1741 and 1850.[5] During that surge, the central government was unable to provide social services with the local bureaucracies. This lag gave local elites the opportunity to assist local government community services such as famine relief, tax collection, and water control, thereby increasing their influence in local society. Commercialization and urbanization had also begun to take their toll on the local government's capacity to manage society, permitting still further expansion of the local elites' sphere of activities.[6] Before the Taiping Rebellion, these societal developments had already become a major concern of the Qing state.

In the late nineteenth century, the lack of government control over local society continued to degenerate. In the arena of managing resources, the Qing government made an attempt in 1853 to reorganize its bureaucracy for the collection of a commercial tax called *lijin*. Although the Qing government did initially make some progress toward reducing the size of its local bureaucracy, thus making it more efficient in tax collection, the program eventually failed due to the conflict it generated between the merchants and the government, and between the local authorities and the central government.[7] More significantly, however, as Kuhn's landmark study has shown, the outbreak of the Taiping Rebellion cut short any government attempt to rejuvenate its strength at the local level. During the rebellion, the court reluctantly encouraged the local elites to form local militia to suppress rebels, and this militarization gave them more opportunities to expand their power. Local elites capitalized fully on the opportunity to entrench their power. After the rebellion, the government was continuously caught in a crisis precipitated by external aggression, internal disturbances, and even power struggles within the imperial court. Therefore, before the end of the nineteenth century, the dynasty had neither the opportunity nor the

[4] Jack A. Goldstone, *Revolution and Rebellion in the Early Modern World* (Berkeley: University of California Press, 1991), 349–415.
[5] Ping-ti Ho, *Studies on the Population of China 1368–1953* (Cambridge, MA: Harvard University Press, 1962).
[6] Rankin, *Elite Activism*, 2.   [7] Mann, *Local Merchants*, 3–7, 94–120.

energy to deal with the local elites and their interference in the local government's official functions.[8]

Shortly after the turn of the century, in September 1908, the Empress Dowager proclaimed her decision to adopt Self-Government, within a framework of constitutionalism.[9] Her objectives were twofold: to alleviate the county government from the multifarious obligations that diverted its attention from its primary duties of managing financial resources and maintaining public order,[10] and to restrain the local elites' activities and prevent them from interfering in the functioning of the government.[11] Among all other measures embodied in the New Policies and recently adopted constitutionalism, Self-Government was the pivotal component of the Qing government's twentieth-century effort to strengthen the power of the state.

Even though, the name Self-Government implied the notion of self-rule, the mission of the institution, as it was intended, was to enable a high degree of government control. Feng Guifeng, a magnate in Suzhou, suggested using Self-Government to delimit the boundary of local elites' activities and power, and thus enable the county government to function without much interference. Feng's ideas were popularized by his writings during the reform period and were eventually approved by the Qing government.[12] The primary responsibilities of Self-Government, unequivocally designated by the government guideline, were to foster a modern style of education, public hygiene, road construction, local commerce, welfare programs, and community affairs management, in addition to raising funds for those projects.[13] Furthermore, the blueprint compelled the chief officers of each institution to obtain confirmation by the state authority after they had been elected by the public. This last stipulation reveals the true intent behind the Self-Government plan had nothing to do with self-governing *(zizhi)*.[14]

Local elites generally participated in Self-Government with exuberance because they presumed the institutions would provide them the opportunity to obtain official acknowledgement of their preeminent

[8] Kuhn, *Rebellion and Its Enemies*, 211–25.
[9] Sheng, "Qingmo difang zizhi sixiang de shuru," 159–82. See also Philip Kuhn's article "Local Self-Government," 268–80.
[10] Kuhn, "Local Government," 330–40.
[11] Kuhn, "Local Self-Government," 276.
[12] Ibid., 268–80. [13] Shen, "Difang jingying," 193. [14] Ibid., 194.

status.[15] John Fincher has described a situation in which the assembly-men felt from the beginning that they were equal to the provincial officials. It can be imagined that at the local level similar situations must have existed in which the local elites also felt they were equal to the local officials. As this was happening, it was natural that the local elites began to challenge the authority of the local government.[16] Eventually, with the opportunities provided by the Qing program, the local elites challenged dynastic authority through provincial assemblies, chambers of commerce, educational associations, and private societies, a result exactly contrary to that desired by the central government.

Besides depending on Self-Government, the Qing government formulated other schemes to control local society. One method was to modernize its local administration, especially the police departments. During the first decade of the twentieth century, new police offices were added to each county government in Henan. In some counties, more extensive police headquarters were instituted. New branches were created under individual police departments, such as the Department of Illegal Business Supervision and the Department of Investigation. Modifications to the police department stood a good chance of elevating the efficiency of the government's administration of local affairs, especially since the police assumed most of the burden of dealing with the swelling tax resistance and anti-Manchu ferment at the end of the Qing.[17]

The Qing dynasty ended in the midst of widespread tax defiance, military mutiny, and urban insurrection, after many of the kingdom's local rural constituencies had turned against the regime.[18] As discussed in

---

[15] "Nanzhao xianzhi," 26; *Huojia xianzhi*, 9 (1991): 16–17; Chen, *Tangyin xianzhi*, 10; and Shen, "Difang jingying," 193–4. For a brief discussion of the local elites' response to the government initiatives under the New Policies, see Kuhn's essay, "Local Self-Government," 335–40.

[16] Fincher, *Chinese Democracy*, 218–50.

[17] "Nanzhao xianzhi," 25; *Huojia xianzhi*, 6 (1991): 17; Wang, *Henan xinhai geming*, 144; *Nanyang shizhi*, 28; Wang, *Henan jindai dashi ji*, 103–4; Chen, *Shiyu zougao*, (January 14, 1910), 1: 4–7; *Yongan shangshu zouyi* (September 1903), 21; *Yuzhe huicun* 55; *Mingqing dangan* (April 8, 1903); *Dagong bao*, (November 19, 1903); *Dagong bao* (November 24, 1903); and *Yangwu xianzhi*, 1: 12.

Bernhardt observes a similar pattern for the rise of tax resistance in Jiangsu province between 1902 and 1911–1912. This rising tide of protest was also seen by Bernhardt to be the effect of the sudden increase of taxes in the beginning of the twentieth century by the Qing court. See Bernhardt, *Rents, Taxes, and Peasant Resistance*, 156–9.

[18] Xin Zhang, "Reconsidering the 1911 Revolution: The Case of Henan," *Chinese Historians* 7, no. 1–2 (1994): 1–43.

Chapters 3 and 4, the 1911 Revolution offered immediate opportunities to the political contenders who were already competing for the country's political mandate. At the local level, political authority was absent, and the local elites rushed to fill the vacuum. In northern Henan, local elites took over and created an interim authority in the county, which prevented the chaos from escalating. Both the county assemblies and the bureaus of public funds began to defy the authority that county governments exerted over a variety of issues pertaining to taxation, corruption, and the use of public funds.[19]

From the beginning of the early Republican period, therefore, the modern state makers were confronted with the immense undertaking of exerting greater control over local society while steering clear of obstructions created by the emergence of modern technology and urbanization throughout the country (railroads, newspapers, telecommunications) and by the amplification of elite activism as an effect of the increase in communication among diverse social groups as well as within the local elite stratum.[20] In addition, the state makers were also faced with the task of bringing the entire population, including the local elites, into its political system. The ultimate goal of modern state making, which differed from the state strengthening pursued by a traditional state such as the Qing, was to expand the political basis of the state to the public and to transform the population under its control into citizens of a modern nation. The modern state makers, therefore, could no longer regard the local elites as a target of control but rather as the critical bridge through which the state could reach the public.[21]

The modern state emerged in Europe during the early eighteenth century in the presence of a homogeneous culture, a large peasant base, and a decentralized but uniform political structure. The Western European states also benefited from the extensive development of industri-

---

[19] Xiao, *Xiuwu xianzhi*, 7 (1931): 1, 42; Han, *Xinxiangxian xuzhi*, 1 (1923): 81; "Neixiang xianzhi: dashi ji," 13; *Xixia xianzhi* (1990), 17; and *Anyang xianzhi*, (Minguo), 37–40.

[20] Kuhn, "Local Self-Government," 281. My research discussed in Chapters 5 and 6 also shows that the local elites in Henan gained political sophistication through the exchange of ideas among different groups and locations, as well as through increased networking due to the convenience of travel and communications. These developments added a great deal of difficulty to the state's attempt to control them.

[21] S. N. Eisenstadt, *The Political Systems of Empires* (London: Free Press of Glencoe, 1963), 360–70. Harumi Befu, "The Political Relation of the Village to the State," *World Politics* 19 (1967): 601–20.

Those who also believe imperial China to be a traditional state are Shimizu Morimitsu (1939) and Martin Yang (1945).

alization, commercialization, and capitalism.[22] In early twentieth-century China, however, the once uniform political edifice of the late Qing disintegrated as that homogeneous culture encountered the challenges of diversification posed by foreign intrusion, the demise of the dynasty, and the rise of various social forces. In addition to these challenges, the conditions on which modern European states relied were absent. Industrialization, for instance, was not fully developed in China until later in the century. And although there had been extensive commercialization and urbanization since the mid-Ming, capitalism did not burst into full bloom before the foreign intrusion of the late nineteenth century. A modern state in China had to be based on conditions quite different from those that supported the modern state in Europe. The history of the modern state in northern Henan is typical of its progress throughout the country.

NORTHERN HENAN

The 1911 Revolution that toppled the Qing dynasty also brought a surge of elite activism in local society, due to the dissolving of government control and the rise of a wide range of societal activities in the country, many deeply rooted in nationalistic and anti-Manchurian sentiments. As discussed in Chapter 7, in northern Henan these changes had at least two results at the beginning of Yuan Shikai's era: a restructuring began in most elite communities, and the local elites started to challenge the authority of county government.

The Early Republican Period

In the beginning of the early Republican period, the reorganization took place in the elite community to redefine the leadership within such institutions as the chambers of commerce, county assembly, and bureau of public funds. At the same time, secret societies vigorously recruited members and staged local insurrections. These militant societies included the Red Spear, the Heavenly Gate Society, the Blue Path Society, Yellow Tassel, White Tassel, Green Tassel, and Blue Tassel. In the midst of these developments, local elites became a strong voice in community affairs. County assemblies and chambers of commerce became the pivot of county decision making. For example, when Xinxiang County was raided

---

[22] Charles Tilly, ed., "Reflections on the History of European State-making," in *The Formation of National States in Western Europe*, Charles Tilly, ed., 3–83.

by a secret society, the local elites decided to call in nearby government troops rather than wait for the county government to take action. In most counties, the local elites did not even confer with county magistrates before initiating such a step. The influence of local elites in northern Henan during this period conformed to a countrywide trend (noted by Keith Schoppa in his study of Zhejiang) toward an increasingly active role in local society.[23] An election for the provincial assembly, held in the region in 1912, only added to their political fervor.[24]

Even before Yuan Shikai assumed the presidency, he was fully cognizant of the ease with which local elites had been taking over the counties' authority. On January 2, 1912, while Yuan was still president of the Qing cabinet, he ordered then governor of Henan, Qi Yaolin, to disband the provincial assembly because Yuan claimed that the assembly was secretly supporting the revolutionaries. On July 12 he authorized Zhang Zhenfang, the new governor, to abolish the Office for Preparation for Self-Government in every county. In the second half of 1913, further endeavors were made by the provincial government. And in 1914 the government issued a directive for the abolition of all the county assemblies and any remaining Self-Government institutions. With these government measures, the momentary upsurge of elite activism was quickly halted.[25]

As Yuan Shikai's regime ended, elite activism started to rebound vigorously, gathering momentum until 1927, when Feng Yuxiang again took control of Henan.[26] First, northern Henan saw an unprecedented rise in vigor among the local elites in 1916, inspired not by a wave of nationalism but by the slackening of government control.[27] Then, in 1918, local elites from the entire region formed a Negotiation Committee for Tax Reduction to petition against the excessive tariffs imposed by Feng

---

[23] Schoppa, *Chinese Elites*, 73–5.

[24] Wang, *Chongxiu Huaxian zhi*, 32; Xiao, *Xiuwu xianzhi*, 15 (1931): 8; *Xiuwu xianzhi*, 9: 44; Yang, *Xiuwu xianzhi*, (1986), 14, 155; Han, *Xinxiangxian xuzhi*, 1 (1923): 34, 81; Han, *Xinxiangxian xuzhi*, 2: 32–3; *Xinxiangxian xuzhi*, 5: 74; Chen, *Tangyin xianzhi*, 10, 322, 363; Zi Zhen, "Fan feng zhangzheng zhong zhi yubei tianmenhui" (Heavenly Gate Society during the War Against the Feng Army), in *Henan shizhi ziliao*, 6 (1984): 57–66, 82–3, 164–7; and *Shen bao* (November 23, 1912).

[25] Wang, *Henan jindai dashi ji*, 144, 150; Chen, *Tangyin xianzhi*, 247, 322; Yang, *Xiuwu xianzhi* (1986), 155; and Zhang, *Huojia xianzhi* (1991), 17.

[26] Wang, *Chongxiu Huaxian zhi*, 20: 7–8; Han, *Xinxiangxian xuzhi*, 2 (1923): 33; *Xinxiangxian xuzhi*, 1: 81; and Zou, *Huojia xianzhi*, 7 (1934): 9.

[27] Keith Schoppa's study shows the rise of the local elites' vigor was inspired by nationalism. See Schoppa, *Chinese Elites*, 74–5.

Guozhang's government. After the committee had sent a delegation to Beijing, the government conceded a reduction in tax rates. Inspired by their victory, local elites in Xinxiang County thwarted the selling of a piece of public land by the Commissioner for Government Property to treasure hunters. Elites in Huojia County, united as the Bureau of Public Funds, blocked a similar transaction. Challenges from local elites to the authority of warlord governments soon became widespread throughout the region.[28]

Aside from the endeavors previously described, some minor elites affiliated with secret societies, contributing to the rapid growth of such organizations as the Tianmenhui, and arousing great concern among government officials. In Hui County the Tianmenhui at one time boasted nearly 300,000 members. In 1926 in Ji County a Tianmenhui chapter fomented a riot over excessive taxes imposed on the people. The organization, joined by groups from Qi and Hui counties, surrounded the county seat until the army announced a reduction in the tax rate. To control such rebellions, the county governments sometimes had to rely on provincial troops, which occasionally were defeated by the secret societies.[29]

The interval between the regimes of Yuan Shikai and Feng Yuxiang was undeniably a time of "local-elite triumph."[30] One reason for the elites' success, according to Ch'i Hsi-sheng, may have been the prevailing absence of commitment in the local society from the warlord governments during this period, a time Ch'i has categorized as the second (1919–24) and (partially) third phase (1924–8) of the warlord period. Because most warlords in the county were preoccupied with warfare against other military powers, Ch'i contends, they were unable to pay much attention to "internal consolidation."[31] My research, however, suggests the provincial administrations instituted by the warlords were

---

[28] *Chen bao* (May 30, 1921); Zou, *Huojia xianzhi*, 5 (1934): 13; *Huojia xianzhi*, 7: 2; Xiao, *Xiuwu xianzhi*, 9 (1931): 5; *Xiuwu xianzhi*, 6: 37; Han, *Xinxiangxian xuzhi*, 4 (1923): 39; Han, *Xinxiangxian xuzhi*, 2: 55; *Xinxiangxian xuzhi*, 1: 33; Xinxiang shi hongqi qu shizhi bianchuan weiyuan hui, *Hongqi quzhi (Gazetteer of Hongqi District)* (Xinxiang: Shenghuo, Dushu, Xinzhi Sanlian Shudian, 1991), 15; and Chen, *Tangyin xianzhi*, 695.

[29] *Huixian wenshi ziliao*, 2 (1990): 13–14; "Jixian dashi ji," 28; and *Henan shizhi ziliao*, 6 (1984): 94–5.

[30] Lenore Barkan argues the central state had completely disintegrated during this period. With never any opposition from the bottom of the societal pyramid, local elites were able to concentrate on building up their local communities. See Barkan, "Patterns of Power," 203–6.

[31] Ch'i, *Warlord Politics*, 206–32.

engaged at the local level, but those efforts were not sufficient to prevent the local elites from pursuing their political ambitions.[32]

We may also attribute the swell of elite activism to political developments in the large cities that were all within easy reach by the railroad (e.g., Hankou, Tianjin, Beijing). For instance, when student demonstrations occurred in Shanghai during the May Thirtieth Incident, similar demonstrations were held in Xiuwu and Tangyin counties shortly thereafter. In all, about 200,000 people from the area, many of them students, joined the demonstrations. And organizations similar to the Workers Union, the Nationalist Party, and the Communist Party appeared in the region at almost the same time they did in Kaifeng.[33] Although some of these social elements posed challenges to the values shared by the local elites, these developments helped bring about a social environment conducive to any elite activities.

Owing to the rise of the power of secret societies toward the end of the early Republican period, Feng Yuxiang encountered extraordinary defiance to his authority when he instituted a government in Henan. In Anyang, Tangyin, and Hua counties, for example, the Tianmenhui and the Red Spear instigated several tax-resistance incidents. A negotiator sent by Feng's army was killed in one of them. In another incident in Hua County even a magistrate was driven away by the Red Spear. Feng's government also obtained many reports from the county administrations that secret societies had deprecated tax officials and fomented factional skirmishes among their ranks thus creating obstacles to their control by the government.[34]

Feng Yuxiang's first response to the threatening power of the secret societies was to order the members of the elite community to dissociate

[32] *Minguo ribao* (June 6, 1920), 88; Wang, *Chongxiu Huaxian zhi*, 33; and *Tangyin wenshi ziliao (Local History of Tangyin County)*, 1 (Tangyin: Zhongguo renmin zhengzhi xieshang huiyi, Henansheng Tangyinxian weiyuan hui wenshi ziliao weiyuan hui, 1988): 23–6.

[33] "Ge xian xianzhang hanbao congzheng ganxiang zhaiyao" (Selections from the County Magistrate's Report of Their Thoughts on the Administrative Duty), *Henan zhengzhi (Political Affairs in Henan)* 4, no. 7 (1934): 2; Chen, *Tangyin xianzhi*, 13; Yang, *Xiuwu xianzhi* (1986), 16; "Jixian dashi ji," 28–9; *Jiaozuo xinghuo (The Revolutionary Spark in Jiaozuo)*, Zhonggong Henan dangshi zhuanti ziliao congshu (Zhengzhou: Zhonggong dangshi chuban she, October 1991), 29–35; and *Xinxiang xianzhi* (1991), 329.

[34] *Huixian wenshi ziliao,* 2 (1990): 13–18; Zi, "Yubei tianmenhui," 57–66, 82–3, 164–7; Wang, *Chongxiu Huaxian zhi*, 20: 8–9; Wang, *Chongxiu Huaxian zhi*, 17: 27, 40; and Chen, *Tangyin xianzhi*, 363.

themselves from the secret societies. However, this moderate gesture was received as a sign of weakness, and complaints continued to arrive at Feng's headquarters from the local administrations about the secret societies' insolence toward Feng's army officers and local elites' involvement in those incidents. Such insults against the Northern Army *(beijun)* were common, as the Red Spear considered themselves invincible. Feng thus resolved to take stern action against the secret societies, and by doing so to subdue the uncooperative local elites.[35]

A sequence of bloody events aimed at suppression began around July 1927. An army commander, Jie Hongchang, led his division of soldiers by train into northern Henan. When the train approached Tangyin station, the officers, mistakenly thinking it their destination, started to slay everyone they suspected to be Red Spear members. Before they had realized their error, thirty innocent people had lost their lives. A month later, another unit of the Nationalist Revolutionary Army entered Hua County to enforce martial law and ended by killing some Red Spear members. Soon afterward, Jie Hongchang's division appeared in Anyang County to retaliate for its soldiers having been attacked by the White Spear. After the army encircled the county seat, it massacred several hundred people they assumed to be White Spear members. A reign of terror soon followed under Feng Yuxiang's regime, as anyone suspected of being a member of a secret society could receive a maximum penalty of death. For example, a cotton-factory owner used Feng Yuxiang's troops to settle a salary dispute with his workers. He simply reported to the army that the workers were members of the White Spear. As a result, dozens of workers were killed.[36]

Feng Yuxiang's method worked in two ways to curb the influence of secret societies and to intimidate local elites. His massive display of power caused any local challenge to the government's authority to vanish on sight, and it ensured the resumption of local elites' cooperation with county government. In Huojia County, for instance, the Bureau of Wagon and Horse voluntarily placed itself under the authority of the Bureau of Finance, a new office within the county government. In Hua County, the Chamber of Commerce was converted into a government

---

[35] Chen, *Tangyin xianzhi*, 533 and Wang, *Chongxiu Huaxian zhi*, 20: 8; and *Zhongzhou jingu*, 6 (1988): 15.

[36] Chen, *Tangyin xianzhi*, 13, 363, 533, 696–7; Wang, *Chongxiu Huaxian zhi*, 41; There are three versions of this incident. See *Anyangxian wenshi ziliao*, 1 (1988): 85–93; *Henan shizhi ziliao*, 6 (1984): 169–70; *Weihui wenshi ziliao*, 3 (1991): 65–71; and "Jixian dashi ji," 29.

agency without dissension from its members. When Feng's army entered Hui County to search out members of the Red Spear, the elite community expressed no objection, even when the soldiers were executing their fellow villagers and clan members. Having been silenced, many local elites redirected their energy to activities acceptable to the county government, such as founding schools, managing factories, and organizing community projects.[37]

After the county governments were strengthened, many of them proceeded to diminish the size of local militias and disband peasant associations that were dominated by local elites. In some cases, as in Hua County, these undertakings were backed by Feng Yuxiang's troops. These efforts further undercut the vigor of such elite-controlled organizations. Although Self-Government organizations were permitted to remain after they were restored by Feng Yuxiang, they were restricted to carrying out community responsibilities (e.g., overseeing the reversal of foot binding) for the rest of Feng's rule.[38] The decline of elite activism in northern Henan was thus a direct result of Feng Yuxiang's state-making efforts.[39]

Before we continue, I shall discuss briefly the role of local elites in their communities and the position of the county magistrate in this region. During the early Republican period the local elites functioned as brokers between the county government and the village community, and the county magistrate played an intermediary role between the higher levels of government and local society. In most scholarship on China the word *intermediary* has been associated with the local elites, and a similar tendency among local officials has been overlooked. But let us first consider the brokerage role of local elites.

The Role of Local Elites. Ramon Myers has shown that, in northern Chinese villages during the late imperial and early Republican period, there were tax brokers who had not been formally appointed by the tax office. Nor did they receive a fixed salary; they lived on brokerage fees

---

[37] Zou, *Huojia xianzhi*, 6 (1934): 2; Wang, *Chongxiu Huaxian zhi*, 32; Wang, *Chongxiu Huaxian zhi*, 20: 8; *Henan wenshi ziliao*, 15 (1985): 120–1; and Chen, *Tangyin xianzhi*, 598.

[38] Wang, *Chongxiu Huaxian zhi*, 33, 42; Xiao, *Xiuwu xianzhi*, 6 (1931): 36–7; Zhang, *Xiuwuxian xinzhi*, 49; and Qing, *Anyang xianzhi* (1933), 1123.

[39] Lenore Barkan's study of Rugao County in Jiangsu Province shows the Communists and Nationalists' attack on the local elites caused a general decline in elite activism. See Barkan, "Patterns of Power," 193, 206–8.

and bribes. But their authority to oversee tax payments and arbitrate disputes between villagers was never questioned by the peasants.[40] In general agreement with Myers's earlier observation, Prasenjit Duara also shows that entrepreneurial brokers had existed during the late imperial period and that they survived into the twentieth century, despite state attempts to minimize their roles. The state was unsuccessful in bureaucratizing these subadministrative personnel and in giving the responsibilities of tax collection directly to village community leaders – not only because the very process of state strengthening had destroyed the protective character of the community leaders, but also because the entrepreneurial state brokers had managed to gain access to community leadership over the years.[41]

Duara has identified two types of brokerage role for local elites in the Republican period: entrepreneurial and protective. He associates the entrepreneurial brokerage role with clerks, runners, and others who assisted official duties for a profit. The protective brokerage role was usually performed by community organizations that had been formed to protect the interest of the community against the entrepreneurial brokers. In practice, the line between the two brokerage roles was often blurred, although in theory the former was discharged predominantly for profit whereas the latter concentrated primarily on protecting the village community.

Although the entrepreneual brokers were not incorporated into the state bureaucratic system, Duara further argues, they acquired a great deal of power in the village communities by working for the state as contractors. Their responsibilities ranged from enforcing tax payments to supervising community projects. They could also monopolize the flow of information between state and villagers. The activities of "state brokers" in local society posed an insoluble problem for state makers; nevertheless they were invaluable to the state in terms of resource extraction and the management of village communities.[42]

My sources have also shown that "entrepreneurial" brokerage was indeed a prominent role of local elites during the early Republican period, especially when *tanpai* was present, as illustrated by a dialogue between two officers of Wu Peifu's army. One officer related that local elites had set up ad hoc collecting stations and acted as tax brokers for

[40] Myers, *Peasant Economy*, 64, 86–7, 99.
[41] Duara, *Culture, Power, and the State*, 42–3, 51, 242–3.
[42] Ibid., 42–57.

the army.[43] However, the brokers collected more than the amount being solicited by the army and kept the excess as their profit. This supports Hsi-sheng Ch'i's discovery that the warlord government was using the local elites as tax brokers when the local bureaucracy was absent or failed to meet the government's demands.[44] As for the protective role, the local elites in northern Henan seemed to rely greatly on secret societies to protect their village communities from the warlord government. They joined these organizations not only to use them as a means of popular control but also to enhance their own influence among the ordinary peasants. Sometimes, as studies of other locations have shown, local elites could even use the societies as a bargaining chip in their constant struggle against the warlord regimes.[45] Such cases can certainly be found in northern Henan.

The Position of County Magistrate. John Watt portrays the county magistrates in late imperial China as the highest-ranking state officials who still had close contact with the local people. As the outsiders in village communities, they had to rely on local elites to assist their administration while at the same time maintaining authority over them. As Watt's study shows, a magistrate's function was determined by his responsibilities in preserving public order, exercising justice, and collecting taxes on behalf of the state.[46] During the early Republican period, from the perspective of northern Henan, these responsibilities remained largely the same. However, it was now much harder to fulfill them because of the uncertainty of the magistrate's position as well as the general lack of state support.[47]

---

[43] Li Binzhi, "Gen Zhang Fulai ren canmou zhang de huiyi" (My Experience of Being a Chief of Staff under Zhang Fulai), in *Henan wenshi ziliao (Henan Local History)*, 33 (1990): 3.

[44] Ch'i, *Warlord Politics*, 153.

[45] See Maurice Freedman, *Lineage Organization in Southeastern China* (London: Athlone, 1958); Kuhn, *Rebellion and Its Enemies*; Morton H. Fried, *The Fabric of Chinese Society* (New York: Praeger, 1953); and Hsiao-tung Fei, "Peasantry and Gentry: An Interpretation of Chinese Social Structure and its Changes," *American Journal of Sociology* 52, no. 1 (1946): 1–17.

[46] Watt, *District Magistrate*, 11–22.

[47] Schoppa also notes that during the 1911 Revolution, official responsibilities of the magistrate were generally similar throughout the province of Zhejiang, but their roles in dealing with the local elites differed from zone to zone. Immediately after the 1911 Revolution, some magistrates in the inner core seemed to become subordinate to the county assembly. But under Yuan Shikai's state-making efforts, their power was strengthened in almost all aspects. See Schoppa, *Chinese Elites*, 78–9.

Table 8.1. *Length of Magistrates' Terms in Xinxiang County (1911–23)*

Name	Year Appointed	Length of Term (year)	Origin
Xu Yinyuan	1911–12	1	Zhilu
Tang Huaiyuan	1912–13	1	Sichuan
Liu Qingxuan	1913–14	1	Henan
Lu Qu	1914–15	1	Jiangsu
Lu Xiangcen	1915–16	1	Shandong
He Jiashu	1916–18	2	Zhejiang
Ju Yun	1918–18	less than 1	Jiangxi
Yang Wenhuan	1918–19	1	Shaanxi
Han Bangfu	1919–20	1	Shandong
Lu Yiao	1920–20	less than 1	Shandong
Guo Xuanhe	1920–21	1	Henan
Li Jialin	1921–22	1	Jiangsu
Qu Shitan	1922–23	1	Anhui
Jiang Xunchuan	1923–		Jingyao

Source: Han Bangfu et al., *Xinxiangxian xuzhi* (Gazetteer of Xinxiang County) (Kaifeng: 1923), 2; 3, 4.

The uncertainty of the magistrate's position was first evident in its high turnover rate. Because most magistrates were appointed by whoever controlled the region, they were often victimized by the frequent changes in the higher levels of authority. According to several surveys, many magistrates were appointed for short terms. In fact, as Table 8.1 shows, between 1911 and 1923, only one magistrate served for more than a year.

So it was in every county. The average term for a magistrate in Huojia County between 1911 and 1916, for example, was one year and from 1917 to 1932, less than a year. In Xiuwu County only two magistrates held their positions more than two years. Most magistrates were therefore less interested in their duties than in making a quick profit while still in office.[48] Even those magistrates who aspired to serve their communities had little opportunity to do so.[49]

---

[48] Han, *Nongcun diaocha*, 95; Han, *Xinxiangxian xuzhi*, 1 (1923): 33; and Han, *Xinxiang-xian xuzhi* (1923), 44, 48.

[49] Kathryn Bernhardt has recently shown some magistrates to have been sympathetic toward peasants (they sometimes joined landlords in lobbying the provincial government for rent reduction). But because they were also concerned about promotion, they worked hard to ensure that the provincial government's demands were met. See Bernhardt, *Rents, Taxes, and Peasant Resistance*, 175–7.

The instability of the position also affected the sensitive relationship that existed between magistrates and local elites during the early Republican period. On the one hand, both parties were mutually dependent in maintaining each other's power and prestige; on the other hand, each posed a threat to the other because their interests constantly conflicted. A magistrate had to closely supervise the local elites to prevent tax evasion and other unlawful activities, but the elites continually intimidated, slandered, and accused magistrates of abusing power as well as corruption. This situation was therefore similar to the late imperial period.[50]

Lacking support from above, magistrates had to rely increasingly on local elites in order to fulfill their responsibilities, and often had to depend on the financial support of wealthier peasants to carry out county projects such as building bridges.[51] But because they lacked supervision from the administration above them, magistrates were likely to abuse their power. That abuse aggravated tension between magistrates and local elites, who often represented the village communities in complaints. Although as Schoppa perceives it, the antagonistic aspect of the relationship might be "symbolic" whereas the common interest was "substantive," major confrontations did occur from time to time. Whenever they did, they usually weakened the magistrate's position, as well as that of the higher authority.[52]

Therefore, during the early Republican period, it became more difficult for the magistrates to strike a balance between their duties to the state and their relationship with the local community. In a 1914 dispute between the people of Xiuwu County and a British coal mine owner, the county magistrate received instructions from the provincial authority to grant the British mining rights. In order to fulfill his official duty but also to maintain his relationship with the local community, which strongly resented the foreigners, he secretly arranged with local elites for a public protest to be staged in front of his government office. After the protest, he reported to the higher authority that the people in the county had refused to comply with the order.[53] For his own survival, a magistrate had

---

[50] As T'ung-tsu Ch'u has argued, however, the conflict between the two groups was never serious enough to alter the local power structure because the clashes occurred only between individuals. See Ch'u, *Local Government*, 168–92.

[51] Wang, *Chongxiu Huaxian zhi*, 20: 7–8; and Han, *Xinxiangxian xuzhi*, 4 (1923): 30.

[52] Schoppa, *Chinese Elites*, 79.

[53] *Xiuwu wenshi ziliao*, 3 (1987): 4–9.

to be an agent of the state one minute and a protector of the local interest the next.

The Nanjing Decade

By the end of 1928, the Nationalist government faced a situation in northern Henan quite different from what its predecessors had confronted. At the same time, Feng Yuxiang's severity toward secret societies had dampened elite activism to its lowest level since the end of the Qing. The government, however, was not satisfied, and it became determined to convert the local elites from "objects" of state control into "agents" that would facilitate government supervision, intervention, and control of local society and to prevent the local elites from challenging its authority in the future.[54] The provincial government thus issued the County Organizational Law and instituted an election for both ward chief and *baojia* head at the village level. It also instructed village communities to hold elections for the subcounty wards (although county magistrates also were permitted to appoint their own choices for ward chief and *baojia* head).[55]

A village survey conducted at that time indicated the election of subcounty ward officials depended on two background elements: land holding and education. At least 70% of the new ward chiefs included in the survey were wealthy landlords. Furthermore, of the seventy-six ward chiefs in the survey, 16% were graduates of middle school, another 16% came from normal school or primary school background or were degree holders, and the rest were completing their education. This preference for landed and educated elites for the subcounty level of bureaucratization is confirmed by several later government reports.[56]

Once the ward chiefs had assumed their positions, the government began to indoctrinate them with its own ideas of governing. Meanwhile, the county government closely supervised their performance and atti-

---

[54] Kuhn offers that as an agent, a member of a local elite group "was counted on to perform services that were essential to the economic and political stability of local society. . . . As object, he was a man who could use his considerable local influence in opposition to the state, either in his own or in his community's interest." See Kuhn, "Local Self-Government," 260.

[55] Han, *Nongcun diaocha*, 94–5.

[56] Ibid., 75–6, 94, 99; "Henansheng zhengfu ershiwu niandu xingzheng jihua" (Henan Provincial Government's Administrative Plan for 1936), *Zhengzhi yuekan* 6, no. 3 (1936): 5; and "Fenshu huiyi an," (1939), Archival no. 28-10-18: 11.

tude toward authority, and dismissed those who demonstrated uncooperative tendencies.[57] These methods quite effectively turned ward chiefs in this region into "purely administrative arms of the county government." Gradually but surely, as the Nationalist government had started to notice, some new ward chiefs had little or no administrative knowledge but behaved instead like local despots.[58] In order to enforce regulations they had enacted, some ward chiefs even maintained their own militias. Since the ward chief had the authority to replace any *bao* chief or *li* chief, they were viewed from below as wielding the equivalent power of a county magistrate.[59]

Ward chiefs' abuse of power in taxation was also a grave concern of the government. According to previous custom, the villagers relied on tax farmers to pass information on land and households to the county government and then to handle tax collection, allowing those ad hoc agents to benefit personally from the process by manipulating both the villagers and the government. As Yeh-chien Wang points out, the old system of land registration, tax assessment, and tax collection was very inefficient and confused.[60] During the early Republican period, however, the old system of taxation remained because the state was unable to change the local tax structure. As tax farming continued, so did the corruption and inefficiency in the local tax system. Because the tax farmer did not receive an official salary, but relied on tax collections for a living, corruption was a constant temptation. Furthermore, the government was virtually powerless to prevent the many ways peasants had devised to evade taxes.[61] Thus, the Nationalist government initiated a system that put the chiefs of the town, village, and ward in charge of tax collection.[62] And once the system was backed by the county police, it became much more efficient. However, for the moment the new system allowed the ward chief too much power in taxation. These ward chiefs, to use Philip Huang's words, enjoyed the power of two systems, that of the state and of society. As a part of the state, they had the county government and its police on their side. But since they still were a part of the local society,

---

[57] "Yi yue lai zhi minzheng," 2, no. 3 (March 1932): 3; and Han, *Nongcun diaocha*, 94.

[58] Kuhn, "Local Self-Government," 286–7. See also Duara, *Culture, Power, and the State*, 62.

[59] Duara, *Culture, Power, and the State*, 92.

[60] Wang, *Land Taxation*, 21–48.

[61] Myers, *Peasant Economy*, 268–72.

[62] Henansheng minzheng ting, "Shicha Anyangxian zhengzhi baogao" (Report on the Political Situation in Anyang County), *Henan minzheng yuekan* (1932): 101.

they had the personal connections needed to overcome any resistance from within the community.[63]

Shortly after the ward chief was given the responsibility for taxation, local officials and villagers alike flooded the provincial administration with complaints. In Anyang County, for instance, an official report indicated the local elites were given opportunities to assist in tax collection. These powerful elites usually occupied the position of village chief, town chief, or ward chief. Some were also in charge of the local militia. The report added that they usually increased the tax burden on the people in the form of *tanpai*. Some local elites even used force to coerce payment. Many ward chiefs ignored government regulations and kept as much as half their collections for themselves.[64] Occasionally, some ward chiefs became so powerful that even the county magistrates were unable to control them.[65]

This pattern of corruption fits well into Prasenjit Duara's theory of state involution, which he based on his examination of state expansion under the Nationalist government. The crucial reason for the state's loss of control over local society, in Duara's opinion, was its constant dependence on lower-level functionaries, such as the ward chiefs and *baojia* heads, who acted as state tax collectors but no longer identified themselves with the state's goals. Meanwhile, many former state brokers bought their way into these positions in order to line their own pockets, hence, the simultaneous success and failure in state expansion during the Republican period.[66]

By 1932, the Nationalist government had come to realize that subcounty ward offices were used by the local elites, many of whom had become ward chiefs, as arenas for activities beyond the pale of government approval. The government launched a campaign to curb the power of the ward chiefs, especially over militia and taxation. It also discontinued the subcounty ward system and replaced it with a *baojia* system. The provincial government ordered these offices dissolved immediately; some persisted nevertheless. At the same time, the government divided local elites into two categories, the "righteous gentry" *(xiansheng* or *zhengsheng)* and the "local bullies and evil gentry" *(tuhao liesheng)*, and went after those in the latter category. During the first provincial con-

---

[63] Huang, *Peasant Economy*, 286–9; Myers, *Peasant Economy*, 65–6.
[64] "Yi yue lai zhi minzheng," (June 1932): 90, 96, 109.
[65] Wang, "Henan lishi."
[66] Duara, *Culture, Power, and the State*, 73–7.

ference of militia organization, for example, a government official mentioned in a speech that one important goal of the *baojia* system was to eliminate the influence of local bullies and evil gentry. The speaker clearly distinguished between "good" and "bad" gentry and suggested the government should promote the influence of the former and eliminate the latter.[67] More findings can confirm Philip Kuhn's claim that the Nationalist government began to deal with the so-called local bullies and evil gentry from the beginning of its regime. Its efforts, such as the ward division of the 1930s, aimed at depriving the bullies not only of control over local militia but also of their dominance of local resources.[68]

Although previous scholarship is replete with discussions of "local bullies and evil gentry," it will be useful to examine the issue from the perspective of the relationship between state and society in northern Henan. According to Kuhn, this colorful term reflects a popular conception about some local elites. As opposed to urban elites and "upper elites" in the rural community, the bullies and evil gentry usually relied on coercive and illegal methods to maintain their wealth, power, and influence. There is no doubt these individuals were powerful members of the local elite community. But why did local officials file so many reports against them in particular, and why were they considered "bullies" and "evil?" A government report suggested that these local elites not only established dominance in their village communities but also were able to "manipulate legal procedures" *(baolan cisong)* against local officials, or, in other words, they often challenged the officials through the legal process. The report urged officials to avoid association with these undesirable members of the local elite community.[69]

The following illustrative case took place in Anyang County in January 1932. Before then, a conflict between tax officials and villagers had resulted in the previous magistrate dismissing the officials for corruption. When the officials were restored to their positions by the new magistrate, Zhou Pengnian, tension began to mount between the magistrate and the people in the county, especially after the magistrate collected millions of *yuan* from the people for the Nationalist Army. Under the leadership of some elites, a riot took place in front of the county government office. The magistrate ordered the speedy arrest of the local elites responsible

---

[67] "Yi yue lai zhi minzheng," 2, no. 10 (November 1932): 2; and *Baojia yundong huiyi congkan*, 16.

[68] Kuhn, "Local Self-Government," 295–8.

[69] "Shicha Anyangxian zhengzhi baogao," (June 1932): 100, 105.

for the incident. During the provincial court hearings, however, the magistrate, not the elites, was found guilty, sentenced to three years in jail, and barred from office for five years.[70] As the event suggests, local elites were capable of using the government legal system against local officials, threatening the officials' position and interest. Thus, terms such as *bullies* and *evil* not only reflected the popular perception of some of those powerful local elites, but it revealed the deepening tension between local elites and local officials, who frequently used these terms to describe the elites.

Aware of this tension, the government closely supervised the activities of the local elites to prevent any mobilization of public force that might directly challenge government authority.[71] In 1932 a recently organized Anti-Japanese Militia Group in Tangyin County was ordered by the provincial government to disband. When the leaders of the group refused to follow the order, they were immediately arrested. In addition to its own surveillance, the government also encouraged different social groups to join its effort against the so-called local bullies and evil gentry. In public speeches, many provincial officials called for unification of China, by which they meant that the country should unify against those local elites who had gained control of local society and carved the countryside into their own small domains.[72]

At the same time, one of the primary tasks the government projected was to reestablish a harmonious relationship with the local elites. To accomplish that goal, the government appointed a few distinguished community leaders to high positions to show its willingness to incorporate the representatives of the local communities into its political system (and in the meantime, to co-opt those possible leaders of elite discontent). For this reason, Wang Yinchuan, one of the most prestigious scholars in northern Henan, was appointed to several official posts by the Nationalist government. After he had been appointed chief of the provincial government in Anhui, he was designated general secretary of the provincial government. This departure from previous policy was accompanied by an unprecedented responsiveness on the part of the provincial government to the complaints of the local elite community. When the Sino-Japanese War prompted the need for

---

[70] Qing, *Anyang xianzhi* (1933), 1126.

[71] As Kuhn rightly points out, during the 1930s the Nationalist government was concerned that any public mobilization would overturn its efforts at state control. See Kuhn, "Local Self-Government," 287–98.

[72] *Tangyin wenshi ziliao*, 1 (1988): 72; and *Baojia yundong huiyi congkan*, 1–17.

public support, the government even allowed some forms of peasant mobilization.[73] The Nationalist government thus employed both control and accommodation to deal with the local elite community.

Although its attempt to bureaucratize village communities in northern Henan into a subcounty ward system was unsuccessful, the government's state-making efforts generated important changes in local society – for example, the politicization of local elites. Due to the state's efforts, local society became an extension of the conflict of interest between the government and the GMD at both the national and provincial levels. One result of that extension was a widespread factionalism among local elites during the 1930s. Unlike that in the past, this partisanism involved government officials and agencies and was concerned mostly with political issues far removed from matters that concerned the villagers. In my investigation, I have chosen factionalism as the indicator of the impact of state making.

Factionalism: The Case of Northern Henan. Previous studies have basically focused on factionalism as a part of political culture in both the Nationalist Party and the government. It was not only "endemic" in the Nationalist Party but also one of the prevailing characteristics of the Nationalist government, "the most sensible alternative" to a government system that lacked a central authority.[74] According to Lloyd Eastman, factionalism was a way to enhance personal interest. Those within the government or party who joined one faction or the other usually were not committed to any political course but rather regarded it as an avenue to promote personal interest or maintain their influence.[75] Bradley Geissert, on the other hand, perceives the most important source of conflict between the Nationalist government and landlords as being the dissension among the different factions of the Nationalist government and between the government and the GMD. Geissert maintains that leftists

[73] "Shicha Anyangxian zhengzhi baogao," (June 1932): 95; *Henan wenshi ziliao*, 15 (1985): 124; "Mishu chu geke gongzuo gaiyao," 3–4; *Zhengfu gongbao*, 503 (1932): 3; and Li Zonghuang, *Zizhi congshu (Books on Self-Government)*, 28: *Li Zonghuang huiyilu: bashi sannian fendou shi (Reminiscence of Li Zonghuang: The History of Eighty Three Years of Striving)* (Taipei: Zhongguo difang zizhi xuehui, 1972): 321.

[74] See Joseph Fewsmith, *Party, State, and Local Elites in Republican China: Merchant Organizations and Politics in Shanghai, 1890–1930* (Honolulu: University of Hawaii Press, 1985), 181–95; and Hung-mao Tien, *Government and Politics in Kuomintang China, 1927–1937* (Stanford: Stanford University Press, 1972), 45–72.

[75] Lloyd E. Eastman, Jerome Ch'en, Suzanne Pepper, and Lyman Van Slyke, eds., *The Nationalist Era in China: 1927–1949* (Cambridge: Cambridge University Press, 1990), 26–32; Eastman, *Abortive Revolution*, 303–6.

and rightists treated the local elites differently because of their divergent political views. In fact, all the policies of the Nationalist government, including its views toward the local elites, were greatly influenced by this widespread factionalism.[76] Why did this highly politically oriented factionalism become a local phenomenon in the 1930s? From one perspective, it seems to be the by-product of state making.

My sources show that many different factions had existed earlier in this region, but on a much smaller scale. That is, although there were major factions within elite communities, often divided across such lines as education at the proper institutions or location of residence, none were deeply involved with government agencies or national politics. For instance, different groups had evolved almost in every county as a result of the competition for the management of schools, a position that provided a dependable income.[77] This situation changed in the 1930s, as the following cases demonstrate.

In 1931 two major factions, each containing both community leaders and county officials, emerged within the elite community in Tangyin County. The factions were divided, at first, by residence of their elite members. Those who lived east of the Beijing-Hankou Railroad belonged to the *Ludong* (East of the Railroad) faction, and those who lived on the west, to the *Luxi* (West of the Railroad) faction. The *Ludong* faction consisted mostly of school teachers, school principals, and education officers in the county government; members of the *Luxi* faction were mostly rich landlords. A third group soon came into being that included a few ward chiefs and county officials. These factions shared very different views on almost every major issue concerning the community as well as the policies of county government. The involvement of the county officials encouraged the rivalry among the factions.

Soon, as a result of a power shift within the elite community, the three factions merged into two larger groups: the *Wushi* (Fifth Normal School) faction (named for the site of its meetings) and the *Jingzhong* (Mighty Loyalty) faction (named for the school at which its leader was principal). The former group embraced such diverse members as ward chiefs, rich peasants, lower-level officials, and school teachers. The other group was supported financially by the business owners in the county and included

---

[76] Bradley Kent Geissert, "Power and Society: The Kuomintang and Local Elites in Kiangsu Province, China, 1924–1937," Ph.D. Dissertation (University of Virginia, 1979), 47–57.

[77] *Zhengzhi yuekan* 2, no. 12 (January 1933): 2–3.

many distinguished members of the elite community. In the beginning, both the *Wushi* and *Jingzhong* factions opposed county officials for various reasons. Members of the *Jingzhong* faction accused county officials of such sins as ignoring the law, delaying payment of a teacher's salary, and neglecting the demands of the people. The *Wushi* faction filed complaints against the chief of the Finance Bureau and a ward chief. All the accused officials were relieved of their positions.

Gradually, members of each faction used their influence with county officials to promote the financial interest of its members. Once, the members of the *Jingzhong* faction collected a sum of money from the general public with a surtax called the *Caotou gongyi juan* (Caotou Public Welfare Contribution), disregarding the fact the provincial government had already prohibited such a random collection. Members kept two-thirds of the fund for the Jingzhong High School and relinquished the remainder to the county government. Because county officials had participated, the matter was not investigated.[78]

As the years progressed, the disunity within the elite community deepened. In May 1936, when the Nationalist government promulgated the Constitution of the Republic of China and organized local elections for delegates to the National Congress, the *Wushi* and *Jingzhong* factions fought over the position of county representative. After Qin Jiwu, a member of the *Wushi* faction, was elected, the *Jingzhong* faction publicly criticized him as being too young. Qin was replaced by a member of the other faction.

As the GMD gradually became the center of political power in Tangyin County and established its headquarters there, the party secretary, Guo Zhengmin, also joined the *Jingzhong* faction in its fight against the *Wushi* faction. Guo was informed by the members of the *Jingzhong* faction that he was held in disrespect by the *Wushi* faction because of his lack of education, and so he forbade anyone associated with the *Wushi* to be permitted to join the GMD. A little later, Guo announced that no one without party membership could become a community leader in any capacity. By relying on the political power of the GMD, Guo and other members of the *Jingzhong* faction finally dominated the county's elite community.[79]

In Xinxiang County, factional hostilities surfaced as open conflict between the two local chapters of the Blue Shirts and the Reform Clique

---

[78] *Tangyin wenshi ziliao*, 1 (1988): 78–80.
[79] Ibid., 61–9.

– a conflict in which the GMD provincial headquarters intervened consistently. Two factions ultimately emerged, along with a newspaper, the *Northern Henan Daily*, first published by GMD county headquarters in September 1929. At that time, the provincial headquarters of the GMD sent three officials to organize the party in the county – Han Gongfu, Xu Jibin, and Yang Yaowu – replacing Lu Xiangliu and Lu Yunru, who were known to belong to a political faction, the *gaigepai* (Reform Clique), within the national organization of the GMD. This change in the GMD county party apparatus reflected similar changes in the provincial party organization. Under the leadership of the new party officials, the newspaper was published as an internal newsletter for party members. With the endorsement of Guo Zhongkui, who had retired earlier, the paper received financial support from the elite community, including Wang Yanqing, head of the county Chamber of Commerce and a wealthy bank owner. It was printed by the printing shop owned by Wang's bank, Tongheyu. A month later, the leadership of the GMD organization in the province was returned to those belonging to the Reform Clique. Consequently, Lu Xiangliu and Lu Yunru were reinstated as the county leaders of the party. In midst of this shuffling, the newspaper ceased operations.[80]

In November 1931, again with the endorsement of Guo Zhongkui, the paper resumed publication. It was no longer an internal newsletter for the GMD, however, but a public newspaper that opposed Japanese aggression in Manchuria. It was now controlled entirely by the local elites, with Guo as chairman of its board of directors. As before, the newspaper was financially supported by local businesses and other institutions, including the Tongheyu Bank, the Chamber of Commerce, and the Zhongyuan Coal Company. It was expanded from two to four pages and began to report most of the events that occurred throughout the country. Between 1931 and 1932 the newspaper operated smoothly.

Shortly after 1932, however, the newspaper was taken over by former GMD branch leader Han Gongfu, who again brought in the newspaper to the center of factional confrontation between the Blue Shirts and the Reform Clique, which was then in control of the county party headquarters.[81] Although Han headed the newspaper, the paper was independent from the party and followed the principles set by the board

---

[80] *Xinxiang xianzhi* (1991), 330; and Guo, "Huiyi *Yubei ribao*," 29–31.

[81] For the various names given to the organization known to Western readers as the Blue Shirts, see Eastman, *Abortive Revolution*, 61.

of directors, most of whom were distinguished elite members of the county. Therefore, it mostly reflected the interests of the elite community rather than the GMD. In 1935, when Liu Zhi, the former chairman of the provincial government, was replaced by Shang Zhen, the newspaper published an essay supporting the decision. The Blue Shirts immediately informed Liu about the essay. Liu, who still held a position in the provincial government, was enraged, and under his direct order the Blue Shirts quickly seized the paper and stopped its operations.

The causes of such factionalism during the late Republican period were several. First, many state efforts to bureaucratize local elites followed the patterns of preexisting elite factions. Government reports indicate the appointment decisions of ward chiefs, for instance, were mostly made in that way. This practice further divided the elite community, creating conflicts like the one in Tangyin County. Second, due to the success of state expansion, government officials became more involved with the local community than ever before. As also shown in the Tangyin case, their deep involvement with local society promoted factionalism among the different elite groups because the new members often carried with them diverse personal views and interests. Third, as the Xinxiang case illustrates, the increase of the state influence seems to have corresponded with the level of politicization of the local polity. The greater the influence of the provincial government in northern Henan, the more politicized the factionalism became, and local society was no longer able to determine its own destiny but instead became a venue for the confrontation between different political interests in the provincial or national government or the GMD.[82] For these reasons, the intensification of factionalism in northern Henan was the direct consequence of state making, indicating, from the viewpoint of state penetration, that the Nationalist government had succeeded initially in its goal.

Paradoxically, however, this initial success created a barrier for the Nationalist government to reach its final aim in state making because the intensification of factionalism had left local society in turmoil since the mid-1930s. In 1935, for example, an officer of the Nationalist army, Shi Yousan, confiscated rice from a grain merchant, Chen Gaoxiang. Chen petitioned the county assembly to compensate him by adding surcharges to the land tax collected by the provincial authority. Previously, such a request would have seemed unreasonable. But this time,

---

[82] "Yi yue lai zhi minzheng," (June 1932), 109–11; Li, *Zizhi congshu*, 28 (1972): 294.

with county officials heavily involved in different factions in the elite community, Chen was able to exploit personal relationships to secure the desired result. Not long thereafter, Chen's case became an issue of contention between two government agencies then at odds with each other, the county police and county security. The local elites, divided in their loyalties to the two factions, also became embroiled in open conflict. As in many such cases, factionalism in local society had paralyzed local government.[83]

It was previously assumed the Nationalist government was incapable of penetrating below the county level to organize social reform. Below that level, the local elites were thought to be in control.[84] I have shown the Nationalist government was able to penetrate to at least the sub-county level. Although in the end such an effort was undermined by the local elites, it allowed the state to intervene somewhat in local society. Thus, the intensification of factionalism in northern Henan should be seen as an indication of both the success and the failure of state making. On the one hand, the Nationalist government achieved greater influence than had any of the early Republican states through state penetration. On the other hand, the Nationalist state was unable to expand its political base among the local elites. Instead, it turned local society into a political battleground, which sowed the seeds for state's ultimate failure in the ensuing decade.

Above all, in its endeavor to build a modern state, the Nationalist government, unlike its predecessors, regarded the local elites as more than a target of state control. It attempted to incorporate them into its political system through the bureaucracy of its subcounty wards. But the undertaking was sabotaged by local elites. Through a combination of control and accommodation, the government finally succeeded, albeit to a limited degree, in achieving greater control of local society.

SOUTHWESTERN HENAN

Southwestern Henan has always posed immense difficulty to state makers for at least two apparent reasons. Its remoteness from Kaifeng, the

---

[83] *Weihui wenshi ziliao*, 3 (1991): 48–50.
[84] See John Fairbank, Edwin Reischauer, and Albert Craig, eds., *East Asia: Tradition and Transformation* (Boston: Houghton Mifflin, 1973), 787–8, 793; Eastman, *Abortive Revolution*, chapters 1, 3, 5; and Tien, *Government and Politics*, chapters 5, 6.

customary location of the provincial authority, made it difficult for any higher level of government to administrate the area. Furthermore, during the Republican period, the region was controlled by a group of newly risen elites who resisted any state attempt to exert its influence there. As previous chapters have shown, these elites were capable of using local militia and other elite organizations as an avenue of their own social control. They capitalized on a public yearning for a stable life, secure from banditry, to create an "environment of conflict" that was counterproductive to state making.[85] In order to compete for control of this region, each regime during the Republican period had to negotiate, compromise, and bargain with the local elites in addition to using every available means of forceful confrontation. To comprehend this intricate relationship between state and society, let us examine not only local elite resistance to state making but the state's attempt to overcome that resistance to achieve its modern transformation.

The Early Republican Period

After Yuan Shikai's government took control of southwestern Henan in April 1912 by driving away a small army called *luefenyongjun* from the city of Nanyang, its first task was to restrain the bandits who plagued the region, a task that occupied much of its time and effort before 1914. On January 22, 1914 Yuan relieved Gao Wengui – the Commissioner of Nanyang Regional Security – of his position for failing to accomplish his mission in controlling the bandits led by Bai Lang. As soon as the campaign against bandits produced results, the government promptly shifted its attention to reducing the influence of the local elites. In Nanyang City, for example, a county council formed earlier by the *luefenyongjun* was abolished after a Commissioner of Nanyang Regional Security was sent there to set up a regional garrison headquarters. Similar action was taken by the local government in every county. On May 20, the regional gov-

---

[85] Joel S. Migdal offers an alternative to the early models of European state building: the traditional-modern, stages of growth, and center-periphery models. Migdal considers the state merely one social organization among many (e.g., lineage, clan, kinship) that competed to achieve the same goal of social control. In Migdal's model, resistance from other social organizations or individuals is the main reason for the failure of the state to achieve predominance. Instead of examining the state's penetration into society and its success in extracting resources, Migdal scrutinizes the "environment of conflict" in which the state and other social organizations struggled to impose their own rules on society. See Migdal, *Strong Societies and Weak States*, 24–41, 261.

ernment ordered the merger of various private militia groups in every county with the one sponsored by the county government. Although, initially, the order was received with enthusiasm as the local elites saw the opportunity to legitimize their power, it soon became clear the government's true intention was to limit their activities. Therefore, many ignored the order. All these undertakings increased the government's administrative capability in the region.[86]

When Yuan Shikai's regime was over, and throughout the rest of the early Republican period, southwestern Henan descended into a statelessness. This confusion in the state's authority arose from the lack of stable government in the country and from sporadic state-making efforts by different warlord regimes and armies passing through the region. In 1923, for example, a small army called the *yijun* formed a county government in Neixiang. Less than a year later, when the Nationalist Revolutionary Army moved into the county, it replaced that regime with one of its own. Shortly thereafter, Wu Peifu's army occupied the region, followed by the *jianguoyujun*, both of which created their own county government agencies. In three years alone, therefore, Neixiang County experienced at least four different county administrations, established by disparate self-proclaimed authorities – in addition to those designated by the provincial authorities in Kaifeng.

Furthering the chaos, various organizations such as secret societies, the Communist Party, and the Nationalist Party also appeared in the region during this period. These political changes, along with the prevailing banditry crisis, added to the local society's vulnerability to exploitation and agitation.[87] This confusion contributed to a long-term "cultural crisis" in local society.[88]

One manifestation of the crisis was the "ruthlessness, boldness, and Machiavellian suppleness" of certain local elites, especially the newly

---

[86] *Xichuan xianzhi* (1990), 479; *Nanyang shizhi*, 29; *Nanyang xianzhi* (1990), 23; "Neixiang xianzhi: dashi ji," 17; and *Xichuan wenshi ziliao* (1989), 110.

[87] *Shanghai minbao* (*Shanghai People's Tribune*), (Shanghai, April 22, 1923), 192; *Nanyang xianzhi* (1990), 26, 31; and *Nanyang shizhi*, 31.

[88] Guy S. Alitto has argued, with specific reference to southwestern Henan, that the disintegration of the political system in the country caused a profound cultural crisis in the peripheral areas. The crucial indication of that crisis was that the local elites, along with the rest of the local population, no longer identified with any legitimizing authority but rather considered themselves, the people, the source of legitimacy. This transition provided the rationale for the new elites to take local matters into their own hands and to respond to every predicament with coercion and even bloodshed. See Alitto, "Rural Elites," 218–63.

risen elites.[89] In general, the local elites' challenge to authority was much more aggressive than it was in the north; in the southwest it usually ended in violence. During a tax riot in Nanyang County, for example, the participants totally destroyed the county office responsible for the collection of stamp duties. In Neixiang County, local elites plotted the assassination of a county official who was responsible for the program against opium farming. Public humiliation of county officials was also common. The local elites immediately perceived any government failure to respond to these challenges as a sign of weakness.[90]

Often, the local elites' challenges were centered around the issue of authority over the local militia, indicating that military power had become a crucial source of legitimacy. After one large militia led by Bie Tingfang began to emerge in Neixiang County, it denied the authority of the Bureau of Bandit Pacification – a county government agency responsible for commanding the county militia – and proclaimed itself the only legitimate militia group in the county. In Xichuan County, when the magistrate asked him to protect the county government, Chen Shunde took advantage of the opportunity and assumed leadership of the county militia.[91]

Max Weber's and Reinhard Bendix's analyses of the relationship between social actions and a general conception of a legitimate order shed light on this crucial change during the early Republican period. "Action," says Weber, "and especially social actions which involve social relationship, may be governed in the eyes of the participants by the conception that a legitimate order exists."[92] That order, in Bendix's understanding, "endures as long as the conception of its legitimacy is shared by those who exercise authority and those who are subject to it."[93] The developments in southwestern Henan indicate no such conception of a legitimate order, and that lack brought about the disappearance of pre-

[89] Alitto, "Rural Elites," 263.
[90] *Nanyang xianzhi* (1990), 24; Ibid. (1989), 30; "Neixiang xianzhi: dashi ji," 17; *Nanyang shizhi*, 30; and Henan dangshi gongzuo weiyuan hui, *Wusi qianhou de Henan shehui (Society in Henan Before and After the May Fourth Movement)* (Zhengzhou: Henan renmin chuban she, 1986), 481; and *Xichuan xianzhi* (1990), 411.
[91] "Neixiang xianzhi: dashi ji," 16; *Xixia xianzhi* (1990), 19; and *Xichuan xianzhi* (1990), 24–5.
[92] Max Weber, *The Theory of Social and Economic Organization* (New York: Oxford University Press, 1947), 124.
[93] Reinhard Bendix, *Nation-Building and Citizenship: Studies of Our Changing Social Order* (New York: Wiley, 1964), 16.

vious social norms and moral standards in the area. The change in individual behavior affected local society for the rest of the Republican period.[94]

An obvious sign of the change was the escalation of the power struggle within the elite community. Local elites were led to believe that whoever possessed power, especially military power, had legitimacy on his side. Various undertakings of the major and minor state makers at the local level, as well as the progress of warlordism throughout the country only aggravated the situation. The story of Bie Tingfang's confrontation with Zhang Hexuan and his defiance of state authority is instructive here.

In 1920 the county magistrate, Teng Yanan, reorganized all private militia groups into a county militia with three large divisions. He then appointed Zhang Hexuan, Bie Tingfang, and Nie Guozheng, to be the division chiefs. Afterward, Teng himself became the county militia chief but appointed another member of the local elite community, Jin Xin, to the position of deputy chief. Soon, Teng was accused by the local elites of embezzling from the tobacco tax fund and was dismissed from his position by the military authority of *fengtianliuyuxianfengdui*. Before Teng left Neixiang, he relinquished his position as county militia chief to Jin, who was later arrested by the Nanyang Garrison Commander of *yijun*, Ma Zhimin. Ma had also been accused of involvement in stealing government funds. The leadership of the county militia then naturally fell into the hands of Zhang Hexuan.[95]

After he rose to power in Neixiang County, Bie was often called upon by the provincial authority to assist its campaign against bandits. His stature thus grew within the elite community, and 1923 saw considerable expansion of his militia unit. By the end of the year, Ma Zhimin went to Neixiang County to reappoint Zhang Hexuan, Bie Tingfang, and Nie Guozheng as division chiefs. He also added a fourth division, with Luo Jiwu in charge. Zhang Hexuan considered his appointment as division chief to be a setback in his political career. However, it was not until Ma Zhimin appointed Bie as county militia chief – a position that was above

---

[94] Edward McCord argues that Chinese warlords emerged in the special context of the continuing crisis of political authority. That crisis, which started after the fall of the Qing dynasty, was caused by the difficulty of the nation to redefine its political authority. As the crisis persisted, military force became the only viable means to resolve the crisis, and the result was warlordism. See McCord, *Power of the Gun*, 309–15.

[95] Zhang, "Bie Tingfang," 83–4; See also *Bie Tingfang shilu*, 22; and "Neixiang xianzhi: dashi ji," 18.

Zhang's – in order to win his support for Ma's army that Zhang and Bie began to regard each other as principal rivals for power.[96]

The friction between Bie Tingfang and Zhang Hexuan first began to mount when Zhu Taosheng returned to his native Neixiang County. Zhu was sent back by Wu Peifu with the official title Chief Commander of the Military Units in the Four Southwestern Counties to organize grass-roots support for Wu's army. For a short while, Zhu was received by the elite community as the representation of government authority because he carried an official seal and a flag from Wu Peifu's government and was accompanied by twenty soldiers. As Zhu arrived in the county, Bie Tingfang initially decided to follow his instructions, even though Zhu appointed Zhang Hexuan chief of the county militia, relegating Bie Tingfang to a secondary position as division chief. The arrival of Zhang Zhigong, a garrison commander of the region sent by Wu Peifu, further confirmed Zhu's arrangement, which angered Bie, who had assumed that Zhu's arrangement was only temporary.[97]

The final showdown between Bie Tingfang and Zhang Hexuan occurred in 1926 when Zhang Zhigong's army was leaving the city of Nanyang. When Zhang Zhigong instructed Zhang Hexuan to lead a militia group to garrison Nanyang City, the latter requested Bie to bring a division of militiamen with him. Bie defied Zhang's order, arguing that Zhang did not have the proper authority. Bie then plotted to have Zhang assassinated, but the plot was uncovered and Zhang immediately moved his militiamen to the walled county seat. Subsequently, Zhang arrested Zhu Taosheng for his involvement in the plot. Open confrontation became unavoidable as Bie learned of Zhu's arrest.[98]

During his confrontation with Zhang Hexuan, Bie realized that the main source of his power was his local militia, not the endorsement of officials. He, therefore, no longer felt the need for Zhu Taosheng to legit-imize his position, although he still believed Zhu's seal and flag would convince others of his right to power. While Bie and Zhang were still at loggerheads, Zhu suddenly became very ill. Before Zhu died, Bie went to his home and demanded the seal. Zhu refused and died soon after-ward, but Bie was able to obtain the seal from Zhu's wife. With the seal in hand, Bie Tingfang proclaimed himself the only legitimate command-

[96] "Neixiang xianzhi: dashi ji," 20; Zhang, "Bie Tingfang," 85; and "Xixia xianzhi" (Unpub-lished), 12.
[97] *Bie Tingfang shilu*, 24–7; and Zhang, "Bie Tingfang," 85.
[98] Zhang, "Bie Tingfang," 85–7; and *Bie Tingfang shilu*, 26–9.

ing officer of all the militia units of four counties: Neixiang, Xichuan, Deng, and Zhenping.[99]

Bie Tingfang's success corresponded with the end of Wu Peifu's influence in Neixiang County, brought about by Feng Yuxiang's troops moving into the county by April 1927, two months before they seized Nanyang City. As soon as Feng's commanding officer, Sun Lianzhong, saw Bie's militia, his interest was piqued. After Sun's troops defeated Wu Peifu's at Nanyang, Sun had been instructed by his superior to co-opt Bie's militia. Having done that, Sun made Bie General Commander of the Neixiang Militia Regiment, conferring on him the responsibility for helping to rid the Neixiang area of bandits.[100]

A few months later, Feng Yuxiang announced the formation of four divisions of militia in Henan, to be known collectively as the Henan People's Militia. Feng appointed Bie Tingfang brigade commander, together with Peng Yuting and Zhao Zhiting, and made Wang Jinsheng, Chen Shunde, and Ding Shuheng regimental commanders. All four of the new divisions were placed under the authority of the southern Henan regiment. Despite Feng's appointments, Bie Tingfang continued to proclaim himself commander-in-chief of all the militia groups in southwestern Henan. Now that Bie controlled all the militia in the four-county area, Bie no longer felt subordinate to any authority. His militia headquarters began to take over the county government, acting as if it was the only local authority. It issued orders, collected taxes, and settled lawsuits or disputes, all in the name of the county government. By fall 1927, when a county magistrate sent by the provincial government, Yuan Shengan, started to question Bie's right to appropriate these duties, he was killed in an incident allegedly staged by a group of bandits. Then several other county officials who shared Yuan's distrust died in a similar incident. In another case, Bie Tingfang ordered the assassination of several county officials on November 19, 1928. Among them were the County Inspector of Education and County Bureau Chief of Education. It can be easily imagined these liquidations were carried out for reasons similar to the previous assassinations. In the following years, no one in the county government dared question Bie's power.[101]

---

[99] Chen, *Xianhua wanxi*, 126.
[100] Zhang, "Bie Tingfang," 86.
[101] Zhang Zhenjiang, "Feng Yuxiang zai Henan zuzhi mintuan jun de qingkuang" (Account of Feng Yuxiang's Organizing the People's Militia in Henan), in *Henan wenshi ziliao (Henan Local History)*, 8 (1983): 61–3; Ibid., 27 (1988): 89–93; *Nanyang xianzhi* (1990), 26; "Neixiang xianzhi: dashi ji," 24; and Zhang, "Bie Tingfang," 87.

Bie Tingfang's growing domination finally alarmed Feng Yuxiang's administration. It perceived Bie's large militia as a threat to its control of the county. Soon a local complaint was filed against Bie by Zhang Qiaochu, Hu Gongchen, and Qin Bichen. Zhang had been appointed by the previous county magistrate as head of a ward militia unit and a county inspector of education. Like Zhang, Hu had been the principal of a normal school for many years. Unlike Zhang and Hu, Qin was not involved in education but he was a head of the powerful Qin lineage. In this local opposition, Feng saw his chance to curb the influence of Bie Tingfang. As the complaint was received by Feng's government, the garrison commander of Nanyang District, Shi Yousan, immediately sent troops into Neixiang County to Disarm Bie's militia. Informed of the troop's approach, Bie and his militia hid in the mountains. After the troops left without touching Bie or his men, Bie began to flagrantly defy authority.[102]

The Neixiang experience strongly suggests that a sense of legitimate order had disappeared from southwestern Henan during the early Republican period because the region had been rendered totally stateless. The situation was further aggravated by sporadic attempts at state making by different military authorities that continued to create confusion in the local community. Because of these random interventions, the power struggle among local elites intensified. In a large sense, therefore, state making was counterproductive to the social development of the local society at this time.

As a consequence of these changes, local elites began to take matters into their own hands and completely ignored county authority. In this regard, my findings diverge from any of the existing models that explain the relationship between the local elites and state authority. To see how different the two approaches are, let us examine the preexisting models on local elites.

The Role of Local Elites. As Chung-li Chang has argued, local leaders often assisted, advised, or negotiated with the officials in different ways to protect their community's interests. The gentry would work with state officials, Chang suggests, when they perceived their interest to correspond with that of the government. If the two interests collided, the

---

[102] Zhang, "Bie Tingfang," 87; and *Bie Tingfang shilu*, 43–5.

gentry would oppose the government's actions without seriously challenging its authority.[103]

Agreeing with Chang, Kung-chuan Hsiao identifies two types of village leaders: the official leader, who received official appointment or was elected; and the informal leader, who relied for his power and influence on a number of factors – usually, age, wealth, learning, kin status, and personal capacity for leadership. Village leaders, Hsiao contends, sometimes served as intermediaries between villagers and the government. They sometimes openly opposed the government when their personal interest or the interest of their home areas were jeopardized.[104]

Following this line of thought, T'ung-tsu Ch'u perceives the influence of the local elites to fall generally into two spheres, the sphere of commoners and the sphere of local officials. In the former sphere, elites functioned as social leaders who settled disputes, raised funds for community projects, and headed local militias. In the latter, they influenced the decisions of local officials. Local elites were the intermediaries between the local officials and common people. Magistrates, generally unfamiliar with the details of county functioning, relied on them for important assistance such as transmitting orders and obtaining responses from the people. In return, local elites needed the magistrate's backing to maintain their influence and privileges. Their conflict with the officials was always on the level of individuals within the same power group, never between two groups.[105]

Observing local elites from the same angle, Hsiao-tung Fei considers Chinese rural society a two-layered structure. The central authority constituted the top layer and the local governing unit, the bottom. Fei contends the gentry played a decisive role in the bottom layer. Their function often went beyond the limit of local management to the extent that they exerted pressure on government from the bottom up. Through their relatives and friends, they could have their opinion heard by local government officials and even by the central authority.[106]

A variation of this model is a brokerage model, which stresses the "transmitter" function of the local elites in taxation and their protective role in village organization.[107] As discussed earlier, Prasenjit Duara has identified the subadministrative personnel and the individuals assisting

---

[103] Chang, *Chinese Gentry*, 51–70.   [104] Hsiao, *Rural China*, 264–322.
[105] Ch'u, *Local Government*, 175, 180–1, 190–2.
[106] Fei, *China's Gentry*, 79–88.   [107] Ch'u, *Local Government*, 187.

the county government in taxation as well as community projects as "entrepreneurial brokers." Meanwhile, he also acknowledges that other local elites organized themselves among villages to protect the community interest, often against the entrepreneurial brokers. Sometimes, however, the protective brokers also acted as entrepreneurial brokers.[108]

Offering a different perspective, Marianne Bastid-Bruguiere has analyzed the rise of a generation of "novel rural oligarchy" in various regions since the Taiping Rebellion. These rural parvenus were created by the social changes of the late imperial period. They were neither the traditional scholar elites nor did they assume the traditional ritual functions within local communities. They exercised their power through local militias and depended on government support to maintain their personal interests, such as appropriating large sections of public land in border areas and uncultivated zones for themselves.[109]

Keith Schoppa, through his "rural oligarchy" model of peripheral Zhejiang elites, proposes that many local elites chose to work within the government institutions to enhance their status. They assisted magistrates in all kinds of local matters and usually performed minor official duties to the extent that their role and that of the officials became blurred. Schoppa finds the relationship of these peripheral elites with magistrates to be less antagonistic than in the other areas of Zhejiang, citing the evidence that fewer petitions for the impeachment of magistrates were filed by the local elites in the periphery than elsewhere.[110]

In Edward McCord's "strongmen" model, the main source of power of the local elites in Xinyi County of Guizhou is closely associated with their control of the local militia. And they held power through the conducting of local defense, not the holding of degrees. By their suppression of the Taiping rebels, the local elites rose to power through the government's honoring of official titles and brevet offices.[111]

Johanna M. Meskill argues that the local elites were more powerful than the government because of their special ties to local society. Deeply rooted in local soil, they "represented a local, but economically differ-

---

[108] Duara, *Culture, Power, and the State*, 42–57.
[109] Marianne Bastid-Bruguiere, "Currents of Social Change," in *The Cambridge History of China: Late Qing, 1800–1911, Part II*, vol. 11. John K. Fairbank and Kwang-ching Liu, eds. (New York: Cambridge University Press, 1980), 579–601.
[110] Schoppa, *Chinese Elites*, 116–18, 132–4.
[111] McCord, "Local Military Power," 168–72.

entiated, group that combined personal prowess, local prestige, wealth, and at least marginal legitimacy in the eyes of the government." But, the relationship between these strongmen and the government was ambivalent. They could either lead rebellion against the government or they could assist the government in legitimizing themselves.[112]

How do these models fit the local elites in southwestern Henan? The evidence from the present study strongly suggests that none of the models fit well, although most contain some applicable aspects. For example, most models presuppose the existence of a (more or less) stable, or at least identifiable, government institution, both central and local – a condition obviously lacking in southwestern Henan.

The gentry model assumes a two-tier structure, with the government in the upper tier and the village community in the lower. A stable government was a necessary foundation for the existence of such a structure. According to the oligarchy model, local elites either depended heavily on government support or chose to work under the government's institutions in order to maintain their power. Even the strongmen in McCord's study relied on government recognition for their status. In southwestern Henan a stable county government no longer existed, and even when it did, it was paralyzed by the local elites' efforts to take over its function and replace it with their own institution (see Chapter 6). Through self-legitimization, the local elites reduced state influence to a minimum. They thus had little interest or desire to assist the county government in local affairs.

Although the brokerage model does not necessarily share the same presuppositions – as one can argue local elites could perform a brokerage role without a stable or identifiable government in existence – it does not describe the role of the local elites (see previous discussion). The closest existing description of the local elites in southwestern Henan is Meskill's model, based on her study of eighteenth- and nineteenth-century Taiwan, in which the relationship between the government and the local elites falls into the first category – to lead a rebellion against the state. However, the local elites in this region were far more politically sophisticated than those in Taiwan.

Based on the discoveries of the differences in realities of southwestern Henan and other areas of the country, I suggest that in future research we follow an "intertextural" approach recognizing the unique-

---

[112] Meskill, *Chinese Family*, 88–91, 102, 260.

ness of each locale in its social structure and the elements of its community culture.[113] Such conditions could vary from time to time, or location to location, especially during the early Republican period, when the political situation was generally fluid. As many of my sources show, even in similar peripheral areas, considerable variations existed among different counties, as they did in the relationship between the local elites in those counties and the various state authorities.

The Position of County Magistrate. To shed further light on the relationship between state authority and local society in southwestern Henan, we may also need to examine the changes that occurred in the type of person who occupied the position of county magistrate. As my sources indicate, the magistrates appointed by Yuan Shikai's and Li Yuanhong's regimes were mostly well educated and had administrative experience. Afterward, a wider variety of people, including army officers and other local elites, were selected for the position.[114] Although, the tension between the local people and magistrates continued when nonnatives occupied the post, the usual link between magistrate and gentry that existed in the imperial period was replaced by a special tie between the local community and its natives who became county officials.[115] Because the natives usually had their own interests and feelings toward the community, they were more likely to disobey orders from above and to preserve their ties to, and personal interest in, the community, although they became more susceptible to bribery or other corruption than outsiders. This change in the origin of magistrates decreased the state's influence in the local society.[116]

Throughout the early Republican period, changes also transpired in the capacity of magistrates to perform their official duties. Because there was little administrative support for magistrates from higher levels of administration, the magistrates often had to depend on the local elites to either restore or preserve the status quo. This put the magistrate at a

---

[113] Vivienne Shue argues for a process approach to Chinese politics. Examining both social and cultural elements simultaneously, she claims, leads to an "analysis of the entire, intricate social intertexture that forms the stuff of political life." See Vivienne Shue, *The Reach of the State: Sketches of the Chinese Body Politic* (Stanford: Stanford University Press, 1988), 25–9.

[114] *Henan tongguan lu (Officials in Henan)* (Kaifeng, 1921); and *Nanyang xianzhi* (1990), 120–1.

[115] Kuhn, "Local Self-Government," 262; and Ch'u, *Local Government*, 176.

[116] *Xichuan xianzhi* (1990), 25; and "Ge xian xianzhang hanbao," 4, no. 7 (1934): 10.

disadvantage while he was competing with the local elites for public support.[117] One magistrate from Xichuan County wrote: "Xichuan County is located in a remote area; the situation there is unusual. Everything is very difficult [for the magistrate]." The comments from his superior in the provincial administration are even more revealing: "What the local bullies and evil gentry rely on is the support of the public, and they use that against the government. If we can educate the people . . . not to support the local bullies and evil gentry, we will be able to carry out the government's orders there." If the magistrate was not a native, such influence was always hard to come by.[118]

Finally, by contrast with the north, southwestern Henan suffered from an even higher turnover rate among magistrates due to the frequent fluctuation in state authority (see Table 8.2).

As Table 8.2 indicates, most magistrates in Nanyang County served less than a year in their positions, many for less than six months. A similar situation occurred in other counties as well. At least seven magistrates served in Neixiang County within one five-month period. A brigade commander of Feng Yuxiang's army, Wei Fenglou, entering Neixiang County in May 1927, arrested the former county magistrate and appointed a succession of his own officers to the post. Similar actions were constantly taken by the warlords or other military authorities. Shortly thereafter, the provincial government began to appoint its own magistrates. My findings confirm James Sheridan's assertion that during the warlord period there was a particularly high turnover of magistrates in rural China.[119] As a result of such instability, few county magistrates were taken seriously by the people.[120] Given the shaky status of most county magistrates in this region, it was no wonder that state influence was severely compromised at the local level, eventually resulting in a weak state presence and strong resistance from local elites to the state-making process.[121] After it established its provincial administration in Kaifeng, the Nationalist government thus faced a serious challenge to its reinstatement of state influence in southwestern Henan.

---

[117] Wakeman, *Strangers at the Gate*, 30.

[118] "Ge xian xianzhang hanbao," 4, no. 7 (1934): 8.

[119] James Sheridan, "The Warlord Era: Politics and Militarism under the Peking Government, 1916–28," *The Cambridge History of China*, John K. Fairbank, ed. vol. 12 (New York: Cambridge University Press, 1983), 290–1.

[120] "Neixiang xianzhi: dashi ji," 23.

[121] My findings thus differ significantly from those in Keith Schoppa's study of the peripheral zone of Zhejiang. Schoppa, *Chinese Elites*, 115–41.

Table 8.2. *Length of Magistrates' Terms in Nanyang County (1912–48)*

Name	Year Appointed	Length of Term	Origin
Zhu Shenxiu	1912	two months	
Han Bangfu	1912, Feb.–Jun.	less than one year	Shandong
Zhao Bingwen	1913	five months	Jiangsu
Zhu Zhengben	1913, May–	one month	Anhui
Jing Xingcheng	1913, Jun. 30–	one month	Henan
Zhang Bin	1913, Aug.–	less than one year	Shanxi
Cao Mushi	1914, Mar.–	nine months	Shandong
Cui Wen	1914, Dec.–	one year	Jiangsu
Shen Jiaxin	1915, Dec.–	nine months	Beijing
Cheng Changxin	1916, Sep.–	six months	Anhui
Wang Chonglu	1917, Mar.–Jun.	three months	Shandong
Tian Pei			Tianjin
Zhang Shoutian	1919	about one year	Hubei
Wang Sidan	1920, Oct.–	about one year	Zhejiang
Du Ziji	1921		
Wu Guoxing			
Tai Fusan			
Zhang Xidian			
Li Shuying	1923, Nov.–	three months	Zhili
Lu Xiaoxian			Shaanxi
Yu Hualou	1926		
Li Tiemin			
Chen Ruyu	1927, Sep.–	less than one year	
Dong Guoqing	1927	about one year	Henan
Zhu Yanzu	1928	one year	
Cui Songtao	1929	less than one year	
Liu Kan			
Zhou Ruilin	1929	less than one year	
Deng Feimin	1929	less than one year	
Chen Zijian	1930, Jan.–	four months	Shaanxi
Mi Zanchen	1930, Mar.–May	two months	Shaanxi
Du Baotian	1930, May–Nov.	six months	Shaanxi
Hao Peiyun	1930–1931	four months	Henan
Lu Zongxian	1931, Mar.–Aug.	three months	Zhejiang
Li Yaguang	1931, Aug.–Dec.	four months	Hebei
Zhang Lie	1931, Dec.–	less than one year	Zhejiang
Wei Xiaoru	1932, May–Aug.	three months	Henan
Mao Longzhang	1932, Oct.–	eight months	Zhili
Wang Youqiao	1933, Jun.–	eleven months	Henan
Luo Zhen	1934, May	three years	Henan (Nanzhao)
Zhu Jiuying	1937	less than one year	Hunan

(Continued)

Table 8.2. *(Continued)*

Name	Year Appointed	Length of Term	Origin
Zhang Keming	1937	about one year	Henan (Xichuan)
Tao Wenjing	1938, Apr.–Dec.	eight months	Henan (Nanyang)
Li Zijing	1939–1940	one year	Henan (Deng)
Fan Xiaochun	1941–1943	two years	Henan
Chen Yi	1943–1944	one year	Henan
Feng Boqing	1944, Apr.–	nine months	
Zhao Zhiting	1945, Jan.–	about two years	Henan (Nanyang)
Guo Zibin	1946–1948		Henan

Source: Nanyang difang shizhi bianchuan weiyuan hui, *Nanyang xianzhi (Gazetteer of Nanyang County)* (Zhengzhou: Henan renmin chuban she, 1990), 120–2.

The Nanjing Decade

As the Nationalist government took control of Henan at the end of 1928, southwestern Henan was in the midst of a series of political developments that culminated in the emergence of the Southwestern Henan Four-County Self-Government.[122] As the previous chapters have shown, Self-Government was antagonistic toward the state. From its early days, the Nationalist government had to deal with not only the leaders of the organization but also a large number of hostile militiamen, and the control of these military forces turned out to be its greatest concern. As soon as Liu Zhi became the chairman of the provincial government, he took steps to suppress the local elites' defiance of the provincial government. Liu perceived the local elites in four counties (Neixiang, Zhenping, Xichuan, and Deng) in southwestern Henan as being the least cooperative toward the provincial government. His first target was these four counties.[123]

---

[122] For detailed information on the Self-Government organization and its quite sophisticated elite activism, refer to Zhang Xin, "Elite Activism in the Periphery: Henan, 1900–1937," *Republican China*, 19, no. 2 (1994): 67–103.

[123] Henan sheng zhengfu mishu chu tongji shi, *Wunian lai shizheng tongji: baoan (Statistics of the Last Five-year Administration: Security)* (Kaifeng: Henansheng zhengfu mishu chu, 1935), 1; Liu Zhi, *Wo de hui yi (My Memoir)* (Taipei: Rongtai yinshu guan, 1966), 117–20.

To reduce the leverage of the local elites and strengthen its own influence, initially the government fortified its administrative control of the area outside the four counties. Here the government suspended the county magistrate in Nanyang for his inability to control unauthorized Self-Government. Subsequently, Liu Zhenhua, then Nanyang regional security chief officer, ordered the execution of the president of the county Chamber of Commerce and the head of the county militia, for participating in the founding of Self-Government. For a similar crime, the Nanyang County government also confiscated the land of several elites. In Xinye and Tanghe counties, government troops detained several elites for organizing Self-Government there.[124]

By 1933, the government began to target the local elites in the four counties. It ordered its troops to arrest Peng Yuting for failure to comply with its orders and for resisting government taxation, but the order was rescinded for lack of soldiers. Later, more attempts were made to arrest Bie Tingfang for defying government authority. Liu Zhi once planned to dispatch troops to Neixiang County, only to be contradicted by the chief of the department of interior, Li Jingzhai. If the government troops were unable to match the local militia, Li argued, the government would completely forfeit its authority in the area. Also in 1933 the provincial government adopted a gun control law that forced gunsmiths to give up their private practices or face severe penalties. But the law was completely ignored by the local elites in the four-county area.[125]

When it failed to achieve control over the leaders of Self-Government, the provincial government tried to co-opt them. Liu Zhenhua, then Nanyang District Chief, invited Peng Yuting to assist in the training of functionaries for a government-sponsored Self-Government organization founded in Nanyang County. By late 1933, Zhu Jiuying and Luo Zhen, two new commissioners of Nanyang District, visited Neixiang County to praise Bie for contributing to the stability and economic development of the county. Zhu then offered Bie his personal friendship. In December 1933 Bie Tingfang received his first official appointment from the Nationalist government, Chief Commander of the Guerrilla Force in

---

[124] *Zhengfu gongbao*, 153 (1931): 4–5; *Nanyang xianzhi* (1990), 28; and *Henan sheng nongcun diaocha*, 106.
[125] *Yi yue lai zhi caizheng*, 3, no. 3 (April 1933): 6; Ibid., 2, no. 12 (January 1933): 15; and Chen, *Xianhua wanxi*, 57.

Nanyang District. But suspicious of the government's intention to restrict his activities, Bie renounced the title.[126]

Bie's uncooperativeness greatly enraged Liu Zhi, who therefore revived his plan to arrest him. In 1934, in order to lure Bie to Kaifeng, Liu appointed him division commander of the provincial militia in Kaifeng and insisted that Bie appear in person to receive the appointment. Suspecting foul play, Bie sent his lieutenants, Yang Jiesan and Tian Ziyue, with nearly one thousand militiamen. As soon as Yang and Tian arrived in Kaifeng, the two were detained and subsequently executed, and their bodyguards were arrested. Having failed in his attempt to trap Bie, Liu Zhi himself led troops into Neixiang County to arrest him. On his march, however, the garrison commander of Nanyang District, Pang Binxun, fearing a regionwide rebellion of militiamen, persuaded Liu not to carry out his plan. Liu thus returned to Kaifeng without Bie.[127]

Ironically, while the local elites' relationship with the provincial government was going sour, their relationship with local officials started to improve. The district commissioner, Zhu Jiuying, for instance, became very sympathetic toward Self-Government after he became acquainted with its leaders. In an effort to ease the tension between himself and Bie Tingfang, Liu Zhi later reluctantly appointed Bie commander-in-chief of the Self-Defense Army in the Sixth District of Henan Province. Meanwhile, the garrison commander of Nanyang District, Pang Binxun, had also become very friendly with Bie, having at times depended on the support of Bie's militia to fulfill his duty of controlling banditry. Pang's overtures of friendship to Bie may have been motivated by the fact that by the time Pang became garrison commander, Bie already had about forty thousand men under his command.[128] Nevertheless, this cordial relationship between local officials and local elites greatly helped to maintain stability in the region.

To understand this interesting phenomenon, I refer to Joel Migdal's concept of "accommodation," which can be applied to the compromises made by the three holders of power in local society: state officials, local political figures, and strongmen. As Migdal has also observed in India, Mexico, and other Third World countries at present, none of the parties

---

[126] *Nanyang shizhi*, 33; *Bie Tingfang shilu*, 59–62; and *Xixia xianzhi* (1990), 23.

[127] "Xixia xianzhi: renwu pian," 122; Zhang, "Bie Tingfang," 103–4; *Bie Tingfang shilu*, 57–8; and "Neixiang xianzhi: dashi ji," 32.

[128] *Bie Tingfang shilu*, 47–8, 62.

in such a "triangle of accommodation" was able to monopolize power; each had to compromise with the others.[129]

In southwestern Henan, the triangle was different in that it existed only among the Nationalist government, local officials, and local elites. Because local elites had the upper hand, the local officials were the most accommodative and the local elites were the least, whereas the provincial government was forced to make unwilling concessions. The following events illustrate this relationship. Bie Tingfang planned to conduct a local trial for several dozen bandits and secret-society members waiting to be transferred from the county jail to the provincial jail. The provincial government agreed to let the trial take place, but insisted that the prisoners be turned over to the provincial jail after the trial. During the trial, Bie ignored the government's order and demanded the prisoners be executed. After the execution, Bie informed the provincial police headquarters, but the police never responded.[130]

The local elites' dominance was also evident in their way of dealing with local officials. A magistrate resigned from his position in Xichuan County, for instance, because the local elites had interfered with his official duties. Other magistrates complained that their personal residences were always guarded by militiamen sent by the local elites to prevent anyone from approaching them privately, although the elites claimed that the guards were to protect them from bandits.[131]

This is not to say the local elites never accommodated the Nationalist government or local officials. Bie Tingfang assisted government troops in rescuing Zhenping County from bandits in February 1932. In 1933 he also sent two regiments of his own militiamen to help government troops in their fight against bandits. On December 12, 1936, Bie even dispatched his militiamen as reinforcements for Chiang Kai-shek's army, which was surrounded in southern Shangchen County. And when the Ninety-Fifth Route Army was passing through Neixiang County on its way to Shaanxi province to rescue Chiang, Bie also volunteered to provide the army with food and other supplies.[132] Local elites accommodated Nationalist government and local officials, however, only when they perceived their

---

[129] Migdal, *Strong Societies and Weak States*, 247–56.

[130] Chen Yuchun, "Bie Tingfang yanxing jianwen suoji" (Anecdotes about Bie Tingfang), in *Henan wenshi ziliao (Henan Local History)*, 33 (1990): 127.

[131] Wu Kai, "Yang Jiahui xianzhang de youlai" (The Reason for Yang Jiahui Becoming a County Magistrate), in *Xichuan wenshi ziliao (Xichuan Local History)* (1989): 130; and Chen, "Bie Tingfang yanxing," 128.

[132] "Neixiang xianzhi: dashi ji," 30–31, 34.

own interests coincided with those of the other members of the triangle.

Of the three sides of the triangle, local officials were in the most accommodative position, a situation virtually unchanged since the end of the early Republican period. Once in Deng County, for instance, Bie Tingfang's militiamen killed some suspected bandits. After the killing was reported to Liu Zhenhua, there was no response nor any action taken. In 1936, when the Xichuan County government received many complaints about Self-Government using force to collect various fees, county officials pretended the complaints had never been received.[133]

The position of the Nationalist government in the relationship deserves more discussion. It is first worth noting that the government's influence had gradually increased in this region since the beginning of the 1930s, although most of the influence was limited to the areas outside the four counties. For instance, in 1932 the provincial government sent an inspector to Nanzhao County to investigate a complaint filed by the chief of the county's Education Bureau against the county magistrate for neglecting his responsibility. And in 1935, after a Nanyang County judge had been assassinated, the state police immediately arrested ten suspects and executed part of the group.[134]

In addition, the Nationalist government had been making considerable efforts to maintain its influence by accommodating the local elites outside the four-county area. In April 1930, a tax riot broke out in response to a county magistrate's excessive levying. During the riot, the county police chief ordered the police to open fire on the protesters after they had destroyed the police station at Sanlitun. Afterward, local elites and nearly two thousand locals joined together in protest. Under pressure, the provincial government agreed to execute the police chief and the assistant magistrate.[135]

Within the four-county area, however, state influence was still very limited. In order to assess the success of the Nationalist government's state-making plan, I have chosen the politicization of factionalism as my criterion. As I indicated earlier, such factionalism in northern Henan was a product of state involvement in local society. Because of the lack of state involvement in southwestern Henan, this type of factionalism never developed there on a scale comparable to that in the north.

[133] *Bie Tingfang shilu*, 56–7; and Wang, "Xichuanxian difang zizhi," 29.
[134] "Mishu chu geke gongzuo gaiyao," 3 (1990): 29.
[135] *Nanyang xianzhi* (1990), 27, 619; and Ibid. (1989), 32, 216–17.

In a 1933 conflict of local elites in Deng County, one group was headed by the militia leader Dai Huanzhang and the other was joined by many powerful elites. The second group saw Dai expanding his militia following and decided to curb his power. They sent a message to Bie Tingfang requesting his assistance. Bie soon arrived in Deng County with four thousand militiamen to surround the headquarters of Dai's militia. As soon as Liu Zhi heard the news, he sent a delegate to mediate between the two groups. Bie refused to let Dai leave and his men launched an attack, but Dai finally escaped.[136]

On another occasion, tension had existed between Bie Tingfang and a former Tongmenhui member and regionally known political activist, Wang Gengxian, who was always critical of Bie. By the time Bie's militia had taken over Deng County, Wang was residing in Kaifeng. After receiving an invitation from Bie's antagonists to lead their opposition, Wang hastened back to Deng County. On learning of Wang's return, Bie persuaded the county magistrate to arrest him for conspiracy against the county government. Wang was soon killed by Bie's men.[137]

Factionalism in the southwest in the late Republican period obviously had little to do with the political issues that concerned the rest of the country, neither did it involve the political organizations that challenged each other in the north. Factionalism here derived mostly from the competition for power among different groups of local elites, or resulted from the way local elites formed their "web of defined relationships" to ensure their own interests, both of which situations grew naturally in the local soil.[138] Nor were any of the factional conflicts related to any of the personnel changes in the government or the Nationalist Party. This missing linkage between factionalism as a local phenomenon and as a part of national politics should be considered an indication of the lack of impact of state making.

Reconciliation of State and Society. The beginning of the Sino-Japanese War marked the turning point of the government's policy toward the

---

[136] *Bie Tingfang shilu*, 43.   [137] Ibid., 51–3.

[138] Discussing factionalism in the Republican period, Andrew Nathan points out that most Chinese viewed themselves in a "web of defined role relationships" and acted accordingly. The practical reason for establishing such relationships was to ensure stability between each party in a relationship; it also provided a base line by which one party could gauge the other. See Andrew J. Nathan, "A Constitutional Republic: the Peking Government, 1916–28," in *The Cambridge History of China (Republican China 1912–1949, Part I)*, vol. 12, ed. John K. Fairbank (Cambridge: Cambridge University Press, 1983), 271–4.

local elites in southwestern Henan. Considering it a strategic location for retreat, the Nationalist government reassessed the region's significance and realized the advantage of having a large number of local militiamen working for its political agenda. The government thus reversed its previous antagonistic stance and embraced the local elites and their organization, Self-Government. This important gesture removed the major obstacle that had prevented the local elites from supporting the Nationalist state in its political aims.

In the summer of 1937 the provincial government appointed Bie Tingfang the security chief of the entire Nanyang District and invited him to move his militia headquarters into Nanyang City. Commissioner Zhu Jiuying then authorized a Self-Government institution be established in every county as a part of Four-County Self-Government. The following year, when Li Zonghuang, then chairman of the GMD in Henan, arrived in Kaifeng, he was told that Bie Tingfang and other local elites in southwestern Henan were resisting provincial authority – they even refused to allow the GMD to maintain an office in the area. But Li decided to take a different approach to the local elites in southwestern Henan than his predecessors had. He invited Bie Tingfang to meet him in Kaifeng to discuss a common course of action against the Japanese. Since the invitation, Li had been a key advocate of a lenient policy toward the local elites because he valued their support for the Nationalist government's political agenda above any reconciling of political differences between the elites and local officials. To win the assistance of the local elites, Li tried to persuade other officials to put aside their personal views, arguing that the elites were unintentionally following Sun Yat-sen's idea of social reform.[139]

In March 1938 Bie Tingfang and Li Zonghaung finally met in Kaifeng. Li assuaged Bie's suspicions of his intentions by assuring him the government considered his activities to be legitimate. Li also praised Bie for his courage in carrying out such an extensive organizational program as Self-Government. After conferring with Li for several days, Bie decided to cooperate with the government and volunteered to establish a Nationalist Party chapter in the four-county area. The provincial government then appointed Bie commissioner of the Nationalist Party in Zhenping, Neixiang, and Xichuan counties. After that, most of the local elites involved with Self-Government were offered

---

[139] "Nanzhao xianzhi," 47; Li, *Zizhi congshu*, 28 (1972): 326, 328; and Chen, "Bie Tingfang yanxing," 125.

official positions. Self-Government was thus fully legitimized by the government.[140]

The high point of the new relationship between the Nationalist government and the local elites occurred in the summer of 1938 when Chiang Kai-shek decided to meet with Bie Tingfang in Wuhan. During the meeting, Chiang praised Bie and granted him the new title of Commander in Chief of National Resistance and of the Self-Defense Army of the Sixth District of Henan. As a result of the meeting, the Nationalist government acknowledged Neixiang County as one of three model counties in China. As a friendly gesture, Chiang Kai-shek even sent a secret service officer to help Bie organize a secret service branch in Neixiang County. Liu Zhi's words about the Nationalist government's intention, contained in an internal government document, are very telling. Liu wrote that Bie Tingfang was a local despot who ignored the government and that he should be eliminated. However, because he was too powerful to be liquidated, the government should co-opt him to support its agenda, especially when the Sino-Japanese War made that support more necessary than ever. Thus, out of expedience, the Nationalist government finally reached out to the local elites in the southwest.[141]

Such events were typical of the pattern of weak state presence versus strong social resistance that existed in southwestern Henan during the Republican period. This pattern began to emerge immediately after Yuan Shikai's administration, as part of the political evolution of local society. One important aspect of that evolution was the persistence of a profound cultural crisis resulting from the absence of a conceptualization of legitimate order, and which contributed to an intensified competition for influence among local elites throughout the end of the early Republican period. Because military power was perceived as the only source of authority, that competition centered mainly around the issue of the leadership of the local militia and resulted in the concentration of local power among a few military elites.

The emergence of the elite organization known as Self-Government was a natural outcome of the earlier political evolution among the local elites, but it in return institutionalized their dominance of the area. The existence of Self-Government greatly hindered the Nationalist govern-

---

[140] Li, *Zizhi congshu*, 28 (1972): 328–9; "Neixiang xianzhi: dashi ji," 36; and Sheng, *Wanxi Chen Shunde*, 105–9. For Li Zonghuang's experience in Nanyang, See Li Zonghuang, *Li Zonghuang huiyilu* (Reminiscence of Li Zonghuang) (Taipei, 1972).

[141] "Neixiang xianzhi: dashi ji," 37; and *Bie Tingfang shilu*, 63–4.

ment's reinstatement of its authority in the region. In order to cope with the local elites, the government tried every method at its disposal, including suppression, co-optation, and accommodation.[142] But all failed due to the strong resistance from the local elites and internal dissension among the state officials.

The Sino-Japanese War forced the Nationalist government to embrace the local elites. This strategic move, which secured the support of local elites for the government's political course, brought the government closer to its goal of state making. The Nationalist government thus achieved its original aim – to expand its political base to include the local elites. In comprehending the reason for the Nationalist government's sudden reversal in policy toward the local elites in southwestern Henan, Joel Migdal's theory is instructive. Migdal notes that the rise of a strong state and successful state building requires one important condition in addition to efficient and loyal bureaucrats and wise state leaders. That condition is a "massive societal dislocation," such as the spread of world economy, revolution, or massive migration – a disruption that could destroy the old bases of social control and weaken other social organizations sufficiently to allow the state to achieve dominance through state building, or, an external military threat that could trigger state-building efforts and force the state to deal with the strongmen who instigated it.[143] In the southwestern Henan experience, the Sino-Japanese War served as just such a condition, forcing the Nationalist government to reach out to the local elites in the region.

Did this change in policy mean that the Nationalist government accomplished its goal of creating a modern state? The answer is "no," but on this subject there has been much previous discussion. According to Theda Skocpol, for example, the Nationalist government was an urban-based regime, unlike the peasant-based CCP, and it failed to consolidate centralized state power because it lacked the administrative and military resources needed for the task of penetrating rural society. Even though the Nationalist state established unchallenged military and administrative control in the provinces, it was unable to influence village-level politics and break the power structure of the local elites.[144]

---

[142] For a discussion of the "oppositional" model of state making, see David Nugent, "Building the State, Making the Nation: The Bases and Limits of State Centralization in 'Modern' Peru," *American Anthropologist* 96, no. 2 (1994): 333–69.

[143] Migdal, *Strong Societies and Weak States*, 269–77.

[144] Skocpol, *States and Social Revolutions*, 242–52.

Disagreeing with Skocpol, Lloyd E. Eastman attributes the Nationalist government's failure to the lack of any social base. Its hegemony was based neither on the landholding class in the countryside nor on capitalists in the urban areas. Its policies originated from no political group or institution outside the government, but only from the welfare of its own members. The Nationalist state, therefore, existed only to aggrandize its own bureaucrats' personal interests.[145]

Dissenting from both Skocpol and Eastman, Bradley K. Geisert interprets the relationship between the local elites and the Nationalist government as being rather complex. There was not only antagonism but also cooperation between the two, both based on their mutual interests. But overall, Geisert believes, an alliance existed between the Nationalist government and the local elites. Because of that affiliation, the chance of the Nationalist government establishing a genuinely modern state was jeopardized, for a modern state depended largely on the support of its entire citizenry, not merely a particular social group. In Geisert's understanding, an iron bond between state and citizen was crucial to the emergence of a modern state, and the strong alliance between the government and the elites made such a bond impossible. The Chinese state thus remained a garrison state, dependent for its control of local society on suppression rather than mass mobilization of its citizenry.[146]

My research supports Geisert's view that the Nationalist government had extended its arms only to the local elites, not to the general rural population, which was the essential task for creating a modern state. Even toward the local elites, as the evidence from southwestern Henan indicates, the Nationalist government still remained suspicious and cautious. The Nationalist government had never felt comfortable with the local elites in the southwest. As soon as the evacuation of provincial administration was over, the chairman of the provincial government, Wei Lihuang, called for a meeting to relieve the local elites, especially Bie Tingfang, of their official positions. Subsequently, the provincial government appointed its own officials to the top positions in the local militia, which angered Bie Tingfang and probably brought on his death soon thereafter.[147] In other words, even after Chiang Kai-shek's meeting with Bie Tingfang, there is still little indication the GMD had a genuine alliance with the local elites. The GMD's inability to destroy the local

---

[145] Eastman, *Abortive Revolution*, 286.
[146] Geisert, "Power and Society," (dissertation), 261–3.
[147] Li, *Zizhi congshu*, 28 (1972): 329; Chen, *Xianhua wanxi*, 17.

elite establishment thus remained one of the main reasons for its assuming a cooperative strategy toward the local elites. This halfway transformation of the Nationalist government into a modern state therefore planted the seeds of the government's ultimate failure when facing a Communist challenge based on a mobilization of the rural population from the ground up, during and after the Sino-Japanese War.

SUMMARY

This study has suggested two distinctive patterns of relationship between the state and local society in Henan during the Republican period: in northern Henan a strong state presence versus a weak social resistance pattern, and in the southwest, exactly the reverse.[148] The northern Henan pattern emerged right after Yuan Shikai issued his order to end the county assemblies and Self-Government. It continued during Feng Yuxiang's regime, with roughly a ten-year hiatus due to the very absence of a stable state. As soon as the Nationalist government took over the province, it took steps to prevent the local elites from challenging its authority by combining co-optation measures with campaigns against the so-called local bullies and evil gentry. But after the government grasped the increasing tension between itself and the local elites, it modified its policy from one of confrontation to one of accommodation.

The pattern of relationship between state and society in southwestern Henan, however, evolved even before the end of the Qing dynasty, while the local society was beset by a banditry crisis. As a profound cultural crisis – manifested in the lack of a general conceptualization of legitimate order among the population of peripheral areas like southwestern Henan – continued during the early Republican period, the local elites took advantage of the social conditions to supplant the state authorities throughout the region. Even the Nationalist government had to relinquish its attempts to suppress the local elites, shifting to a policy of co-optation and accommodation, and finally to fully recognizing the legitimacy of local elites' dominance of the area.[149]

---

[148] According to James Scott, one common characteristic of peasant life is resistance to a formal power such as the state. See Scott, "Everyday Forms of Resistance," 3–33.

[149] My conceptualization of what constitutes opposition between the state and society is based on David Nugent's notion of that relationship in Peru. According to Nugent, co-optation and accommodation were also part of oppositional measures for state making. See Nugent, "Building the State," 333–69.

By reviewing the formation of these two patterns, one inevitably sees that modern state making was not simply a top-down process but an interaction between the state and local society, and that its outcome was often predetermined by the long-term process of social transformation that occurred before and during state making. To take the Nationalist government's experience in southwestern Henan as an example, the success of state making was preconditioned by the social development that transpired before the arrival of that government. Even though the government had the commitment and military resources, it was unable to reverse the outcome of the state-making efforts of its predecessors precisely because gradual changes in the local power structure had already led to the establishment of a militarily and politically powerful elite organization called Self-Government. Given these preexisting conditions, the Nationalist government was forced to resort to the only methods by which the state could deal with strong societal resistance to its state-making efforts (as Charles Tilly has also noted in the European state-making experience): bargaining, accommodation, and compromise with the local elites.[150] After even those measures failed, the Nationalist government was forced to yield completely to the local elites and only then, ironically, did it accomplish its initial goal of extending its political base to those individuals. From this vantage point, therefore, we can see that modern state making was part of a "mutually transforming and engaging" process between the state and society.[151]

---

[150] Charles Tilly notes that one of the important ways for any state to deal with massive resistance from society is to bargain with the forces providing that resistance. Although there are many methods of bargaining, including war and repression, that process is responsible for what finally becomes the core of "citizenship." See Charles Tilly, *Coercion, Capital, and European States, AD 990–1990* (Cambridge, MA: Basil Blackwell, 1990), 101–3.

[151] Migdal, "State in Society," 9–23.

Conclusion

DURING the turbulent period from 1900 to 1937, Chinese society underwent a transition that propelled it toward modernity. That process, however, was undergirded neither by capitalist development nor industrialization – both of which have been essential in the experience of modern Western societies, but were lacking in the conditions of Chinese local society. Because this transformation evolved from within the society itself – as a part of its long-term political, social, and economic changes – I consider it to have been a genuine self-transformation.

TRANSFORMATION AT THE INDIVIDUAL LEVEL

The social transformation process was first visible through changes at level of the individual as illustrated by the developments in Henan, which have been the focus of this book. During the first decade of the twentieth century, significant changes occurred in the local power structure of northern and southwestern Henan. Those changes transferred power from those community leaders who had based their influence essentially on personal status and prestige (usually associated with state-conferred degrees, family wealth, and strength of lineage) to those who came from diverse personal backgrounds and had broad political, business, or military experience, but were capable of taking advantage of the fluctuating situation to enhance their influence in the communities. This development was initiated by changes in the social conditions in each area that confronted its inhabitants with many unprecedented social, economic, and even religious issues. Meanwhile, these regional changes coincided with the abolition of the examination system and subsequent demise of the Qing dynasty, which in many ways heralded the ending of a traditional social and cultural system upon which the status, power, and influence of the elite stratum had rested. All these changes, however, opened doors for the people in the lower social echelons, even the most ordinary members of the local communities, to enter the competition for community leadership by demonstrating their capability in a wide range of arenas to deal with the new societal challenges, or to use these new social circumstances for their own advantage. As the local communities welcomed these individuals into its power structure, the community value system began to alter. As a result, the traditional value that had associated wealth, status, and prestige with power and influence in the local communities started to fade away. Personal ability to provide community leadership as well as achievement in helping the local community to deal with various situations began to be recognized. This shift in values was an important component of the modern development of China's society and had been initiated by the rising need of most people to contend, on a local level, with the challenges imposed by the changes in their social environment.[1]

A modification of the traditional value system, however, was not the only significant development in the local society of northern and southwestern Henan. The structures of community leadership in both regions soon were affected. As more and more of the later generation of power holders entered the competition for power, the old power structure gradually dissolved. In northern Henan, this transition of power was facilitated by the gradual opening of the area due to the construction of railroads, the constant exodus of many of the most influential elites to the cities, and the emergence of new social groups, including students of the modern schools, workers, and political party activists. These developments converted local society in that region into a battleground for the power struggle that was joined by many different social forces, not merely the local elites. This competition created conditions favorable to the dominance of the secret societies until Feng Yuxiang moved into Henan.

In southwest Henan, however, social disarray and the lack of legitimate authority provided ample opportunities for the rise of a new generation of community leaders. These local parvenus based their dominance not only on military skills and their leadership of local militias, but also on extensive administrative experience and organizational

---

[1] Such changes in the traditional Chinese value system have been considered by those associated with modernization theory to be one of the most significant developments that occurred during modernization. See Burke, *History and Social Theory*, 132–3.

talent. Despite their disparate personal backgrounds, they all climbed to the top of the community leadership by wielding coercive force. The rise of these community leaders concentrated a great deal of power into the hands of a few local elites.

TRANSFORMATION AT THE SOCIETAL LEVEL

Judging from developments at the individual level, both regions witnessed an appreciable expansion of elite activism during the Republican period. In southwestern Henan, the changes gave rise to the Self-Government movement, under which three major changes in the local communities can be identified: the acceleration of the crisis of legitimacy, the rise of localism, and the formation of a local identity among the local elites. In northern Henan, however, a different picture was emerging, as some local elites engaged in extensive networking activities, extending their sphere of personal relations from the local to the regional level, and then from the regional to the national level. Accompanying the activities of the northern elites, considerable changes also occurred in the way personal ties were formed. Relationships that traditionally had been personal and face-to-face gradually became impersonal, detached, and indirect – a significant modern development that also transpired as a result of these local elites' networking activities.[2]

The activities of the local elites in both areas produced other unintended consequences. The Self-Government movement in southwestern Henan induced an exclusive pattern of elite dominance over the local communities. In northern Henan, the networking activities finally enabled the local elites to penetrate the state. Two concurrent trends of social development thus became increasingly visible during the Republican period: one, the upward extension of elite activism in northern Henan, which finally led to the local elites' ability to influence political development at the provincial level; the other, the localization of elite dominance in southwestern Henan, which enabled the local elites to mobilize the communities, as well as local resources, for their own political goals. Along with the latter trend, there surfaced a highly institutionalized and politically sophisticated elite activism, comparable to that

---

[2] Talcott Parsons and Anthony Giddens have both considered the replacement of personal with impersonal relationships to be a major portent of modern development. See So, *Social Change*, 21–3.

found in the cities or commercialized areas. Within the new complex activism, local elites not only demonstrated their enormous capacity to form extensive personal ties and incorporate new ideas from their counterparts in other areas to enhance their own elite institutions, they also showed immense flexibility in adapting to the concept of modern bureaucracy, and using political indoctrination, in combination with the traditional system of *baojia*, for the purpose of local control. Developments in the elite activism of both regions, therefore, clearly signaled an increasing differentiation and complexity of Chinese local rural society spawned by internal changes within the local communities.[3]

MODERN STATE MAKING AND SOCIAL TRANSFORMATION

The societal changes I have discussed largely predetermined the outcome of state making by the Republican state. In my view, the Chinese state in the early Republican period was a fluid and transitory entity that varied from time to time and place to place and that encompassed any political or military power holder who ever established authority over the two areas under study. In order to understand how the process of social transformation interconnected with the process of state making, I first examined the state-making endeavors of Yuan Shikai, the warlords, Feng Yuxiang, and the Nationalist government, focusing on the bureaucratic expansion and fiscal extension of the state, both from top to bottom and from center to periphery. As the findings of my research indicate, almost all the Republican regimes attempted to create a powerful state, a state able to exercise a high degree of supervision, intervention, and control over the local society. But their efforts yielded uneven results that, in turn, depended on the aforementioned social developments in the local communities, including the different strengths of the elite communities. In northern Henan, state making was generally successful, not only because the area was easily accessible from the outside but, more importantly, fierce competition for power within the local communities as well as the drain of able elites to the cities

---

[3] As I discussed in the first chapter, one of the most important results of modernization – in the opinion of many Western theoreticians, including Herbert Spencer, Emile Durkheim, Max Weber, Talcott Parsons, S. N. Eisenstadt, and Anthony Giddens – is the increasing complexity and differentiation of society. See Chapter 1 for details. Furthermore, to describe the development I have observed in Henan, I believe the term *social differentiation*, coined by Eisenstadt, is more suitable than any others previously used by social scientists. See Eisenstadt, "Social Differentiation," 376.

weakened community leadership. The state failed to penetrate south-western Henan, however, because of strong resistance from an elite community that refused to recognize the legitimacy of any state authority. Even after the Nationalist government had established a centralized administration and made considerable efforts to reach out for the local elites in the area, it still could not, before the outbreak of the Sino-Japanese War, reverse the experience of its predecessors. Meanwhile, although the Nationalist government succeeded in establishing tight bureaucratic and fiscal control in northern Henan, it still failed to prevent state involution from taking place there as the local elites had affixed themselves to the local bureaucracy.

To further analyze the reasons for such drastically opposite results of state making, I further investigated the mutual engagement of the state and society, the interaction between the process of social transformation and modern state making. My conceptualization of modern state making is based on the notion that such an effort requires the state to expand its political base to, and therefore to share its goal with, the population being governed – in addition to being able to penetrate the local society for the maintenance of social order and the mobilization of resources. In order to create a modern state, a regime was forced to deal with the rural population, especially the local elites. It is thus inevitable that state making interact with the process of social transformation. As research shows, almost every state during the Republican period attempted to control the local elites, albeit only a few – Yuan Shikai, Feng Yuxiang, and the Nationalist government – succeeded in northern Henan. Among those who succeeded, however, only the Nationalist government had endeavored to expand its political base, and then only to the local elites, not to the rural population. Even so, the Nationalist government was forced to reach out to the rural communities in southwestern Henan after it had failed in all other means of engagement, including suppression, co-optation, and accommodation, especially when it was under the additional pressure of the Sino-Japanese War. This lack of vision in the creation of a modern state could only result in a partial transformation of the Nationalist state, making it vulnerable to future destruction by the Communists. From the vantage point of local society, therefore, one can discern two distinctive trends of state making during the Republican period, one progressive and the other impeded, and two patterns of relationship between state and society, a strong state presence versus a weak social resistance in northern Henan, and vice-versa in the southwest. These two opposite trends, and the two contrasting state-making patterns, strongly suggest that modern social transformation in China has been a multilinear rather than a unilinear process.

SOCIAL TRANSFORMATION AND CHINA'S MODERN TRANSITION

This study intends to offer the above notion of social transformation not as a restrictive model or grand theory but as an analytical framework to help understand China's transition from a traditional to a modern society during the period between 1900 and 1937. Rather than examining this transition from the various aspects of elite mobility, social mobilization, and state making, I have incorporated the three under one theme. In this way, I seek to gain a holistic, contextualized view of what I consider the three main aspects of a single historical process, China's societal self-transformation, and thus to observe the important correlations among them.

As the evidence I have uncovered demonstrates, the process of modern transition unfolded in China under a combination of conditions that were distinctive to each locale during the particular period under examination. To take northern and southwestern Henan as examples, those conditions were created by an amalgam of exogenous and endogenous factors, including intensified commercialization and the intrusion of foreign economic interests in the north; the banditry crisis; and the deterioration of peasant living conditions in the southwest. In addition, major political, social, and economic changes in the country – such as the demise of the Qing dynasty, warlordism, and the rise of new social forces – also affected the two areas directly and indirectly. Given the influence of all these conditions, Chinese modern transition evolved within the social, political, and economic context of each locale.

The driving forces for that transformation were the desires of the members of Chinese society to meet the challenges to their livelihood, welfare, and previous lifestyle that arose from the changes in the social environment that occurred in this decisive period. These desires propelled individuals to survive these fluctuations or even to better their station by taking advantage of the opportunities available to them through conducting, or enlarging the scope of, their various activities. In dealing with these changes, many inhabitants in both areas, especially the local elites, followed various paths that led not only to the dissolution of an old social structure – within which they used to form their personal relations, maintain their status, or define their personal roles in their village communities – but also to the emergence of a diversified, or even polarized, yet increasingly complex society.[4]

In shaping the modern changes, Chinese tradition played an important role. From its beginning, traditional symbols and methods have been used in the competition for power among various social forces and in the expansion of elite activism. To take the networking activities of the northern Henan elites as an example, much of the maneuvering among different circles of relationships was undertaken within the realm of tradition, albeit even though these undertakings unexpectedly led to modern developments. In southwestern Henan, the later generation of community leaders emerged in the same way as the previous influential elite members – by relying on the traditional methods for acquiring power – although the success of the later leaders depended mostly on the changes in the value system of the community. Furthermore, as one can notice, once these newly risen elites established themselves in the community leadership, they immediately attempted to restore traditional values to their local communities. It was obvious, throughout the process of modern transition, that Chinese tradition either persisted or was rejuvenated, even while it was being modified.

The present study also clearly demonstrates that the arrival of Chinese modernity was a multilinear process, interwoven by different political trends, social undertakings, and economic developments simultaneously proceeding in all directions. This multiplicity was brought about by different attempts and activities by various social and political entities, particularly the state authorities, the local elites, and other social forces. Vertically there were intersecting motions between top-down endeavors aimed at creating a modern nation and bottom-up attempts to penetrate the state. Horizontally, there was a constant interchange of ideas between areas of core and periphery while there were developments in various dimensions that continuously polarized those regions. Even within each village community, there were multiple currents not only generated by power competition but also by different individual interests. Since China's transition to modernity is crisscrossed by multilinear processes, it is crucial that we observe the fundamental differences in the condi-

---

[4] My conception of how the actions of individuals are based on their needs, desires, and perceptions of opportunity comes from theoreticians such as Anthony Giddens. See Layder, *Social Theory*, 125–50, 207–23. I also owe a debt to Ronald S. Burt for an understanding of the dialectic relationship between social change and individual action. See Burt, *Theory of Action*, 9.

tions, as well as the very process of China's transition, from that of the Western European countries. The presuppositions that place industrialization and capitalist development as the prerequisite conditions for Chinese modernity reflect only a universalistic, unidirectional, and unilinear view of the world, which is far from the reality.

Appendix

Table A.1. *Provincial Authorities Located in Kaifeng*

Under Yuan Shikai	
February 15, 1912*	Qi Yaolin (governor)
March 23, 1912	Zhang Zhenfang (military governor *[Dudu]* and the governor *[Minzheng zhang]*)
February to March, 1914	Zhang Zhenfang (concurrent governor of Henan *[Dutu]*)
February 12, 1914	Tian Wenlie (governor *[Minzheng shi]*)
September 20, 1914	Zhao Ti (military governor *[jiangjun]*) Tian Wenlie (governor *[Xunan shi]*)
Under Li Yuanhong	
July 6, 1916	Zhao Ti (military governor *[Dujun]*) Tian Wenlie (governor *[Shengzhang]*)
Under Feng Guozhang	
December 4, 1917	Zhao Ti (military governor and concurrent governor)
Under Xu Shichang	
October 1918	none
February 16, 1920	Wang Yinchuan (governor)
March 4, 1920	Zhao Ti (military governor)
July 2, 1920	Zhang Fengtai (governor)
May 10, 1922	Feng Yuxiang (military governor *[Dujun]*)
Under Li Yuanhong	
October 31, 1922	Zhang Fulai (commissioner of military affairs *[Duli junwu shanhou shiyi]*)
December 12, 1923	Li Jichen (governor)

(continued)

Table A.1. *(Continued)*

Under Huang Fu (performing president function ad interim between November 24, 1924)	
November 3, 1924	Hu Jingyu (commissioner of military affairs)
November 7, 1924	Sun Yue (governor)
Under Cao Qun	
October 1923	none
Under Duan Qirui	
April 10, 1925	Yue Weijun (commissioner of military affairs)
August 28, 1925	Yue Weijun (concurrent governor)
Under Wu Peifu	
March 11, 1926	Kou Yinhua (military governor *[Duli]*)
March 17, 1926	Jin Yue (concurrent governor)
June 3, 1926	Xiong Bingqi (governor)
November 17, 1926	Zhang Yinghua (governor)
January 18, 1927	The position of military governor was abolished when Kou Yinhua resigned
February 1927	Chen Shantong (acting governor)
Under Feng Yuxiang	
June 13, 1927	Feng Yuxiang (chairman of Henan provincial government)
Under Chiang Kai-shek GMD Government	
December 12, 1928	Han Fuqu (concurrent chairman of the provincial government)
June 13, 1929	Han Fuqu (chairman of the provincial government)
May 31, 1930	Zhang Fang (acting chairman of the provincial government)
October 20, 1930	Liu Zhi (chairman of the provincial government)
January 1, 1936	Shang Zhen (chairman of the provincial government)
February 3, 1938	Cheng Qian (chairman of the provincial government)
October 5, 1939	Wei Lihuang (chairman of the provincial government)
January 5, 1942	Li Peiji (chairman of the provincial government)

Appendix

* The dates indicate when the new appointments were made.

Sources: Wang Tianjiang et al., *Henan jindai dashi ji: 1840–1949 (Henan: A Chronology of the Modern Period: 1840–1949)* (Kaifeng: Henan renmin chuban she, 1990). *Henan lishi mingren cidian (Dictionary of Historically Known Persons in Henan)*, Wang Tianxiang et al., eds. (Zhengzhou: Zhongzhou guji chuban she, 1988). *Zhongzhou lishi renwu cidian (Historically Known Persons in the Central Plain)*, Guo Remin et al., eds. (Kaifeng: Henan daxue chuban she, 1991). *Henan dashi ji ziliao congbian: 1840–1918 (Collection of Resources on the Major Events in Henan: 1840–1918)*, Wang Tianjiang, ed. (Zhengzhou: Henan difang shizhi bianchuan weiyuan hui, 1984). Li Chunshou, "Qingmo he beiyang junfa tongzhi shiqi Henansheng junzheng jiguan yange ji renshi bianqian" (Military, Civil Administration, and Personnel Changes in Henan Province during the End of the Qing and the Northern Warlord Period), in *Henan wenshi ziliao (Henan Local History)*, 9 (Zhengzhou: Wenshi ziliao weiyuan hui, 1984): 30–44. Xinsheng Sun, "Minguo shiqi Henansheng zhengfu ji ge tingchu zuzhi yange ji guanyuan genti" (Chronology of Henan Provincial Government Administration and Personnel Changes during the Republican period), in *Henan shizhi ziliao*, 7 (Zhengzhou: Henansheng difang shizhi bianchuan weiyuan hui, 1984): 86–90. *Biographical Dictionary of Republican China*, Howard L. Boorman and Richard C. Howard, eds. (New York: Columbia University Press, 1970). Xin Ping, *Minguo jiangling lu (Biographical Information of Army Generals during the Republican Period)* (Shenyang: Liaoning renmin chuban she, 1991).

Appendix

Table A.2. *Regional Authorities Located in Nanyang City*

Date	Commander	Authority
1900–1912	Xie Baosheng	Qing provincial troops, reserve force *(xunfangjun)*
February 1912	Bao Binyao	*luefenyongjun** led by Ma Yunqing and later Wang Tianzong
April 1912	Zhang Zhenfang	under Yuan Shikai
April–July 1912	Ma Jizeng	under Yuan Shikai
August 1912	Tian Zuolin	under Yuan Shikai
1914	Guo Zhencai	under Yuan Shikai
winter 1915	Wu Qingtong	under Yuan Shikai
August 1920	Li Zhiyun	*fengtian yijun*
October 1921	Li Zhiyun	*fengtianliuyuxianfengdui*
winter 1923	Ma Zhimin	*yijun*
December 1925	Zhang Zhigong	Wu Peifu
January 1926	Zhang Mutong	Wu Peifu
June 1926	Fan Zhongxiu	*jianguoyujun*
February 1927	Xu Shouchun	Wu Peifu Ma Wende
June 1927	Fang Zhenwu	Feng Yuxiang
summer 1927	Wu Peifu	stayed for two months
fall 1927	Wang Huafu	Feng Yuxiang
September 1927	Yue Weijun	*jianguoyujun*
summer 1928	Shi Yousan	Feng Yuxiang
October 1929–April 1930	Yang Hucheng	Nationalist government
March 1931	Ge Xiaoxian	Nationalist government
May 1931	Wan Pinyi	Nationalist government
July 1931	Song Tiancai	Nationalist government
winter 1931	Li Yujie	Nationalist government
spring 1932	Liu Zhenhua	Nationalist government
1933–July 1934	Zhang Fang	Nationalist government Wang Lingyun
fall 1934	Pang Binxun	Nationalist government
spring 1935	Bai Fengxiang	Nationalist government Li Fuzhi
fall 1936	provincial	Nationalist government security force

* *Note*: The *luefenyongjun* (Army of Bravery of the Henan Natives in Hubei) was a small army organized by the Henanese native soldiers in the Hubei Civilian Army *(hubei minjun)*. These soldiers, nearly 2,000 strong, elected Ma Yunqing as their leader and returned to Henan in 1911 to assist the revolution there. In January 1912 the army defeated the garrison troops in Nanyang County and took control of the city. By late 1912 the army was incorporated into the government army under Yuan Shikai.

Sources: Nanyang difang shizhi bianchuan weiyuan hui, *Nanyang xianzhi (Gazetteer of Nanyang County)* (Zhengzhou: Henan renmin chuban she, 1990), 163–4. Nanyang shi difang shizhi bianchuan weiyuan hui, *Nanyang shizhi (Gazetteer of Nanyang City)* (Zhengzhou: Henan renmin chuban she, 1989). Xin Ping, *Minguo jiangling lu (Biographical Information of Army Generals during the Republican Period)* (Shenyang: Liaoning renmin chuban she, 1991). Henansheng renwu zhi bianji zu, "Henansheng renwu zhi" ("Historical Figures in Henan Province"), (Unpublished manuscript).

Table A.3. *Governing Entities in Neixiang County*

Date	Person in Authority	Authority
February 1912	Wang Tianzong	
	Xiang Chunyuan et al.	*minjun* of Red Gang from Deng County
1912		Yuan Shikai
1913		Yuan Shikai
July 1913	Bai Lang	(bandit leader)
fall 1913–	Tian Zuolin	Yuan Shikai
January 1916		Yuan Shikai
1917		Feng Guozhang
1918	Zhao Ti	Feng Guozhang
1918		Duan Qirui
spring 1919		*liuyuxianfengdui** (Duan Qirui)
1921		Xu Shichang
1922		Li Yuanhong
1923	Ma Zhimin	*yijun*
1924	Ma Zhimin	*yijun*
1924	Zhu Taosheng	GMD's Nationalist Revolutionary Army
1925	Zhang Zhigong	Wu Peifu
April 1926 (a few days)		
	Fan Zhongxiu	*jianguoyujun*
1926		(the year of confusion in leadership)
May 1927	Sun Lianzhong	Feng Yuxiang
1927	Fan Zhongxiu	*jianguoyujun*
	Sun Lianzhong	Feng Yuxiang
	Ma Wende	Wu Peifu
August 1928		Feng Yuxiang
winter 1928	Shi Yousan	Feng Yuxiang
May 1929 (one day)	Shi Yousan	Nationalist government
November 1929	Yang Hucheng	Nationalist government
winter 1929	Liu Ruming	Feng Yuxiang
June 1930	Liu Ruming	Feng Yuxiang
1932–May 1933	Liu Zhenhua	Nationalist government
1934	Liu Zhi	Nationalist government
1935		Nationalist government
1936		Nationalist government
1937	Bie Tingfang	Nationalist government

* *Note*: *Liuyuxianfengdui* belonged to Zhang Zuolin's Fengtian army. However, in 1918 Zhang lent his army to support Duan Qirui. The army was under Duan's command. See *Biographical Dictionary of Republican China*, Howard L. Boorman and Richard C. Howard, eds. (New York: Columbia University Press, 1970), 117.

Sources: "Neixiang xianzhi: dashi ji" ("Neixiang Local Gazetteer: Major Events"), (Neixiang, Unpublished). Xixia xianzhi bianchuan weiyuan hui, *Xixia xianzhi (Gazetteer of Xixia County)* (Zhengzhou: Henan renmin chuban she, 1990). *Henan lishi mingren cidian (Dictionary of Historically Known Persons in Henan)*, Wang Tianxiang et al., eds. (Zhengzhou: Zhongzhou guji chuban she, 1988). *Zhongzhou lishi renwu cidian (Historically Known Persons in the Central Plain)*, Guo Remin et al., eds. (Kaifeng: Henan daxue chuban she, 1991). Henansheng renwu zhi bianji zu, "Henansheng renwu zhi" ("Historical Figures in Henan Province"), (Unpublished manuscript).

Table A.4. *Troops Stationed in Xichuan County*

1909	The Qing government reduced its troops in Xichuan County to one colonel *(fujiang)*, one lieutenant *(qianzong)*, two sublieutenants *(bazong)*, one sergeant *(waiwei)*, fourteen security guards, and ten soldiers.
1912	One battalion of soldiers from the newly co-opted provincial army from the known bandit leader Wang Tianzong's gang was sent by Zhang Zhenfang to stay in Xichuan County. A little later, two battalions of soldiers from a small army called *luefenyongjun* came from Hubei to Xichuan County and remained for a few months.
1917	Two battalions of the Fengtian Army were stationed in Xichuan County since it was feared that a single 500-man battalion would be useless against an onslaught of bandits.
November 1925	A small army from Shaanxi province, the *Shaanxilujun,* led by Zhang Zhigong, entered Xichuan County. It stayed there a few months and left.
1927	Feng Yuxiang's Nationalist Revolutionary Army retreated into Xichuan County after it was defeated by Jiang Jieshi, but left shortly afterward. The same year, the 14th division of Feng's army was also stationed at the Xichuan county seat. It set up a temporary military school and recruited students.
Summer 1927	Yue Weijun led his division of the Second Group Army to stay in Xichuan County.
1928	One brigade from Feng Yuxiang's army was stationed in Xichuan County until nearly the end of the year.
1929	One brigade from Feng Yuxiang's army again entered Xichuan County until its commander, Shi Yousan, left Feng to serve under Jiang Jieshi. The army then left for Nanyang. In October 1929, one unit of Feng Yuxiang's army arrived in Xichuan County. The army co-opted some bandits and remained at the county seat for a while. On November 26 Jiang Jieshi's army, led by Yang Hucheng, drove Feng's army out of Xichuan and remained there for a short period.
1930	Feng Yuxiang's army, led by division commander Liu Ruming, entered Xichuan while fighting the Nationalist army. After the war between Feng and Jiang Jieshi, Liu's division left.
1931	One company of Feng Yuxiang's army under Liu Ruming returned to Xichuan County and left in the autumn.

Sources: Xichuanxian difang shizhi bianchuan weiyuan hui, *Xichuan xianzhi (Gazetteer of Xichuan County)* (Zhengzhou: Henan renmin chuban she, 1990). *Henan lishi mingren cidian (Dictionary of Historically Known Persons, in Henan)*, Wang Tianxiang et al., eds. (Zhengzhou: Zhongzhou guji chuban she, 1988). *Zhongzhou lishi renwu cidian (Historically Known Persons in the Central Plain)*, Guo Remin et al., eds. (Kaifeng: Henan daxue chuban she, 1991). Henansheng renwu zhi bianji zu, "Henansheng renwu zhi" ("Historical Figures in Henan Province"), (Unpublished manuscript).

Bibliography

Chen bao 晨報 (*Morning Post*). Peking, 1927.

Dagong bao 大公報 (*L'Impartial*). Tianjin, 1927.

Dazhong minbao 大中民報 (*Minli Daily*). 1912.

Hankou minguo ribao 漢口民國日報 (*Hankou Republican Daily*). Hankou, 1927.

Henan guanbao 河南官報 (*Henan Government News*). Kaifeng, 1905.

Henan guanbao 河南官報 (*Henan Government News*). Kaifeng, 1908.

Huibao 匯報 (*Reporter*). Shanghai, 1905.

Jianghan ribao 江漢日報 (*Jianghan Daily*). Hankou, 1908.

Juewu: Minguo ribao 覺悟民國日報 (*Consciousness: A Republican Daily*). Shanghai, 1928.

Minguo ribao 民國日報 (*Republican Daily*). Shanghai, 1926.

Shanghai minbao 上海民報 (*Shanghai People's Tribune*). Shanghai, 1923.

Shanghai minguo ribao 上海民國日報 (*Shanghai Republican Daily*). Shanghai, 1929.

Shangwu guanbao 商務官報 (*Business Government News*). Beijing.

Shen bao 申報 (*Shanghai Newspaper*). Shanghai, 1919–27.

Shi bao 時報 (*The Eastern Times*). Shanghai, 1919.

Shuntian shibao 順天時報 (*Peking Times*). Peking, 1925.

Xin zhongzhou bao 新中州報 (*New Central Plains News*). Kaifeng, 1924.

Ziyou bao 自由報 (*Freedom News*). 1912.

Alba, Richard D. and Gwen Moore. 1983. "Elite Social Circles." In *Applied Network Analysis: A Methodological Introduction*, Ronald S. Burt and Michael J. Minor, eds. Beverly Hills: Sage Publications.

Alitto, Guy S. 1979. *The Last Confucian: Liang Shu-ming and the Chinese Dilemma of Modernity*. Berkeley: University of California Press.

———. 1979. "Rural Elites in Transition: China's Cultural Crisis and the Problem of Legitimacy." Pp. 218–63 in *Selected Papers from the Center for Far Eastern Studies*, vol. 3, 1978–79, Susan Mann Jones, ed.

Anderson, Benedict. 1983. *Imagined Communities: Reflections on the Origin and Spread of Nationalism*. London: Verso.

Anderson, Perry. 1974. *Lineages of the Absolutist State*. London: N.L.B.

———. 1977. *Passage from Antiquity to Feudalism*. London: N.L.B.

Antony, Robert J. 1989. "Peasants, Heroes and Brigands: The Problems of Social Banditry in Early Nineteenth-century South China." *Modern China* (April): 123–48.

Anyang wenshi ziliao (Local History of Anyang County). vols. 1–44. Anyang: Anyang shi weiyuan hui wenshi ziliao weiyuan hui, 1989.

Anyang xianwei dangshi ban. 1986. "Yijiu erqi nian Anyang qianghui yundong de chubu diaocha" 一九二七年安陽槍會運動的初步調查 (General Survey of the Spear Movement in 1927 in Anyang County). In *Henan dangshi yanjiu* 河南黨史研究, vol. 2. Zhengzhou: Henansheng dangshi ban.

Averill, Stephen C. 1981. "The New Life in Action: The Nationalist Government in South Jiangxi, 1934–1937." *China Quarterly*, no. 88 (December): 594–628.

———. 1987. "Party, Society and Local Elite in the Jiangxi Communist Movement." *Journal of Asian Studies*, 46 no. 2 (May): 279–303.

———. 1990. "Local Elites and Communist Revolution in the Jiangxi Hill Country." Pp. 282–304 in *Chinese Local Elites and Patterns of Dominance*, Joseph Esherick and Mary Rankin, eds.

Baker, Hugh D. R. 1977. "Extended Kinship in the Traditional City." Pp. 499–520 in *The City in Late Imperial China*, G. William Skinner, ed. Stanford: Stanford University Press.

Barkan, Lenore. 1990. "Patterns of Power: Forty Years of Elite Politics in a Chinese County." Pp. 191–215 in *Chinese Local Elites and Patterns of Dominance*, Joseph W. Esherick and Mary Backus Rankin, eds.

Bastid-Bruguiere, Marianne. 1980. "Currents of Social Change." Pp. 579–610 in *The Cambridge History of China: Late Qing, 1800–1911*, Part II, vol. 11, John K. Fairbank and Kwang-Ching Liu, eds. Cambridge: Cambridge University Press.

Beal, Edwin G. Jr. 1958. *The Origins of Likin, 1853–1964*. Cambridge, MA: Harvard University Press.

Beattie, Hilary J. 1979. *Land and Lineage in China: A Study of T'ung-Ch'eng County, Anhwei, in the Ming and Ch'ing Dynasties*. Cambridge: Cambridge University Press.

Bedeski, Robert E. 1981. *State-Building in Modern China: The Kuomintang in the Prewar Period*. China Research Monograph. Berkeley: University of California, Center for Chinese Studies.

Befu, Harumi. 1967. "The Political Relation of the Village to the State." *World Politics* 19: 601–20.

Bendix, Reinhard. 1964. *Nation-Building and Citizenship: Studies of Our Changing Social Order*. New York: Wiley.

———. 1967. "Tradition and Modernity Reconsidered." *Comparative Studies in Society and History* 9: 292–346.

———. 1978. *Kings or People: Power and the Mandate to Rule*. Berkeley: University of California Press.

Berger, Peter L. 1986. *The Capitalist Revolution: Fifty Propositions about Prosperity, Equality, and Liberty*. New York: Basic Books.

Bergère, Marie-Claire. 1968. "The Role of the Bourgeoisie." Pp. 229–95 in *China in Revolution: The First Phase, 1900–1913*, Mary Wright, ed.

———. 1986. *The Golden Age of the Chinese Bourgeoisie: 1911–1937*. New York: Cambridge University Press.

Bernhardt, Kathryn. 1992. *Rents, Taxes, and Peasant Resistance*. Stanford: Stanford University Press.

Bianco, Lucien. 1986. "The Peasant Movements." Pp. 270–328 in *The Cambridge History of China: Republican China 1912–1949*, Part 2, vol. 13, John K. Fairbank and Albert Feuerwerker, eds. Cambridge: Cambridge University Press.

Billingsley, Phil. 1981. "Bandits, Bosses, and Bare Sticks: Beneath the Surface of Local Control in Early Republican China." *Modern China* 7, no. 3 (July): 235–87.

———. 1988. *Bandits in Republican China*. Stanford: Stanford University Press.

Boorman, Howard L. and Richard C. Howard, eds. 1970. *Biographical Dictionary of Republican China*. New York: Columbia University Press.

Bourdieu, Pierre. 1977. *Outline of a Theory of Practice*, vol. 1, Jack Goody, ed. Richard Nice, trans. Cambridge Studies in Social Anthropology. Cambridge: Cambridge University Press.

Britan, Gerald M. and Ronald Cohen. 1980. "Toward an Anthropology of Formal Organizations." P. 14 in *Hierarchy and Society*, Gerald M. Britan and Ronald Cohen, eds. Philadelphia: Institute for the Study of Human Issues.

Brook, Timothy. 1990. "Family Continuity and Cultural Hegemony: The Gentry of Ningbo, 1368–1911." Pp. 27–50 in *Chinese Local Elites and Patterns of Dominance*, Joseph Esherick and Mary Rankin, eds.

Brown, Peter. 1971. *The World of Antiquity, A.D. 150–750*. New York: Harcourt Brace Jovanovich.

Buck, John L. 1930. *Chinese Farm Economy*. Nanking: University of Nanking Press.

———. 1937. *Land Utilization in China*. Chicago: University of Chicago Press.

Burgess, John S. 1928. *The Guilds of Peking*. New York: Columbia University Press.

Burke, Peter. 1992. *History and Social Theory*. Ithaca: Cornell University Press.

Burt, Ronald S. 1982. *Toward a Structural Theory of Action: Network Models of Social Structure, Perception, and Action*. New York: Academic Press.

Calhoun, Craig. 1991. "Indirect Relationship and Imagined Communities: Large-Scale Integration and the Transformation of Everyday Life." Pp. 95–121 in *Social Theory for a Changing Society*, Pierre Bourdieu and James S. Coleman, eds. (Boulder, CO: Westview Press, 1991).

Ch'an, Wellington K. K. 1977. *Merchants, Mandarins, and Modern Enterprise in Late Ch'ing China*. Cambridge, MA: Harvard University Press.

Ch'en, Jerome. 1972. *Yuan Shih-k'ai*, 2nd ed. Stanford: Stanford University Press.

Ch'i, Hsi-sheng. 1976. *Warlord Politics in China: 1916–1928*. Stanford: Stanford University Press.

Ch'u, Tung-tsu. 1962. *Local Government in China under the Ch'ing*. Cambridge, MA: Harvard University Press.

Chang, Chung-li. 1955. *The Chinese Gentry: Studies on Their Role in Nineteenth-Century Chinese Society*. Seattle: University of Washington Press.

———. 1962. *The Income of the Chinese Gentry*. Seattle: University of Washington Press.

Chang, Hao. 1971. *Liang Ch'i-ch'ao and Intellectual Transition in China, 1890–1907*. Cambridge, MA: Harvard University Press.

Chang, Jianqiao, et al. 1985. *Henan sheng dili* 河南省地理 (The Geography of Henan Province). Zhongguo dili congshu. Zhengzhou: Henan jiaoyu chuban she.

Chang, P'eng-yuan. 1976. "Comments from Authors Reviewed." *Modern China* 2, no. 2 (April): 185–8.

Chen, Bozhuang. 1936. *Pinghan yanxian nongcun jingji diaocha* 平漢沿線農村經濟調查 (Village Survey along the Peking-Hankou Railroad). Shanghai: Zhonghua shuju.

Chen, Duxiu. 1926. "Hongqiang hui yu Zhongguo de nongmin yundong" 紅槍會與中國的農民運動 (Red Spear and the Chinese Peasant Movement). In *Xiangdao* 響導, 4: 158.

Chen, Kuilong. 1904. *Yongan shangshu zouyi* 庸庵尚書奏議 (Yongan Ministry of Foreign Affairs President Report). vol. 4. Peking, November 29.

Chen, Shunde, et al. 1979. *Xianhua wanxi ji* 閒話宛西集 (Recollections of Southwestern Henan). Taipei: Weiqin chuban she.

Chen, Zifeng, et al. 1987. *Tangyin xianzhi* 湯陰縣誌 (Gazetteer of Tangyin County). Kaifeng: Henan renmin chuban she.

Chesneaux, Jean, ed. 1972. *Popular Movements and Secret Societies in China, 1840–1950*. Stanford: Stanford University Press.

———. 1973. *Peasant Revolts in China*, 1840–1949. New York: Norton.

Chiang, Siang-tseh. 1954. *The Nien Rebellion*. Seattle: University of Washington Press.

Chongxiu Linxian zhi 重修林縣誌 (Recompilation of Lin County Gazetteer), 14 vols. Linxian, 1932.

Chongxiu Runan xianzhi 重修汝南縣誌 (Recompilation of Runan County Gazetteer). Runan: Runanxian weiyuan hui, 1983.

Chow, Yung-teh. 1966. *Social Mobility in China: Status Careers among the Gentry in a Chinese Community*. New York: Atherton Press.

Cihai bianji bu. 1980. *Ci hai* 辭海: *lishi fence* 歷史分冊, *Zhongguo gudai shi* 中國古代史 (Encyclopedia: History, Traditional China), 434.

Coatsworth, John H. 1981. *Growth against Development: The Economic Impact of Railroads in Porfirian Mexico*. DeKalb: Northern Illinois University Press.

Cohen, Paul A. 1984. *Discovering History in China: American Historical Writings on the Recent Chinese Past*. New York: Columbia University Press.

Collins, Randall. 1988. *Theoretical Sociology*. San Diego: Harcourt Brace Jovanovich.

———. 1994. *Four Sociological Traditions*. rvsd. ed. New York: Oxford University Press.

Collins, Randall and Michael Makowsky. 1989. *The Discovery of Society*. 4th ed. New York: Random House.

Cook, Karen, et al. 1983. "The Distribution of Power in Exchange Networks:

Theory and Experimental Results." *American Journal of Sociology* 89, no. 2: 275–305.

———. 1990. "Exchange Theory: A Blueprint for Structure and Process." P. 165 in *Frontiers of Social Theory: The New Syntheses*, George Ritzer, ed. New York: Columbia University Press.

Coser, Lewis A. 1971. *Masters of Sociological Thought: Ideas in Historical and Social Context*. New York: Harcourt Brace Jovanovich.

Cui, Xiaying. 1992. "Xunzheng shiqi Henan zhengzhi zhi yanjiu" 訓政時期河南省政治研究 ("Analysis of political affairs in Henan during the Republican period"). M.A. thesis.

Curran, Thomas D. 1993. "Educational Reform and the Paradigm of State-Society Conflict in Republican China." *Republican China* 18, no. 2 (April): 26–63.

Curtin, Philip D. 1984. *Cross-cultural Trade in World History*. Cambridge: Cambridge University Press.

Dahl, R. A. 1956. *A Preface to Democratic Theory*. Chicago: University of Chicago Press.

———. 1961. *Who Governs? Democracy and Power in an American City*. New Haven: Yale University Press.

———. 1977. *Polyarchy*. New Haven: Yale University Press.

de Bary, Theodore. 1975. "Introduction." In *The Unfolding of Neo-Confucianism*. New York: Columbia University Press.

Dengxian wenshi ziliao weiyuan hui. 1985. *Dengxian wenshi ziliao* 鄧縣文史資料 (Local History of Deng County). 2 vols. Dengxian: Zhengxie Dengxian weiyuan hui.

Deng, Zhiyuan, ed. 1925. *Henan shengzhi* 河南省誌 (Provincial Gazetteer of Henan).

Dengzhou shi difang shizhi zongbian shi. "Dengxian zhi: renwu" 鄧縣誌：人物 ("Local history of Deng County: Personages"). Dengxian, Unpublished manuscript (review copy).

d'Entreves, Alessandro Passerin. 1967. *The Notion of the State*. London: Oxford University Press.

Des Forges, Roger V. 1973. *Hsi-liang and the Chinese National Revolution*. New Haven: Yale University Press.

Deutsch, Karl W. 1961. "Social Mobilization and Political Development." *American Political Science Review* 55 (September): 494.

Dittmer, Lowell and Samuel S. Kim. 1993. "In Search of a Theory of National Identity." In *China's Quest for National Identity*, Lowell Dittmer and Samuel Kim, eds. Ithaca: Cornell University Press.

Dongfang zazhi 東方雜誌 (Eastern Miscellany), 24 vols. Shanghai: 1927.

Duan, Deren, et al. 1984. *Henan dashi ji ziliao congbian: 1840–1918* 河南大事紀資料叢編: 1840–1918 (Chronology of Henan: 1840–1918). Kaifeng: Local History of Henan Publisher.

Duara, Prasenjit. 1988. *Culture, Power, and the State: Rural North China, 1900–1942*. Stanford: Stanford University Press.

———. 1990. "Elites and the Structures of Authority in the Villages of North

China, 1900–1949." Pp. 261–81 in *Chinese Local Elites and Patterns of Dominance*, Joseph W. Esherick and Mary Backus Rankin, eds.

———. 1993. "De-Constructing the Chinese Nation." *Australian Journal of Chinese Affairs*, no. 30 (July).

———. 1995. *Rescuing History from the Nation: Questioning Narratives of Modern China*. Chicago: University of Chicago Press.

Eastman, Lloyd E. 1984. *Seeds of Destruction: Nationalist China in War and Revolution, 1937–1949*. Stanford: Stanford University Press.

———. 1988. *Family, Field, and Ancestors: Constancy and Change in China's Social and Economic History, 1550–1949*. New York: Oxford University Press.

———. 1990. *The Abortive Revolution: China under Nationalist Rule, 1927–1937*. Cambridge, MA: Harvard University Press.

———. 1990. "State Building and the Revolutionary Transformation of Rural Society in North China" (Review of Prasenjit Duara's *Culture, Power, and the State: Rural North China, 1900–1942*). *Modern China*, no. 2 (April): 226–34.

Eastman, Lloyd E., Jerome Ch'en, Suzanne Pepper, and Lyman Van Slyke, eds. 1990. *The Nationalist Era in China: 1927–1949*. Cambridge: Cambridge University Press.

Eberhard, Wolfram. 1962. *Social Mobility in Traditional China*. Leiden: Brill.

Eisenstadt, S. N. 1954. "Social Differentiation, Integration and Evolution." *American Sociological Review* (June): 376.

———. 1959. "Primitive Political Systems: A Preliminary Comparative Analysis." *American Anthropologist* 61.

———. 1963. *The Political Systems of Empires*. London: Free Press of Glencoe.

———. 1973. *Tradition, Change and Modernity*. New York: Wiley.

———. 1974. "Studies of Modernization and Sociological Theory." *History and Theory* 13: 225–52.

Eisenstadt, S. N. and Stein Rokkan, eds. 1973. *Building States and Nations: Models and Data Resources*, vol. 1. Beverly Hills: Sage Publications.

Eisenstadt, S. N. and Louis Roniger. 1980. "Patron-Client Relations as a Model of Structuring Social Exchange." *Comparative Studies in Society and History* 22.

Elias, Norbert. 1939. *The Civilizing Process: The Development of Manners*, Edmund Jephcott, trans. New York: Urizen.

Elman, Benjamin A. 1990. *Classicism, Politics, and Kinship: The Ch'ang-chou School of New Text Confucianism in Late Imperial China*. Berkeley: University of California Press.

Elster, Jon, ed. 1986. *Karl Marx: A Reader*. Cambridge: Cambridge University Press.

———. 1990. "Merton's Functionalism and the Unintended Consequences of Action," Pp. 120–9 in *Robert K. Merton: Consensus and Controversy*, Jon Clark, Celia Modgil, and Sohan Modgil, eds. London: Falmer Press.

Elvin, Mark. 1973. *The Pattern of the Chinese Past*. Stanford: Stanford University Press.

———. 1974. "The Administration of Shanghai, 1905–1914." Pp. 239–62 in *The*

Chinese City between Two Worlds, Mark Elvin and G. William Skinner, eds. Stanford: Stanford University Press.

———. 1976. "Comments from Authors Reviewed." *Modern China* 2, no. 2 (April).

Emerson, Richard M. 1972. "Exchange Theory, Part II: Exchange Relations and Networks." Pp. 58–87 in *Sociological Theories in Progress*, 2nd ed., J. Berger et al. Boston: Houghton Mifflin.

Esherick, Joseph. 1976. *Reform and Revolution in China: The 1911 Revolution in Hunan and Hubei*. Berkeley: University of California Press.

———. 1987. *The Origins of the Boxer Uprising*. Berkeley: University of California Press.

———. 1990. *Chinese Local Elites and Patterns of Dominance*. Berkeley: University of California Press.

Esherick, Joseph W. and Mary Backus Rankin, eds. 1976. "A Symposium on the 1911 Revolution." *Modern China* 2, no. 2 (April): 139–84.

Fairbank, John K. 1976. *The United States and China*. Cambridge, MA: Harvard University Press.

Fairbank, John K., Edwin O. Reischauer, and Albert M. Craig. 1965. *East Asia: The Modern Transformation*. Boston: Houghton Mifflin.

———. 1973. *East Asia: Tradition and Transformation*. Boston: Houghton Mifflin.

Fei, Hsiao-tung. 1939. *Peasant Life in China: A Field Study of Country Life in the Yangtze Valley*. London: Routledge and Kegan.

———. 1946. "Peasantry and Gentry: An Interpretation of China's Social Structure and its Changes." *American Journal of Sociology* 52, no. 1 (July): 1–17.

———. 1953. *China's Gentry: Essays in Rural-Urban Relations*. Chicago: University of Chicago Press.

———. 1992. *From the Soil, the Foundations of Chinese Society*. Translation of Fei Xiaotong's Xiangtu Zhongguo, with an introduction and epilogue. Gary G. Hamilton and Wang Zheng, trans. Berkeley: University of California Press.

Fen, Zigang, et al. 1934. *Nanyang nongcun shehui diaocha baogao* 南陽農村社會調查報告 (Report of a Village Survey in Nanyang). Shanghai: Li ming chuban she.

Feng, Wengang. "Peng Yuting" 彭玉廷 ("Peng Yuting"). Unpublished manuscript.

Feng, Yuxiang. 1974. *Wo de shenghuo* 我的生活 (My Life). Bowen shuju.

Feng yu zheng cheng 風雨征程 (History of Revolutionary Movements in Nanzhao County). Zhengzhou: Henan renmin chuban she, 1991.

Feuerwerker, Albert, ed. 1969. *History in Communist China*. Cambridge, MA: M.I.T. Press.

———. 1970. *China's Early Industrialization: Sheng Hsuan-huai and Mandarin Enterprise*. New York: Atheneum.

Fewsmith, Joseph. 1985. *Party, State, and Local Elites in Republican China: Merchant Organizations and Politics in Shanghai, 1890–1930*. Honolulu: University of Hawaii Press.

Fincher, John H. 1981. *Chinese Democracy: The Self-Government Movement in Local, Provincial and National Politics, 1905–1914*. New York: St. Martin's Press.

Fisher, D. H. 1976. "The Braided Narrative: Substance and Form in Social History." Pp. 109–34 in *The Literature of Fact: Selected Papers from the English Institute*, Angus Fletcher, ed. New York, Columbia University Press.

Fitzgerald, John. 1990. "The Misconceived Revolution: State and Society in China's Nationalist Revolution, 1923–1926." *Journal of Asian Studies* 49, no. 2 (May): 323–43.

Folsom, Kenneth E. 1968. *Friends, Guests, and Colleagues: The Mu-Fu System in the Late Ch'ing Period*. Berkeley: University of California Press.

Foucault, Michel. 1977. *Discipline and Punish: The Birth of the Prison*. New York: Pantheon Books.

Freedman, Maurice. 1958. *Lineage Organization in Southeastern China*. London: Athlone.

Fried, Morton H. 1953. *The Fabric of Chinese Society*. New York: Praeger.

Friedman, Edward. 1974. *Backward toward Revolution: The Chinese Revolutionary Party*. Berkeley: University of California Press.

Fung, Edmund S. K. 1975. "Military Subversion in the Chinese Revolution of 1911." *Modern Asian Studies* 9, no. 1.

Gamble, Sidney. 1954. *Ting Hsien: A North China Rural Community*. Berkeley: University of California Press.

Gasster, Michael. 1968. "Reform and Revolution in China's Political Modernization." Pp. 67–96 in *China in Revolution: The First Phase 1900–1913*, Mary C. Wright, ed.

———. 1969. *Chinese Intellectuals and the Revolution of 1911*. Seattle: University of Washington Press.

Geertz, Clifford. 1961. "Studies in Peasant Life: Community and Society." *Biennial Review of Anthropology*, Bernard J. Siegel, ed. Stanford: Stanford University Press.

———. 1983. *Local Knowledge: Further Essays in Interpretive Anthropology*. New York: Basic Books.

Geisert, Bradley Kent. 1979. "Power and Society: The Kuomintang and Local Elites in Kiangsu Province, China, 1924–1937." Ph.D. dissertation. University of Virginia.

Gellner, Ernest. 1983. *Nations and Nationalism*. Ithaca: Cornell University Press.

———. 1988. "Introduction." In *Europe and the Rise of Capitalism*, Jean Baechler, John A. Hall, and Michael Mann, eds. Oxford: Basil Blackwell.

Gerth, Hans H., ed. 1951. *The Religion of China: Confucianism and Taoism*, Hans H. Gerth, trans. Glencoe, IL: Free Press.

Giddens, Anthony. 1981. *A Contemporary Critique of Historical Materialism*. Berkeley: University of California Press.

———. 1982. *Sociology: A Brief but Critical Introduction*. 2d ed., Robert K. Merton, ed. San Diego: Harcourt Brace Jovanovich.

———. 1984. *The Constitution of Society*. Berkeley: University of California Press.

———. 1987. *Social Theory and Modern Sociology*. Stanford: Stanford University Press.

———. 1990. *The Consequences of Modernity*. Stanford: Stanford University Press.

———. 1991. *Modernity and Self-Identity: Self and Society in the Late Modern Age*. Stanford: Stanford University Press.

———. 1992. *The Transformation of Intimacy: Sexuality, Love and Eroticism in Modern Societies*. Stanford: Stanford University Press.

———. 1995. *Politics, Sociology and Social History: Encounters with Classical and Contemporary Social Thought*. Stanford: Stanford University Press.

Goldstone, Jack A. 1991. *Revolution and Rebellion in the Early Modern World*. Berkeley: University of California Press.

Goodman, Bryna. 1995. *Native Place, City, and Nation: Regional Networks and Identities in Shanghai, 1853–1937*. Berkeley: University of California Press.

Goody, Jack. 1996. *The East in the West*. Cambridge: Cambridge University Press.

Grieder, Jerome. 1972. "The Question of Politics in the May Fourth Era." Pp. 95–102 in *Reflections on the May Fourth Movement: A Symposium*, Benjamin Schwartz, ed.

Guan, Weilan, comp. 1956. *Zhonghua minguo xingzheng quhua ji tudi renkou tongji biao* 中華民國行政區劃及土地人口統計表 (Demarcation of Administrative Districts and Surveys of Population and Landholding in the Republic of China). Taipei: Beikai chuban she.

Guo, Renmin, et al. 1991. *Zhongzhou lishi renwu cidian* 中州歷史人物辭典 (Historically Known Persons in the Central Plain). Kaifeng: Henan daxue chuban she.

Guo, Wenxuan and Qiao Jiabao. "Henan jindai minzhu geming xianqu Guo Zhongkui yishi" 河南近代民主革命先區郭仲隗軼事 (Revolutionary Martyr in Modern Henan: The Story of Guo Zhongkui) in *Wenshi ziliao* (Local History), vol. 1 (1987), 7–20.

Guo, Xuyin and Chen Xingtang. 1987. *Aiguo jiangjun Feng Yuxiang* 愛國將軍馮玉祥 (Patriotic General Feng Yuxiang). Zhengzhou: Henan renmin chuban she.

Guo, Yingsheng, ed. 1989. *Zhongzhou jingu* 中州今古 (Present and Past of Henan). 6 vols. Zhengzhou: Zhongzhou jingu bianji bu.

Gusfield, Joseph R. 1967. "Tradition and Modernity: Misplaced Polarities in the Study of Social Change." *American Journal of Sociology* 72: 351–62.

Habermas, Jürgen. 1975. *Legitimation Crisis*, Thomas McCarthy, trans. Boston: Beacon Press.

———. 1976. *Communication and the Evolution of Society*, Thomas McCarthy, trans. Boston: Beacon Press.

Hall, John A. 1985. *Powers and Liberties: The Causes and Consequences of the Rise of the West*. Oxford: Basil Blackwell.

———. 1988. "States and Societies: The Miracle in Comparative Perspective." Pp. 20–8 in *Europe and the Rise of Capitalism*, Jean Baechler, John A. Hall, and Michael Mann, eds. Oxford: Basil Blackwell.

Han, Bangfu, et al. 1934. *Henan sheng nongcun diaocha* 河南省農村調查 (Henan Village Survey). Shanghai: Shangwu yinshu guan.

Harrell, Stevan. "The Decline of Ethnicity and the Transformation of the North

Taiwan Local Elites." Paper presented at the Conference on Chinese Local Elites and Patterns of Dominance. Banff.

Hassinger, Edward. 1961. "Social Relations Between Centralized and Local Social Systems." *Rural Sociology* 36: 354–64.

Hawkins, Joyce M. and Robert Allen, eds. 1991. *Oxford Encyclopedic English Dictionary*. Oxford: Clarendon Press.

Held, David. 1982. "Crisis Tendencies, Legitimation and the State." In *Habermas Critical Debates*, John B. Thompson and David Held, eds. Cambridge, MA: M.I.T. Press.

Henan dangshi renwu zhuan 河南黨史人物傳 (Communist Personages in Henan). 4 vols. Hou Zhiyin, et al., eds. Zhengzhou: Henan renmin chuban she, 1989.

Henan difang zhi zhengwen ziliao xuan 河南地方誌徵文資料選 (Collected Essays on the Local History of Henan). Zhengzhou: Henan sheng difang zhi bianchuan weiyuan hui zong bianji shi, 1983.

"Henan geming lishi wenjian huiji" 河南革命歷史文件匯集 ("Collection of historical materials on the revolution in Henan"). CCP Internal Document. Unpublished manuscript.

Henan minzheng yuekan 河南民政月刊 (Monthly Report of Civil Administration in Henan). Henan sheng minzheng ting, ed. Kaifeng: Henan sheng zhengfu chuban she, 1932–1933.

Henan quansheng baojia yundong huiyi congkan 河南全省保甲運動會議叢刊 (Minutes from the Henan Provincial Conference on the *Baojia* Movement). Kaifeng: Henan sheng zhengfu chuban she, 1931.

Henan quansheng mianye diaocha baogao shu 河南全省棉業調查報告書 (Report on Survey of the Cotton Industry in Henan province), Henan sheng shiye ting, ed. Kaifeng, 1925.

Henan sheng anyang xianzhi 河南省安陽縣誌 (Gazetteer of Anyang County in Henan), Qing Guitai, et al., eds. Anyang: Anyang wenxian bianji weiyuan hui, 1933.

"Henan sheng disan qu xingzheng ducha zhuanyuan gongshu linshi huiyi jilu" 河南省第三區行政督察專員公署臨時會議紀錄 (Minutes of the Emergency Meeting Held by the Special Commissioner's Office of the Henan Provincial Government, Third Administrative District). No. 2 National Archives. Nanjing, 1939.

"Henan sheng renwu zhi" 河南省人物誌 ("Historical figures in Henan Province"), Henan sheng renwu zhi bianji zu, ed. Unpublished manuscript.

Henan sheng zhengfu gongbao 河南省政府公報 (Communique of the Henan Provincial Government). Issues. 275–301 Kaifeng: Henan Provincial Government, 1931–1932.

"Henan sheng zhuanyuan fenshu huiyi an" 河南省專員分署會議案 (Minutes of the Henan Provincial Government, Special Commissioner's Office). No. 2 National Archives. Nanjing, 1939.

Henan shizhi ziliao 河南史誌資料 (Local History of Henan). 7 vols. Zhengzhou: Henan sheng difang shizhi bianchuan weiyuan hui, 1984.

Henan tongguan lu 河南同官錄 (Officials in Henan). Kaifeng, 1921.

Henan wenshi ziliao 河南文史資料 (Local History of Henan). 33 vols. Henan wenshi ziliao bianji bu, ed. Zhengzhou: Henan renmin chuban she, 1990.

Henan xianqing 河南縣情 (Henan County History), Qu Mingjing, et al., eds. Zhengzhou: Henan renmin chuban she, 1990.

Henan zhengzhi 河南政治 (Political Affairs in Henan), no. 2–6. Kaifeng: Henan sheng zhengfu bianyi chu, 1933–1936.

Henan zhengzhi yuekan 河南政治月刊 (Monthly Report of Political Affairs in Henan). 6 vols. Kaifeng: Henan sheng zhengfu bianyi chu, 1932–1936.

Hermassi, Elbaki. 1978. "Changing Patterns in Research on the Third World." *Annual Review of Sociology* 4.

Ho, Ping-ti. 1962. *The Ladder of Success in Imperial China: Aspects of Social Mobility, 1368–1911*. New York: Columbia University Press.

———. 1962. *Studies on the Population of China 1368–1953*. Cambridge, MA: Harvard University Press.

Hobsbawm, E. J. 1963. *Primitive Rebels: Studies in Archaic Forms of Social Movement in the 19th and 20th Centuries*. New York: Praeger.

———. 1990. *Nations and Nationalism Since 1780: Programme, Myth, Reality*. Cambridge: Cambridge University Press.

Hofheinz, Roy. 1969. "The Ecology of Chinese Communist Success: Rural Influence Patterns 1923–1945." Pp. 3–77 in *Chinese Communist Politics in Action*, A. Doak Barnett, ed. Seattle: University of Washington Press.

———. 1977. *The Broken Wave: The Chinese Communist Peasant Movement, 1922–1928*. Cambridge, MA: Harvard University Press.

Honig, Emily. 1992. *Creating Chinese Ethnicity: Subei People in Shanghai, 1850–1980*. New Haven: Yale University Press.

———. 1992. "Migrant Culture in Shanghai: In Search of a Subei Identity." Pp. 239–65 in *Shanghai Sojourners*, Frederic E. Wakeman, Jr. and Wen-hsin Yeh, eds. Berkeley: University of California, Berkeley.

Hongqi quzhi 紅旗區誌 (Gazetteer of Hongqi District). Xinxiang: Shenghuo, Dushu, Xinzhi Sanlian Shudian, 1991.

Hoogvelt, Ankie M. M. 1982. *The Third World in Global Development*. London: Macmillan.

Houn, Franklin. 1959. *Central Government of China, 1912–1928: An Institutional Study*. Madison: University of Wisconsin Press.

Hsiao, Kung-chuan. 1960. *Rural China: Imperial Control in the Nineteenth Century*. Seattle: University of Washington Press.

Hsieh, Winston. 1972. "Triads, Salt Smugglers, and Local Uprisings: Observations on the Social and Economic Background of the Waichow Revolution of 1911." In *Popular Movements and Secret Societies in China, 1840–1950*, Jean Chesneaux, ed.

———. 1978. "Peasant Insurrection and the Marketing Hierarchy in the Canton Delta, 1911–1912." Pp. 79–102 in *Studies in Chinese Society*, Arthur P. Wolf, ed.

Hsu, Immanuel C. 1990. *The Rise of Modern China*. 4th ed. New York: Oxford University Press.

Huang, Philip C. C. 1985. *The Peasant Economy and Social Change in North China*. Stanford: Stanford University Press.

———. 1991. "The Paradigmatic Crisis in Chinese Studies." *Modern China* 17, no. 3 (July): 303.

———. 1993. "'Public Sphere'/'Civil Society' in China? The Third Realm between State and Society." *Modern China* 19, no. 2 (April): 216.

Huixian wenshi ziliao 輝縣文史資料 (Local History of Hui County), 2 vols. Xuexi wenshi wenyuan hui, ed. Huixian: Zhengxie huixian shi weiyuan hui, 1990–1991.

"Huixian zhi" 輝縣誌 ("Gazetteer of Hui County"). Huixian, Unpublished manuscript.

Huntington, Samuel. 1976. "The Change to Change: Modernization, Development, and Politics." Pp. 25–61 in *Comparative Modernization: A Reader*, Cyril E. Black, ed. New York: Free Press.

———. 1977. *Political Order in Changing Societies*. New Haven: Yale University Press.

Huojia fangzhi bao 獲嘉方誌報 (Huojia County Local Gazetteer News). Huojia: Huojia xian shizhi bangong shi, 1984.

Huojia xianzhi 獲嘉縣誌 (Gazetteer of Huojia County). 17 vols. Zou Guyu, et al., eds. Kaifeng, 1934.

Huojia xianzhi 獲嘉縣誌 (Huojia County Gazetteer), Zhang Aiguo, et al., eds. Beijing: Sanlian shudian, 1991.

Hymes, Robert. 1986. *Statesmen and Gentlemen: The Elite of Fu-chou, Chiang-hsi, in Northern and Southern Sung*. Cambridge: Cambridge University Press.

Ichiko, Chuzo. 1968. "The Role of the Gentry: An Hypothesis." Pp. 297–318 in *China in Revolution: The First Phase 1900–1913*, Mary Clabaugh Wright, ed.

Jen, Yu-wen. 1973. *The Taiping Revolutionary Movement*. New Haven: Yale University Press.

Jiaozuo xinghuo 焦作星火 (The Revolutionary Spark in Jiaozuo). Zhonggong Henan dangshi zhuanti ziliao congshu. Zhengzhou: Zhonggong dangshi chuban she, 1991.

Jinian xinhai geming qishi zhounian qingnian xueshu taolun hui lunwen xuan 紀念辛亥革命七十周年青年學術討論會論文選 (Collection of Essays from the Young Scholars' Conference in Commemoration of the Seventieth Year Anniversary of the Republican Revolution), 2 vols. Beijing: Zhonghua shuju, 1983.

"Jixian dashi ji" 汲縣大事記 ("Major events in Ji County"). Jixian: Henan sheng jixian zhi zongbianji shi, Unpublished manuscript.

"Jixian shehui zhi" 汲縣社會誌 ("Social history of Ji County"). Jixian: Henan sheng jixian zhi zong bianji shi, Unpublished manuscript.

Jixian wenshi ziliao 汲縣文史資料 (Local History of Ji County), 3 vols. Jixian: Zhengxie Henansheng Jixian weiyuan hui, 1988–1990.

"Jixian zhi: renwu" 汲縣誌：人物 ("Gazetteer of Ji County: Personages"). Jixian, Unpublished manuscript.

Johnson, Chalmers. 1962. *Peasant Nationalism and Communist Power: The Emergence of Revolutionary China, 1937–1945*. Stanford: Stanford University Press.

Jones, Susan Mann. 1978. "The Organization of Trade at the County Level: Brokerage and Tax Farming in the Republican Period," Pp. 70–99 in

Selected Papers from the Center for Far Eastern Studies, vol. 3, Susan Mann Jones, ed.

———, ed. 1978–79. *Select Papers from the Center for Far Eastern Studies*, vol. 3. Chicago: University of Chicago.

Juexiang xinghuo 菊鄉星火 (Revolution in Neixiang County). Neixiang: Zhonggong Neixiangxian dangshi gongzuo weiyuan hui, 1987.

Kadushin, C. 1966. "The Friends and Supporters of Psychotherapy: On Social Circles in Urban Life." *American Sociological Review* 31.

———. 1968. "Power, Influence and Social Circles: A New Methodology for Studying Opinion Makers." *American Sociological Review* 33: 685–98.

Kahn, Harold and Albert Feuerwerker. 1969. "The Ideology of Scholarship: China's New Historiography." In *History in Communist China*, Albert Feuerwerker, ed.

Kapp, Robert A. 1973. *Szechwan and the Chinese Republic: Provincial Militarism and Central Power, 1911–1938*. New Haven: Yale University Press.

Kennedy, Thomas. 1974. "Self-Strengthening: An Analysis Based on Some Recent Writings." *Ch'ing-shih wen-t'i* 3, no. 1 (November).

Kohli, Atul and Vivienne Shue. 1994. "State Power and Social Forces: On Political Contention and Accommodation in the Third World." In *State Power and Social Forces: Domination and Transformation in the Third World*, Joel S. Migdal, Atul Kohli, and Vivienne Shue, eds. Cambridge: Cambridge University Press.

Kuhn, Philip. 1970. *Rebellion and Its Enemies in Late Imperial China: Militarization and Social Structure, 1796–1864*. Cambridge, MA: Harvard University Press.

———. 1975. "Local Self-Government under the Republic: Problems of Control, Autonomy, and Mobilization." In *Conflict and Control in Late Imperial China*, Frederic Wakeman and Carolyn Grant, eds.

———. 1978. "Local Taxation and Finances in Republican China," Pp. 100–36 in *Selected Papers from the Center for Far Eastern Studies*, vol. 3, Susan Mann Jones, ed.

———. 1986. "The Development of Local Government." Pp. 329–60 in *The Cambridge History of China: Republican China 1912–1949*, Part 2, vol. 13, John K. Fairbank and Albert Feuerwerker, eds. Cambridge: Cambridge University Press.

Lapidus, Ira M. 1975. "Hierarchies and Networks: A Comparison of Chinese and Islamic Societies." Pp. 26–42 in *Conflict and Control in Late Imperial China*, Frederic Wakeman and Carolyn Grant, eds.

Lary, Diana. 1974. *Region and Nation: The Kwangsi Clique in Chinese Politics, 1925–1937*. Cambridge: Cambridge University Press.

Lauer, Robert H. 1971. "The Scientific Legitimation of Fallacy: Neutralizing Social Change Theory." *American Sociological Review* 36: 881–9.

Lavely, William. 1989. "The Spatial Approach to Chinese History: Illustrations from North China and the Upper Yangzi." *Journal of Asian Studies* 48 (February): 100–13.

Layder, Derek. 1994. *Understanding Social Theory*. London: Sage Publications.

Levenson, Joseph. 1958–1964. *Confucian China and Its Modern Fate*. 3 vols. Berkeley: University of California Press.

Levy, Marion J. 1967. "Social Patterns (Structures) and Problems of Modernization." In *Readings on Social Change,* Wilbert Moore and Robert M. Cook, eds.
Englewood Cliffs, NJ: Prentice-Hall.

Lewis, Charlton. 1976. *Prologue to the Chinese Revolution: The Transformation
of Ideas and Institutions in Hunan Province, 1897–1907.* Cambridge, MA:
Harvard University Press.

Li, Dazhao. 1959. *Li Dazhao xuanji* 李大釗選集 (Selected Essays of Li Dazhao).
Beijing: Renmin chuban she.

Li, Tengxian. 1936. *Peng Yuting yu zhenping zizhi* 彭玉廷與鎮平自治 (Peng Yuting
and Self-Government in Zhenping County). Zhenping: Difang jianshe cujing-
weiyuan hui.

Li, Zonghuang. 1972. *Li Zonghuang huiyilu: bashi sannian fendou shi*
李宗黃回憶錄：八十三年奮鬥史 (Recollections of Li Zonghuang: The History of
Eighty Three years of striving). vol. 28 of *Zizhi congshu* 自治叢書 (Books on
Self-Government). Taipei: Zhongguo difang zizhi xuehui.

Lin, Furui and Chen Daiguang. 1981. *Henan renkou dili* 河南人口地理 (Population Geography in Henan). Zhengzhou: Henan sheng kexue yuan dili yanjiu
suo.

Lin, Yu-sheng. 1979. *The Crisis of Chinese Consciousness: Radical Antitradition-
alism in the May Fourth Era.* Madison: University of Wisconsin Press.

Lipset, S. M. 1959. *Political Man.* London: Mercury Books.

Little, Daniel and Joseph W. Esherick 1989. "Testing the Testers: A Reply
to Barbara Sands and Ramon Myers's Critique of G. William Skinner's
Regional Systems Approach to China." *Journal of Asian Studies* 48 (February): 90–9.

Liu, Boang. "Huiyi zha huanghe tieqiao de yumou" 回憶炸黃河鐵橋的預謀
(Recollection of the Plans for Destroying the Yellow River Bridge). In
Xinhai geming huiyi lu 辛亥革命回憶錄 (Recollections of the Republican
Revolution).

Liu, Jinxiang, ed. 1929. *Henan xinzhi* 河南新誌 (Henan New Gazetteer). Kaifeng.

Liu, K. C. 1978. "The Ch'ing Restoration." Pp. 409–90 in *The Cambridge History
of China: Late Ch'ing 1800–1911*, Part I, vol. 10 John K. Fairbank, ed. Cambridge: Cambridge University Press.

Liu, Zhi. 1966. *Wo de hui yi* 我的回憶 (My Memoir). Taipei: Rongtai yinshu guan.

———. 1966. *Wo de huiyi* 我的回憶 (Personal Memoirs). Taipei: Self-printed.

Lust, J. 1972. "Secret Societies, Popular Movements and the 1911 Revolution."
In *Popular Movements and Secret Societies in China, 1840–1950*, Jean Chesneaux, ed.

MacKinnon, Stephen R. 1980. *Power and Politics in Late Imperial China: Yuan
Shi-kai in Beijing and Tianjin, 1901–1908.* Berkeley: University of California
Press.

Mandelbaum, Maurice. 1971. *History, Man, and Reason: A Study in Nineteenth-
Century Thought.* Baltimore: Johns Hopkins University Press.

Mann, Michael. 1986. *The Sources of Social Power: A History of Power from the
Beginning to A.D. 1760.* Cambridge: Cambridge University Press.

———. 1993. *The Sources of Social Power: The Rise of Classes and Nation-States,
1760–1914.* Cambridge: Cambridge University Press.

Mann, Susan. 1987. *Local Merchants and the Chinese Bureaucracy, 1750–1950*. Stanford: Stanford University Press.

Marks, Robert. 1984. *Rural Revolution in South China: Peasants and the Making of History in Haifeng County, 1570–1930*. Madison: University of Wisconsin Press.

Marsden, Peter. 1987. "Elements of Interactor Dependence." In *Social Exchange Theory*, Karen S. Cook, ed. Beverly Hills: Sage Publications.

McCord, Edward. 1990. "Local Military Power and Elite Formation: The Liu Family of Xingyi County, Guizhou." In *Chinese Local Elites and Patterns of Dominance*, Joseph W. Esherick and Mary Backus Rankin, eds.

———. 1993. *The Power of the Gun: The Emergence of Modern Chinese Warlordism*. Berkeley: University of California Press.

McDonald, Angus W., Jr. 1978. *The Urban Origins of Rural Revolution: Elites and the Masses in Hunan Province, China, 1911–1927*. Berkeley: University of California Press.

McKnight, Brian E. 1971. *Village and Bureaucracy in Southern Sung China*. Chicago: University of Chicago Press.

McNeill, William H. 1982. *The Pursuit of Power: Technology, Armed Force, and Society Since A.D. 1000*. Chicago: University of Chicago Press.

Merelman, R. M. 1966. "Learning and Legitimacy." *American Political Science Review* 60.

Meskill, Johanna. 1979. *A Chinese Pioneer Family: The Lins of Wu-feng, Taiwan, 1729–1895*. Princeton: Princeton University Press.

Metzger, Thomas. 1973. *The Internal Organization of Ching Bureaucracy: Legal, Normative, and Communication Aspects*. Cambridge, MA: Harvard University Press.

———. 1977. *Escape from Predicament: Neo-Confucianism and China's Evolving Political Culture*. New York: Columbia University Press.

Michael, Franz H. 1966–1971. *The Taiping Rebellion: History and Documents*, Margery Anneberg, et al., trans. Seattle: University of Washington Press.

Migdal, Joel. 1987. "Strong States, Weak States: Power and Accommodation." In *Understanding Political Development*, Myron Weiner and Samuel P. Huntington, eds. Boston: Little, Brown and Company.

———. 1988. *Strong Societies and Weak States: State-Society Relations and State Capabilities in the Third World*. Princeton: Princeton University Press.

———. 1994. "The State in Society: An Approach to Struggles for Domination." In *State Power and Social Forces: Domination and Transformation in the Third World*, Joel S. Migdal, Atul Kohli, and Vivienne Shue, eds. Cambridge: Cambridge University Press.

Miliband, R. 1969. *The State in Capitalist Society*. New York: Basic Books.

Min Tu-ki. 1989. *National Polity and Local Power: The Transformation of Late Imperial China*, Philip Kuhn and Timothy Brook, eds. Cambridge, MA: Harvard University Press.

Minami Manshu tetsudo kabushiki kaisha Hokushi keizai chosajo. *Hokushi noson gaikyo chosa hokoku* (Report on the Investigation of General Conditions of North China Villages). 1940.

Moore, Barrington Jr. 1966. *Social Origins of Dictatorship and Democracy.* Boston: Beacon Press.

Murphey, Rhoads. 1974. "The Treaty Ports and China's Modernization." Pp. 17–72 in *The Chinese City Between Two Worlds*, Mark Elvin and G. William Skinner, eds. Stanford: Stanford University Press.

Myers, Ramon H. 1970. *The Chinese Peasant Economy: Agricultural Development in Hopei and Shantung, 1890–1949.* Cambridge, MA: Harvard University Press.

Nandu xuetan 南都學壇 (Academic Forum of Nandu: Scholarly journal of Nanyang Normal College), Yang Mengli, et al., eds. Nanyang: Nanyang shifan zhuanke xuexiao, 1990.

Nanyang dangshi renwu zhuan 南陽黨史人物傳 (Biographies of Communist Historical Figures in Nanyang County), vol. 1, Yaojun Li, et al., eds. Zhengzhou: Henan renmin chuban she, 1987–1989.

Nanyang shizhi 南陽史誌 (Gazetteer of Nanyang City). Zhengzhou: Henan renmin chuban she, 1989.

Nanyang shizhi tongxun 南陽史誌通訊 (Nanyang Historical Newsletter). Nanyang: Neibu kanwu, 1991.

Nanyang wenshi ziliao 南陽文史資料 (Local History of Nanyang County). 6 vols. Nanyang: Zhengxie Nanyang weiyuan hui, 1986–1990.

Nanyang xian wenshi ziliao 南陽縣文史資料 (Local History of Nanyang County). 5 vols. Nanyang: Wenshi ziliao bianchuan weiyuan hui, 1987–1988.

Nanyang xianzhi 南陽縣誌 (Gazetteer of Nanyang County). Zhengzhou: Henan renmin chuban she, 1990.

Nanyang xianzhi: bingfang 南陽縣誌：兵防 (Gazetteer of Nanyang County: Military Defense) (Nanyang: [Guanxu] [During the years of Guanxu]).

Nanyang yinglie pu 南陽英烈譜 (Revolutionary Martyrs in Nanyang County), vol. 1. Nanyang: Nanyang diqu xianzhi bianchuan weiyuan hui, 1985.

Nanzhao wenshi ziliao 南召文史資料 (Local History of Nanzhao County). Nanzhao: Zhengxie Henan sheng Nanzhao xian weiyuan hui, 1989–1989.

Nanzhao wenshi ziliao: Nanzhao difang zizhi zhuanji 南召文史資料：南召地方自治專集 (Local History of Nanzhao County: Special Edition on local Self-Government). 4 vols. Nanzhao: Zhengxie Nanzhao xian weiyuan hui, 1989.

"Nanzhao xianzhi: dashi ji" 南召縣誌：大事記 ("Gazetteer of Nanzhao County: Major events"). Nanzhao, Unpublished manuscript.

"Nanzhao xianzhi: renwu" 南召縣誌：人物 ("Gazetteer of Nanzhao County: Personages"). Nanzhao, Unpublished manuscript.

"Nanzhao xianzhi renwu zhi" 南召縣誌人物誌 ("Personages in Nanzhao County history"). Nanzhao, Unpublished manuscript.

Naquin, Susan. 1976. *Millenarian Rebellion in China: The Eight-Trigrams Uprising of 1813.* New Haven: Yale University Press.

Naquin, Susan and Evelyn S. Rawski. 1987. *Chinese Society in the Eighteenth Century.* New Haven: Yale University Press.

Nathan, Andrew J. 1983. "A Constitutional Republic: The Peking Government, 1916–28." Pp. 259–83 in *The Cambridge History of China: Republican China 1912–1949*, Part I, vol. 12, John K. Fairbank, ed. Cambridge: Cambridge University Press.

———. 1986. *Chinese Democracy*. Berkeley: University of California Press.

Neixiang wenshi ziliao 內鄉文史資料 (Local History of Neixiang County). Neixiang: Neixiang xian weiyuan hui, 1986–1989.

Neixiang wenshi ziliao: Bie Tingfang shilu 內鄉文史資料：別廷芳實錄 (Local History of Neixiang County: Special Edition on Bie Tingfang). Neixiang: Zhengxie, Neixiangxian weiyuan hui, 1985.

"Neixiang xianzhi: dashi ji" 內鄉縣誌：大事記 ("Neixiang local gazetteer: Major events"). Neixiang, Unpublished manuscript.

"Neixiang xianzhi: renwu" 內鄉縣誌：人物 ("Neixiang local gazetteer: Personages"). Neixiang: Neixiang xianzhi zongbianji shi, Unpublished manuscript.

Neixiang yinglie 內鄉英烈 (Revolutionary Martyrs in Neixiang County). Neixiang: Neixiang xianzhi zongbianji shi, 1985.

Nisbet, Robert. 1969. *Social Change and History: Aspects of the Western Theory of Development*. New York: Oxford University Press.

Nugent, David. 1994. "Building the State, Making the Nation: The Bases and Limits of State Centralization in 'Modern' Peru." *American Anthropologist* 96, no. 2: 333–69.

Parsons, Talcott. 1966. *Societies: Evolutionary and Comparative Perspective*. Englewood Cliffs, NJ: Prentice-Hall.

———. 1968. *The Structure of Social Action*. New York: Free Press.

———. 1971. *The System of Modern Societies*. Englewood Cliffs, NJ: Prentice-Hall.

Peng, Yuting. 1933. *Peng Yuting jiangyan ji* 彭玉廷講演集 (Speeches by Peng Yuting). Zhenping.

Perdue, Peter C. 1987. *Exhausting the Earth: State and Peasant in Hunan, 1500–1850*. Cambridge, MA: Harvard University Press.

Perkins, Dwight. 1969. *Agricultural Development in China, 1368–1968*. Chicago: Aldine Press.

———. 1975. "Introduction: The Persistence of the Past." In *China's Modern Economy in Historical Perspective*, Dwight Perkins, ed. Stanford: Stanford University Press.

Perry, Elizabeth J. 1980. *Rebels and Revolutionaries in North China: 1845–1945*. Stanford: Stanford University Press.

———. 1983. "Social Banditry Revisited: The Case of Bai Lang, a Chinese Brigand." *Modern China* 9 (July): 355–82.

———. 1984. "Collective Violence in China, 1880–1980." In *Theory and Society*. 13, no. 3 (May): 427–54.

Polanyi, Karl. 1957. *The Great Transformation*. Boston: Beacon Press.

Pomeranz, Kenneth. 1993. *The Making of a Hinterland: State, Society, and Economy in Inland North China, 1853–1937*. Berkeley: University of California Press.

Popkin, Samuel L. 1979. *The Rational Peasants: The Political Economy of Rural Society in Vietnam*. Berkeley: University of California Press.

Poulantzas, N. 1973. *Political Power and Social Classes*. London: New Left Books.

Price, Don. 1974. *Russia and the Roots of the Chinese Revolution, 1896–1911*. Cambridge, MA: Harvard University Press.

Pye, Lucian. 1971. *Warlord Politics: Conflict and Coalition in the Modernization of Republican China*. New York.

Qin, Jun. "Jianzhi yange" 建制沿革 ("The history of the governmental system"). Unpublished manuscript.

———. "Peng Yuting shilue" 彭玉廷事略 ("Stories about Peng Yuting"). Unpublished manuscript.

———. "Wo suo liaojie de Li Yiwen" 我所了解的李益闻 ("What I know about Li Yiwen"). Nanyang, Unpublished manuscript.

Rankin, Mary. 1971. *Early Chinese Revolutionaries: Radical Intellectuals in Shanghai and Chekiang, 1902–1911.* Cambridge, MA: Harvard University Press.

———. 1986. *Elite Activism and Political Transformation in China: Zhejiang Province, 1965–1911.* Stanford: Stanford University Press.

———. "The Origins of a Chinese Public Sphere: Local Elites and Community Affairs in the Late Imperial Period." Unpublished manuscript.

Rankin, Mary, John K. Fairbank and Albert Feuerwerker. 1986. "Introduction: Perspectives on Modern China's History." In *The Cambridge History of China: Republican China 1912–1949*, Part 2, vol. 13, John K. Fairbank and Albert Feuerwerker, eds. Cambridge: Cambridge University Press.

Rawski, Evelyn. 1979. *Education and Popular Literacy in Ch'ing China.* Ann Arbor: University of Michigan Press.

Redfield, Robert. 1965. *Peasant Society and Culture.* Chicago: University of Chicago Press.

Reischauer, Edwin O., John K. Fairbank, and Albert M. Craig. 1965. *East Asia: The Modern Transformation.* Boston: Houghton Mifflin.

Rhoads, Edward. 1974. "Merchant Associations in Canton, 1895–1911." Pp. 97–118 in *The Chinese City Between Two Worlds*, Mark Elvin and G. William Skinner, eds. Stanford: Stanford University Press.

———. 1975. *China's Republican Revolution: The Case of Kwangtung 1895–1913.* Cambridge, MA: Harvard University Press.

Riggs, Fred W. 1964. *Administration in Developing Countries: The Theory of Prismatic Society.* Boston: Houghton Mifflin Company.

Ritzer, George. 1992. *Sociological Theory.* 3rd ed. New York: McGraw-Hill.

Rokkan, Stein. 1975. "Dimensions of State Formation and Nation-Building: A Possible Paradigm for Research on Variations within Europe." Pp. 562–600 in *The Formation of National States in Western Europe*, Charles Tilly, ed. Princeton: Princeton University Press.

Ropp, Paul. 1981. *Dissent in Early Modern China: Ju-lin Wai-shih and Ch'ing Social Criticism.* Ann Arbor: University of Michigan Press.

Rowe, William T. 1984. *Hankow: Commerce and Society in a Chinese City.* Stanford: Stanford University Press.

———. 1985. "Approaches to Modern Chinese Social History." Pp. 236–96 in *Reliving the Past*, Oliver Zunz, ed. Chapel Hill: University of North Carolina Press.

———. 1989. *Hankow: Conflict and Community in a Chinese City, 1796–1895.* Stanford: Stanford University Press.

———. 1990. "The Public Sphere in Modern China." *Modern China* 16, no. 3.

Runkel, Philip J. and Margaret Runkel. 1984. *A Guide to Usage for Writers and Students in the Social Sciences.* New Jersey: Rowman & Allanheld.

Rozman, Gilbert, ed. 1981. *The Modernization of China*. New York: Free Press.

Sanderson, Stephen K. 1990. *Social Evolutionism: A Critical History*. Cambridge, MA: Basil Blackwell.

———. 1995. *Social Transformation: A General Theory of Historical Development*. Cambridge, MA: Basil Blackwell.

Sands, Barbara and Ramon Myers. 1986. "The Spatial Approach to Chinese History: A Test." *Journal of Asian Studies* (August).

———. 1990. "Economics and Macroregions: A Reply to Our Critics," *Journal of Asian Studies* (May): 344–6.

Schoppa, Keith. 1973. "The Composition and Functions of the Local Elite in Szechwan, 1851–1874." *Ch'ing-shih wen-t'i* (November).

———. 1976. "Local Self-Government in Zhejiang, 1909–1927." *Modern China* 4, no. 2 (October): 503–30.

———. 1977. "Province and Nation; The Chekiang Provincial Autonomy Movement, 1917–1927." *Journal of Asian Studies* 36, no. 4: 661–74.

———. 1982. *Chinese Elites and Political Change: Zhejiang Province in the Early Twentieth Century*. Cambridge, MA: Harvard University Press.

———. 1992. "Contours of Revolutionary Change in a Chinese County." *Journal of Asian Studies* 51, no. 4 (November): 770.

Schram, Stuart. 1966. *Mao Tse-Tung*. New York: Simon and Schuster.

Schutz, Alfred. 1967. *The Phenomenology of the Social World*, George Walsh and Frederick Lehnert, trans. Evanston, IL: Northwestern University Press.

Schwartz, Benjamin I., ed. 1972. *Reflections on the May Fourth Movement: A Symposium*. Cambridge, MA: Harvard University Press.

Scott, James. 1972. "Patron-Client Politics and Political Change in Southeast Asia." *American Political Science Review* 66.

———. 1976. *The Moral Economy of the Peasant: Rebellion and Subsistence in Southeast Asia*. New Haven: Yale University Press.

———. 1989. "Everyday Forms of Resistance." In *Everyday Forms of Peasant Resistance*, Forrest D. Colburn, ed. Armonk, NY: M. E. Sharpe.

Seybolt, Peter J. 1996. *Throwing the Emperor from his Horse: Portrait of a Village Leader in China, 1923–1995*. Boulder, CO: Westview Press.

Shen, Qingbi. 1976. *Wanxi Chen Shunde xiansheng zhuan* 宛西陳舜德先生傳 (The Story of Chen Shunde). Taipei: Hongdao wenhua shiye chuban she.

Shen, Songqiao. 1978. "Jingji zuowu yu jindai Henan nongcun jingji: 1906–1937" 經濟作物與近代河南農村經濟 (Cash Crops and Peasant Economy in Modern Henan: 1906–1937). In *Jindai Zhongguo nongcun jingji shi lunwen ji* 近代中國農村經濟史論文集. Taipei: Zhongyang yanjiu yuan jindai shi yanjiu suo.

———. 1992. "Difang jingying yu guojia quanli: minguo shiqide Wanxi zizhi, 1930–1943" 地方精英與國家權力：民國時期的宛西自治 (Local Elites and State Power: Wanxi Self-Government during the Republican Period, 1930–1943). In *Zhongyang yanjiu yuan jindai shi yanjiu suo jikan* 中央研究院近代史所季刊, vol. 21. Taipei: Zhongyang yanjiu yuan jindai shi yanjiu suo.

Sheqi renwu 社旗人物 (Personages in Sheqi County). Sheqing: Sheqi xian difang zhi zong bian shi, 1986.

"Sheqi xianzhi renwu pian" 社旗縣誌人物篇 ("Local history of Sheqi County: Personages"). Sheqi, Unpublished manuscript.

Sheridan, James. 1966. *Chinese Warlord: The Career of Feng Yu-hsiang*. Stanford: Stanford University Press.

———. 1975. *China in Disintegration: The Republican Era in Chinese History, 1929–1949*. New York: Free Press.

Shue, Vivienne. 1988. *The Reach of the State: Sketches of the Chinese Body Politic*. Stanford: Stanford University Press.

Skinner, G. William. 1964. "Marketing and Social Structure in Rural China: Part I." *Journal of Asian Studies* 24, no. 1 (Nov. 1964): 3–43.

———. 1965. "Marketing and Social Structure in Rural China." *Journal of Asian Studies* 24 no. 2 (February): 195–228.

———. 1971. "Chinese Peasants and Closed Community: An Open and Shut Case." *Comparative Studies in Society and History* 13, no. 3.

———. 1976. "Mobility Strategies in Late Imperial China: A Regional Systems Analysis." Pp. 324–64 in *Regional Analysis*, vol. 1. Carol A. Smith, ed. New York: Academic Press.

———. 1977. "Cities and the Hierarchy of Local Systems." In *The City in Late Imperial China*, G. William Skinner, ed. Stanford: Stanford University Press.

———. 1978. "Cities and the Hierarchy of Local Systems." Pp. 1–78 in *Studies in Chinese Society*, Arthur P. Wolf, ed.

Skocpol, Theda. 1979. *States and Social Revolutions: A Comparative Analysis of France, Russia, and China*. New York: Cambridge University Press.

Smelser, Neil. 1964. "Toward a Theory of Modernization." In *Social Change*, Amitai Etzioni and Eva Etzioni, eds. New York: Basic Books.

Smith, Arthur H. 1899. *Village Life in China*. New York: Fleming H. Revell.

Smith, Anthony D. 1973. *The Concept of Social Change: A Critique of the Functionalist Theory of Social Change*. London: Routledge and Kegan Paul.

So, Alvin Y. 1990. *Social Change and Development: Modernization, Dependency, and World-System Theories*. Newbury Park: Sage Publications.

Spencer, Herbert. 1876–1885. *The Principles of Sociology*. New York: D. Appleton.

———. 1972. *Herbert Spencer on Social Evolution: Selected Writings*, J. D. Y. Peel, ed. Chicago: University of Chicago Press.

———. 1974. *The Evolution of Society: Selections from Herbert Spencer's Principles of Sociology*, Robert L. Carneiro, ed. Chicago: University of Chicago Press.

Strand, David. 1989. *Rickshaw Beijing: City People and Politics in the 1920s*. Berkeley: University of California Press.

———. 1990. "Mediation, Representation, and Repression: Local Elites in 1920s Beijing." Pp. 216–38 in *Chinese Local Elites and Patterns of Dominance*, Joseph W. Esherick and Mary Backus Rankin, eds.

Tangyin wenshi ziliao 湯陰文史資料 (Local History of Tangyin County). vol. 1. Tangyin: Tangyin xian weiyuan hui wenshi ziliao weiyuan hui, 1988.

Tawney, Richard H. 1932. *Land and Labor in China*. Boston: Beacon Press.

Thaxton, Ralph. 1983. *China Turned Rightside Up: Revolutionary Legitimacy in the Peasant World*. New Haven: Yale University Press.

———. 1997. *Salt of the Earth*. Berkeley: University of California Press.

Tien, Hung-mao. 1972. *Government and Politics in Kuomintang China, 1927–1937*. Stanford: Stanford University Press.

Tilly, Charles, 1975. "Reflections on the History of European State-making." Pp. 3–83 in *The Formation of National States in Western Europe*, Charles Tilly, ed. Princeton: Princeton University Press.

————. 1975. "Western State-Making and Theories of Political Transformation." In *The Formation of National States in Western Europe*, Charles Tilly, ed. Princeton: Princeton University Press.

————. 1990. *Coercion, Capital, and European States, A.D. 990–1990*. Cambridge, MA: Basil Blackwell.

Tipps, Dean C. 1976. "Modernization Theory and the Comparative Study of Societies: A Critical Perspective." In *Comparative Modernization: A Reader*, Cyril Black, ed. New York: Free Press.

Toa, Dobunkai, comp. 1919. *Shina Shobetsu Zenshi: Seko-sho* (A Gazetteer of all Provinces of China). vol. 13. Tokyo.

Tong, Kunhou. "Wang Xiaoting xiansheng nianpu" ("A chronicle of Mr. Wang Xiaoting's life." Unpublished manuscript.

Tongheyu yinhao de chuangban yu fazhan 同和裕銀號的創辦與發展 (The History of Tongheyu Bank), Zhang Yufeng, et al., eds. Zhengzhou: Henan renmin chuban she, 1985.

Tongxu xianzhi 通許縣誌 (Tongxu County Gazetteer). 11 vols. Tongxu: Tongxu-xian weiyuan hui, 1983.

Tu, Wei-ming, ed. 1994. *China in Transformation*. Cambridge, MA: Harvard University Press.

Turner, Bryan S. 1993. *Max Weber: From History to Modernity*. London: Routledge.

Turner, Jonathan. 1986. *The Structure of Sociological Theory*. 4th ed. Chicago: Dorsey.

————. 1990. *The Past, Present, and Future of Theory in American Sociology*. Pp. 371–92 in *Frontiers of Social Theory: The New Syntheses*, George Ritzer, ed. New York: Columbia University Press.

Wakeman, Frederic. 1966. *Strangers at the Gate: Social Disorder in South China, 1839–1861*. Berkeley: University of California Press.

————. 1975. *The Fall of Imperial China*. New York: Free Press.

————. 1975. "Localism and Loyalism during the Ch'ing Conquest of Kiangnan: The Tragedy of Chiang-Yin." Pp. 43–85 in *Conflict and Control in Late Imperial China*, Frederic Wakeman and Carolyn Grant, eds.

————. 1991. "Models of Historical Change: The Chinese State and Society, 1839–1989." In *Perspectives on Modern China: Four Anniversaries*. Kenneth Lieberthal, et al., eds. Armonk, NY: M. E. Sharpe.

————. 1993. "The Civil Society and Public Sphere Debate: Western Refections on Chinese Political Culture." *Modern China* 19, no. 3 (April): 108–38.

Wakeman, Frederic and Carolyn Grant, eds. 1975. *Conflict and Control in Late Imperial China*. Berkeley: University of California Press.

Wallace, Water L. 1994. *A Weberian Theory of Human Society*. New Brunswick: Rutgers University Press.

Wallerstein, Immanuel. 1984. "Patterns and Prospectives of the Capitalist World-Economy." In *The Politics of the World-Economy*. New York: Cambridge University Press.

Wang, Fuzhou. 1970. "Lu bu shi yi ye bu bi hu ji wanxi" (No One Pockets Anything Others Lost on the Road and No One Closes the Door at Night: Recollections of Southwestern Henan). In *Zhuanji wenxue* 傳紀文學 (Biographical Literature), (Taipei) 16, no. 4.

Wang, Guolin. 1987. *Zhenping xian wenshi ziliao: Peng Yuting yishi* 鎮平縣文史資料：彭玉廷軼事 (Local History of Zhenping County: The Story of Peng Yuting). Zhenping: Zhenpingxian weiyuan hui.

Wang, Puyuan, et al., eds. 1932. *Chongxiu Huaxian zhi* 重修滑縣誌 (Gazetteer of Hua County). 20 vols. Kaifeng: Kaifeng Xinyu Printing Shop.

Wang, Quanying. "Henan jindai jingji ziliao: meikuang ye" 河南近代經濟資料：煤礦業 ("Collection of materials on the modern economy in Henan: coal industry"). Unpublished manuscript.

———. "Henan jindai jingji ziliao: jindai gongye ji shou gongye" 河南近代經濟資料：近代工業及手工業 ("Collection of materials on the modern economy in Henan: modern industry and handicrafts"). Unpublished manuscript.

———. "Henan jindai jingji ziliao: jindai wenhua ziliao" 河南近代經濟資料：近代文化資料 ("Collection of materials on the modern economy in Henan: modern culture"). Unpublished.

———. "Hongqiang hui ziliao hui ji" 紅槍會資料匯集 ("Collection of materials on the Red Spear"). Unpublished.

Wang, Tianjiang. "Henan lishi: si" 河南歷史：四 ("History of Henan: part 4"). Unpublished manuscript.

———. "Henan lishi: zhongpian, xihua de beiju" 河南歷史：中篇，西化的悲劇 ("History of Henan: part 2, tragedy of Westernization"). Unpublished manuscript.

———, ed. 1984. *Henan dashi ji ziliao congbian: 1840–1918* 河南大事記資料叢編 (Collection of Resources on the Major Events in Henan: 1840–1918). Zhengzhou: Henan difang shizhi bianchuan weiyuan hui.

———, ed. 1986. *Henan xinhai geming shishi changbian* 河南辛亥革命史事長編 (Collection of the Historical Records on the Republican Revolution in Henan). vol. 1. Zhengzhou: Henan renmin chuban she.

Wang, Tianxiang, et al., eds. 1988. *Henan lishi mingren cidian* 河南歷史名人辭典 (Dictionary of Historically Known Persons in Henan). Zhengzhou: Zhongzhou guji chuban she.

Wang, Xitong. "Minguo xianren" 民國閒人 ("Man of leisure during the Republic"). Unpublished diary.

———. "Yan yu ping zong" 燕豫萍蹤 ("My life in Henan and Hebei"). Unpublished diary.

Wang, Yeh-chien. 1973. *Land Taxation in Imperial China, 1750–1911*. Cambridge, MA: Harvard University Press.

Wang, Zhongchen, et al. 1979. *Xinxiang Tongheyu yinhao shimo* 新鄉同和裕銀號始末 (The Rise and Fall of Tongheyu). vol. 1. Zhengzhou: Henan renmin chuban she.

Watson, Andrew, tr. 1972. *Transport in Transition: The Evolution of*

Traditional Shipping in China. Ann Arbor: University of Michigan, Center for Chinese Studies.

Watt, John. 1972. *The District Magistrate in Late Imperial China.* New York: Columbia University Press.

Weber, Max. 1947. *The Theory of Social and Economic Organization.* New York: Oxford University Press.

———. 1951. *The Religion of China: Confucianism and Taoism*, Hans H. Gerth, ed. Glencoe, IL: Free Press.

———. 1983. *Max Weber on Capitalism, Bureaucracy and Religion: A Selection of Texts*, Stanislav Andreski, ed. London: George Allen and Unwin.

Weigert Andrew J., J. Smith Teitge, and Dennis W. Teitge. 1986. *Society and Identity: Toward a Sociological Psychology.* Cambridge: Cambridge University Press.

"Wei Xichuan xian difang zizhi sannian jihua gaiyao" 僞淅川縣地方自治三年計劃概要 (Three-Year Plan of Self-Government in Xichuan County). In Archive at the Xichuan Public Security Bureau, Archive No: Dewei juan, wenlin 1. Xichuan: Archival Office of the District Government.

Weihui wenshi ziliao 衛輝文史資料 (Local History of Weihui). 3 vols. Weihui: Zhengxie Weihui shi weiyuan hui, Xuexi wenshi weiyuan hui, 1991.

Wenshi ziliao 文史資料 (Local History), 2 vols. Xinxiang: Zhengxie Xinxiang weiyuan hui, 1987–1990.

Wenshi ziliao xuanji 文史資料選集 (Collection of Essays from Local History of Henan), 47 issues. Zhengzhou: Henan renmin chuban she, 1967.

Williamson, A. 1866. *Journey in North China.*

Wolf, Arthur ed. 1974. *Religion and Ritual in Chinese Society.* Stanford: Stanford University Press.

———. ed. 1978. *Studies in Chinese Society.* Stanford: Stanford University Press.

Wolf, Eric R. 1969. "Kinship, Friendship, and Patron-Client Relations in Complex Societies." A.S.A. Monographs, no. 9. In *The Social Anthropology of Complex Societies*, Michael Banton, ed. London: Tavistock Publications.

Wong, Young-Tsu. 1977. "Popular Unrest and the 1911 Revolution in Jiangsu." *Modern China* 3, no. 3 (July).

Wou, Oderic Y. K. 1978. *Militarism in Modern China: The Career of Wu P'ei-fu, 1916–39.* Dawson: Australian National University Press.

———. 1984. "Development, Underdevelopment and Degeneration: The Introduction of Rail Transport into Honan." *Asian Profile* (Hong Kong) 12, no. 3 (June).

———. 1994. *Mobilizing the Masses: Building Revolution in Henan.* Stanford: Stanford University Press.

———. "The Impact of Differential Economic Change on Society in Honan in the 1920s and 1930s." Unpublished manuscript.

Wright, Mary C., ed. 1968. *China in Revolution: The First Phase 1900–1913.* New Haven: Yale University Press.

Wrigley, E. A. 1972–1973. "The Process of Modernization and the Industrial Revolution in England." *Journal of Interdisciplinary History* 3: 225–59.

Wunian lai Henan zhengzhi zong baogao: caizheng 五年來河南政治總報告

(General Report of Political Affairs in Henan for the Last Five Years: Finances). Kaifeng: Henan sheng zhengfu mishu chu, October 1935.

Wunian lai shizheng tongji: caizheng 五年來施政統計：財政 (Statistics of Last Five-year Administration: Finances), Henan sheng zhengfu mishu chu tongji shi, ed. Kaifeng: Henan sheng zhengfu mishu chu, 1935.

Wusi qianhou de Henan shehui 五四前後的河南社會 (Society in Henan Before and After the May Fourth Movement). Zhengzhou: Henan renmin chuban she, 1986.

Wusi yundong zai Henan 五四運動在河南 (The May Fourth Movement in Henan). vol. 3 of *Henan difangzhi ziliao congbian* 河南地方誌資料叢編, Pang Shouxin, et al., eds. Zhengzhou: Zhongzhou shuhua she, 1983.

Wuzhi xianzhi 武陟縣誌 (Wuzhi County Gazetteer). vol. 2. Wuzhi: Wuzhixian weiyuan hui, 1984.

Xiangcun gongzuo taolun huibian: xiangcun jianshe shiyan 鄉村工作討論彙編：鄉村建設試驗 (Collection of Discussions of Village Work: The Rural Construction Experiment), 3 vols. Shanghai: Zhonghua shuju, 1937.

Xichuan wenshi ziliao 淅川縣誌 (Local History of Xichuan). 4 vols, Wenshi ziliao yanjiu weiyuan hui, ed. Xichuan: Xichuanxian weiyuan hui, 1987–1989.

"Xichuan xianzhi" 淅川縣誌 ("Gazetteer of Xichuan County"). Xichuan: Xichuan xianzhi bianchuan weiyun hui, Unpublished manuscript.

Xichuan xian lishi ziliao huibian 淅川縣歷史資料彙編 (Collection of Historical Documents in Xichuan County). Xichuan: Xichuan xianzhi zongbianji shi, 1983–1985.

Xichuan xianzhi 淅川縣誌 (Gazetteer of Xichuan County). Zhengzhou: Henan renmin chuban she, 1990.

"Xichuan xianzhi: difang zizhi" 淅川縣誌：地方自治 (Gazetteer of Xichuan County: Self-Government). Xichuan: Xichuan xianzhi bianchuan weiyuan hui, Unpublished manuscript.

"Xichuan xianzhi: renwu" 淅川縣誌：人物 (Gazetteer of Xichuan County: Personages). Xichuan: Xichuan xianzhi bianchuan weiyuan hui, Unpublished manuscript.

Xin, Ping. 1991. *Minguo jiangling lu* 民國將領錄 (Biographical Information about Army Generals during the Republican Period). Shenyang: Liaoning renmin chuban she.

Xinxiang wenshi ziliao 新鄉文史資料 (Local History of Xinxiang County), 4 vols. Xinxiang: Xinxiang wenshi ziliao weiyuan hui, 1987–1990.

Xinxiang xianzhi 新鄉縣誌 (Local Gazetteer of Xinxiang County). Xinxiang: Shenghuo, Dushu, Xinzhi Sanlian Shudian, 1991.

Xinxiangxian wenshi ziliao 新鄉縣文史資料 (Local History of Xinxiang County), 6 vols. Xinxiang: Xinxiangxian zhengxie wenshi ziliao weiyuan hui, 1987–1991.

Xinxiangxian xuzhi 新鄉縣續誌 (Gazetteer of Xinxiang County). 2 vols. Han Banfu, et al., eds. Xinxiang, 1923.

Xiuwu wenshi ziliao 修武文史資料 (Local History of Xiuwu County), 5 vols. Xiuwu: Zhongguo renmin zhengzhi xieshang huiyi Xiuwuxian weiyuan hui, 1988.

Bibliography

Xiuwu xianzhi 修武縣誌 (Gazetteer of Xiuwu County). vol. 1, Xiao Guozhen, et al., eds. Xiuwu, 1931.

Xixia xianzhi 西峽縣誌 (Gazetteer of Xixia County). Xixia: Henan renmin chuban she, 1989–91.

"Xixia xianzhi: renwu pian" 西峽縣誌：人物編 (Gazetteer of Xixia County: Personages). Xixia: Xixia xianzhi bianchuan weiyuan hui, Unpublished manuscript.

Xu Anyang xianzhi: bingfang zhi 續安陽縣誌：兵防誌 (Sequel to the Gazetteer of Anyang County: Military Defense). Anyang, Minguo (During the Republican period).

Xu Anyang xianzhi: renwu biao 續安陽縣誌：人物表 (Sequel to the Gazetteer of Anyang County: List of Personages). Anyang, Minguo (During the Republican period).

Xu Wuzhi xianzhi 續武陟縣誌 (Continuation of Wuzhi County Gazetteer) (Wuzhi).

Xuchang xianzhi 許晶縣誌 (Xuchang County Gazetteer). vol. 4. Xuchang: Xuchang weiyuan hui, 1983.

Yamagishi, Toshio. 1987. "An Exchange Theoretical Approach to Network Positions." In *Social Exchange Theory*, Karen S. Cook, ed. Beverly Hills: Sage Publications.

Yang, Martin C. 1945. *A Chinese Village: Taitou, Shantung Province*. New York: Columbia University Press.

Yang, Mayfair Mei-hui. 1994. *Gifts, Favors, and Banquets: The Art of Social Relationships in China*. Ithaca: Cornell University Press.

Yao, Xueyin. 1945. *Changye* (The Long Night). Chongqing.

Yeh, Wen-Hsin. 1990. *The Alienated Academy: Culture and Politics in Republican China, 1919–1937*. Cambridge, MA: Harvard University Press.

Yin, Gengyun. *Yujun jilue: tufei qi* 豫軍記略：土匪，七 (Brief History of the Henan Army: Bandits, VII).

———. *Yujun jilue: huifei er* 豫軍記略：會匪，二 (Brief History of the Henan Army: Heterodox Societies II).

"Yizhan shiqi nongmin yundong" 一戰時期農民運動 (The Peasant Movement in Henan during World War I). In *Zhonggong Henan dangshi ziliao congshu* 中國河南黨史資料叢編, Hu Wenlan, et al., eds. Zhengzhou: Dangshi gongzuo weiyuan hui, 1986.

Yongan shangshu zouyi 庸庵當書奏議 (Report of the President of the Yongyan Ministry of Foreign Affairs). vol. 4. Beijing, 1904.

Young, Ernest P. 1977. *The Presidency of Yuan Shih-K'ai*. Ann Arbor: University of Michigan Press.

"Yubei Lin Hua Tang tianmenhui" 豫北林滑湯天門會 (The Heavenly Gate Society in Lin, Hua, and Tang counties of Northern Henan). vol. 2. In *Henan shizhi luncong* 河南史誌論叢. Yang Jingqi, et al., eds. Zhengzhou: Henan renmen chuban she, 1990.

Zeitlin, Irving M. 1973. *Rethinking Sociology: A Critique of Contemporary Theory*. Englewood Cliffs, NJ: Prentice-Hall.

Zeitlin, M., et al. 1980. "On Classes, Class Conflict, and the State: An Introductory Note." In *Classes, Class Conflict and the State: Empirical Studies in Class Analysis*, M. Zeitlin, ed. Cambridge, MA: Winthrop.

Zelin, Madeleine. 1984. *The Magistrate's Tael: Rationalizing Fiscal Reform in Eighteenth-Century Ch'ing China*. Berkeley: University of California Press.

Zhang, Fang. "Henan xinhai geming de huiyi lu" 河南辛亥革命的回憶錄 (Recollections of the Republican Revolution in Henan). In *Xinhai geming huiyi lu* 辛亥革命回憶錄 (Recollection of the Republican Revolution).

Zhang, Hexuan. "Wo de ba shi nian" 我的八十年 ("My eighty years"). Neixiang, Unpublished.

———. "Wo de zi zhuan" ("My autobiography"). Unpublished.

———. "Zhang Hexuan you pai dangan cailiao" 張和宣右派檔案材料 ("Archival material of the rightist, Zhang Hexuan"). Neixiang: Neixiangxian dang'an guan, Unpublished manuscript.

Zhang, Kaiyuan and Liu Wang Ling. 1985. "The 1911 Revolution: The State of the Field in 1982." *Late Imperial China* 6, no. 1 (June).

Zhang, Renjun. 1903. *Yuzhe huicun* 諭摺匯存 (Collection of Imperial Reports) 55, no. 1. Peking, June 4.

Zhang, Xin. 1991. "Elite Mobility, Local Control, and Social Transformation in Modern China: 1900–1937." Ph.D. dissertation, University of Chicago.

———. 1994. "Elite Activism in the Periphery: Henan, 1900–1937." *Republican China* 19, no. 2 (April): 67–103.

———. 1994. "Reconsidering the 1911 Revolution: The Case of Henan." *Chinese Historians* 7, no. 1–2 (Spring and Fall): 1–44.

Zhao, Chun. "Nanyang tanghe jian de nongcun xianzhuang" 南陽唐河間的農村現狀 ("The present situation in the villages located between Nanyang and the Tang River"). Unpublished manuscript.

Zhaoge renwu zhuanlue 朝歌人物傳略 (Personages in Qi County), 2 vols. in *Qixian wenshi ziliao* 淇縣文史資料 (Local History of Qi County). Qixian: Zhengxie Qixian wenshi ziliao weiyuan hui, 1988.

Zhenping wenshi ziliao 鎮平文史資料 (Local History of Zhenping County). Zhenping: Zhenpingxian weiyuan hui.

Zhenping zizhi gaikuang 鎮平自治概況 (Self-Government in Zhenping). Zhenping, 1933.

Zhenpingxian zizhi gaikuang 鎮平縣自治概況 (Self-Government in Zhenping County). Beiping: Jingcheng chuban she, 1932.

Zhonggong Xichuan xian dangshi ziliao 中共淅川縣黨史資料 (Chinese Communist Party, Xichuan County Party Archives). vol. 2. Xichuan: Xichuanxian dangshi ziliao zhengji bianji weiyuan hui, 1987.

Zhonghua renmin gongheguo fensheng ditu ji 中華人民共和國分省地圖集 (Atlas of the People's Republic of China). Beijing: Ditu chuban she, 1974.

Zhongyuan dadi fa chun hua 中原大地發春華. vol. 1. Zhengzhou: Henan renmin chuban she, 1991.

Zhongyuan wenxian 中原文獻 (Local History of Henan). 20 vols. Taipei: Zhongyuan wenxian chuban she, 1980.

Zi, Zhen. 1927. "Fanfeng zhanzheng zhong zhi yubei tianmenhui" 反馮戰爭之豫北

天門會 (Tianmenhui in Northern Henan during the War against Feng's army). In *Xiangdao zhoubao* 嚮導週報 (Xiangdao Weekly News), 197.

Zou, Lu. "Guangfu zhiyi" 光復之役 (The Battle to Reclaim the Nation). In *Zhongguo guomindang shigao* 中國國民黨史稿 (The History of the Nationalist Party).

Zurndorfer, Harriet T. 1989. *Change and Continuity in Chinese Local History: The Development of Hui-chou Prefecture, 800–1800*. Leiden: E. J. Brill.

Index

311